DUMBARTON OAKS
MEDIEVAL LIBRARY

*Daniel Donoghue, General Editor*

THE LIFE OF
SAINT PETER OF ATROA

SABAS

DOML 85

# The Life of
# Saint Peter of Atroa

## SABAS

Edited and Translated by

## IOANNIS POLEMIS and
## ATHANASIOS MARKOPOULOS

### with RICHARD P. H. GREENFIELD

DUMBARTON OAKS
MEDIEVAL LIBRARY

HARVARD UNIVERSITY PRESS
CAMBRIDGE, MASSACHUSETTS
LONDON, ENGLAND
2024

First Printing

*Library of Congress Cataloging-in-Publication Data*
Names: Sabas (Monk), active 9th century, author. | Polemēs, I., editor,
    translator. | Markopoulos, A., editor, translator. | Greenfield, Richard
    P. H., editor, translator. | Sabas (Monk), active 9th century. Life of
    Saint Peter of Atroa. | Sabas (Monk), active 9th century. Life of Saint
    Peter of Atroa. English.
Title: The life of Saint Peter of Atroa / Sabas ; edited and translated by
    Ioannis Polemis and Athanasios Markopoulos, with Richard P. H.
    Greenfield.
Other titles: Dumbarton Oaks medieval library ; 85.
Description: Cambridge : Harvard University Press, 2024. | Series:
    Dumbarton Oaks medieval library ; DOML 85 | Includes
    bibliographical references and index. | Text in Greek with English
    translation on facing pages; introduction and notes in English.
Identifiers: LCCN 2024003690 | ISBN 9780674295643 (cloth)
Subjects: LCSH: Peter, of Atroa, Saint, 773–837 — Biography — Early
    works to 1800. | Christian saints — Byzantine Empire — Biography —
    Early works to 1800.
Classification: LCC BX4700.P474 S23 2024 | DDC 270/.092
    [B] — dc23/eng/20240513
LC record available at https://lccn.loc.gov/2024003690

# Contents

# Introduction

## THE LIFE OF SAINT PETER OF ATROA

Saint Peter of Atroa was born in the city of Elaia in western Asia Minor, near Pergamon (modern Bergama), in 773 CE, according to the indications offered by his biographer Sabas.[1] His father held a military rank and was, in all probability, quite wealthy. The saint, whose baptismal name was Theophylaktos, showed his zeal for the solitary life from an early age: he abandoned his family and joined the company of Paul, an ascetic on Mount Dagouta in Phrygia. Paul conferred upon him the monastic name of Peter in 794 and took care to ordain the young Peter as a priest. Together they founded a new monastery, dedicated to the prophet Zechariah, in the plain of Atroa, east of Mount Olympos in Bithynia in northwestern Asia Minor. After Paul's death in 805 or 806, Peter became abbot of the small monastic community that had gathered there.

The late eighth and early ninth centuries were still difficult times for the Byzantine Empire, which had in many ways been forced to reinvent itself following the loss of its eastern and southern regions to the Arab expansion a century before. Following a period of relative political stability for much of the eighth century under the Isaurian em-

perors, the now much-reduced empire came under renewed pressure in the early 800s from powerful Arab, Slav, and Bulgarian neighbors, while internally the regime in Constantinople grew increasingly fragile, a situation that would persist for most of Peter's life. For many, this catastrophic and persistent disruption of the earlier Byzantine world was seen as divine punishment, and a possible cause for God's wrath was held by some to be the use and veneration of religious images, or icons, in worship. From 726 until 787 it became the policy of the imperial regime in Constantinople to oppose and to some extent attempt to eradicate this practice, a policy that historians have labeled Iconoclasm (literally, "the breaking of images"). The result was a series of clashes with and persecution of those who supported icons (the iconodules, or "venerators of images"), a conflict that for many surviving sources, particularly those with religious connections, came to characterize the period.

After a period of toleration, the emperor Leo V the Armenian (813–820) renewed Iconoclasm in 815 and initiated persecution of those monastic communities that refused to obey his decisions. Peter advised his spiritual sons to disperse all over the areas of Bithynia and Phrygia, abandoning the convent of Saint Zechariah. After making a pilgrimage to the famous shrines of John the Evangelist in Ephesus and of the archangel Michael in Chonai, Peter traveled to Cyprus and visited the most famous churches there. Afterward he returned to Bithynia and rejoined his community, which was gathered at the monastery of Saint Zechariah once more. The saint took the opportunity to visit his native city of Elaia, to meet his brother Christophoros

and persuade him to embrace the monastic life, renaming him Paul.

Being a wandering monk, Peter did not remain in his monastery for long, departing for Lydia, to the south, where he founded a new monastic community on the so-called Kalonoros (Good Mountain). The saint was arrested by the Iconoclasts while visiting the abbot Athanasios, who was imprisoned in the fortress of Plateia Petra in Lydia. After being harassed by the infamous Lamaris, an imperial official who was an ardent supporter of Iconoclasm, the saint spent some time in prison together with his brother Paul, but was liberated and returned to Kalonoros.

The assassination of emperor Leo V at Christmas in 820 brought a degree of easing of the persecution against the Iconophiles. The community of Saint Zechariah was re-established, and Peter spent his time traveling between the convents of Saint Zechariah, Kalonoros, Saint Porphyrios, and Valentia. These travels are recorded by the saint's biographer, Sabas, who does not fail to mention several miracles Peter performed in those places. Peter also visited the famous leader of the Iconophiles, Saint Theodore of Stoudios, who had been exiled to Asia Minor. After this visit, Theodore wrote a letter to his followers, castigating them for not recognizing Peter's ascetic achievements (on which see further, below).

The resumption of persecution under the emperor Theophilos (829–842) forced Peter to renew his anxious efforts to keep together the monastic communities he had founded. In the last phase of his life as an itinerant monk he was joined by the former bishop of Anchialos, Jacob, who

had participated in the Seventh Ecumenical Council (787). After visiting his friend Saint Ioannikios, another famous ascetic of Bithynia in this period, Saint Peter died in the small hermitage of Saint Nicholas on New Year's Day 837. His body was buried with all proper honors, and his tomb became famous for the miraculous healings that took place there.

<br>

### Sabas, the Author of the Life of Saint Peter

*The Life of Saint Peter of Atroa* was written by the monk Sabas, a well-known figure of the middle ninth century. Sabas was, so to speak, the official biographer of the two great Bithynian saints of his times, that is, Ioannikios and Peter of Atroa.[2] He was an eyewitness of several incidents he narrated in *The Life of Saint Peter,* being himself a spiritual son of the saint. Sabas describes some other incidents on the basis of the information given to him by several companions of the saint who had witnessed them. He was thus a conscientious compiler of his material, which he tried to ascertain and verify as exhaustively as possible.[3] The information he provides concerning himself is rather meager. His family must have maintained a residence in Constantinople, since in chapter 48 of *The Life of Saint Peter,* Sabas informs us that he planned to take refuge there from an Arab raid. The argument that he was born after 815, because he calls Methodios of Constantinople "the first orthodox patriarch of our generation," seemingly ignoring Nikephoros, who had been patriarch until 815, is rejected by Vitalien Laurent, the first editor of the *Life.*[4] He might have been born around 818, according to a recent reconstruction of his biography, al-

though we have some doubts concerning the grounds for giving such a precise date for the hagiographer's birth.[5]

An ardent iconophile, Sabas took care to present these two men, Saints Ioannikios and Peter, as staunch, uncompromising defenders of the orthodox faith. He was particularly interested in presenting the two as equal to the great ascetics of the past: like the old abbots of Egypt or Palestine who, by the sheer fame of their achievements, were able to gather crowds of people around them, both abandoned the world at a very early age and led solitary lives, performing many miracles and advising those in need. Despite his zeal for preserving his heroes' memory, Sabas did conceal occasional details that could harm their reputations. Fortunately, we possess another *Life of Saint Ioannikios,* written by a certain Peter, in which the saint is presented as an opponent of the Studites, if not of Saint Theodore himself, and as a supporter of the iconophile patriarch Methodios, installed in 843, who restored the cult of the images but did not persecute the iconoclasts as vigorously as the Studites might have wished. This detail is not even mentioned in the *Life* written by Sabas. Therefore, it is possible that *The Life of Saint Peter* might also be a tendentious document, not revealing all aspects of its protagonist, although such a contention is very difficult indeed to prove. For example, it might be tempting to see the incident of Saint Peter's meeting with Theodore the Studite as an invention of Sabas's, since he was positively biased toward the Studites, but the event is mentioned in other sources as well.[6] Sabas also gives us a reliable chronological frame of the saint's life: he takes care to indicate several events by the year of the reign of the emperor as well as by the years that have passed since the saint's birth (or his

embracing of monasticism). Thus, even if Sabas did conceal certain details of the life of Saint Peter, generally speaking, he has left us a trustworthy document, replete with prosopographical, topographical, and other details related to the saint's life and his social and political milieu, which contribute to what appears to be a quite accurate reconstruction of his monastic career.

Sabas seems to be a rather unsophisticated author. His numerous mistakes in the use of Attic Greek suggest that his education was far below the level usually required from authors dealing with ecclesiastical subjects. In spite of his limitations, the author does sometimes try to elevate his style by using learned quotations; this is the case, for example, in the introduction (chapter 1), which creates an impression of erudition for the audience, through his use of a quotation from pseudo–Dionysius the Areopagite. But Sabas's strength lies in his simple yet powerful narrative style. We shall give just one example: In chapter 48 he describes his own anxiety because of the impending invasion of the Arabs, succinctly presenting the saint's address to him in dialogue with his own thoughts, given in direct speech. The apprehension of the moment is captured in a manner that is both vivid and convincing.

Sabas also takes care to construct his text in a meaningful manner through the use of various motifs, which are repeated in some crucial passages of the text. It is thus evident, for instance, that Sabas deliberately describes the death of Paul, Saint Peter of Atroa's spiritual father, so as to mirror the death of his disciple, many years afterward: Paul entrusts Peter with the guidance of his monastic community before his death in a way that almost anticipates Peter's

own last instructions to his disciples before his death. Saint Peter is the lawful successor of Saint Paul, who urges him to care about his brethren at the time of his death (chapter 11.1). But the brother of Saint Peter becomes the lawful successor of the saint in his turn, after being entrusted with the leadership of the community by the saint (chapters 83–84). Therefore, the motif of the spiritual sonhood, which functions as a confirmation of the legality of the leadership of most Byzantine monastic communities, helps Sabas to give a broader dimension to his text, likely as a way of enhancing the authority of the (probable) current abbot of the community, Jacob, who was a nephew of Saint Peter's, and is mentioned in both the preamble of the text (chapter 1.2) and later on as well (chapters 103–4).

The text begins (chapter 1.2) with a description of a miracle of Saint Peter, who appeared to the author in a dream, dressed as a priest and inside a church, and gave him a cup of oil to drink, thus encouraging him to write down his *Life*. It is not by chance that a similar miracle precedes the death of Saint Peter, who appeared to Saint Ioannikios in a dream: both men were in the church of Saint Nicholas when suddenly a great mountain appeared, the peak of which reached the sky, and two men guided Saint Peter to the sky (chapter 81). The episode recounts a kind of "ascension" of Saint Peter, closely following the New Testament descriptions of the ascension of Jesus; the mountain is none other than the so-called cosmic mountain, the *axis mundi* (world axis), the place where the divinity encounters human beings. Saint Ioannikios's vision serves as a reminder of Sabas's dream as described in the preamble to the text. Placed as it is between these two supernatural visions, the whole narrative func-

tions as a divine apocalypse: the writing of the text has been ordained by the saint himself inside a church, and the text comes to its conclusion with the departure of the saint, which takes place on two levels, a supernatural one in chapter 81 and a natural one (the saint's death) in chapter 85.[7]

## The Two Versions of The Life

*The Life of Saint Peter of Atroa,* which was written by Sabas shortly after the saint's death, survives in two manuscripts: Marcianus gr. 583 (henceforth, Marc.), offering an integral version of the text, and Glascuensis BE 8.x.5 (henceforth, Glasc.), preserving the text with some gaps due to the loss of several folios and including, in addition, certain posthumous miracles of the saint absent from Marc. The text was published first by Laurent on the basis of Marc., but, after he realized that the text was also preserved by Glasc., he proceeded to a partial edition of those parts of Glasc. that were missing in Marc., concurrently offering a sort of critical apparatus to all the chapters of his previous edition and enumerating the different readings of Glasc.[8] Laurent argued that both Glasc. and Marc. were produced by the author of the text himself, who revised his original version (Marc.), written a short time after the saint's death, producing a corrected and augmented version of his text (Glasc.) some years later.

In our view, neither Glasc. nor Marc. is to be identified with the original text produced by Sabas. There are significant discrepancies between the two manuscripts, and there are several cases in which the original version of the text is preserved either by Glasc. or by Marc. Generally speak-

ing, Glasc. is more accurate, offering the correct reading of many passages, while Marc.'s contribution to the restoration of the original text, while not negligible, is less substantial. However, the degree of accuracy with which the text is preserved by the two manuscripts is not the only difference between them, nor even the most significant. On the one hand, it is obvious that Glasc. represents a much more complete version of the text, while Marc. omits several episodes or significant details, which are preserved in full only in the version of Glasc. On the other hand, several passages that deal with the same material in both manuscripts are preserved by Marc. with substantial reworking: indeed, almost the entire text of the *Life* seems to have been reworked by a subsequent author, probably a monk of the monastery of Saint Peter, and this reworking is reflected in Marc. However, a certain degree of reworking may be detected in Glasc. as well, since in some cases Marc. seems to offer a more original form of the text, while the version of Glasc. is either deficient or wrong. We present here a small sample of the differences between Glasc. and Marc., grouped into various categories, so that the reader may grasp the peculiarities of each version. Glasc. is much closer, though not identical, to the original text as written by Sabas, while Marc. is an abbreviation of it.

1. Textual differences arising from scribal error.

An example of a false computation of time, which is most likely attributable to a scribal error, is encountered in chapter 4.1: Marc. specifies that at the time of his escape from his paternal house the saint was twenty-eight years old. Lau-

rent realized that such an age would be far too late for somebody who was described as little more than a child at the
time of his decision to embrace the monastic life and accordingly emended the text, writing ιη′ (18) instead of κη′
(28). In our view Glasc. may offer the saint's correct age,
since it states explicitly that he was twenty years old (εἰκοστὸν ἔτος ἄγων τῆς ἡλικίας) at the time he took the monastic habit.

However, there are some cases in which Marc. seems to
preserve the original reading. In chapter 51 Glasc. writes,
Λαβὼν ὁ ὅσιος μετ᾽ αὐτοῦ Φιλόθεον καὶ Βαρνάβαν τοὺς
ἀξιομνημονεύτους ὑπηρέτας αὐτοῦ, ἔτι τε καί τινα ἕτερον
ἐπίσκοπον, Κύπριον τῷ γένει καὶ τῇ ἀρχῇ, Ἰωάννην καλούμενον, ὅσπερ καὶ τῷ ὁσίῳ πατρὶ ταπεινοφρονῶν ὑπετάττετο πρὸς πᾶσαν διακονίαν τοῖς κατὰ τὴν μονὴν ἐπιτηδεύων (The holy one, taking with him those distinguished
servants of his, Philotheos and Barnabas, as well as another
man, a bishop called John who hailed from and held office
on Cyprus, who had made himself subordinate to the holy
father because of his humility and performed every kind of
service for those in the monastery).The sentence lacks a
verb. The version of Marc. provides one: Λαβὼν μετ᾽ αὐτοῦ
Φιλόθεον καὶ Βαρνάβαν τοὺς ὑπηρέτας αὐτοῦ, αἰτεῖται καί
τινα ἐπίσκοπον, Κύπριον τῷ γένει, Ἰωάννην καλούμενον,
ὃς καὶ ταπεινοφρονῶν τῷ ὁσίῳ πατρὶ ὑπετάττετο πρὸς
πᾶσαν διακονίαν, συνεισελθεῖν μετ᾽ αὐτῶν εἰς τὸν ναὸν τῆς
ὑπεραγίας Θεοτόκου (Taking with him his servants Philotheos and Barnabas, he also asked a certain bishop called
John who hailed from Cyprus, who had made himself subject to the saint because of his humility and performed every
kind of service, to come with them to the church of the all-

holy Theotokos). The verb αἰτεῖται (asked) of Marc. seems to be the original reading, which due to a mistake that occurred, possibly through dictation, was transformed into ἔτι τε (as well as) in Glasc.

2. Differences concerning grammar and syntax: attempts by the two redactors to correct grammatical blunders in the original text.

There is no doubt that the author, Sabas, had difficulties in adhering to the rules of Attic syntax. In many cases, instead of abiding by the learned style employed by most Byzantine authors, he used forms of the vernacular. In some cases, those forms are preserved by both Glasc. and Marc. For example, in chapter 6.8, the accusative (τὸν δοξάσαντα Κύριον σὺν τῷ δοξασθέντι φωνὰς ἠφίει) is employed instead of the dative (τῷ δοξάσαντι Κυρίῳ).[9] However, in certain other cases vernacular forms have been corrected in one of the two versions. Marc. thus corrects several "ungrammatical" forms of Glasc., which seem to be original: for example, in chapter 111, where Glasc. has προσκυλινδοῦσθαι and Marc. προσκυλινδεῖσθαι, or in chapter 79, where Glasc. has ἐπίστανται and Marc. ἐφίστανται. But there are certain cases in which the inverse phenomenon is to be observed, that is, Glasc. seems to correct Marc.: for example, in chapter 1.1, Marc.'s πρᾶξιν καὶ θεωρίαν λελαμπρυσμένου for Glasc.'s πράξει καὶ θεωρίᾳ λελαμπρυσμένου, or in chapter 1.2 Marc. gives τρέψας μοι, and Glasc. τρέψας με. So, we should not rush to the conclusion that one of the two versions is more primitive or more vernacular than the other. As we have seen, very often, one version may employ ver-

nacular forms, which are removed by the other (or vice versa) when describing the same event.

3. Omission of important details or entire events by Marc.

An interesting example of Marc. drastically changing the text of Glasc. occurs in chapter 1.2. While Glasc. mentions the miracles of the saint that had to do with the author himself and the miracles that benefited other people (τῶν εἰς ἐμὲ . . . θαυματουργημάτων τὰ βέβαια, τῶν πολλαχῶς εὐεργετηθέντων . . . τὰ εὔδηλα), Marc. omits any reference to miracles done for the author himself, mentioning only the miracles the saint performed that were reported by other people, who were trustworthy and presumably gave an account of them to the author. It is a clear case of Glasc.'s priority over Marc.: no author would suppress his own testimony concerning a saint in favor of the testimony of other people.

Then, in chapters 6.3–4 and 7, where Glasc. offers us a full transcription of the letters concerning the ordination of the saint exchanged between his spiritual father Paul, the patriarch Tarasios of Constantinople, and Basileios the bishop of Zygos, the documents are omitted altogether by Marc. There can be no doubt that the documents are not forgeries; in all probability they were kept in the archive of the monastery of the saint, where the author of his *Life* found and transcribed them.

One of the most important amplifications by Glasc. is to be found in chapters 12.1–3, where there is a long theological digression on the value of icons. That text, which seems to be a pastiche of the doctrinal commonplaces of iconophile

literature, is omitted by Marc. One might be tempted to consider the digression in Glasc. as a later addition to the text, since such interpolation was rather common in hagiographic texts: redactors embellished them by inserting digressions here and there irrelevant to the original. But in this case the opposite occurred: a later redactor (in Marc.) omitted a digression that disturbed the sequence of events and potentially confused the reader. This becomes clear, as in chapter 12.2 Glasc. states that, after Leo V took power (κατασχόντι δὲ Λέοντι τῷ τυράννῳ τὸ σκῆπτρον), the Evil One revolted against God once more (ἐπαρθέντι γὰρ αὐτῷ κατὰ Θεοῦ), inventing a heresy and deciding to destroy the icons and ruin them altogether (οὐκ ἄλλην τινὰ αὐτῷ παρέδειξεν αἵρεσιν . . . τὴν εἰκόνα λιθάζων, ἐκμοχλεύων, καταστρέφων, συμπατῶν τε καὶ κατακαίων). A version of this extract is the only part of this long passage in Glasc. that is also preserved by Marc., but there it is condensed and totally transformed by the redactor: Κατασχόντος δὲ τοῦ τυράννου τὰ σκῆπτρα καὶ κατεπαρθέντος τοῦ Κτίσαντος, καταστρέφει καὶ ἐκμοχλεύει καὶ συμπατεῖ καὶ κατακαίει πᾶσαν τὴν τῶν σεπτῶν εἰκόνων θέαν (As soon as the tyrant had seized the scepter, he acted arrogantly toward the Creator; he tore down and overthrew and trampled upon and burned every appearance of the sacred icons). Readers who have only the version of Marc. before them may get the impression that the originator of the destruction of the icons was Leo V, not the devil, as is explicitly stated in Glasc. That the variant of Marc. is not the original one is proved even by the syntax of that version, which is rather muddled: the genitive absolute, κατασχόντος, refers to Leo, who is also the subject of the verbs that come afterward.

There are also, however, some cases in which Marc. may preserve an original detail omitted by Glasc. This is the case in chapter 44, where Marc. adds that the nephew of the saint, after being cured by him, remained in the monastery, and gave glory to the Lord. According to Laurent, the fact that Glasc. does not specify whether this man remained in the monastery or not indicates that by the time of the redaction of Glasc. the saint's nephew had abandoned the monastery. This might be possible, but there is no proof for the hypothesis.

4. Different ways of expressing the same thing in Glasc. and Marc.

In several places in the two manuscripts we come across different terms or different expressions employed to describe the same event, with both forms seeming to be of equal value. For example, in chapter 14.3 the offering of the divine gifts by Saint Peter is referred to as a ζωοθυσία by Marc., and as a θεοθυσία by Glasc. Both terms seem to be equally applicable in this context. We have no way of determining which of the two versions is the original.

## Were Both Versions of the Text Written by Sabas?

While Laurent believed that both Marc. and Glasc. were produced by the hand of the monk Sabas himself, it is difficult to understand how he came to this conclusion, which is rather tenuous and far from certain. A plausible explanation is that he was working within the confines of the editorial techniques of his day, which held that most hagiographic

texts presented a homogeneous, closed tradition, and any
interventions were best explained as conscious attempts by
their authors to improve their style. At that time the idea of
an "open" text would not have crossed his mind. To do jus-
tice to Laurent, we must note that he did not reject the pos-
sibility of the redactor of Glasc. being someone other than
the author himself; he even adduced some arguments that
might give credence to such a view. For example, in certain
cases where Sabas speaks about himself in personal terms in
Marc., Glasc. chooses a more impersonal tone, watering
down the autobiographic elements of the text. However,
Laurent did not develop those arguments, instead prefer-
ring to attribute the discrepancies between Marc. and Glasc.
to Sabas himself. He argues that Glasc. adds several episodes
that could hardly have been known to anyone else except
Sabas, who was a constant companion of the saint and had
firsthand knowledge of his adventures. And he contends
that the public recitation of his text during the office of Matins (see chapter 98) gave Sabas the opportunity to observe
the reaction of the audience and revise his text accordingly.
That Glasc., while recording a miracle of the saint, refers
to the recitation of the *Life* of the saint during Matins is a
proof for Laurent that Glasc. is later than Marc.; in his view
the text recited at Matins could be none other than Marc.

However, none of Laurent's arguments are conclusive or
strong enough to make us believe that both versions of the
text were written by Sabas himself. One might doubt that
the theological digression of Glasc.'s chapters 12.1–3 was
part of the original text, but can there truly be any doubt
concerning the originality of the letters exchanged between
the monk Paul and patriarch Tarasios settling the matter of

Peter's ordination? Why would Sabas omit these important texts while composing Marc., adding them only later, when he supposedly prepared his Glasc. version? In our view their omission by Marc. can more easily be explained as an attempt by a later redactor to abbreviate a text that was too long for him.

The issue of Saint Peter's posthumous miracles, which are to be found only in Glasc., is an exceptionally thorny one, but important in this context.[10] Laurent insisted that Sabas himself added the miracles to his text in a later phase; that is, that the "original" text—represented for Laurent by Marc.—lacked any reference to the posthumous miracles of the saint. But one may adopt another solution and suggest that Marc. omitted those miracles because of its author's general tendency to abbreviate the text. Therefore, the epilogue of Marc., in which it is stressed that no one can give a satisfactory account of the numerous miracles the saint performed after his dormition, may have been written by a redactor and not the author himself. Beginning his account of the posthumous miracles of Saint Peter, Sabas says (Glasc., chapter 86.2), "Since, then, by the grace of the good God we have reached the end of our poorly worded description of our father Peter's miracles when he was alive, I will turn my discourse to those after his dormition as I, wretch that I am, promised." Laurent believed that this promise was given by Sabas in the lost part of Glasc.,[11] but he failed to notice that the promise was actually given a few lines before, in chapter 86.1: "This is the final point, brothers, of the struggles and miracles of Father Peter's earthly life. What came afterward we are going to expound separately for those of you who are faithful and loyal." At this point Sabas disrupts his narrative, asking his audience to praise the Father, the Son, and the

Holy Spirit and ending his account at the close of chapter
86.1 with the word "amen," a clear indication that the text
has been completed.

In fact, in Glasc., as it now stands, we are presented with
two different texts, which were mistakenly published by
Laurent as one and the same chapter (chapter 86, which, in
our edition, is broken into two parts, 86.1 and 86.2).[12] The
part of the text that ends with an "amen" is the original epilogue to the *Life* of the saint. The text that follows is the
prologue to a new text, that is, the Appendix to the original *Life,* which refers to the posthumous miracles of Saint
Peter. Both texts, *Life* and Appendix, were written by Sabas
himself, but at different times. It is clear that Sabas ended
his *Life* of the saint, promising at the same time to continue
it afterward by composing a new text narrating in a separate treatise the miracles that took place after the saint's
dormition.

In this interpretation the epilogue preserved by Marc. is
to be considered a secondary composition, written by a redactor who avoided any mention of the posthumous miracles of the saint: he speaks about healings of people blind,
deaf, leprous, and possessed by demons, in a most general
manner and without giving any further specifications. One
is tempted to consider that part of Marc. as a short, rather
impressionistic account written by somebody who had read
the posthumous miracles of the saint preserved in Glasc.

If the distinction we have made between the two, originally independent, parts of chapter 86 is correct, we may
explain the reference in chapter 98 to the reading of *The Life
of Saint Peter* at Matins on his feast. Sabas there refers to his
own *Life* as having been read during the feast—a *Life* that
had no posthumous miracles, since the Appendix had not

yet been written. We are not in a position to determine the time that elapsed between the writing of the epilogue to *The Life of Saint Peter* and the composition of the new text, the Appendix of posthumous miracles. Laurent, who argued that the time between Sabas's versions was rather lengthy, may be correct. We would perhaps not be far from the truth if we maintained that the posthumous miracles were written around the years 860 to 865 by Sabas, in fulfillment of the promise he had given earlier to his monastic audience in the epilogue of his *Life* of the saint.

To conclude, neither Marc. nor Glasc. represent the original form of *The Life of Saint Peter* as written by the monk Sabas. Each version (Marc. to a greater extent) exhibits several inaccuracies, omissions of important details, and textual errors, which can be corrected only on the basis of the other version. It would be unreasonable to attribute all those mistakes to an author who supposedly undertook the task of correcting his text at a later stage, as Laurent insisted. Marc. has a tendency to drastically abbreviate the original text, while Glasc. is much more conservative. Because of its tendency to omit important details for the sake of brevity, we consider Marc. to be less trustworthy than Glasc., although, in some cases, Marc. seems to preserve the original form of the text when Glasc. does not.

## The Translation

The translation in this volume is based on the version of Glasc. but, following our approach to the text (see the Note on the Text), the parts missing in that manuscript (notably chapters 15–37 and 52–78) are translated from the relevant sections of Marc. In accordance with the style requirements

of the DOML series, the changes of source are not indicated in the text and translation themselves, but are made clear in the Notes to the Translation. Text and translation of passages where Marc. differs significantly from, or adds to, Glasc. are also provided in those notes. The inclusion of sections from Marc. has necessitated keeping intact the numbering of Laurent's edition, but the version of Glasc. divides the text into several chapters bearing titles, which, though probably not written by the author himself, represent an attempt to make the reading of the text easier. We have also translated those titles, offering the reader the option to construct the text in a different way from that of the first editor.

Again, in accordance with series style, we have kept Notes to the Translation to a minimum, providing only necessary indications concerning the chronology of the events, the topography, and some prosopographical details. Finally, we should note that an anonymous modern Greek translation of the text (according to Marc.) was published in 2013.[13]

We wish to thank our colleagues, Professors Alexander Alexakis and Sofia Kotzabassi, for reading the text and making several suggestions. Richard Greenfield contributed by enhancing the translation and polishing the notes and Introduction. We also wish to thank Nicole Eddy, the managing editor of the series, for her meticulous copy editing and helpful suggestions.

## NOTES

1 The best modern account of the saint's life (in German) is to be found in *PmbZ*, no. 6022 (Petros von Atroa).

2 For a brief account of Sabas and his work, see Martin Hinterberger,

"The Byzantine Hagiographer and His Text," in *The Ashgate Research Companion to Byzantine Hagiography*, vol. 2, *Genres and Contexts*, ed. Stephanos Efthymiadis (Farnham and Burlington, VT, 2013), 224–25. Sabas is not to be confused with his namesake, the biographer of Saint Makarios of Pelekete. See also Óscar Prieto Domínguez, *Literary Circles in Byzantine Iconoclasm: Patrons, Politics and Saints* (Cambridge, 2020), 394, and 400–401, who identifies him with a recipient of some letters of the patriarch Photios, on rather dubious grounds. On the (equally dubious in our view) attribution to him of some other works, for example unpublished biographies of Saint Ilarion of Dalmatos and of the patriarch Methodios, see Domínguez, *Literary Circles*, 407–24.

3 Cyril Mango, "The Two Lives of St. Ioannikios and the Bulgarians," in "Okeanos: Essays Presented to Ihor Ševčenko on His Sixtieth Birthday by His Colleagues and Students," ed. Cyril Mango and Omeljan Pritsak, special issue, *Harvard Ukrainian Studies* 7 (1983): 403–4, analyzing Sabas's *Life of Saint Ioannikios,* had serious doubts concerning his credibility, however.

4 See Vitalien Laurent, ed. and trans., *La vie merveilleuse de saint Pierre d'Atroa (†837),* Subsidia hagiographica 29 (Brussels, 1956), 11.

5 See Domínguez, *Literary Circles,* 393. Generally speaking, the biography of Sabas reconstructed by Domínguez (pp. 391–427) lacks a sound factual basis. In our view it is not possible to identify the biographer of Saints Peter and Ioannikios with an abbot of the monastery of Pissadinoi, a recipient of some letters of the patriarch Photios, and an abbot of the monastery of Stoudios, simply because they have the same name.

6 We refer mainly to the two versions of the *Life of Saint Theodore the Studite*, A (*BHG³* 1755, PG 99:220CD) and B (*BHG³* 1754, PG 99:316D). For the latter, see Robert H. Jordan and Rosemary Morris, eds. and trans., *The Life and Death of Theodore of Stoudios,* Dumbarton Oaks Medieval Library 70 (Cambridge, MA, 2021), 172–75.

7 The supernatural level is stressed in another episode of the saint's *Life:* in chapter 41.1 the saint, though being absent in Bithynia, appears in a church in Lydia, saving the nuns of a monastery from their enemies.

8 Vitalien Laurent, ed. and trans., *La "Vita retractata" et les miracles posthumes de saint Pierre d'Atroa,* Subsidia hagiographica 31 (Brussels, 1958), 13.

9 The addition of πρὸς here by Laurent seems unnecessary, since there

are other vernacular forms in both versions. See, for example, chapter 50.1, πάλιν τὸ αὐτὸ πλήρης (instead of πλῆρες), or chapter 84.1, τὸν τῆς μονῆς (ἡμῶν added in Marc.) οἰκονόμον καὶ σὸν ἀδελφὸν Παῦλον ἡμῶν ἐγχείρισον τὴν κυβέρνησιν.

10 For a brief discussion of these miracles and their recipients, see Stephanos Efthymiadis, "Collections of Miracles (Fifth–Fifteenth Centuries)," in Efthymiadis, *Ashgate Research Companion,* vol. 2, p. 120.

11 Laurent, *La "Vita retractata,"* 134n2: "Cette promesse n'a pu être formulée que dans la seconde partie de la Vie et dans la partie perdue, car la fin de la première édition (cf. ch. 86) laisse nettement entendre que l'auteur renonce à relater les miracles posthumes en raison même de leur nombre. Sabas est donc en définitive revenu sur son propos."

12 Laurent, *La "Vita retractata,"* 135.

13 Ὅσιος Πέτρος τῆς Ἀτρώας, Ἄγνωστα Συναξάρια [*sic*] 1 (Thessaloniki, 2013).

# THE LIFE OF
# SAINT PETER OF ATROA

Βίος καὶ πολιτεία τοῦ ὁσίου καὶ θαυματουργοῦ πατρὸς ἡμῶν καὶ ὁμολογητοῦ Πέτρου, ἡγουμένου μονῆς τοῦ Ἁγίου Ζαχαρίου, συγγραφεὶς παρὰ Σάβα μοναχοῦ.

## Προοίμιον

*Οἱ τῶν τοῦ Θεοῦ μυστηρίων ἱεροφάνται, ἄλλοι μὲν ἄλλως καὶ ἄλλα κατὰ καιροὺς ἰδίους ἕκαστος κατὰ τὸ δοθὲν αὐτῷ χάρισμα συνεγράψαντο, οἱ μὲν τῆς ἀρχιφώτου καὶ θεαρχικωτάτης Τριάδος τὴν ἁπλουμένην ἑνότητα καὶ τὴν ἑνουμένην ἁπλότητα, οἱ δὲ τὴν τοῦ Θεοῦ Λόγου πρὸς σῶμα ἀδιάσπαστόν τε καὶ ἀσύγχυτον καθ᾽ ὑπόστασιν ἕνωσιν, οἱ δὲ τὴν τῶν μαρτύρων ἀριστείαν καὶ εὐκλεᾶ μέχρις αἵματος* πρὸς τὴν εἰδωλολατρείαν καὶ τοὺς τυράννους ἀντικατάστασιν, καὶ ἀγγελικῶς ἄλλοι τῶν ἐπὶ γῆς βιωσάντων τὴν ἄσκησιν, καὶ πολλοὺς τοῦ σκότους τῆς ἀσεβείας ῥυσάμενοι, τῷ φωτὶ Χριστοῦ τῆς εὐσεβείας ἐπύρσευσαν καὶ πρὸς τὸν ὅμοιον ζῆλον ἀθλήσεως λέγω διήγειραν ἢ ἀσκήσεως. Οὐ γὰρ ὀνίνησιν ὅλως τὸν μάρτυρα τοῦ μαρτυρίου ἡ συγγραφὴ ἢ τὸν ἀσκητὴν τῆς ἀσκήσεως, ἀλλ᾽ ἡμῶν πρὸς μνήμην ἐγγράφονται διηνεκῆ καὶ ὠφέλειαν, ἵνα τὸν λόγον μεταθέντες εἰς πρᾶξιν, κοινωνοὶ τῶν ἐκείνοις ἡτοιμασμένων γενώμεθα ἀγαθῶν. Ὅθεν κἀγὼ ὁ ἀνάξιος ἀνδρὸς θεοφόρου καὶ θαυματουργοῦ, πράξει καὶ θεωρίᾳ λελαμπρυσμένου, καὶ τὸ τοῦ Χριστοῦ λογικὸν ἀπλανῶς ποιμάναντος

Life and conduct of our holy and miracle-working father and confessor Peter, the superior of the monastery of Saint Zechariah, written by the monk Sabas.

## Preface

*The hierophants of the mysteries of God,* each of them in his own way and in his own time, in accordance with the talent given to them by God, wrote various things about the simplified unity and the unified simplicity of the most divine Trinity, the source of light. Others wrote about the unbroken and unconfused hypostatic union of God the Word with flesh; others described the prowess and the glorious resistance of the martyrs against the idolaters and the tyrants, *to the point of shedding their own blood;* and others again wrote about the struggle of those living angelically on earth and, after rescuing many people from the darkness of impiety, inflamed them with the light of the pious faith in Christ, rousing them, I mean, to the same zeal for contest and asceticism. For the description of his martyrdom is of no profit at all to a martyr, nor that of his struggles to an ascetic; rather, it is for us that these descriptions have been written as a perpetual reminder and assistance, so that, by putting the words into practice, we may come to share the good things prepared for them. For this reason, when I, unworthy man that I am, was ordered by the most holy father Jacob, who became the leader of his flock a short time afterward, to com-

3

ποίμνιον προσταγεὶς βίον συντάξαι θεόληπτον παρὰ τοῦ
μικρὸν ὕστερον καθηγησαμένου τούτου τῆς ποίμνης ὁσιωτάτου πατρὸς Ἰακώβου, ὤκνουν δι' ἀπορίαν λόγου πρὸς
τὴν ἐγχείρησιν, τὸ ὕψος τῆς εὐσεβείας καὶ θαυμαστῆς πο-
λιτείας τοῦ πατρὸς ὑφορώμενος, ὡς αὐτοῖς ὀφθαλμοῖς
κατενόησα, καὶ τὸ βάθος τῆς ταπεινώσεως, δι' ἧς καὶ
οὐρανοπολίτης ἐγένετο, καὶ τὸ πλοῦτος τῆς πρὸς τὸν Θεὸν
ἀγάπης καὶ τὸν πλησίον, καὶ πρός γε τούτοις τὴν ἀθλη-
τικὴν μονιὰν καὶ τὴν ἀσκητικὴν παλαίστραν καὶ τοὺς πολλοὺς ἐκείνους ὑπὲρ Χριστοῦ διωγμοὺς καὶ τῶν θεοδωρή-
των σημείων τὸ ἄπειρον.

1.2 Περὶ τοῦ ἐν ἀποκαλύψει ὑπὸ τοῦ πατρὸς Πέτρου τῷ
ἐξηγητῇ δοθέντος λόγου

Καὶ γὰρ τούτῳ τῷ φωστῆρι τῶν φωστήρων κατηξιώθην
στοιχειωθῆναι πρὸς τὴν τοῦ μονήρους βίου διαγωγὴν ὁ
πανελάχιστος ἔγωγε, ἔχων ἀεὶ ἐν καρδίᾳ τὰ αὐτοῦ ψυχωφελῆ κατορθώματά τε καὶ θαύματα, ἅπερ καὶ ἀναγκαίως
ἐπείγομαι λέγειν διὰ τὸ τῆς παρακοῆς ἐπικίνδυνον κατὰ
καιρὸν τὸν προσήκοντα. Ποῖα δὴ ταῦτα; Τῶν εἰς ἐμὲ
αὐτοῦ θαυματουργημάτων τὰ βέβαια, τῶν πολλαχῶς εὐεργετηθέντων καὶ παρεμοῦ ὁραθέντων τὰ εὔδηλα, τῆς παρ'
ἑτέρων εὐαποδέκτων ἀνδρῶν ἀψευδοῦς διδαχῆς τὰ εὔ-
πιστα, καὶ πρό γε τούτων ἁπάντων καὶ σὺν τούτοις τῆς
ἐνθέου ζωῆς αὐτοῦ τὸ ἀκρότατον. Πρὸς οὖν τὴν τούτων
λοιπὸν διήγησιν, ἀδελφοί, ὡρμημένῳ μοι καὶ ἀπορουμένῳ,
ὡς ἀεὶ πᾶσι πτωχὴ ποιεῖν εἴωθεν διάνοια, εἰς λιτὴν τὴν

pose a divinely inspired life of a man who was possessed by God and a miracle worker, who had distinguished himself by his actions and his spiritual contemplation, and had governed the rational flock of Christ without error, I hesitated because of the deficiency of my speech for this task, for I looked with awe at the height of the piety and the admirable conduct of our father, something which I observed with my own eyes; at the depth of his humility, through which he became a citizen of heaven; at the fullness of his love *of God* and *his neighbor;* and, in addition to these, at his solitary competition and ascetic contest, his numerous trials for the sake of Christ, and his innumerable God-given wonders.

1.2 On the gift of speech given by our father Peter to the narrator through revelation

Though wholly insignificant, I was deemed worthy of being introduced to the monastic life by this luminary among luminaries, and, having always kept in my heart his spiritually beneficial achievements and miracles, I was now being forced to narrate them at the appropriate time, because disobedience is dangerous. Which are they? Those indisputable instances of the miracles he performed for my sake, those manifest instances of the benefactions which he worked in many ways and which were seen by me, those most credible instances in the truthful account of other well-respected men, and, before everything else and in addition to these, the loftiness of his divine life. So, my brothers, when I had set about my narration of these matters and was at a loss, as is always the case with every poor mind, I turned

συγγραφὴν μεταθέμενος, τῷ πατρὶ τῶν πατέρων ἐν ἐκτε-
νίᾳ ἱκέτευσα δοθῆναί μοι λόγον ἐν ἀνοίξει τοῦ στόματός
μου. Ὁ δὲ ὢν ἀεὶ πολύσπλαγχνος πατὴρ ἡμῶν καὶ ὑπή-
κοος, εἰς ὕπνου τινὰ λεπτοτάτου ἔμφασιν τρέψας με, ἀποκαλύπτει μου εὐθὺς τῆς διανοίας τὰ ὄμματα, καὶ ὁρῶ ναὸν
μέγαν, φαιδρόν τε καὶ περικαλλῆ, οὗ τὸ κάλλος ἀνέκφρα-
στον καὶ ἡ δόξα ἀνεκδιήγητος, καὶ αὐτὸν πρὸς τῷ δεξιῷ
μέρει τοῦ θυσιαστηρίου ἑστῶτα τὴν ἱερατικὴν ἐνδεδυμέ-
νον στολήν. Ὃς καὶ λαβὼν ἐκ τῆς θείας τραπέζης κρατῆρα
θεῖον (ἦν δὲ οὗτος ἐλαίου μεστὸς εὐώδους), ἐκ τούτου
μοι μεταδίδωσιν. Ἐξ οὗ καὶ διυπνισθεὶς ὁ ταλαίπωρος,
πρὸς τὴν τῶν μεμελημένων συγγραφὴν εὐθαρσῶς κατε-
τόλμησα, περὶ ὧν καὶ τοῦ λέγειν ἀπάρχομαι.

2.1 Περὶ τοῦ πόθεν ὥρμητο καὶ ποταπῶν γεννητόρων
ἐξέφυ

Ὁ θεῖος καὶ οὐρανοπολίτης οὗτος ἀνήρ, <ὁ> οὐρανίᾳ ζωῇ
ἐν σαρκὶ ὡς οὐρανὸν οἰκήσας τὴν γῆν καὶ πρὸς ἑαυτὸν
διὰ τοῦτο τὰς ἀγγελικὰς χορείας ἐπισπασάμενος, ὁ ἐν τῇ
βίβλῳ τῶν πρωτοτόκων τῶν ἀπογεγραμμένων ἐν οὐρανοῖς
πολιτογραφηθεὶς ὡς πρωτότοκος καὶ ἐν τῇ τούτων ἐκκλησίᾳ εἰσδεδεγμένος ὡς ἄξιος, ὁ ὁσιώτατος Πέτρος, ὥρματο
χώρας μὲν Ἀσίας, κώμης δὲ καλουμένης Ἐλαίας, Κοσμᾶ
καὶ Ἄννης γέννημα χρηματίσας, τοῦ μὲν ἐπὶ ῥώμῃ σώματος καὶ στρατείᾳ πρὸς τῇ λοιπῇ καλοκαγαθίᾳ τεθαυμα-
σμένου καὶ τιμωμένου, τῆς δὲ κατίχνως τῆς προφήτιδος
Ἄννης ὡς συνωνυμούσης κατὰ πάντα πορευομένης, ἐλπίδι

my writing into an entreaty, and I fervently beseeched the father of the fathers to give me speech *when I opened my mouth.* And our father, being always most merciful and eager to listen, made me experience the outward appearance of a light sleep and immediately opened my mind's eye. I saw a great church, radiant and very beautiful, the loveliness of which was indescribable and the glory ineffable. I also saw him standing at the right side of the holy altar, wearing his priestly vestments. He took from the holy altar a holy vessel (which was full of fragrant olive oil), and gave me a share of it. When I, wretch that I am, woke up, filled with confidence, I dared to undertake the writing of the matters about which I was concerned, and about which I shall now proceed to speak.

### 2.1 On where he came from and from what kind of parents he sprang

This divine man, this citizen of heaven, who dwelt on earth as if it were heaven through the heavenly conduct of his life in the flesh and thus attracted the angelic orders to himself, this man who, being himself firstborn, was enrolled as a citizen in the book *of the firstborn who are registered in heaven* and who was received into their *church* as worthy of it, this most holy Peter came from the land of Asia, from a village called Elaia, being a child of Kosmas and Anna. His father was admired and honored because of his physical strength as well as for his military achievements, while his mother followed the way of the prophetess Anna, being synonymous with her in all respects, in her hope and her faith in unwavering prayer. That pious woman who, in a similar way, experienced

τὲ καὶ πιστῇ ἀδιακρίτῳ προσευχῇ, ἧς καὶ τῶν λυπηρῶν
ὁμοιοτρόπως αὕτη ἡ εὐσεβὴς κληρονόμος καὶ κοινωνὸς
ἐχρημάτισεν ὡς οἶμαι, κατὰ θείαν οἰκονομίαν. Συνοικοῦσα
γὰρ αὕτη τῷ ταύτης ἀνδρί, ἕως καιροῦ ἠτεκνωμένη διέμει-
νεν λυπουμένη τὴν ἀπαιδίαν καὶ τῷ Κυρίῳ προσάξειν ὑπ-
ισχνουμένη τὸ γεννησόμενον, ὡς σωθῆναι ἀποστολικῶς
διὰ τὴν τεκνογονίαν ἐλπίζουσα. Ὁ δὲ τρισυπόστατος Κύριος, ταύτην παρ' αὐτῆς εὐκτικῶς δεξάμενος τὴν ὑπόσχεσιν, τριάδα τέκνων αὐτῇ κατακαιροὺς ἀποδίδωσι, διαρρήξας αὐτῆς τὰ δεσμὰ τῆς στειρώσεως.

## 2.2 Περὶ γεννήσεως, ἀναγεννήσεως, προσαγωγῆς καὶ ἱε-
ρωσύνης αὐτοῦ

Λαβούσης δὲ αὐτῆς ἐν γαστρί, καὶ τεκούσης τὸν μέγα
τοῦτον φωστῆρα τῶν φωστήρων, ὅ τε πατὴρ καὶ αὐτὴ καὶ
ἅπασα ἡ συγγένεια, τὴν τῆς ἀτεκνίας ζοφερὰν λύπην ἀπο-
βαλλόμενοι, τῇ τῆς εὐτεκνίας λαμπηδόνι χαρμονικῶς
κατηστράπτοντο, δι' ὃ ἀνάγουσιν ὁμαδὸν τὸ παιδίον ἐν τῷ
ἱερῷ τῇ ὀγδόῃ ἡμέρᾳ, ὡς ἔθος ἐστὶ Χριστιανοῖς, *περιτομῇ
καρδίας περιτεμνόμενον καὶ θείῳ Πνεύματι ἐλλαμπόμε-
νον*, ὡς αὕτως πάλιν τῇ τεσσαρακοστῇ τὴν αὐτὴν χάριν
δεχόμενον ἐκτυπώτερον. Εἶθ' οὕτως τῇ μυστικῇ καὶ τε-
λειοποιῷ τοῦ θείου βαπτίσματος ἀναγεννήσει προσάγου-
σιν, θεοβουλήτως καλέσαντες αὐτὸν Θεοφύλακτον, ὡς
Θεῷ προεγνωσμένον καὶ εἰς πολλῶν σωτηρίαν τετηρημέ-
νον. Ὡς δὲ τοῦτον ἡ μήτηρ ἀπεγαλάκτισεν, πληροῦσα
αὐτῆς τῆς προσευχῆς τὴν ὑπόσχεσιν, τῷ ἱερῷ προσφέρει,

the sorrow of that prophetess, is to be reckoned her heir and partner, in my view, because of divine dispensation. For although she lived together with her husband, after she had remained childless for a long time, she was distressed because of her childlessness and promised to offer to the Lord the child which would be born, hoping to be saved, as the Apostle says, through childbearing. The triune Lord, after receiving this promise from her through her prayers, gave her a triad of children, each one in its own time, after breaking the bonds of her sterility.

2.2  On his birth, his baptism, his presentation and priesthood

As soon as she became pregnant and gave birth to that great luminary among luminaries, his father, Anna, and all their relatives, cast away the dismal grief of childlessness and beamed joyfully with the radiance caused by having a child. For that reason, as a group, they all took the child to the church on the eighth day, as is Christian practice, and there he was circumcised with *a circumcision of the heart* and illuminated by the divine Spirit. In the same way, on the fortieth day the child received the same grace more clearly. Afterward they brought him to the mystical and perfecting regeneration of the holy baptism, naming him Theophylaktos by the will of God, because the child was known by God in advance and was preserved by him for the salvation of many people. And when his mother weaned him, fulfilling the promise of her prayer, she presented the child to the church

καὶ τῷ ἀρχιερεῖ προσάγει ὡς ἄλλον Σαμουὴλ τὸν πρωτό-
τοκον, ἀνθομολογουμένη Κυρίῳ.

2.3 Ὁ δὲ ἱεράρχης ἱερολογήσας τὸ τηνικαῦτα, στεφάνῳ
ἱερατικῷ τὴν κεφαλὴν τοῦ παιδὸς περικείρει καὶ τοῖς τῷ
Θεῷ ἀφιερωμένως δουλεύουσι συγκαταριθμεῖ. Ἐξ οὗ δὴ
καθεκάστην *προέκοπτεν τὸ παιδίον σοφίᾳ καὶ ἡλικίᾳ, ὥστε*
θαυμάζειν πάντας τὴν σύνεσιν, τὴν προσευχήν, τὴν ἄσκησιν, τὴν εὐλάβειαν αὐτοῦ, τὴν ἐν τῷ ναῷ τοῦ Θεοῦ προσεδρίαν, τὴν μακροθυμίαν, τὴν πραότητα, καὶ λέγειν, "ἀληθῶς *Πνεῦμα Θεοῦ ἐστιν ἐν αὐτῷ·* οὐδέπω γὰρ τοσαύτην
ἀρετὴν ἐν τοιαύτῃ σώματος κατείδομεν ἁπαλότητι." Ἐν
δευτέρᾳ γὰρ ἡλικίᾳ ἤδη καθίστατο, ἤγουν δωδεκαετίᾳ.

3 Περὶ τοῦ φθόνου τοῦ πρόσμονος καὶ ἀσφαλείας τῆς
θεομήτορος τοῦ ναοῦ καὶ τῆς ἐν αὐτῷ τοῦ πατρὸς παρα-
δόξου εἰσόδου

Ταύτης περὶ αὐτοῦ τῆς φήμης πανταχόσε ἐξηχηθείσης, ὁ
τοῦ ναοῦ τῆς θεομήτορος προσμονάριος, ἐν ᾧ ἐποιεῖτο
τὴν προσεδρίαν καὶ ἀδιάλειπτον προσευχὴν ὁ μακάριος
ὑπὸ τοῦ πονηροῦ δαίμονος φθόνῳ καὶ ὑποψίᾳ τρωθείς, ὡς
μὴ τῇ πολλῇ εἰς τὸν ἄνδρα πίστει καὶ πληροφορίᾳ τοῦ τῆς
ἐκκλησίας πληρώματος, τὴν αὐτοῦ ἐγχειρίσαντος λειτουργίαν, αὐτὸν ἐκεῖνον ταύτης ἐξώσειεν, ἐν θυμῷ πολλῷ
τοῦτον ἀπελάσας τῆς ἐκκλησίας πύλας τε ταύτης κλείσας
τε καὶ σφραγίσας, εἰς τὰ οἰκεῖα τὰς κλεῖς ἐπιφερόμενος
ἐπορεύετο. Κατὰ δὲ τὸν καιρὸν τῶν ἑωθινῶν ὕμνων ὡς
εἰώθει ὁ ὅσιος ἐπὶ τὸν προλεχθέντα ναὸν τῆς Θεοτόκου

THE LIFE OF SAINT PETER OF ATROA

and offered her firstborn to the archpriest as a new Samuel, giving praise to the Lord.

2.3 At that time the hierarch recited a prayer, clipped the child's hair in the shape of a priestly crown, and registered him among those consecrated to serving God. From that time onward the child *increased in wisdom and stature* every day and thus all admired his prudence, prayers, ascetic conduct, piety, constant presence in the church, forbearance, and gentleness. They said, "Truly *the Spirit of God* is in him. We have never seen such virtue in such a tender body." The saint was already in the second phase of his life, that is, twelve years old.

3 On the envy of the warden of the church, our father's protection by the mother of God and the miraculous entrance of our father into the church

After this rumor about Theophylaktos spread everywhere, the warden of the church of the mother of God, in which the blessed father was pursuing his diligent way of life and ceaseless prayer, was wounded with envy and suspicion by the evil demon. He feared that, because of the great faith and confidence of the church community in the man, they would dismiss him [the warden] and entrust the job to Theophylaktos. Enraged, the warden drove the saint out of the church and, after closing and locking the doors, went to his house carrying the keys with him. When it was time for the hymns of matins, the holy one went as usual to the previously mentioned church of the Theotokos, reciting the

πορεύεσθαι, ᾤχετο τὸ τοῦ Δαβὶδ ἀποστηθίζων ψαλτήριον, καὶ δὴ εὗρεν αὐτοῦ κεκλεισμένας τὰς θύρας καὶ αὐτὸς εὑρέθη τὸ τοῦ Δαβὶδ στιχολογῶν ῥητόν· Ἀνοίξατέ μοι πύλας δικαιοσύνης· εἰσελθὼν ἐν αὐταῖς ἐξομολογήσομαι τῷ Κυρίῳ. Καὶ σφραγίσαντος αὐτοῦ τῷ ζωοποιῷ τοῦ σταυροῦ τύπῳ, αὐτοματὶ ἠνοίγησαν αὐτῷ αἱ πύλαι τοῦ ἱεροῦ καὶ εἰσιόντι πάλιν ἐκλείσθησαν, σώας ἑαυτῶν ἀποσώζουσαι τὰς σφραγίδας. Μετὰ δὲ ταῦτα καταλαβὼν ὁ τὰς κλεῖς τοῦ ἱεροῦ ἐπιφερόμενος προσμονάριος καὶ ἀνοίξας, εὗρεν ἔνδον τὸν ὅσιον προσευχόμενον, καὶ θάμβος ἐξαίσιον ἔλαβεν αὐτὸν τῆς εἰσόδου αὐτοῦ τὸν τρόπον ἀμηχανήσαντος. Ὅθεν πίπτει πρηνὴς πρὸς τὸ ἔδαφος, καὶ γίνεται ἱκέτης ὁ πρότερον διώκτης, αἰτεῖ τὲ συγγνώμην περὶ τῆς εἰσαυτὸν παραυτοῦ τολμηθείσης δαιμονιώδους καὶ φθονηρᾶς ἀγνωμοσύνης. Λαμβάνει λοιπὸν τοῦ σφάλματος τὴν συγχώρησιν καὶ διαβεβαιοῦται μηκέτι τούτῳ τοῦ ἱερωτάτου ναοῦ ἀποκλείειν τὴν εἴσοδον.

4.1 Περὶ τῆς ἑπταημέρου νηστείας καὶ προσευχῆς αὐτοῦ καὶ πρώτου πρὸς αὐτὸν τῆς Θεοτόκου χρησμοῦ

Οὕτως κατ' ἐκείνου καιροῦ καὶ τόπου ὁ μακάριος διαλάμπων καὶ οὐδὲ μέρος τι ἀρετῆς ἐπιτελεῖν λογιζόμενος, ἀφάτῳ ταπεινοφροσύνῃ, ἀΰπνῳ προσευχῇ καὶ ἐπιτεταμένῃ νηστείᾳ, τὴν τῶν ἁπάντων δέσποιναν Θεοτόκον ἐξιλεοῦτο, ἐν τῷ ταύτης τεμένει, μηδὲν βεβρωκὼς τὸ παράπαν ἢ πεπωκὼς ἐν ἡμέραις ἑπτά, ἀποκαλυφθῆναι αὐτῷ τὰ πρὸς σωτηρίαν αὐτοῦ. Καὶ πληρουμένων τῶν ἑπτὰ

psalms of David. However, at the same moment as he found the doors closed he found himself reciting the saying of David: *Open the gates of righteousness for me, that I may enter through them and give thanks to the Lord.* After he had made the life-giving sign of the cross on them, the doors of the church opened by themselves for him and shut again when he had entered, while their locks stayed intact. Following this, the warden arrived, carrying the keys of the church. When he opened the doors and found the saint praying inside, he received a great shock as he could not understand how he had entered. As a result, he fell prostrate on the floor, and the former persecutor became a supplicant, requesting forgiveness for having dared to display his demonic and envious misunderstanding of Theophylaktos. He then received absolution for his fault and assured the saint that he would not bar the doors of the most holy church to him again.

4.1 On the seven-day fast, his prayer, and the first prophecy of the Theotokos to him

The blessed man thus shone in that place at that time. But, since he thought he was not fulfilling even a small part of virtue by his indescribable humility, vigilant prayer, and prolonged fasting, he begged the queen of all, the Theotokos, to make a revelation concerning his salvation in her own church, neither eating nor drinking anything for seven days. Once the seven days were completed, the mother of God

ἡμερῶν, φησὶ πρὸς αὐτὸν κατόναρ ἐν χρηματισμῷ ἡ μη-
τρόθεος· "τὸ πρὸς ἀρετὴν σύντονόν τε καὶ ξένον ἰδοῦσά
σου, κατένευσα πρὸς τὴν αἴτησιν. Δι' ὃ ἀναστὰς ἔξελθε,
καὶ ἰδοὺ μοναχός τις ὀνόματι Ἰάκωβος παροδεύει· συν-
οδοιπόρησον αὐτῷ." Διαναστάντος δὲ αὐτοῦ ἀπὸ τοῦ
ὕπνου, καὶ εὑραμένου τὸν μοναχὸν ὃν αὐτῷ ἡ θεομήτωρ
ἐχρησμοδότησεν, ἐπιπλείστας ἡμέρας τούτῳ συνώδευσεν
τὴν πορείαν ποιουμένῳ πρὸς τὸ Ὀλύμπιον ὄρος, μηδενὶ
τοπαράπαν τὰ κατ' αὐτὸν ἀναθέμενος, καίπερ εἰκοστὸν
ἔτος ἄγων τῆς ἡλικίας καὶ ἐν αὐτῇ ὢν τῇ ἀκμῇ τῆς νεότητος. Τούτου οὖν γεγονότος, ἐπένθησαν αὐτὸν οὐ μικρῶς
οἱ γεννήτορες, τῆς ἡλικίας τὸ νέον καὶ τοῦ κάλλους τὸ
ὡραῖον καὶ τῆς περὶ πάντα καλλονῆς αὐτοῦ τὴν μνήμην
ἀνεπίληστον ἔχοντες καὶ τί ἂν ἀθρόως γέγονεν μὴ γινώ-
σκοντες.

## 4.2 Περὶ τοῦ δευτέρου χρησμοῦ καὶ ὁδηγίας αὐτοῦ

Πορευομένου δὲ αὐτοῦ καταπάροδον, τῇ ἐπιούσῃ νυκτὶ
ἐπιφαίνεται αὐτῷ πάλιν καθ' ὕπνους ἡ Θεοτόκος λέγουσα·
"Ἀκολούθει μοι." Ὁ δὲ κατόπιν, ὡς ἔφη, ταύτης ἐβάδιζεν,
καὶ πρὸς τὰ Φρύγια ὄρη ἐλθοῦσα, ἤγουν τῆς ἐπονομαζο-
μένης Δαγούτης, δείκνυσιν αὐτῷ τόπον καλούμενον
Κρυπτὰ καὶ ἀναχωρητικὸν κελλίον καὶ τὸν ἐν αὐτῷ ἀγω-
νιζόμενον γέροντα Παῦλον καλούμενον. Καὶ φησίν·
"Παρὰ τούτῳ δεῖ σε σωθῆναι τῷ ἀσκητῇ." Καὶ πρὸς
ἐκεῖνον ἐπιστραφεῖσα ἡ πάναγνος, "δεῦρο," λέγει, "ἐπιλα-
βοῦ τῆς χειρὸς αὐτοῦ, καὶ ποίμανον αὐτὸν καὶ Πέτρον

14

spoke in response to him in a dream, "I have seen your extraordinary eagerness for virtue and granted your request.
So, get up, go outside, and lo and behold, a monk named
Jacob will be passing by. Travel with him." Theophylaktos
woke up, found the monk mentioned by the mother of God
in her prophecy, and traveled with him for many days, making the journey to Mount Olympos. He did not discuss his
decision with anybody at all, although he was twenty years
old, in the prime of youth. When this occurred, his parents
lamented him greatly, since they could not erase from their
memory his young age, his good looks, and his virtue in all
respects and did not know what might have unexpectedly
happened to him.

4.2 On the second prophecy and the directions given to
him

In the course of his journey, when night was falling the
Theotokos appeared to him once more in his sleep, and said,
*"Follow me."* As he told the story, he walked along behind her
and when she reached the mountains of Phrygia, in the region called Dagouta, she showed him a place called Krypta,
and a hermit's cell, and the elder, called Paul, who was con-
testing spiritually in it. And she said, "You are to be saved
alongside that ascetic." Then, turning to the elder, the all
pure one said, "Come, take his hand, be his shepherd, and

αὐτὸν ἐπονόμασον, ὅτι στερρὸν οὗτος σκεῦος τῆς εὐσεβείας ἀναδειχθήσεται." Ἔξυπνος δὲ γενόμενος ὁ ἀοίδιμος,
ὁρᾷ καὶ ἰδοὺ ὑπῆρχεν τὸ τούτου ἐνύπνιον προσχηματίζον
οὕτως ἀλήθειαν. Ὡς γὰρ ἐχρηματίσθη, ἐπιλαβόμενος τῆς
ὁδοῦ τοῦ συνοδεύσαντος αὐτῷ μοναχοῦ τὴν ἑτέραν πορευομένου, κατέλαβεν τὸν ὑποδειχθέντα τόπον ὀνομαστί,
εὗρέν τε τὸ κελλίον τοῦ γέροντος, καὶ αὐτὸν ἐκεῖνον τῆς
κέλλης τὴν θύραν προσμένοντα. Καὶ ὡς ἴδεν αὐτὸν ὁ
γέρων, χαριέντως προσεφώνησεν· "Καλῶς ἦλθες, τέκνον
ἐμὸν τὸ γλυκύτατον· ἡ Θεοτόκος μοι τὰ κατὰ σὲ ἀπεκάλυ-
ψεν, ὡς σήμερον ἔρχῃ πρός με, καὶ τὴν σήν μοι ἐπίκλησιν
ἐπιδέδωκεν." Ὁ δὲ φησίν· "Κἀμοῦ ὁδηγός, πάτερ, ἡ αὐτὴ
πρὸς τὴν σὴν ἁγιωσύνην ἐγένετο." Καὶ εἰκότως, ἀδελφοί,
καὶ μάλα δικαίως ἡ θεία χάρις ἡ ἀεὶ χειραγωγοῦσα τὸν
ὅσιον καὶ πρὸς τοῦτον τὸν μέγαν τῆς ἐγκρατείας στύλον
ὡς ἄλλον Ἰσραὴλ καθωδήγησεν, ὅλην αὐτοῦ τὴν ζωὴν
πρακτικῶς ἐν ἑαυτῷ ἀπομάξασθαι, καὶ ὡς ἄλλον Ἐλισ-
σαῖον τῷ Καρμηλίῳ Ἠλίᾳ μαθητευθῆναι, καὶ σοφώτερον
γενέσθαι περὶ τὰ τοιάδε ὡς σοφόν. "Δίδου γὰρ σοφῷ ἀφορ-
μὴν καὶ σοφώτερος ἔσται," φησὶ Σολομῶν.

5 Περὶ τῶν κατὰ τὸν ὅσιον Παῦλον τὸ πόθεν καὶ πῶς εἰς
τὴν τῆς Φρυγίας κατήντησεν ὑπουρίαν

Ἀλλ' ἐπειδὴ τοῦ πανοσίου Παύλου τούτου ἐμνήσθημεν,
ἀναγκαίως ᾠήθημεν διασαφῆσαι τὰ κατ' αὐτόν, ἐκ μέρους
τὸ ὅλον ἐπιδεικνύντες καὶ τὰ πάντα αὐτοῦ κατορθώματα
δι' ὀλίγων προσβεβαιοῦντες. Χώρας μὲν οὗτος ἦν τῶν

name him Peter, because he will prove to be a sturdy vessel of piety." When the renowned man woke up, lo and behold, his dream prefigured the truth. For, as he had been told by the prophecy, taking another route from that of the monk who had traveled with him, Peter reached the place indicated to him by name. He found the elder's cell and the elder himself waiting for him at the door of the cell. As soon as the elder saw him, he called out happily to him, "Welcome, my dearest child! The Theotokos gave me a revelation about you, that you were coming to me today, and she told me your name." The saint replied, "And it was she, father, who guided me to your holiness." And of course, my brothers, and quite rightly, the divine grace, which always guided the saint, led him as if he were a new Israel, to that great pillar of continence, in order that he might actively receive in himself the impression of that man's whole life, and, like another Elisha on Carmel, become a student of Elijah, becoming wiser concerning such spiritual matters, since he was already wise, because, as Solomon says, *"Give instruction to the wise man, and he will be wiser still."*

5  On matters concerning holy Paul: how and from where he reached the foot of the mountains of Phrygia

Since we have mentioned all-holy Paul, we think it is necessary to tell his story, showing the whole through a part and confirming all his achievements through a few. This man

Βουκελλαρίων, ἐν μονῇ τῶν ἐκεῖσε καλουμένῃ Μαντή-
νιον, ἐκ παιδόθεν ἀποταξάμενος καὶ τὸν μοναδικὸν ὑπ-
ελθὼν βίον, καὶ μέχρι χρόνων τῇ κοινοβιακῇ διαρκέσας
παλαίστρᾳ καὶ διαλάμψας καὶ πᾶσαν ἐν αὐτῇ διακονησά-
μενος διακονίαν. Ὅθεν καί τινες αὐτῶν τῶν ἐκεῖσε ὄντων
πλησιοχώρων ἡσυχαστῶν παρὰ τοῦ τηνικαῦτα προεστῶτος τῆς Μαντηνίου μονῆς, ἐξῃτήσαντο ἐπιδοθῆναι
αὐτοῖς τοῦ παρ' αὐτοῦ τὰ χρειώδη διακονεῖσθαι ἑκάστοτε.
Δι' ὃ μετὰ τῆς τοῦ προεστῶτος εὐχῆς καὶ σκέπης ἀπολυ-
θείς, τρισὶν ὁσίοις γέρουσιν ὑπηρέτει ἐπὶ χρόνους ἀνολι-
γώρως, Εὐστρατίῳ τινί φημὶ Θεοδώρῳ καὶ Γεωργίῳ. Οἵτι-
νες τὸ φιλήσυχον καὶ πρᾷον καὶ καταρετὴν ὑψηλότατον
θεώμενοι τοῦ ἀνδρός, ἀνάξιον ἔκριναν τοσαύτην ἀρετὴν
ἐν ὑποτακτικῷ διατελεῖν ἰδιώματι, ὡς οὐδὲ τὸν λύχνον ἐπι-
φερόμενον ἑαυτῷ μόνῳ πρὸς φωτοδοσίαν ἀρκεῖν, ἀλλὰ
καὶ τοῖς ἐφεπομένοις εὐαγγελικῶς καταλάμπειν. Ὅθεν
αὐτὸν καὶ πρὸς τὸ τῆς ἡσυχίας στάδιον ἔκπαλαι τοῦτον
διψῶντα θεοβουλήτως ἐξέπεμψαν. Ὁ δὲ ὢν ἀεὶ φιλόθεος
καὶ μισόδοξος, ὡς πᾶσαν ἄνωθεν πρακτικῶς τὴν πρὸς
Θεὸν ἐπινοήσας ἐγγύτητα, καὶ τοῦτο εὐσεβῶς μετὰ πάντων προστίθησιν, καὶ ξενητεύει σώματι ὁ προξενητεύσας
θελήματι, καὶ γίνεται κοινωνὸς καὶ συνέμπορος τοῦ δι'
ἡμᾶς καθ' ἡμᾶς ὑπὲρ ἡμᾶς πρὸς ἡμᾶς ξενητεύσαντος Θεοῦ
Λόγου, Κυρίου δὲ ἡμῶν Ἰησοῦ Χριστοῦ, καὶ ἔρχεται πρὸς
ταύτην τῆς Φρυγίας τὴν ὑπουρίαν τὴν ἐπονομαζομένην
Κρυπτά, ἐν ᾗ ἄθλοις ἄθλα συμπλέκων διεκαρτέρει, ἐν ᾗ
καὶ ὑπὸ τῆς Θεοτόκου χρηματισθείς, τὸν ὅσιον πατέρα
ἡμῶν Πέτρον, ὡς ἀνωτέρω γέγραπται, προσεδέξατο.

came from the area of Boukellarioi. From his childhood, he had renounced the world and adopted the monastic life in one of the monasteries there, called Mantenion. For a while he endured the spiritual struggles in the monastic community, shining and serving in all its services. Then some of the hesychasts from the neighboring area asked the abbot of the monastery of Mantenion at the time to give them Paul in order to serve them in all that was necessary. For this reason, he was released with the blessing and under the protection of the abbot and eagerly served three holy elders, I mean Eustratios, Theodore, and George, for many years. Realizing the great extent of this man's love of solitude, gentleness and virtue, the three decided that it was inappropriate for such virtue to remain in the status of a servant, since it is not enough for a man carrying a lamp to shine light only on his own person, but he must illuminate all those following him, according to the gospel. For this reason, by the will of God they sent him out into the stadium of solitude, for which he had long been thirsting. Paul, who had always loved God and hated fame and, as he had from the start, had actively sought complete closeness to God, also piously added this achievement to all his others. He who had previously made himself an exile from the world in his will, thenceforth made himself an exile in his body as well, and became a participant and fellow traveler of the Word of God, Jesus Christ our Lord, who made himself an exile because of us, among us, for us, and in regard to us. So Paul came to this foothill of Phrygia called Krypta, where he persevered, engaging in contest upon contest. It was in this place that he received the revelation from the Theotokos and welcomed our holy father Peter, as has been narrated above.

6.1 Περὶ τῆς κοσμικῆς ἐσθῆτος ἀποβολῆς καὶ τῆς τοῦ μονήρους περιβολῆς τοῦ πατρὸς Πέτρου

Τότε γὰρ τότε κατὰ τὸν ἐπιδοθέντα αὐτῷ χρησμὸν τὸν
ὅσιον προσδεξάμενος, καὶ τί ἂν εἴη οὗτος ὁ νέος ἀπο-
σκοπῶν, ἑώρα αὐτὸν ἄπλαστον ὅλον, καὶ καταρετὴν ποι-
κίλον, καὶ πρὸς τὰς τῶν πειρασμῶν ἐπιφορὰς ἀνδρεῖον.
Ὅθεν οὐ μετὰ πολλὰς ἡμέρας τὸ ἄρμα τὸ ἀποτακτικὸν
ἐνέδυσεν αὐτόν, καὶ Πέτρον αὐτὸν ἐπωνόμασεν, τῇ πράξει
προσαρμόττων ὡς ἀπεκαλύφθη τὴν κλῆσιν, καὶ τῇ ἐνεργείᾳ ἐπάγων τὴν προσωνυμίαν, ὡς πολλαχοῦ δείκνυσιν ἡ
γραφή, καὶ ἡ τῶν ἐν χρησμῷ μετακληθέντων ζωὴ ἐπιβε-
βαιοῖ. Ἐξ οὗ ὁ μακαριώτατος οὗτος Πέτρος, οἷα ὅπλα δυ-
νατὰ πρὸς καθαίρεσιν ὀχυρωμάτων ἐνδεδυμένος, στρατιω-
τικῶς καὶ γενναίως ὑπερεμάχει λογισμοὺς καθαίρων καὶ
πᾶν ὕψωμα ἐπαιρόμενον κατὰ τῆς γνώσεως τοῦ Θεοῦ ἀποστολικῶς, καὶ αἰχμαλωτίζων πᾶν νόημα εἰς τὴν ὑπακοὴν τοῦ
πατρός, καὶ ὡς σίδηρον χαλκεῖ, καὶ ὡς πηλὸν κεραμεῖ,
τοῦτον ἐκδιδοὺς ἑαυτόν, πυροῦν τε αὐτὸν καὶ πλάττειν,
καὶ πρὸς ὅ,τι ἂν βούλοιτο χρᾶσθαι.

6.2 Περὶ ἀνεπιλήπτου βίου καὶ τῆς ἐν τῷ Βυζαντίῳ ἀπο-
στολῆς αὐτοῦ

Τοῦτον ὁρῶν ὁ πανάγαστος ποιμὴν αὐτοῦ Παῦλος, ἔν τε
ἀπαθείᾳ καὶ λογισμῶν ἐγκρατείᾳ, γαστρός τε καὶ θυμοῦ
καὶ γλώσσης χαλιναγωγίᾳ ὑπομονῇ τε καὶ ταπεινώσει καὶ
ὑπακοῇ διαπρέποντα, πρός τε τῷ ἀγγελοειδεῖ τῆς θέας καὶ

### 6.1 On father Peter's casting away of his secular clothes and assumption of the monastic garment

At that particular time, Paul welcomed the holy one according to the revelation given to him. And when he examined who the young man might be, he saw that he was entirely without affectation, possessed a variety of virtues, and was courageous in the face of the attacks of the temptations. Therefore, after a few days, he dressed him in the armor of a hermit and named him Peter, suiting what he was called to in his conduct according to the revelation he had received, and making his name fit his actions, as scripture shows in many places and as the life of those called by revelation confirms. From that time on, the most blessed Peter, as if armed *with powerful weapons capable of destroying strongholds,* fought bravely, as a soldier *destroying evil thoughts and every proud obstacle raised up against the knowledge of God* like the apostle *and capturing every thought in obedience* to his father. He offered himself as iron to the blacksmith and as clay to the potter, to be heated, molded, and used for whatever he was wanted.

### 6.2 On his impeccable behavior and his mission to Byzantion

The most admirable shepherd Paul, since he saw Peter distinguish himself in his dispassion, in the continence of his thoughts, in the control of his belly, of his temper, and his tongue, as well as in his patience, his humility, his obedience, and the likeness and similarity of these things to the

τὴν ἴσην καὶ ὁμοίαν τούτων ἠθέλησεν αὐτῷ ἐγχειρίσαι ἱερατικὴν λειτουργίαν. Τοῦτο δὲ βουληθεὶς καὶ τὸ τῆς ζωῆς ἑαυτοῦ μεταβατικὸν λογισάμενος διὰ τὴν τῆς ἀνθρωπίνης δόξης φυγήν, ἐννοήσας τε τὴν ἱερὰν τῶν κανόνων ἀκρίβειαν, <ὡς> οὐκ ἔνι ὑπερορίᾳ μεταβάντα τὸν ὑπὸ ἐπαρχεώτου ἐπισκόπου χειροτονηθέντα πρεσβύτερον, τὰ τῆς ἱερωσύνης ἐνεργεῖν, ἐπιστέλλει πρὸς τὸν ἐν ἁγίοις Ταράσιον ἀρχιεπίσκοπον Κωνσταντινουπόλεως τότε κρατοῦντα καὶ ὀρθοδόξως διέποντα, γράψας τοιαῦτα.

6.3 Ἐπιστολὴ

"Τῆς τοῦ Χριστοῦ ἐκκλησίας εἰρηνευούσης, καὶ πάντων ἤδη παρὰ τῆς σῆς ἁγιωσύνης εὐλογουμένων πανάγιε, ὤφελον κἀγὼ μετὰ πάντων τῆς εὐλογίας σου μετασχεῖν καὶ ἐπιτυχεῖν τῆς ἐντεύξεως. Ἐπειδὴ δὲ ὡς πολλοῖς ἁμαρτήμασι συμπεφυρμένος προήρημαι ἐν ὄρεσι καὶ σπηλαίοις καὶ ταῖς ὀπαῖς τῆς γῆς ἀποβιῶναι πλανώμενος, τῆς σῆς μοι πεποθημένης θέας καὶ εὐλογίας στερίσκομαι. Οὕτως οὖν ἔχοντί μοι καὶ μεταβατικῶς διαζῶντι καὶ ὑπὸ τῶν θείων κανόνων διὰ τὴν εὐταξίαν κωλυομένῳ μεθ᾽ ἑαυτοῦ φέρειν τὸν ὑπὸ ἐπισκόπου ἐπαρχεώτου χειροτονηθέντα πρεσβύτερον, ὑπερορίως τὰ τῆς ἱερωσύνης μὴ ἐνεργοῦντα, ὡς τῷ θείῳ δοκεῖ Πνεύματι καὶ τῇ σῇ ἁγιωσύνῃ, τοῦ ἱερώσασθαί τινα ἔν τινι τῶν ἐπισκόπων τῇ ἡμετέρᾳ οὐθενότητι κέλευσον."

appearance of the angels, wished to entrust him with the priestly office. But although he wanted to do this, he considered that his own way of life was that of a wanderer because of his avoidance of human glory, and called to mind the strictness of the holy canons, which do not permit a priest who has been ordained by a provincial bishop to cross its borders and act as a priest, and so he sent a letter to Saint Tarasios, who was the archbishop of Constantinople then and who was ruling and governing in an orthodox manner. He wrote the following:

## 6.3  The letter

"Since, most holy one, the church of Christ is at peace and all people are blessed by your holiness, I too, like everyone else, also need to have a share in your benediction and attain your response to an appeal. However, being involved with numerous sins, I have preferred to live *as a vagrant, in mountains, caves, and holes in the ground,* and am thus deprived of your sight and blessing, which I have desired. Since I am in this condition, and live my life moving from one place to another, I am also prohibited by the regulation of the holy canons to bring with me a priest who was ordained by a provincial bishop, since he cannot act as a priest outside those borders, as it seems good to the divine Spirit and your holiness. Please, then, for my own worthless self, give an order for someone to be ordained by one of the bishops."

6.4 Τοῦτο τυπώσας τὸ γράμμα ὁ ὅσιος Παῦλος, καὶ τῷ αὐτοῦ μαθητῇ ἐπιδοὺς Πέτρῳ, εἰς τὴν Κωνσταντινούπολιν πρὸς τὸν προλεχθέντα ἀρχιεράρχην ἐξέπεμψεν. Ὅπερ δεξάμενος ὁ θεοείκελος ἐκεῖνος καὶ ἄγγελος ἐν ἀνθρώποις Ταράσιος, εἰς πέρας ἄγων τῶν γραμμάτων τὴν αἴτησιν, οὑτωσὶ γράφει πρός τινα ἐπίσκοπον τοῦ Ζυγοῦ πάνυ ἐνάρετον Βασίλειον προσαγορευόμενον, τὸ ἐπίκλην Πεζὸν διὰ τὸ μηδέπω αὐτὸν ἐπὶ ζῴου κεκαθικέναι ἀλλ᾽ ἀεὶ χριστομιμήτως πεζοπορεῖν.

6.5 Ἐπιστολὴ πατριάρχου

"Παῦλός τις τῶν περὶ τὴν Φρυγίαν ἡσυχαστῶν, τὴν ἡμετέραν διὰ γράμματος προσεδεήθη εὐτέλειαν, ὡς διὰ τὸ τῆς ζωῆς αὐτοῦ ἀεικίνητον καὶ ἄλλοτε ἀλλαχοῦ περιάγειν τὸν ὑπὸ ἐπαρχεώτου ἐπισκόπου χειροτονηθέντα κωλύεσθαι μεθ᾽ ἑαυτοῦ ἔχειν πρεσβύτερον ὑπερορίως ἀνενέργητον μένοντα κατὰ τὴν τῶν κανόνων ἀκρίβειαν. Λοιπὸν ὃν ἂν ἐπιστείλῃ τῇ ὁσιότητί σου, τὰ ἡμῶν ἀντὶ ἡμῶν ἀποπληρῶν καθιέρωσον."

6.6 Περὶ τῆς ἐκ τοῦ Βυζαντίου τοῦ ὁσίου πατρὸς Πέτρου ἀποπλεύσεως καὶ ζάλης καὶ διοράσεως τὲ καὶ προσευχῆς τοῦ πατρὸς Παύλου ὑπὲρ τούτου καὶ σωτηρίας αὐτοῦ

Τοῦτο τὸ γράμμα ὁ ὅσιος Πέτρος παραλαβών, ἀπέπλει τῆς βασιλευούσης, καὶ ζάλη θαλάττιος κατέσχεν αὐτὸν οὐ μικρά, ὥστε τὸ πλοῖον ὑπὸ τῶν κυμάτων συντρίβεσθαι καὶ

6.4  After holy Paul had written this letter, he gave it to his student Peter, and sent him to Constantinople, to the previously mentioned archbishop. That godlike man, that angel in human form, Tarasios, received him and, fulfilling the petition contained in the letter, without more ado wrote to a certain most virtuous bishop of Zygos who was called Basil, and who had the nickname Pezos because he would never ride on an animal but always went on foot, in imitation of Christ.

6.5  The patriarch's letter

"Paul, one of the hesychasts living in the area of Phrygia, petitioned our humility by letter because, due to his itinerant way of life and his constant movement from place to place, he is unable to take with him a priest ordained by the provincial bishop, as this priest, according to the strictness of the canons, remains unable to act outside the provincial borders. Therefore, ordain as a priest whomever he may send to your holiness, fulfilling my prerogatives in my place."

6.6  On our holy father Peter's setting sail from Byzantion, the storm, the vision and prayer of father Paul concerning him, and his salvation

After receiving this letter, holy Peter set sail from the imperial city, but a great storm overtook him at sea: the ship was being pulverized by the waves and all those in it had given

τοὺς ἐν αὐτῷ ἀπολωλεκέναι τῆς ζωῆς τὰς ἐλπίδας. Τοῦτο διὰ τοῦ Πνεύματος γνοὺς ὁ διορατικώτατος νοῦς ὅσιος Παῦλος τῷ Θεῷ καὶ ἑαυτῷ προσαδολεσχῶν, θᾶττον τῆς καθέδρας ἀναπηδήσας ὑπὲρ τοῦ μαθητοῦ μετὰ βοῶν καὶ δακρύων ἐξιλεοῦτο τὸν Κύριον. Τῶν δὲ ἀδελφῶν ἐκπλαγέντων ἐπὶ τῷ ἀθρόῳ τοῦ πατρὸς πένθει, καὶ τί ἂν εἴη τοῦτο ἐξαπορούντων, καὶ παρακαλούντων τὸ αἴτιον αὐτοῖς ἐξειπεῖν, φησὶ πρὸς αὐτοὺς ὁ ὅσιος· "Τοῦ ἀδελφοῦ Πέτρου ἀποπλέοντος τῆς βασιλευούσης, ζάλη οὐ μικρὰ κατέλαβεν αὐτὸν καὶ τρικυμία θαλάττιος ὥστε μέλλειν ἀπόλλυσθαι. Ἀλλ᾽ ἡ τῶν πιστῶν προστάτις Δέσποινα Θεοτόκος τὸν χειμῶνα ἤδη καταπραΰνασα, τοῦ χαλεποῦ κινδύνου ἐκείνου ἐξείλετο αὐτόν." Οἱ δὲ ἀδελφοὶ ταῦτα ἀκούσαντες, τὸ ἀκαριαῖον τῆς ῥοπῆς ἀκριβώσαντες καὶ τὰ λεχθέντα ταμιευσάμενοι, ἐλθόντι τῷ τρισολβίῳ Πέτρῳ, ἠρώτων εἰ λυπηρὸν αὐτῷ κατὰ τὴν πάροδον συνέβη. Ὁ δὲ κατεῖδος ἐξειπὼν τὰ συμβάντα, τοῖς προλεχθεῖσιν ὑπὸ τοῦ πατρὸς ὡμοφώνησεν καὶ ἀψευδῆ ἐδείχθη τὰ τῆς ὁράσεως.

6.7 Περὶ τῆς χειροτονίας τοῦ πρεσβυτερίου αὐτοῦ καὶ τοῦ ἐν αὐτῷ τότε δαιμονιῶντος ὑγιασθέντος

Οὐ μετὰ πολλὰς δὲ ἡμέρας παραδοὺς ὁ πανόσιος Παῦλος τὸν μακάριον Πέτρον ἑνὶ τῶν ὑποτακτικῶν αὐτοῦ, καὶ τὴν ἐπικομισθεῖσαν ἐπιστολὴν καὶ ἀποσταλεῖσαν παρὰ τοῦ προμνημονευθέντος Ταρασίου ἀρχιεπισκόπου Κωνσταντινουπόλεως πρὸς Βασίλειον τὸν ἐπίσκοπον πρὸς τὸ ὂν

up hope of survival. Holy Paul, that most perceptive mind, found this out through the Spirit while he was himself in conversation with God: he immediately jumped up from his chair and begged the Lord with cries and tears for the sake of his student. The brothers were troubled by their father's sudden grief and, wondering what the reason might be, asked him to reveal it to them. The holy one said to them, "After our brother Peter had set sail from the imperial city, he was overtaken by a great storm and a tempest at sea, and was near death. But the guardian of the faithful, our Lady, the Theotokos, has already calmed the storm and saved him from that great danger." When the brothers heard this, they recorded the exact time and carefully remembered what he had said. When the thrice blessed Peter returned, they asked him if anything disagreeable had happened to him on the way, and he gave them a detailed account of what had happened: his narrative verified what the father had said earlier and proved his vision correct.

6.7 On his appointment to the priesthood and the healing at that time of a man possessed by a demon

Not many days later, the most holy Paul entrusted the blessed Peter to one of his subordinates, along with the letter he had received that had been sent by the previously mentioned Tarasios, archbishop of Constantinople, to the bishop Basil, telling him that he might ordain as priest

ἂν αὐτὸς μαρτυρήσῃ καὶ ἀποστείλῃ καθιερώσασθαι, γράφει πρὸς αὐτὸν καὶ αὐτὸς ἰδίαν ἐπιστολὴν ἧς ἡ περιοχή ἐστιν αὕτη.

6.8 Ἐπιστολὴ

"Ἡ κωλύσασά με αἰτία ἀπελθεῖν πρὸς τὴν βασιλεύουσαν καὶ τὸν ταύτης ἄγγελον ἀρχιεράρχην Ταράσιον δέσποτα, αὕτη μου καὶ νῦν κατέχει τὴν πρὸς τὸ τοιοῦτον ὁρμὴν καὶ τῆς πρὸς σὲ παρρησίας ἀπαξιοῖ. Ὅθεν σοι πνεύματι συμπαρὼν καὶ συλλαλῶν ὁ ἀνάξιος ἔγωγε, μαρτυρῶ Πέτρον τὸν μοναχὸν καὶ ἐμὸν ὑποτακτικόν, ἄξιον ὑπάρχειν κατὰ τὴν τῶν κανόνων ἀκρίβειαν τῆς ἀγγελοπρεποῦς ἱερώσεως. Ὅνπερ δεξάμενος κατὰ τὴν τῆς ἐπιστολῆς τοῦ πατριάρχου ἐγκάνονον κέλευσιν, ἄνευ πάσης ἀναβολῆς καθιέρωσον."

6.9 Ταύτην τὴν ἐπιστολὴν καὶ τοῦ ἀρχιεπισκόπου Κωνσταντινουπόλεως ἐπιδοὺς αὐτοῖς ὁ πανόσιος Παῦλος ἐξέπεμψεν. Καταλαβόντες δὲ οὗτοι πρὸς ὃν ἀπεστάλησαν ἱεράρχην Βασίλειον καὶ τὰς ἐπιστολὰς ἐπιδόντες, παρ' αὐτῷ ἐξενίσθησαν. Αὐτὸς δὲ τὰς ἐπιστολὰς ἀναγνούς, τῇ ἐπαύριον εἰσάγει εἰς τὴν ἐκκλησίαν τὸν μακάριον Πέτρον, καὶ χειροθετεῖ τῆς τριαδικῆς θεότητος ἱερολογῶν τὴν ἐπίκλησιν καὶ τὰ τοῦ κανόνος ἐν τούτῳ διεξάγων καὶ διευθύνων. Τότε δὴ τότε ἄνθρωπός τις ὑπὸ πνεύματος ἐνεργούμενος ἀκαθάρτου ἐλεγχθεὶς καὶ ἀνακραυγάζων ὀνομαστὶ

whomever Paul might attest to and send to him; Paul also sent Basil a personal letter, of which this is the content:

### 6.8 The letter

"My master, the same reason that prevented me from visiting the imperial city and its angel, the archbishop Tarasios, also now restrains my eagerness to visit you and makes me unworthy of speaking directly with you. For this reason, being with you and conversing with you in spirit, I, unworthy man that I am, attest that the monk Peter, my subordinate, is, in accordance with our strict canons, worthy of that priesthood which befits angels. Whom receiving, in accordance with the canonical order contained in the patriarch's letter, please ordain him priest without any delay."

6.9 The most holy Paul gave them this letter, together with the letter of the patriarch of Constantinople, and sent them on their way. When they reached the bishop Basil, to whom they had been sent, and handed him these letters, they were received as guests by him. He read the letters and the next day he led the blessed Peter into the church and ordained him, invoking with priestly words the name of the triadic deity and going carefully through and following in detail the canonical requirements. At that time a man possessed by an impure spirit was exposed: calling out his name,

πυροβολεῖσθαι ὑπὸ τῆς τοῦ ὁσίου Πέτρου χάριτος, αὔθωρον ἀπηλλάγη αὐτοῦ, καὶ τὸν δοξάσαντα Κύριον σὺν
τῷ δοξασθέντι εὐχαριστηρίους φωνὰς ἠφίει, τοῦ θείου
Πνεύματος, ὡς οἶμαι, καὶ διὰ τοῦτο τὸ ἄξιον αὐτοῦ ἐπι-
μαρτυροῦντος, καὶ ὑπέστρεψεν καθιερωμένος πρὸς τὸν
ὅσιον Παῦλον τὸν καθηγητὴν αὐτοῦ.

7 Περὶ τῆς διασώσεως τοῦ ἐρίφου ὑπὸ τοῦ ἀλωποῦ

Καθεζομένου ποτὲ τοῦ ὁσίου πατρὸς ἡμῶν Παύλου ἐν τῇ
χώρᾳ τῆς Δαγούτης, ἐν ὄρει καλουμένῳ Φιλαργύρου, ἐν
τῷ ναῷ τῆς παναγίας Δεσποίνης ἡμῶν Θεοτόκου, συνέβη
τινὰ ποιμένα ἐν μιᾷ τῶν ἡμερῶν συνέρχεσθαι ἐκεῖθεν μετὰ
τῆς ποίμνης αὐτοῦ καὶ ἐᾶσαι ἔριφον αὐτῶν ἀφυπνώσαντος
τοῦ ἐρίφου. Πρὸς δὲ τὰς δυσμὰς τοῦ ἡλίου ἤρξατο ὁ ἔριφος ἀνακράζειν. Λέγει οὖν τις τῶν ἀδελφῶν τοὔνομα Ἰωάννης τῷ ὁσίῳ πατρὶ Παύλῳ περὶ αὐτοῦ. Ὁ δὲ λέγει αὐτῷ·
"Κάλεσον τὴν κατασυνήθειαν ὧδε ἐρχομένην ἀλωπὸν καὶ
εἰπὲ αὐτῇ· Ὁ γέρων λέγει, παραλαβοῦσα τὸν ἔριφον, διά-
σωσον αὐτὸν ἐν τῇ μάνδρᾳ αὐτοῦ.'" Ἡ δὲ παραυτίκα ἐπιλαβομένη αὐτοῦ, διέσωσεν αὐτὸν διὰ τῆς νυκτὸς ἐν τῇ
μάνδρᾳ αὐτοῦ ἀσινῆ καὶ σῶον. Ἀπεῖχεν οὖν ἡ μάνδρα ἐξ
αὐτοῦ ὡς ἀπὸ σημείων τριῶν. Μετ' ὀλίγας δὲ ἡμέρας, θεωρήσας τὸν ποιμένα ὁ αὐτὸς Ἰωάννης, ἠρώτα αὐτὸν λέγων·
"Ἐν τῇδε τῇ ἡμέρᾳ ἀπώλεσας ἔριφον;" Ὁ δὲ λέγει αὐτῷ·
"Ναί πάτερ, καὶ τῷ πρωΐ εὖρον αὐτὸν ἐν τῇ θύρᾳ τῆς μάνδρας στήκοντα." Τότε ἔγνωσαν ὅτι ἐκπεπλήρωκεν τὴν
ἐντολὴν αὐτοῦ τὸ ἀλογώτατον κτῆνος.

he was struck as if by fire by the grace of holy Peter, and at the same moment was rid of the spirit. He uttered words of gratitude to the Lord who had glorified the saint, as well as to the saint who had been glorified by the Lord. In this way, in my view, the divine Spirit also bore witness to Peter's worthiness, and he returned to holy Paul, his teacher, ordained as a priest.

## 7   On the saving of the goat by the fox

One day, when our holy father Paul was staying in the area of Dagouta, on a mountain called Philargyrou, in the church of our most holy Lady and Theotokos, a shepherd happened to pass by there with his flock and he left a goat behind, since this had fallen asleep. At sunset the goat started bleating, and one of the brothers, called John, told the holy father Paul about it. The saint said to him, "Call the fox which is in the habit of coming here and say to her, 'The elder says, take the goat and bring it safely to its fold.'" She immediately took it and brought it to its fold safe and sound in the night. The fold was about three miles away from that place. A few days later, John met the shepherd and asked him, "Did you lose a goat that day?" He replied to him, "Yes, father, but in the morning, I found it standing in the entrance to the fold." Then they realized that that most irrational animal had fulfilled the saint's command.

8 Περὶ τῆς πρὸς τὰ Ἱεροσόλυμα τῶν ὁσίων ὁδοιπορίας
καὶ τῆς ξένης ἐν τῷ Ἄλυ τῷ ποταμῷ διαβάσεως αὐτῶν καὶ
ἀπωλείας τῶν μυσαρῶν

Μετὰ τοῦτο παραλαμβάνει ὁ μέγας ἐκεῖνος ποιμὴν Παῦλος
τὸν πατέρα ἡμῶν Πέτρον ὡς μαθητὴν ἀναντίλογον καὶ
πρὸς τὰ Ἱεροσόλυμα ὁδεύσων ἐπιβλέψαι τοὺς ἁγίους
ἐκεῖσε τόπους τῆς οἰκονομίας Χριστοῦ βουλόμενος καὶ
κατασπάσασθαι. Πορευομένων δὲ αὐτῶν καταπάροδον
καὶ τὸν Ἄλυν ποταμὸν καταλαβόντων, εὗρον αὐτὸν ὑδάτων πεπληρωμένον, καὶ πολὺν ὄχλον παροδιτῶν ἔνθεν καὶ
ἔνθεν πρὸς τὰς ὄχθας καθήμενον τούτου προσμένοντα
τὴν ἐλάττωσιν. Αὐτοὶ δὲ ὡς τὸ κατεικόνα τοῦ Θεοῦ ἀπαρά-
γραπτον ἔχοντες, τούτου τῷ νώτῳ πιστῶς ἐπέβησαν ὡς
ἐπιξηρᾶς, καὶ δι᾽ αὐτοῦ ἀβρόχως ἐπὶ τὴν χέρσον διεβιβά-
σθησαν, ὥστε πάντας ἐκπλαγέντας τοὺς ἐκεῖσε παρόντας
καὶ θεωμένους παροδίτας καὶ ἐγχωρίους, τῶν ἰχνῶν αὐτῶν
ἐφάψασθαι καὶ παρακαλέσαι, τοῖς μὲν τῆς τῶν ὑδάτων
πλημμύρας χαρισθῆναι τὴν καταστόρεσιν καὶ ταχίστην
πρὸς τὰ οἰκεῖα διάβασιν, τοῖς δὲ τῆς κατὰ τῆς χώρας αὐτῶν
ἐπελθούσης λοιμώδους φθορᾶς ποιήσασθαι ἐξανάλωσιν·
ἣν γὰρ πλῆθος μυσαρῶν ἐπισκῆψαν ἐν ἐκείνοις τοῖς τόποις κατὰ βοτανῶν καὶ φυτῶν καὶ βλαστημάτων παντοδαπῶν λυμαντικῶς ἐπερχομένων. Εὐξαμένων δὲ αὐτῶν, ὁ
μὲν ποταμὸς εὐθὺς τὴν ἑαυτοῦ πλείστην συστείλας ῥύμην,
τούτοις ἔδωκεν τὴν δίοδον ἀνενόχλητον, τὸ δὲ πλῆθος
τῶν μυσαρῶν αὔθωρον ἠφανίσθη.

8  On the journey of the holy men to Jerusalem, and their extraordinary crossing of the river Halys and destruction of the rodents

After this, as our father Peter was a most obedient student, that great shepherd Paul took him with him as he was planning to travel to Jerusalem to visit and worship at the holy places of Christ's incarnation. In the course of their journey, when they reached the river Halys, they found that its waters were swollen and a large crowd of travelers were sitting on either side of the river, waiting for it to subside. But since the two holy men preserved *the image of God* unsullied within them, they walked on the surface of the river as if it were dry land, filled with faith, and they were carried across it until they reached solid ground, without getting wet. As a result, all those present who saw this, both travelers and locals, were awe struck and clutched at the holy ones' feet. The former begged them to grant them the subsiding of the flood waters and a speedy return home, the latter to make the disastrous plague which had come upon their country go away, for a throng of rodents had fallen upon those areas, damaging in their onslaught all kinds of herbs, plants, and shoots. After the holy men had prayed, the river immediately withheld its great rush, permitting the travelers to cross it without any inconvenience, while the throng of rodents disappeared at that very hour.

9.1 Περὶ τῆς ἐν χρησμῷ ἀναστροφῆς αὐτῶν καὶ τῆς τοῦ προφήτου Ζαχαρίου ναοῦ ἐρευνήσεως

Βουληθεὶς δὲ ὁ ὅσιος Παῦλος ἐπὶ τὰ πρόσω τὴν ὁδοιπορίαν ποιήσασθαι ὡς ἐξώρμητο, ὑπὸ τῆς τοῦ θείου Πνεύματος χάριτος ἐκωλύθη, τοιαῦτα ῥητῶς παρ' αὐτῆς χρησμωδούμενος· "Οὐ βούλομαί σε ἔτι καθ' ἑαυτὸν ζῆν, Παῦλε, ἀλλ' ἢ εἰς πολλῶν σωτηρίαν ποίμνης ἡγεῖσθαι τῆς ἐμῆς καὶ λογικῶν προβάτων περιποιεῖσθαι, γεωργεῖν τε καρδίας ἀγεωργήτους, καὶ πληθύνειν πράξει καὶ λόγῳ τὰ θρέμματα καὶ αὔξειν ἐν αὐτοῖς τῶν ἀρετῶν τὰ γενήματα, ἀπὸ ταύτης τὲ τῆς μάνδρας εἰς τὴν θείαν αὐτὰ καὶ οὐράνιον παραπέμπειν, καὶ μετὰ σὲ τὸν σὺν σοὶ Πέτρον καταλιμπάνειν διάδοχον. Δι' ὃ ἀνάστρεφε ὅθεν ἐξῆλθες, καὶ περιελθὼν τοῦ Ὀλύμπου τὴν ὑπουρίαν εὑρήσεις μικρὸν εὐκτήριον τοῦ προφήτου Ζαχαρίου ὀνομαζόμενον, κἀκεῖ οἰκήσεις, αὐτοῦ συνάξεις, ἐκεῖσε καταλύσεις τὸν βίον."

9.2 Περὶ τῆς αὐτοῦ τοῦ ναοῦ ἀνευρέσεως καὶ οἰκήσεως, καὶ τῆς μὴ πυρὶ ἀναλωθείσης στολῆς τοῦ πατρὸς Πέτρου

Ὑποστρέψας δὲ ὁ ὅσιος Παῦλος ἐκεῖθεν κατὰ τὴν πρόσταξιν καὶ εὑρὼν τὸν τόπον καὶ τὸ εὐκτήριον, ἐν αὐτῷ συναθροίζει τοὺς τοῦ κόσμου φυγάδας, οὓς πρὸς αὐτὸν ἡ θεία χάρις ὡδήγησεν, πρακτικῶς αὐτῷ ἀκολουθεῖν, καὶ τούτῳ ἐξομοιοῦσθαι ὡς πρὸς ἀρχέτυπον βλέποντας. Καὶ γὰρ πάσῃ ἀρετῇ ὁ ἀνὴρ ἐκεκόσμητο καὶ διακρίσει ἐνθέῳ ἀποστολικῶς πρὸς πάντας ἐπεπολίτευτο, τὰ βάρη ἐπικουφίζων

9.1 On their return due to an oracle and their search for the church of the prophet Zechariah

Although holy Paul wished to proceed farther on the journey as he had set out to do, he was prevented by the grace of the divine Spirit, receiving explicitly from it an oracular utterance something like this: "I do want you not to live by yourself anymore, Paul, but rather to become a shepherd leading many to salvation, to tend my rational sheep, to cultivate uncultivated hearts, to multiply these creatures by word and deed, to increase the fruits of their virtues, and to send them from this fold directly to the divine and heavenly one. I also want you to leave Peter, who is with you, as your successor. So, go back where you came from, and after you have gone round the foot of Olympos, you will find a small chapel, named after the prophet Zechariah. There you will settle, there you will gather your flock, and there you will end your life."

9.2 On the discovery of that church, their living there, and the garment of our father Peter, which was not consumed by fire

After holy Paul returned from there as he was ordered, he found that place and the chapel. In it he gathered the fugitives from the secular world, whom the divine grace led to him so that they might follow him in their practice and imitate him, as if looking at a model. For that man had been adorned with every virtue and divine discretion, and had behaved toward all people like an apostle, alleviating *the*

τῶν ἀσθενῶν καὶ τοὺς αὐτοῦ μαθητὰς πρὸς τὸ τοιοῦτον παιδαγωγῶν.

10 Ἐν μιᾷ γὰρ τῶν ἡμερῶν συνέβη τὸν ὅσιον πατέρα ἡμῶν Πέτρον εἰς τὸ πέραν τῆς μονῆς εὐκτήριον τῆς Θεοτόκου καλούμενον προσιερουργίαν παρὰ τοῦ μεγάλου τούτου ποιμένος ἀποσταλῆναι. Καὶ πληρώσαντα τὰ τῆς θυσίας, καταλαμβάνει αὐτοῦ τὴν ποίμνην τὴν ἱερατικὴν ἐνδεδυμένος στολὴν (ἡ γὰρ κοινοβιακὴ παράδοσις ἐγκελεύεται μήτε ἐνδύεσθαι μήτε ἐκδύεσθαι μήτέ τι ἕτερον ἐπιτελεῖν τὸν ὑποτακτικὸν τῆς τοῦ πατρὸς δίχα εἰδήσεως καὶ εὐχῆς), καὶ εὑρίσκει αὐτοῦ τὸν ποιμένα παρὰ ἀνθρακιὰν καθεζόμενον (ἦν γὰρ ἡ ὥρα χειμέριος), καὶ πίπτει αὐτοῦ πρὸς τοὺς πόδας εὐχὴν ἐξαιτούμενος τοῦ τὴν ἱερατικὴν στολὴν ἀποδύσασθαι. Ἦν δέ τις καταυτὸ τῶν ἀμελεστέρων ἀδελφῶν συνεργείᾳ τοῦ πονηροῦ καταπεσὼν ἐν πτώματι παραβάσεως ἐντολῆς, καὶ τὸν ὅσιον παροργίσας ποιμένα, καὶ ἐπεὶ εἶδεν ὁ ποιμὴν τὸν ἁμαρτήσαντα μὴ ἰσχύοντα αὐτοῦ τὰς ἐπιτιμήσεις βαστάσαι ὀλιγωρήσαντα, τί ποιεῖ ὁ τοῦ Θεοῦ κατὰ ἀλήθειαν μιμητής; Αὐτὸς γὰρ ἁμαρτανόντων ἡμῶν παιδεύει τὴν κτίσιν. Ἀφεὶς τὸν πεσόντα καὶ τραυματισθέντα, τοῦ μηδὲν ἠδικηκότος καθάπτεται ὁσιωτάτου Πέτρου, ἔτι πρηνοῦς αὐτοῦ καὶ ἐπιπρόσωπον κειμένου, διὰ τῆς ὑπομονῆς τούτου δῆθεν τὸν ἁμαρτήσαντα πρὸς μετάνοιαν συνωθούμενος. Τοῦτο οὖν ποιήσας ὁ διακριτικώτατος ἐκεῖνος ποιμὴν καὶ ψυχωφελὴς ἰατρὸς καὶ οὐδ᾽ οὕτως ἐπικαμφθέντα τὸν καταπεσόντα θεώμενος, ἰσχυροτέρου χρᾶται φαρμάκου, καὶ ἐπιπληκτικώ-

*burdens* of the feeble and teaching his students to do the same.

10 One day our holy father Peter happened to be sent by the great shepherd, Paul, to the chapel opposite the monastery, which was dedicated to the Theotokos, to celebrate mass. After he had performed the sacrifice, he went back to his flock wearing his priestly vestment, (since the cenobitic tradition specifies that the subordinate can neither dress nor undress himself nor do anything else without the knowledge and permission of his elder). He found his shepherd sitting in front of the fire, (because it was wintertime), and prostrated himself at his feet, requesting his permission to take off his priestly vestment. One of the more negligent brothers who, with the assistance of the evil one, had fallen into the fault of disobeying orders and had irritated the holy shepherd, was present there. And, since the shepherd realized that the sinner was not strong enough to bear his castigation because he had lost courage, what did that true imitator of God do? For when we sin, God punishes his creation. So Paul left the one who had fallen and been wounded, and instead scolded the most holy Peter who had not done anything wrong, and who was still lying prostrate in front of him, driving the sinner to repentance, I suppose, through that one's patient acceptance. And when, after he had done this, that most perceptive shepherd, that physician of souls, saw that the fallen one was not moved even by this, he applied a stronger medicine. Rebuking the blameless one more

τερον ἐπιτίθεται τῷ μὴ πταίσαντι, ὡς αἰτίῳ ἐκείνου τοῦ σφάλματος, καὶ ὡς κενοδοξοῦντι διαβάλλει περὶ τὴν ἱερατικὴν ἐσθῆτα, ἣν καὶ εἰσπῦρ ῥῖψαι κελεύει ἀποδυσάμενον. Ὁ δὲ καὶ τοῦτο ἀναστὰς μετὰ πολλοῦ τοῦ θράσους καὶ ἀκενοδόξου διανοίας ὁ ὅσιος Πέτρος ἀποπληροῖ. Θεασάμενος δὲ ὁ ἐπταικὼς τὸ παράδοξον, ὅτι ὁ μηδὲν ἠδικηκὼς δι᾽ αὐτὸν ἀδίκως ὑπὸ τοῦ προεστῶτος καταδικάζεται, καὶ ἑαυτὸν συγκαταδικάζει ὡς αἴτιον ὁ ἀναίτιος, οὐ μόνον δὲ ἀλλὰ καὶ πυρὶ τὴν τούτου ἐσθῆτα παραδοθεῖσαν, ῥίπτει ἑαυτὸν πρὸς τὸ ἔδαφος, αἰτεῖται συγγνώμην παρὰ τοῦ πατρὸς ὡς τοῦ σφάλματος αἴτιος, "ἐμόν," λέγων "τὸ τραῦμα πάτερ, ἐμὴ ἡ πληγή· οὐκ ἄγγελος, οὐκ ἄνθρωπος, οὐχ οὗτος ὁ ἱερεὺς τούτου καθέστηκεν αἴτιος, ἀλλ᾽ ἡ ἐμὴ ῥᾳθυμία." Τότε δὴ τότε τὸ τῆς ἀδελφότητος σύστημα ἐκεῖσε παρὸν καὶ ταῦτα ἑωρακός, τοῦ καθηγουμένου τοὺς πόδας ἐφάπτεται, καὶ παρακαλεῖ πρὸς τὸ μὴ πυρὶ ἀναλωθῆναι τοῦ ἱερέως τὸ ἔνδυμα, μιᾶς καίπερ ὥρας διάστημα περὶ τὴν διάλεξιν τελεσθείσης καὶ τῆς ἐσθῆτος τῷ πυρὶ προσομιλούσης. Εἶτα τούτων τὴν ἱκεσίαν δεξάμενος ὁ ἀοίδιμος τοῦ πυρὸς κελεύει τὴν ἐσθῆτα ἀναιρεθῆναι. Τῶν δὲ τοῦτο διατάχους πεποιηκότων, ἀσινὴς ἡ ἐσθὴς ἐκ τοῦ πυρὸς ἐκομίζετο, εἰς ἔνδειγμα ὡς οἶμαι τῆς ἀρίστης ζωῆς καὶ στερροτάτης ὑπομονῆς τοῦ ταύτην ἀμέμπτως τὲ καὶ ἀπαθῶς ἱερέως ἐνδυσαμένου.

severely, as if he were responsible for his brother's fault, and accusing him of being vainglorious because of his priestly clothing, he ordered him to take it off and throw it into the fire. Holy Peter, standing up, executed this order too with great courage and mental humility. When the one who had stumbled saw this strange thing, that the one who had done nothing wrong was being wrongly condemned by the elder because of him, and was accepting the condemnation as if he were responsible, although he was not responsible, and not only that, but that his clothing had been consigned to the fire, he threw himself to the ground and asked the father for forgiveness as the one who was responsible for the fault. "My father," he said, "the damage is mine, the wound should be mine too. Neither angel, nor man, nor this priest is responsible for what happened. It was my negligence." Then, indeed, the whole brotherhood, who were there and saw this, grasped the abbot's feet and begged him not to allow the fire to consume the priest's vestment, even though a whole hour had passed in the discussion during which the garment had been in contact with the fire. Then that man of blessed memory accepted their appeal and ordered the garment to be removed from the fire. They did so immediately and the garment was recovered from the fire, undamaged. I think this was as a sign of the excellent conduct and the enduring patience of the priest who wore that garment in an unblemished and dispassionate way.

11.1 Περὶ τῆς κοιμήσεως τοῦ μακαρίου Παύλου, καὶ ποιμνιαρχίας τοῦ πατρὸς ἡμῶν Πέτρου

Μετ' οὐ πολλὰς δὲ ἡμέρας, ἀποκαλύπτει Κύριος τῷ ὁσίῳ
πατρὶ Παύλῳ ταχεῖαν ἔσεσθαι τὴν ἐκ τοῦ σώματος αὐτοῦ
ἔξοδον. Τοῦτο δὲ ἐγνωκὼς ὁ τρισόσιος, πρὸ τῆς φυσικῆς
αὐτοῦ ἐν μνήματι ταφῆς τὲ καὶ ἀποθέσεως, ἔγκλειστρον
μικρὸν ὡς τάφον κατασκευάσας, εὐτελέστερον ὑπάρχον
τῆς συμμετρίας τοῦ σώματος, ἐν τούτῳ καθεῖρξεν ἑαυτόν.
Καὶ ποιήσαντος αὐτοῦ ἐναυτῷ ἑξαμηνιαῖον χρόνον, ἡ τοῦ
σώματος ἐκδημία, καὶ πρὸς τὸν Χριστὸν αὐτοῦ ἤγγισεν
ἐνδημία, καὶ ἔμελλεν ἤδη ἐκλείπειν ἐλθούσης τῆς ἀποφά-
σεως. Καὶ ἐπεὶ οὐκ ἦν ἐκεῖσε ὁ ἀναντίλογος μαθητὴς
αὐτοῦ ὅσιος Πέτρος, ὃν ἔμελλεν ἀνταυτοῦ ὡς προεχρημα-
τίσθη καταλιμπάνειν διάδοχον, ἀλλ' εἰς διακονίαν ἀπεσταλμένος, ἀφεθῆναι μικρὸν ἑαυτὸν τῷ Χριστῷ καθικέτευσεν.
Ὃς μετὰ τρίτην ἡμέραν τῷ ὁσίῳ Πέτρῳ φησὶν ἐκ τῆς ὁδοιπορίας ἐπανιόντι· "Τέκνον, τὸ τῆς ζωῆς ἐμπρόθεσμον
ἐπληρώθη μου, καὶ ἔμελλον ἕως ἄρτι προστεθῆναι πρὸς
τοὺς πατέρας μου, ἐπεὶ δὲ οὐκ ἧς ὧδε, τὸν Κύριον παρεκά-
λεσα, καὶ τρίτην ἡμέραν ἀφέθην διασὲ ἀφῆς πορεύεσθαι
ἔμελλον." Καὶ ταῦτα εἰπὼν συναθροίζει τὴν ἀδελφότητα
καὶ λέγει· "Τεκνία, ἰδοὺ ἐγὼ τῆς παρούσης ζωῆς ἀπανίστα-
μαι, καὶ τὴν παρακαταθήκην ἀποδίδωμι τῷ Κυρίῳ, καὶ
ὡς γῆ πρὸς τὴν γῆν ἐπανέρχομαι. Νῦν οὖν ἀκούσατέ
μου κηδομένου ὑμῶν τῆς σωτηρίας, καὶ φλεγομένου τὰ
σπλάγχνα τῇ συμπαθείᾳ, καὶ μεταστάντος μου μένετε ἀδι-
άσπαστοι, τῷ φόβῳ τοῦ Κυρίου καθηλωμένοι, καὶ τῇ

11.1 On the dormition of the blessed Paul and our father Peter's assumption of the role of chief shepherd

Some days later, the Lord revealed to the holy father Paul that he was soon to depart from his body. Realizing this, that thrice holy man, before his actual burial and disposal in a tomb, built a little grave-like cell, which was smaller than the dimensions of his body, and confined himself to it. After he had spent six months in it, his departure from his earthly body and his advent to Christ approached, and he was already about to pass away, for the word had arrived. But since his disciple, holy Peter, who never contradicted him and whom, as had been foretold, he was going to leave as his successor, was absent, having been sent out on some service, Paul begged Christ to allow him a little time. After the third day, once holy Peter had returned from his journey, he said to him, "My child, I've reached the appointed end of my life, and, indeed, would already now have been *joined with my fathers,* but since you were not here, I begged the Lord and, as this is the third day which was allowed me on account of your absence, I am about to go." After saying this, he gathered the brotherhood and said, "My children, see, I am departing from this present life, giving my deposit back to the Lord, and, being earth, I am returning to the earth. So listen to me now, since I care deeply about your salvation and my heart burns with my feelings for you. After I have moved on, stay together, transfixed with the fear of God, and

τελείᾳ ἀγάπῃ συνηρμοσμένοι, καὶ τῷ ἐν Κυρίῳ ἐσομένῳ πατρὶ ὡς καὶ ἐμοὶ ἐν πάσῃ ὑμῶν τῇ ζωῇ ἀναντιρρήτως ὑπείκετε· εἰ γὰρ καὶ ὁ κανὼν ὑμῖν ἐπιτρέπει ποιεῖσθαι τῆς ποιμνιαρχίας τὴν ψῆφον, ἀλλ' ἐμοὶ τὸ Πνεῦμα τὸ Ἅγιον ἔδειξεν προπολλοῦ τῆς ἡγεμονίας τὸν ἄξιον, ὅνπερ εὐπειθῶς προσδεξάμενοι ὑποτάσσεσθε κατὰ τὸν θεῖον ἀπόστολον καὶ ὑπείκετε, πᾶσαν αὐτῷ εὐγνωμοσύνην καὶ τιμὴν ἀπονέμοντες." Καὶ φωνήσας τὸν ὅσιον Πέτρον, ἵστησιν αὐτὸν ἐνώπιον αὐτῶν καὶ φησίν· "Ἴδε ὁ πατὴρ ὑμῶν." Τούτου οὖν γενομένου, ὡς ἐξενὸς στόματος ἅπαντες εἶπον· "Εὐλογητὸς ὁ Θεός, ὁ τῶν κρυφίων ἐξεταστής, ὁ τὰ τῆς συνειδήσεως ἡμῶν εἰσπέρας ἐπαγαγὼν διὰ τῆς τοῦ πατρὸς ἡμῶν προοράσεώς τε καὶ διοράσεως, καὶ τὸν ποθούμενον ἡμῖν ἀποκαταστήσας ποιμένα." Ἀκηκοὼς δὲ ταῦτα ὁ ὅσιος πατὴρ ἡμῶν Πέτρος ἤρξατο τοῖς τοῦ πατρὸς προσκυλινδοῦσθαι ποσὶν μετὰ βοῶν καὶ δακρύων καὶ λέγειν· "Ἐλέησόν με πάτερ, τὸν τῆς ἀξίας ἀνάξιον, μή με βαρύνῃς ὑπὲρ τὴν δύναμιν, μή μου δὸς τῇ κουφότητι καὶ ἐλαφρίᾳ πτερὸν ἐπάρσεως τὴν ἀρχήν. Προχείρισαι ἄλλον, προβίβασαι πρᾷον, ἀνάγαγε εἰς αὐτὸ τοῦτο τὸν κατὰ Χριστὸν ταπεινόφρονα, ἔασέ με τῷ χρηστῷ ζυγῷ τοῦ Χριστοῦ εἰσαεὶ δαμάζεσθαι τὸν φιλόδοξον." Ὁ δὲ ὅσιος Παῦλος, "Παῦσαι," φησὶ, "τέκνον μὴ ἀντίλεγε ἐπιτάττοντι τῷ Κυρίῳ, καὶ τῇ τούτου προνοίᾳ μὴ ἀντιβόλει, μήποτε λάβῃς κρίμα ἐπιπολὺ ἀνθιστάμενος, μᾶλλον μὲν οὖν διανάστηθι, καὶ ποίμανον ἐνθέως τὴν ἀδελφότητα λόγου σύριγγι, παιδείας ῥάβδῳ, παρακλήσεως βακτηρίᾳ, ἀπροσ-

remaining united in *perfect love.* Submit your whole life un-
questioningly to the one who is to become your father in the
Lord, as you have to me. For, even if the canon does permit
you to hold a vote for your chief shepherd, the Holy Spirit
showed me long ago the one who is worthy of this leadership. Accept him readily, *be subject* to him in accordance with
the divine apostle, and submit, *showing* him every consider-
ation and *honor.*" Then he called holy Peter, made him stand
in front of them, and said, "See, here is your father!" As soon
as this happened, all said with one voice, "*Blessed be God,* who
scrutinizes our hidden thoughts, who has fulfilled our inner
desires through the foresight and insight of our father, and
has brought back to us the shepherd we want." When he
heard these words, our holy father Peter started rolling before his father's feet, crying, weeping, and saying, "Father,
have mercy on me; I am unworthy of this dignity; do not
burden me with something beyond my power, do not provide my frivolity and levity with even the slightest wings of
pride. Prefer another, promote somebody who is gentle, elevate to this dignity somebody who is humble in accordance
with Christ. Let me, the ambitious one, be tamed under the
easy yoke of Christ forever." But holy Paul said, "Stop, child.
Do not contradict the Lord who gives orders, do not hold
out against his providence, so that you are not condemned
for your constant resistance. Instead, rise up and, divinely
inspired, shepherd the brotherhood with the flute of discourse, the rod of discipline, and the staff of consolation,

παθῶς τε ἅμα καὶ ἀνυστάκτως, ὅπως ἐν Χριστῷ καυχήσῃ ἐκφαντικώτατα· 'ἰδοὺ ἐγὼ καὶ τὰ παιδία ἅ μοι ἔδωκας, ὁ Θεός.'" Καὶ ταῦτα εἰπὼν καὶ πάντας ἐπευλογήσας, παρέδωκεν τῷ Κυρίῳ τὸ πνεῦμα. Οἱ οὖν μοναχοὶ τότε σὺν τῷ ἁγίῳ πατρὶ Πέτρῳ, ἐνδόξως κηδεύσαντες τὸ τίμιον αὐτοῦ λείψανον, μετὰ κηρῶν καὶ λαμπάδων, εὐωδίας τὲ καὶ μύρων ὑμνήσαντες, κατέθεντο ἐν τῷ προμνημονευθέντι εὐκτηρίῳ τοῦ ἁγίου καὶ ἐνδόξου προφήτου Ζαχαρίου, ἐνῷ καὶ αὐτοὶ ἑκάστοτε ἐκκλησίαζον.

11.2 Περὶ τῆς μετὰ τὴν ἡγεμονίαν ἀσκήσεως αὐτοῦ

Ταῦτα δὲ γέγονεν ἐν ἔτει τετάρτῳ τῆς εὐσεβοῦς βασιλείας Νικηφόρου καὶ Σταυρακίου, δωδεκάτῳ δὲ ἔτει τῆς τοῦ ὁσίου πατρὸς ἡμῶν Πέτρου ἐνθέου ὑποταγῆς, καὶ χριστομιμήτου ζωῆς, ὡς καταλειφθῆναι αὐτὸν ὑπὸ τοῦ τρισμάκαρος Παύλου ἀρχηγὸν καὶ ποιμένα τῇ ἑαυτοῦ ποίμνῃ τριάκοντα καὶ δύο χρόνων. Ἐξοῦ δὴ καὶ παρεῖχεν ἑαυτὸν ἀκριβέστερον κανόνα καὶ τύπον καλῶν ἔργων τοῖς ὑπηκόοις, πάσης προπάντων ἀπεχόμενος πονηρίας, ἄρτου καὶ οἴνου, καὶ τυροῦ καὶ ἐλαίου καὶ τῶν λοιπῶν ἐνηδόνων τροφῶν τὸ παράπαν οὐκ ἐφιέμενος, μόνοις λαχάνοις καὶ ὀσπρίοις ἠρκεῖτο, λεπτῇ τροφῇ διαιτώμενος, καὶ ὕδατος ἐνδείᾳ πρὸς τούτοις τὴν σάρκα ἐκπιεζόμενος, καὶ ῥάκεσι τριχίνοις περιβαλλόμενος, καὶ σιδήροις ὡς κατάδικος ὅλος ἐνδεσμούμενος.

impartially and vigilantly, so that you may openly and proudly declare before Christ, '*Behold, my God, I and the children whom you have given me!*'" After he had said this and blessed them all, *he surrendered his spirit* to the Lord. Then the monks, together with the saintly father, Peter, prepared his precious body splendidly for burial, with candles and torches, perfumes and ointments, and, singing hymns of praise, placed it inside the aforementioned chapel of the saintly and glorious prophet Zechariah, in which they always used to attend church.

## 11.2  On his ascetic struggles after becoming abbot

These events took place in the fourth year of the pious reign of Nikephoros and Staurakios, and in the twelfth year of our holy father Peter's godly subjection and his life in imitation of Christ. He was thus thirty-two years old when he was left by the thrice blessed Paul as the leader and shepherd of his flock. From that time on, then, he set himself as a rather strict example and model of good behavior for his subordinates, abstaining completely from every wickedness. He did not permit himself any bread and wine, cheese and oil, or any other delightful foods at all, but was content with only vegetables and pulses, living on light food and insufficient water; in addition to this, he oppressed his flesh, covering himself with rags of haircloth and binding his whole body with irons as if he were a convict.

12.1 Περὶ τοῦ τυράννου Λέοντος, καὶ τῆς Εἰκονομάχου αἱρέσεως αὐτοῦ

Οὕτως εὐσεβῶς διαζῶντι τῷ μακαρίῳ ἐν ὅλοις ἔτεσιν, Νικηφόρου καὶ Σταυρακίου, καὶ τῶν μετεκείνους τὸ κράτος ἀναδησαμένων Μιχαὴλ καὶ Θεοφυλάκτου τῶν πανορθοδόξων δεσποτῶν, καὶ πλατύνων πράξει καὶ λόγῳ καὶ ἐντυχίᾳ τοῦ Κυρίου τὸ ποίμνιον, ἀνακύπτει τὶς ἐκ τῶν τοῦ Ἅιδου πυλῶν τοῦ διαβόλου ἀντίμιμος Λέων τῇ προσηγορίᾳ καὶ τῇ κατὰ τῆς Χριστοῦ ἐκκλησίας ὁρμῇ. Ὃς τυραννικῶς ἐκ τῶν Θρᾳκώων μερῶν μετά τινος συμμορίας, τῇ βασιλευούσῃ τῶν πόλεων ἐπιστὰς οὐκ ὀλίγον αὐτῇ περιέστησε τάραχον. Ὁ δὲ κρατῶν ἔτι τοῦ σκήπτρου Μιχαήλ, ὡς εἰρήναρχος τὴν αὐτοῦ ἐκ Θεοῦ ἐξουσίαν ἐπιδίδωσιν εὐμενῶς τῷ τυράννῳ, μὴ ἀνθιστάμενος ὅλως τῷ πονηρῷ κατὰ τὸν εἰρηκότα Χριστόν.

12.2 Κατασχόντι δὲ Λέοντι τῷ τυράννῳ τὸ σκῆπτρον, ὁ πᾶσαν αἵρεσιν ἀρχῆθεν κατὰ τῆς οἰκονομίας Χριστοῦ ἐπινοήσας διάβολος, καὶ πᾶσαν ἐκκενώσας τὴν καταυτῆς μιαρὰν αὐτοῦ καὶ θεόθραυστον βελοθήκην, πᾶσαν δὲ διασείσας τὴν οἰκουμένην διὰ τῶν κατακαιροὺς ὑπασπιστῶν ἑαυτοῦ καὶ ἐκδίκων, καὶ τοῦτον εὑρηκὼς τὸν ἀλιτήριον τύραννον ὥσπερ τι σκεῦος προσπᾶν ὁτιοῦν καταθύμιον αὐτοῦ εὐπαράδεκτον βούλημα πέλοντα, οὐκ ἄλλην τινὰ αὐτῷ παρέδειξεν αἵρεσιν, ἀλλ᾽ εἰς αὐτὸ τὸ <...> κατὰ Θεοῦ ἀλαζονευσάμενος καὶ πεσὼν προενήρξατο, ἣν καὶ ἕως νῦν οὐ διαλιμπάνει ἐνεργῶν ὁ παμμίαρος, ἀφοῦ πέπτωκεν Θεοῦ τὴν εἰκόνα λιθάζων, ἐκμοχλεύων, καταστρέφων,

## 12.1 On Leo the tyrant and his Iconoclastic heresy

The blessed Peter thus lived piously through all the years of Nikephoros and Staurakios, and of those who were crowned after them, Michael and Theophylaktos, the most orthodox rulers, multiplying his flock through his actions, his words, and his prayers to the Lord. Then that imitator of the devil emerged from the gates of Hades, a Leo in name and a lion in his headlong assault on the church of Christ. This man, who came to the imperial city from the area of Thrace with a gang of conspirators, caused a great disturbance in it by his tyrannical behavior. Michael, who was still wielding the scepter, since he was a peaceful ruler, meekly surrendered the power entrusted to him by God to the tyrant, *not resisting the evil one* at all, in accordance with the word of Christ.

12.2 As soon as the tyrant Leo had seized the scepter, the devil, who has invented every heresy against the dispensation of Christ from the beginning and has emptied his entire unholy quiver against it, although this has been broken by God, the devil who has shaken the whole world by means of his supporters and advocates at each time, found that this abominable tyrant was like a vessel apt for all the wishes of his heart. He thus did not assign to Leo some other heresy, but renewed in him the arrogance against God which he himself had begun before, because of which he fell, and which that most abominable one has not stopped contriving from the time he fell even until now, throwing stones at the image of God, prying it loose, overturning it, trampling on

συμπατῶν τε καὶ κατακαίων, διατὸ μὴ ἐφικνεῖσθαι ὅλως κατισχύειν τοῦ πρωτοτύπου, καὶ μάλα εἰδὼς τὰ τῆς εἰκόνος <πρὸς> τὸ ἀρχέτυπον κατά τε τιμὴν καὶ ἀτιμίαν προσαναγόμενα. Ἐπαρθέντι γὰρ αὐτῷ κατὰ Θεοῦ ὡς ἔφην καὶ πεσόντι καὶ κατὰ τῆς εἰκόνος χωρήσαντι, ὁ τοῦ Θεοῦ καὶ Πατρὸς Υἱὸς καὶ χαρακτὴρ ἀπαράλλακτος διασπλάγχνα ἐλέους μὴ φέρων ὁρᾶν τὴν τῆς εἰκόνος αὐτοῦ ἕως τέλους σατανικὴν ἐπικράτειαν, ἦλθεν ὡς οἶδεν ἐν καιροῖς ἰδίοις, ἐξ ἁγίας παρθένου σεσαρκωμένος ἀληθῶς Θεὸς καὶ ἀψευδὴς ἄνθρωπος πέλων, διπλοῦς τῇ φύσει ἐν μιᾷ ὑποστάσει ταῖς ἐνεργείαις τὰς φύσεις προσβεβαιούμενος (ὡς γὰρ Θεὸς τὰ θεῖα, ὡς δὲ ἄνθρωπος εἰργάζετο τὰ ἀνθρώπινα), παθών τε ὑπὲρ ἡμῶν ἀπαθῶς καὶ ἀναστὰς ἐκ νεκρῶν καὶ ἑαυτῷ τοὺς ἐν ᾍδῃ συναναστήσας, τῷ θρόνῳ τῷ πατρικῷ διὰ τῆς ἀπαρχῆς συγκαθίδρυσεν, καὶ τὸν ἐχθρὸν συμπατεῖσθαι ὑπὸ τοὺς πόδας τοῦ γένους ἡμῶν παραδέδωκεν.

12.3 Ἐκεῖνος δὲ ὢν ἀναιδὴς καὶ μισάνθρωπος καὶ ἀναίσχυντος καὶ φθονερός, μὴ φέρων ὁρᾶν τὸν κάτω ἄνω διὰ φιλανθρωπίαν αὐτὸς πεσὼν ἄνωθεν κάτω, οὐκ ἠπόρησεν τῆς πονηρᾶς ἐπινοίας, ἀλλ᾽ εἰς πόλεμον ἀκήρυκτον παρετάττετο πάλαι, οὐ κατὰ τῆς εἰκόνος μόνης ὁ θεομάχος ὡς πάλαι, ἀλλὰ κατὰ τοῦ Θεοῦ Λόγου ὡς πρόπαλαι τοῦ τὴν ἑαυτοῦ εἰκόνα φιλανθρώπως πτωχεύσαντος καὶ θεώσαντος, βλασφημίας πλήρη ἐπινοῶν δόγματα, καὶ ταῦτα ἐν ταῖς τῶν ὑπασπιστῶν κατακαιροὺς κατασπείρων καρδίαις, τῶν μὲν τὸν ἕνα καὶ διφυῆ εἰς δύο ἀναμέρος διαιρούντων

it, and burning it, since he did not manage to overpower the original, but is well aware that whatever honors or dishonors the image is transmitted to the original. For, since the devil revolted against God, as I have said, and fell, he also turned on the image of God, that is, the Son who is the exact imprint of God and of the Father, who, *thanks to his compassionate heart,* could not bear to see his image under the power of Satan anymore, and came in his own good time, taking flesh from a saintly virgin, being both true God and real man, having two natures in one hypostasis, and offering proof of the plurality of his natures through his energies, (for he performed his divine works as God and his human ones as a man). He suffered for our sake without suffering any injury, rose from the dead, raising with him those in Hades and, enthroning them with him as the first fruit upon the throne of his Father, he gave the enemy over to our race to trample under our feet.

12.3 But the devil, being arrogant, man hating, shameless, and envious, and unable to bear seeing the one who was low elevated by God's compassion when he who had himself been high had fallen low, was not at a loss for wicked plans, but had prepared himself long ago for a truceless war. The enemy of God did not attack only the image as he had done in the past, but now also attacked the Word of God himself who, in the distant past, by making himself poor had also deified his image out of his compassion. He invented doctrines full of blasphemies, and sowed them in the hearts of those who were his advocates at each time: some of them divided the one Christ who had two natures into two different hypostases; another proclaimed that he was to

τὰς ὑποστάσεις, τοῦ δὲ τὸν αὐτὸν ἐν μιᾷ τῇ φύσει κηρύτ-
τοντος, ἑτέρου μὴ ἐκ τῆς Παρθένου τὸ ἱερὸν ἐκεῖνο
Χριστοῦ σῶμα διαπεπλᾶσθαι ληροῦντος, ἀλλ᾽ οὐρανόθεν
τοῦτο κατενηνέχθαι καὶ ἄλλου φάσμα καὶ σκιὰ<ν> τὰ κατὰ
τὴν οἰκονομίαν Χριστοῦ ὀνειρώττοντος, <καὶ> πάντων
τούτων ἐκποδὼν γενομένων ὡς ψευδοδόξων ὑπὸ τῶν
κατὰ καιροὺς συνοδικῶν τε καὶ θεοφθέγκτων δογμάτων,
αὐτοῦ τε Σατὰν τῆς προτέρας πτώσεως καταπεσόντος
σφοδρότερον ὅσον τότε μὲν ἀπουρανοῦ ἐπὶ γῆς, νυνὶ δὲ
ἀπὸ γῆς ὑπὸ γῆν καὶ τῆς θεομάχου προαιρέσεως ἐκπεσόν-
τος, εἰς Εἰκονομάχων αἵρεσιν μετῆλθεν κατασυνήθειαν,
τὴν εἰκονομαχίαν εἰδὼς θεομαχίαν ὑπάρχουσαν, καὶ καθ-
οπλίζει πρὸς τὸ τοιοῦτον ὁ τυραννικώτατος ἄρχων τοῦ
κόσμου, τὸν ἴσον ἑαυτῷ ἐν κακίᾳ τυραννικώτατον τύραννον, ὃς Λέων πέλων τῇ προσηγορίᾳ καὶ λέων ὑπάρχων
ἀτίθασος τῇ ὠμότητι καὶ κατατῆς ἐκκλησίας Χριστοῦ
λεοντιαῖον ὁρμώμενος, τῷ διαβολικῷ τῆς εἰκονομαχίας
δόγματι ψυχὰς λεαίνειν κατήρξατο, μὴ τὸν Χριστὸν ἀν-
θρωπόμορφον δογματίζων ἢ γράφων ἢ σεβόμενος, ἀλλὰ
ψιλῷ μὲν λόγῳ τὴν ἀνθρωπείαν φύσιν ἀναλαβεῖν τὸν
Θεὸν Λόγον ἀνακηρύττων, τὸ δὲ ταύτης ὅλως χαρακτη-
ριστικόν, ἵν᾽ εἴπω καὶ ὀργανικὸν ἀπωθούμενος, καὶ μήτε
στόμα ἐκεῖνο ἐν γραφῇ χαρακτηρίζειν τὸ ἅγιον τὸ φῆσαν
"πάτερ, ἐφανέρωσά σου τὸ ὄνομα τοῖς ἀνθρώποις" καὶ "ἄλλον
παράκλητον πέμψω ὑμῖν τὸ πνεῦμα τῆς ἀληθείας ὃ παρὰ τοῦ
Πατρὸς ἐκπορεύεται" καὶ τῆς τριαδικῆς θεότητος προσβε-
βαιῶσαν τὴν ἔλλαμψιν, μήτε χεῖρας ἐκείνας τὰς ἐπὶ τοῦ
σταυροῦ ὑπὲρ τοῦ ἡμετέρου γένους ταθείσας καὶ τὰς ἐν

be found in only one nature; another foolishly declared that the holy body of Christ was not formed from the Virgin, but was brought down from heaven; and another dreamed that whatever pertained to the dispensation of Christ was a phantom and a shadow. All these were, however, cast out as heretics through the synodal and divinely inspired doctrines at each time, and Satan himself suffered a greater fall than his previous one, since then he had fallen from heaven to earth, but now he fell from earth beneath the earth. As he had failed in his intention to fight God, he switched to the heresy of the Iconoclasts from force of habit, because he knew that iconoclasm was a war against God, and thus the most malevolent tyrant in the world armed that most tyrannical man, who was his equal in evil. He was called Leo, and was indeed an untamed lion in his savagery and in his leonine assault on the church of Christ. He started crushing souls through the diabolical doctrine of iconoclasm, teaching that Christ did not have human form and neither depicting nor worshiping him as such, but declaring that the Word of God had assumed human nature merely as a figure of speech, in this way rejecting completely that nature's most important characteristic or most distinctive trait, so to speak. He would not even portray in an image that holy mouth which said, "*Father, I have revealed your name to men,*" and "*I will send another paraclete, the spirit of truth, that proceeds from the Father,*" verifying the illumination of the triune divinity; nor those hands that were stretched on the cross for the sake of our race, destroying the powers of the air and

τῷ ἀέρι δυνάμεις ἐξολεσάσας καὶ ἀπὸ γῆς ἡμᾶς εἰς οὐρανὸν
ἀνακομισάσας, μήτε πόδας ἀχράντους ἐκείνους τοὺς ἐπὶ
τῆς θαλάσσης ἀβρόχως περιπατήσαντας καὶ σὺν τῇ ξηρᾷ
τὰ ὕδατα ἁγιάσαντας, μήτε τι τοῦ θείου ἐκείνου σώματος
ἕτερον, δι' οὗ ἡ φύσις ἡμῶν ἅπασα ἀνεπλάσθη ὑπὸ τὴν
ἁμαρτίαν πεσοῦσα <. . .>, σκοπῷ τοιούτῳ ὡς οἶμαι τοῦ τὰ
ζιζάνια σπείροντος, ὡς εἰ τὰ εἰς θρίαμβον ὄντα τῆς οἰκονομίας Χριστοῦ ἐξωσθείη τῆς ἐκκλησίας, λήθης βυθοῖς τὰ
τῆς ὠφελείας παραδοθήσεται τὰ κατ' αὐτοῦ τὲ τρόπαια
καὶ ἡ αὐτοῦ αἰσχύνη συγκαλυφθήσεται καὶ πάλιν τοῦ γένους κατακρατήσει ὡς ᾤετο. Ἀλλ' ἐψεύσθη τῆς ἐλπίδος ὁ
μιαρώτατος.

12.4 Περὶ τοῦ διωγμοῦ ὑπὸ τοῦ τυράννου καὶ Εἰκονομάχου Λέοντος

Τὴν γὰρ Χριστοῦ εἰκόνα ἐξεώσας τῆς ἐκκλησίας καὶ ταύτην σὺν τῷ σταυρικῷ τύπῳ τῷ πυρὶ παραδούς, διωγμὸν
μέγα ἐκίνει κατὰ τοῦ πλάσματος καὶ τοὺς μὴ πειθομένους
τῷ δυσσεβεῖ αὐτοῦ δόγματι οὐ ταῖς τυχούσαις ὑπέβαλλεν
τιμωρίαις, τῶν ὑπασπιστῶν αὐτοῦ ἀγωνιζομένων ἐν τούτῳ.
Πολλοὺς γὰρ τότε ὁ δυσσεβὴς καὶ τύραννος ἐκεῖνος Λέων
τῶν ἀπειθησάντων αὐτὸν λογικῶν ποιμένων <καὶ> διδασκάλων διαφόρως ἀπέκτεινεν, καὶ πρὸς ἔρευναν ἔτι τῶν
τοιούτων ἀπέστελλεν.

13.1 Τοῦτο δὴ μαθὼν ὁ μακαρίτης Πέτρος συναθροίζει
τὴν ἀδελφότητα καὶ φησίν· "Τεκνία, ὁ ἀεὶ πολεμῶν
Χριστοῦ τὴν ἐκκλησίαν διάβολος καὶ ἀεὶ τῇ δυνάμει τοῦ

THE LIFE OF SAINT PETER OF ATROA

bringing us from earth back to heaven; nor those unblemished feet, which walked *on the sea* without getting wet and
blessed the water along with the dry land; nor any other part
of that divine body, through which our entire nature, which
had fallen under the power of sin, was created anew. In my
view, the purpose of the one who sowed these *weeds* was the
following: if those things that contributed to the triumph of
the dispensation of Christ were thrown out of the church,
what was of benefit from it would be thrown into the depths
of oblivion, the victories against him and his own humilia-
tion would be covered up and he would be able to take control of our race once more, or so he thought. But the most
abominable one's hopes were vain.

12.4 On the persecution carried out by the tyrant and Iconoclast Leo

After Leo had thrown the icon of Christ out of the church
and consigned it, to the fire, together with the symbol of the
cross, he initiated a great persecution against the image, and
severely punished all those who would not follow his impious doctrine, while his advocates engaged in this struggle.
For that impious tyrant Leo executed in various ways many
of the rational shepherds and teachers who disobeyed him
and he sent out agents to investigate such people.

13.1 As soon as the blessed Peter learned this, he gathered his brotherhood and said, "My children, the devil, who
is always fighting the church of Christ continuously and is

Χριστοῦ ἐκνικώμενος, καὶ τανῦν οὐ διέλιπεν τὰ τοιαῦτα ἐπιτηδεύων· ἀνήγειρεν γάρ τινας δυσσεβεῖς Χριστοῦ τῆς οἰκονομίας τὸ γνώρισμα, ὅπερ παρὰ τῶν θείων ἀποστό-λων ἡ ἐκκλησία κεκόσμητο, ὡς μυσαρὸν ἀποξέοντας καὶ εἴδωλον ὀνομάζοντας, οἳ τοῖς μὴ πειθομένοις τῷ ἀσεβεῖ αὐτῶν δόγματι καὶ φρονήματι ἀφιλανθρώπως αἰκίζουσιν. Λοιπὸν ἀδελφοί, παρὰ τῶν θείων γραφῶν κελευόμενοι ἑαυτοῖς μὴ ἐπιρρίπτειν τοῖς πειρασμοῖς, ἀναδύο ἢ τρεῖς τῷ συνδέσμῳ τῆς ἀγάπης περιδεσμούμενοι, χωρήσωμεν πρὸς τὴν ἔρημον, ὅπως καὶ τὴν πίστιν ἡμῶν ἀμόλυντον συν-τηρήσωμεν, καὶ τὴν κοινοβιακὴν ἡμῶν καὶ ἀγγελοπρεπῆ κατάστασιν μὴ ἐκλείψωμεν." Τότε δὴ τότε τὸ τῆς ἀδελφό-τητος πλήρωμα κατασυστήματα γεγονός, καὶ ὅσον ὅσον κρυπτόμενον τοὺς διώκτας, ἐν τόποις ἀμφιλαφέσιν ἐχώρη-σεν.

13.2 Περὶ τῆς ἐν Ἐφέσῳ καθόδου αὐτοῦ καὶ τῶν δαιμονι-ώντων ἐκεῖσε προελεγμοῦ καὶ ἰάσεως

Ὁ δὲ μέγας πατὴρ ἡμῶν Πέτρος τοὺς τῶν ἁγίων εὐκτηρί-ους ναοὺς ὡς Θεοῦ σκηνώματα λογιζόμενος, καὶ πολλὴν ἄνωθεν ἔχων ἐν τούτοις τοῦ παραβάλλειν τὴν ἔφεσιν, καὶ μάλιστα ὅτιπερ ἔμελλεν μηκέτι ἐπιβαίνειν αὐτοῖς διὰ τὴν τῶν κακοδοξούντων τυραννικὴν ἐπικράτειαν (ὁ γὰρ κανὼν εἰσιέναι ὅλως εἰς ἐκκλησίαν ἀσεβῶν οὐκ ἐπιτρέπει τὸν εὐσεβῆ), παραλαμβάνει καὶ αὐτὸς ἕνα τῶν ἀδελφῶν πάνυ σπουδαῖον καὶ ἐνάρετον Ἰωάννην καλούμενον καὶ πρὸς τὸν ἐν Ἐφέσῳ τοῦ θεολόγου Ἰωάννου ναὸν ἀπήει

always defeated by the power of Christ, has not ceased pursuing his business even now. For he has incited some impious men to scrape off the most distinctive sign of Christ's dispensation, with which the church was adorned by the divine apostles, as though it were something abominable, and to call it an idol. They brutally torture all those who do not accept their impious doctrine and faith. Therefore, my brothers, since we are ordered by the holy scripture not to bring temptations upon ourselves, let us move to the desert in groups of two or three, linked to each other through bonds of love, so that we may keep our faith undefiled and not leave behind our coenobitic way of life, which resembles that of the angels." At that time then the whole brotherhood was divided into small groups and, hiding themselves from the persecutors as best as they could, they moved into some heavily wooded places.

13.2 On his journey to Ephesus, and on how those possessed by the demons there reproached him in advance, and on their healing

Our great father Peter considered the houses of worship of the saints to be God's tabernacles and once again had a great desire to visit them, especially since he was not sure of entering them anymore because of their tyrannical occupation by the heretics (for the canon strictly forbids any pious man from entering a church of those who are impious). He took with him one of the brothers, a very diligent and virtuous man called John, and went to pray at the church of John the

προσεύξασθαι, κἀκεῖθεν εἰς τὸν τοῦ ἀρχιστρατήγου Μιχαὴλ τὸν ἐν Χώναις. Ἐνοῖς καὶ τῶν ἐκεῖσε ὀχλουμένων ὑπὸ
πνευμάτων ἀκαθάρτων τὰ πλήθη τούτου τὴν ἔφοδον προ-
κηρύττοντα μετὰ κραυγῆς καὶ θρήνων πυροβολούμενα
ἔλεγον· "Οὐαὶ ἡμῖν ὅτι ἔρχεται ὁ Πέτρος τοῦ ξενισθῆναι
καὶ ἡμᾶς τοὺς ἀθλίους τῶν ἐνθένδε ἀποδιῶξαι," ὅπερ καὶ
γέγονεν. Παραγενομένου γὰρ αὐτοῦ μετὰ πεντεκαιδεκάτην ἡμέραν, πολλοὶ ἐκ τούτων τῶν δαιμονώντων ἰάθησαν
δι' εὐχῶν αὐτοῦ.

14.1 Περὶ τῆς ἐν Κύπρῳ ἀφίξεως ἀναλύσεώς τε αὐτοῦ καὶ
τοῦ ὁραθέντος γαλακτοειδοῦς ἱδρῶτος αὐτοῦ

Μετὰ ταῦτα ἐπὶ τὴν Κύπρον ἐξώρμησε, ἐνῇ καὶ μῆνας
δέκα περιπολεύσας, καὶ τὰ ἐν αὐτῇ ὡς ἐπόθει κατασπασά-
μενος ἅγια, καὶ πολλῶν φυγαδεύσας τὰς νόσους, πρὸς
τὸ Ὀλύμπιον ὄρος ἐπέστρεψεν, καὶ πρὸς αὐτὴν ἤδη τὴν
κατασυστήματα διεσπαρμένην τῆς ποίμνης αὐτοῦ ἀδελφότητα, καὶ καταλύει ἐν ἑνὶ τῶν ἡσυχαστικῶν αὐτοῦ κελλίων Μεσολύμπῳ καλουμένῳ, καὶ ὁρᾶται ὑπὸ τῶν εὑρεθέν-
των ἐκεῖσε ὡς ἄλλος Μωϋσῆς δεδοξασμένος τὸ πρόσωπον,
γαλακτοειδεῖς ἀποστάζων ἱδρῶτας, τῆς ἐν αὐτῷ ὡς οἶμαι
τοῦ θείου Πνεύματος χάριτος ὡς ὑπερφυῶς τρέχοντος ἐν
τῇ φύσει τὰ κατὰ φύσιν ὑπερφύσιν ἐνδεικνυμένης. Τῇ δὲ
ἐπαύριον μεμαθηκότων τῶν ἄλλοθι ἀλλαχοῦ ἰδιαζόντων
ὑποτακτικῶν αὐτοῦ τὴν ἔλευσιν αὐτοῦ καὶ δίκην πτηνῶν
εὐαγγελικῶς πρὸς τοῦτον συναθροισθέντων ἑνὶ ἑκάστῳ
αὐτῶν τὰ μετὰ τὴν ἐκ τῆς μονῆς ἔξοδον ψυχωφελῆ ὁ

Theologian in Ephesus, and from there to the church of the archangel Michael in Chonai. The multitudes of those disturbed by impure spirits in those churches proclaimed his coming in advance and, being burned, said with cries and laments, "Woe to us, because Peter is coming to stay as a guest and he will cast us wretches out of those who are here." This came to pass, for he indeed arrived after fifteen days, and many of those possessed by demons were healed through his prayers.

14.1 On his arrival on Cyprus, his return, and the milk-like sweat seen upon him

After that, he quickly set out for Cyprus, where he wandered around for ten months. After worshipping at all the holy places on it as he wished and banishing the illnesses from numerous people, he returned to Mount Olympos and to the brotherhood of his flock, which had by this time been scattered in small groups. He stayed in one of his hesychastic cells, which was called Mesolympon, and was seen by those who were there as a new Moses whose face was glorified, for milky sweat was dripping from it. I think that it was the grace of the divine Spirit within him, exhibiting the supernatural through the natural as it was flowing supernaturally in nature. The next day, when his other disciples, who were each living alone in a different place, were informed of his arrival, they flocked all around him like the birds of the gospel. The shepherd asked each one of them about all those things that had profited their souls since he had left

ποιμὴν ἐπυνθάνετο, νουθετῶν, διδάσκων, ἐπιστηρίζων καὶ τοιαῦτα φθεγγόμενος· "Τεκνία, μηδὲν ὑμᾶς ὅλως τῶν γηἵνων περιπλανήσῃ, μὴ βρωμάτων ἡδονή, μὴ δόξης ἐπιθυμία, μὴ ἄλλό τι τῶν ἐπικήρων τὲ καὶ φθαρτῶν, μὴ τοῦ κόσμου παντὸς ἢ αὐτῆς τῆς ποίμνης περιλυπήσῃ ὁ χωρισμός, καὶ μάλα εἰκότως γινώσκοντας τῶν ἐναρέτων κόπων ὑμᾶς παρὰ Θεοῦ ἀποληψομένους τὰς ἀμοιβάς. Μᾶλλον μὲν οὖν διανάστητε καὶ πρὸς τὰς μεθοδείας τοῦ πονηροῦ ἀνθοπλίσασθε ἀσκήσεως εὐτονίᾳ, ἡσυχίας προσεδρίᾳ, καὶ τοῦ βίου παντὸς τοῦ ἐνύλου περιφρονήσει. Μὴ ἐν βρώσει ἢ ἐν πόσει ἢ εὐχῇ ἢ ψαλμῳδίᾳ συνέρχεσθε τοῖς αἱρετικοῖς, *μὴ δὲ χαίρειν λέγετε αὐτοῖς· ὁ γὰρ λέγων αὐτοῖς χαίρειν κοινωνεῖ τοῖς ἔργοις αὐτῶν τοῖς ἀκάρποις.*"

14.2 Περὶ τῆς ἐν τῇ μονῇ τῶν ἀδελφῶν συναθροίσεως καὶ τῆς κατασκευῆς τοῦ τῆς Θεομήτορος ἀντρώδους ναοῦ

Ταῦτα αὐτοῦ παρακατατιθεμένου τοῖς ἀδελφοῖς, ἀπηγγέλη αὐτῷ παραυτῶν μὴ ἐγκρατῆ τὴν μονὴν αὐτῶν γενέσθαι ἔτι ὑπὸ τῶν ἀνιέρων αἱρετικῶν, ἀλλὰ μένειν μεμονωμένην. Τοῦτο μαθὼν ὁ ὅσιος πατὴρ ἡμῶν Πέτρος, καὶ τὴν τῆς φυλακῆς τῆς μονῆς αἰτίαν τὴν τοῦ τρισμάκαρος Παύλου λογισάμενος ἀπαραχώρητον εἶναι πρεσβείαν (ἐν γὰρ τῷ προμνημονευθέντι εὐκτηρίῳ τοῦ ἁγίου Ζαχαρίου κατέκειτο ὁ πανόσιος), τοὺς στερεμνίους εὐθὺς τῶν ἀδελφῶν πρὸς πάντα τε κόπον καὶ ἀγῶνας εὐτονωτέρους ἡσυχάζειν προστάξας, τοὺς ἄλλως πῶς ἔχοντας ἐν τῇ προμνημονευθείσῃ συναθροίζει μονῇ κοινοβιακῶς τούτους ἐγκελευσάμενος διαζῆν, αὐτός τε ἀπὸ σημείου ἑνὸς τῆς μονῆς

the monastery, advising, teaching, supporting them, and saying something like this: "My little children, let no earthly thing distract you, neither nice food, nor the desire for glory, nor any other mortal and perishable thing. Do not let your separation from the whole world or from our flock sadden you, and with very good reason, since you know that you will receive the reward for your virtuous labors from God. It is better for you to be vigilant and arm yourselves against the machinations of the evil one through your intensive spiritual training, your devotion to tranquility, and your contempt for the entire material way of life. Do not join the heretics, either by eating, drinking, praying, or singing with them; and *do not welcome* them. *For whoever welcomes* them *participates in* their barren *deeds.*"

14.2 On the gathering of the brethren in the monastery and the construction of the cave church of the mother of God

After offering this advice to the brethren, he was informed by them that the unholy heretics did not control their monastery anymore, but it had been left deserted. When he learned this, our holy father Peter believed that the preservation of the monastery was due to the constant entreaties of the thrice blessed Paul (since the most holy one was lying in the previously mentioned chapel of Saint Zechariah). He immediately urged the strongest brothers, those who were able to bear all manner of labors and struggles, to continue living as hermits. Then he gathered all those who had a different disposition in the previously mentioned monastery and ordered them to live a cenobitic life. He himself found a cave one mile away from the monastery. He enlarged this by

σπήλαιον εὑρών, καὶ τοῦτο προσλατομήσας οἶκον κυ-
ριακὸν κατεσκεύασεν τῆς Παναγίας Θεοτόκου καλούμενον, καὶ μικρὸν τούτῳ προσαρμόσας κελλίον, ζωὴν ἐναυτῷ
ἰσάγγελον ἐπεδείκνυτο, ποτὲ μὲν ἐκ τούτου τοῖς κατησυχίαν ἀδελφοῖς ἐφιστάμενος, ποτὲ δὲ τοὺς ἐν τῇ μονῇ κοι-
νοβιακοὺς πάλιν ἐπισκεπτόμενος, καὶ τούτους ἱερατικῶς
ἁγιάζων, διὰ τῆς τοῦ κυριακοῦ σώματός τε καὶ αἵματος
μεταδόσεως.

14.3 Περὶ τῆς ἐκ τοῦ ναοῦ τοῦ Ἁγίου Ζαχαρίου παραδό-
ξου ἐξόδου αὐτοῦ

Ὅθεν αὐτῷ μιᾷ τῶν ἡμερῶν ἐν τῇ αὐτῇ μονῇ τὴν ἀναίμα-
κτον θυσίαν ἐπιτελοῦντι, ἐπέστη τίς τῶν αἱμοβόρων αἱρετικῶν μετά τινος συμμορίας κατασχεῖν αὐτὸν θέλων, καὶ
τὸν ναὸν τοῦ Ἁγίου Ζαχαρίου περιστοιχίσας, αὐτός τε
ἐκεῖνος τῆς εἰσόδου περικρατήσας, τὸ τέλος τῆς θείας μυ-
σταγωγίας προσέμενεν. Εὐλαβεῖσθαι γὰρ ἀρετὴν ἐπίστα-
ται καὶ πολέμιος. Ὁ δὲ ὅσιος πατὴρ ἡμῶν Πέτρος, μετὰ τὸ
τελέσαι τὴν ἱερατικὴν ἐκείνην θεοθυσίαν, τῷ ζωοποιῷ τοῦ
σταυροῦ σφραγισάμενος τύπῳ, δι' αὐτῶν διῆλθεν μὴ ἐνορώμενος. Ἐπιπολὺ δὲ ἐκδεξάμενος ἐκεῖνος ὁ ἀλιτήριος, ἐν
τῷ ναῷ εἰσεπήδησεν βρύχων, καὶ τὸν ζητούμενον μὴ
εὑρών, ἀμηχανίᾳ κατείχετο καὶ πάντοθεν τοὺς ὀφθαλμοὺς
περιέστρεφεν, εὑρεῖν βουλόμενος ἔξοδον ἑτέραν, παρ' ἣν
αὐτὸς διεφύλαττεν, καὶ μὴ εὑρηκώς, ἀπεχώρει τῆς ποίμνης, ἄπρακτος, καταπεπληγμένος, κατησχυμμένος.

digging it out and made a church there, named for the Most Holy Theotokos, to which he attached a small cell, where he could be seen living like an angel. He would leave it sometimes to visit the brothers who were living as hermits, and sometimes to look after those who were once again living the cenobitic life in the monastery, sanctifying them as a priest through the communion of the body and blood of the Lord.

14.3 On his wondrous escape from the church of Saint Zechariah

One day, while Peter was performing the bloodless sacrifice in that monastery, one of the bloodthirsty heretics came to him with his gang, wanting to arrest him. This man ordered them to surround the church of Saint Zechariah, while he himself lay in ambush at the entrance, waiting for the end of the holy liturgy, since even the enemy understands that virtue should be respected. Our holy father Peter, however, after he had finished that priestly, divine sacrifice, made the life-giving sign of the cross and passed by them without being seen. After that wicked man had waited for a long time, he rushed into the church with a roar, but, since he did not find the man he was looking for, he was baffled. He looked all round everywhere, wishing to discover another exit from that which he was guarding, but, when he did not find one, he left the flock empty-handed, astounded, and ashamed.

THE LIFE OF SAINT PETER OF ATROA

15.1 Περὶ τοῦ ἰαθέντος νεανίσκου κωφοῦ καὶ ἀλάλου

Τῷ δὲ ὁσίῳ πατρὶ ἐν τῷ ἀποσημείου ἑνὸς τῆς μονῆς ἡσυχαστικῷ σπηλαίῳ ἀπελθόντι καὶ ἡσυχάζοντι προσῆλθόν
τινες φέροντες νεανίσκον ἄλαλον καὶ κωφὸν παρακα-
λοῦντες καὶ λέγοντες· "Ἐλέησον ἅγιε θεράπον Χριστοῦ,
τὴν τυραννηθεῖσαν φύσιν ὑπὸ τοῦ δαίμονος, καὶ τὸν τῆς
ἀνθρωπίνης μέτοχον φύσεως τῆς κτηνώδους ἀλογίας
ἀπόλυσον· δεῖξον καὶ ἐν ἡμῖν ὡς ἐν πολλοῖς ὅσιε τὸ φιλάν-
θρωπον· μὴ κενοὺς ἡμᾶς τῆς αἰτήσεως ἀποπέμψῃς, ὁ ἐκ
Θεοῦ λαβὼν τὸ τάλαντον τῶν ἰάσεων. Δοξασθήτω ὡς
πολλάκις ἐν σοὶ πάτερ, καὶ διατοῦτο ὁ Κύριος." Ταῦτα
αὐτῶν μετοδυρμῶν καὶ βοῶν ἐπειπόντων, φησὶ πρὸς αὐτοὺς σπλαγχνισθεὶς ὁ μακάριος· "Προσαγάγετε αὐτὸν
πρὸς μέ." Καὶ προσήγαγον, καὶ κρατήσας αὐτὸς χειρὶ δε-
ξιᾷ τῆς κόμης τοῦ νεανίου, τῷ παντοδυνάμῳ Θεῷ ἱερατικὴν ἱκετηρίαν ἀνέπεμψεν. Μεθὴν καὶ σφραγίσας τὸ
στόμα τοῦ ἀλάλου φησὶν αὐτῷ· "Τί τὸ ἄλγος σου τέκνον;"
Ὁ δὲ λυθεὶς εὐθὺς τὰ δεσμὰ τῆς ἀλογίας προσέφησεν·
"Τὸν φάρυγγα ἀλγῶ δεινότατα πάτερ ἅγιε." Ὁ δὲ ὅσιος
καὶ τοῦτο ἐξ αὐτοῦ ἀποσοβήσας τὸ ἄλγημα, ὑγιῆ καὶ λά-
λον αὐτὸν ἀπέδωκε τοῖς αἰτήσασιν, αὐτοὶ δὲ τὸν κτηνώδη
ἀποδεξάμενοι λογικόν, καὶ τὸν παραφύσιν καταφύσιν
ἀντιλαβόντες, ἀπήεσαν μετὰ χαρᾶς εἰς τὰ ἴδια δοξάζοντες
τὸν Θεὸν καὶ τὸν ὅσιον αὐτοῦ θεράποντα Πέτρον.

15.1 On the healing of the deaf and mute young man

After our holy father had returned to his tranquil cell in the cave a mile away from the monastery and was living there in tranquility, some people came to him, carrying a young man who was deaf and mute. They begged him, saying, "Saintly servant of Christ, have mercy on this creature that has been tormented by the demon, and free this participant in human nature from his beastly disability. Show us your love for humanity, too, holy one, as you have many others. Do not send us away empty handed, you who have received from God the gift of healing. Let the Lord be glorified in you by this, as he has been so many times." After they had said these things while crying and shouting, the blessed one took pity on them and said, "Bring him to me." They brought him, and after Peter had taken hold of the young man's hair with his right hand, he offered a priestly supplication to almighty God. He then made the sign of the cross on the mute boy's mouth, saying to him, "What's hurting you, child?" Instantly liberated from the bonds of speechlessness, he answered him, "My throat hurts terribly, saintly father." The holy one drove that pain away from him too and gave him back to those who had asked him, healthy and able to speak. After they had welcomed back the one who had been like a beast but was now speaking rationally and the unnaturally disabled one now restored to his natural ability, they went home, giving glory to God and his holy servant Peter.

15.2 Περὶ τῆς τοῦ ἐν κόσμῳ διατρίβοντος ἀδελφοῦ αὐτοῦ ἐν ἐπισκέψει ὁρμῆς καὶ τῆς καταπάροδον ἀεὶ πληθύος τῶν δαιμονώντων ἐλεγχομένης, προσιούσης καὶ ἰωμένης

Ὁ δὲ τοῦ Χριστοῦ ὡς ἀληθῶς μιμητὴς καὶ τοῦ Παύλου ζηλωτής, καὶ τοῦ Μωϋσέως ἰσόρροπος ὅσιος Πέτρος, ὁ θέλων πάντας ἀνθρώπους ὡς ἑαυτόν, μετὰ τὸ ἐν ὄρει τῆς ὑψηλῆς ἀνεληλυθέναι ζωῆς, αὐτήν τε τὴν ἔνθεον καὶ πυρφόρον βάτον τῶν θεωριῶν ἰδεῖν τε καὶ κατακτήσασθαι, καὶ τὴν ἐν κόσμῳ αὐτοῦ συγγένειαν ἠθέλησεν ἐπισκέψασθαι καὶ ταύτην <...>

16.1 Ἐν μιᾷ τῶν ἡμερῶν καταλαμβάνων ὁ μακαριώτατος Πέτρος τὰ τῆς Ἀσίας ὄρη τὰ πλησίον Ἵππου μετὰ τοῦ προμνημονευθέντος διακόνου Ἰωάννου καὶ ἐν ἑνὶ τῶν ἐκεῖσε σπηλαίων προσαναπαυθείς, τῇ ἑξῆς διήνυεν τὴν ὁδὸν αὐτοῦ ταῖς κώμαις μικρὸν οἰκονομικῶς προσεγγίζων. Ὅθεν αὐτῷ ὁδεύοντι κατὰ πάροδον, ἱερεύς τις συμπορευόμενος αὐτῷ, ἐν Αὐγούστῳ μηνί, ἐν ὥρᾳ σταθηρᾶς μεσημβρίας, φλογμοῦ τε καὶ καύσωνος ὄντος μεγάλου, τῷ δίψει κατατρυχόμενος, ἤρξατο αὐτοῦ τὴν φλογώδη ὀδύνην τῷ ὁσίῳ προσαναγγέλλειν. Ὁ δὲ ὅσιος σπλαγχνισθεὶς ἐπ᾽ αὐτῷ καὶ μικρὸν διαστὰς καὶ προσευξάμενος, λέγει τῷ διψῶντι· "Ἴδε ὕδωρ ὧδε, καὶ πιὼν ἀπόπαυσαι τῆς δίψης σου." Ὁ δὲ πρεσβύτερος τοῦ αὐτοῦ χωρίου ὢν καὶ εἰδὼς τὸν τόπον ὅτι οὐδέποτε ὕδωρ ἦν ἐν αὐτῷ, ἠπίστει τῷ μακαρίῳ. Ὁ δὲ προσκαλεσάμενος αὐτὸν πάλιν <...> καὶ προσελθὼν καὶ πιὼν καὶ πλησθεὶς τῆς καινῆς ἐκείνης πηγῆς τοῦ ὕδατος, διηπόρει τὴν ἀνάβλυσιν καὶ τὸ θαῦμα

15.2  On the saint's wish to visit his brother who was living in the world, and the constant multitude of those possessed by demons who were reproved, treated, and cured as he passed by

Holy Peter, who was truly an imitator of Christ, emulator of Paul, and equal to Moses, and who, after ascending the mountain of the exalted life, wanted *all people* to see and acquire the divine and burning bush of contemplation like himself, also wished to visit his family who lived in the world and <. . .>

16.1  One day the most blessed Peter reached the mountains of Asia near Hippos, together with the previously mentioned deacon John, and rested in one of the caves there. The next day he continued his journey, approaching the villages only when necessary. While he was traveling on his way, a certain priest went along with him. As this was in August, and it was high noon when it was swelteringly hot, the priest, being oppressed by his thirst, started to complain to the holy one about the distress he was feeling from the burning heat. The holy one took pity on him, and moving a little way away, prayed. Then he said to the thirsty man, "Look, there's water here, drink and quench your thirst." The elder, who was from that village, knew that place and that there had never been a spring in it, so he did not believe the blessed one. But, when Peter called him again, <. . .> the priest came to him, drank and was filled with the water from that new spring. He could not explain its source, however,

τοῖς ἐντοπίοις ἐδήλωσεν, ἐξ οὗ δὴ καὶ ἡ πηγὴ ἐκείνη μέχρι τῆς σήμερον τὴν ἐπωνυμία ἔσχεν, "τοῦ Ἀββᾶ ἡ πηγὴ" παρ' αὐτῶν ὀνομαζομένη.

16.2 Συνοδοιπορούντων οὖν αὐτῶν τῇ ἐπαύριον, πληροφορίαν εἰληφὼς ὁ πρεσβύτερος ἐκ τοῦ πρώτου θαύματος, παρακαλεῖ τὸν ὅσιον ἔτι προσεύξασθαι καὶ τῆς φθορᾶς τὴν χώραν αὐτοῦ λυτρώσασθαι· ἦν γὰρ ἐπελθὸν ἐν αὐτῇ ἀκρίδων πλῆθος, πᾶν χλωρὸν καὶ πᾶσαν βοτάνην ἐξαναλίσκον. Δυσωπηθέντος δὲ τοῦ ὁσίου καὶ εὐξαμένου, ἀφανισμῷ τὸ τῆς ἀκρίδος ὑπεβλήθη στράτευμα.

17 Καταλαβὼν οὖν ὁ ὅσιος τὴν κώμην τὴν ἑαυτοῦ ἐξ ἧσπερ ἐγεννήθη καὶ ὥρματο, εὑρίσκει ἐκεῖ τινα ἐξ αὐτῆς καί φησιν πρὸς αὐτόν· "Δεῦρο, ἀδελφέ, ποίησόν μοι διακονίαν." Εἶτα λέγει αὐτῷ· "Ἄπελθε ἐπὶ ἕνα τῶν οἰκητόρων τῆς κώμης ταύτης Χριστοφόρον καλούμενον, καὶ εἰπὲ αὐτῷ ὅτι· 'Μοναχὸς ζητεῖ σε, ἰδεῖν σε θέλων.'" Τοῦτο ὁ ἀπεσταλμένος πεποιηκώς, πρὸς τὸν ὅσιον ἤγαγεν τὸν ζητούμενον. Τὸ οὖν κατὰ συνήθειαν ἀποδοὺς σέβας τῷ ὁσίῳ ὁ αὐτοῦ ἀδελφὸς Χριστοφόρος, ἠρώτησεν αὐτὸν ὁ μακάριος· "Ἔστιν σοι μήτηρ καὶ ἀδελφός;" Ὁ δὲ μὴ εἰδὼς τίς ἐστιν ὁ ἐπερωτῶν αὐτῷ, λέγει· "Μήτηρ μοι τέως ὑπάρχει, ἥπερ καὶ ὑγιαίνει, ἀδελφὸν δὲ εἶχον, ἀλλ' οὐ νῦν ἐστιν πρὸς ἡμᾶς· καταλείψας γὰρ ἡμᾶς ἀπέδρασε λεληθότως, μέχρι τοῦ νῦν παρ' ἡμῶν ἀγνοούμενος, καὶ πολλὰ αὐτὸν ἐπιθυμῶ κατιδεῖν καὶ κατασπάσασθαι." Ὁ δὲ ὅσιος λέγει πρὸς αὐτόν· "Εἰ δείξω σοι αὐτόν, τί ἄρα πράξεις;" Ὁ δὲ ἀποκριθείς, φησὶν πρὸς αὐτόν· "Σοὶ μὲν χάριν ὁμολογήσω ὡς εὐεργέτῃ, αὐτοῦ δὲ ἐν πάσῃ τῇ ζωῇ μου

and announced the miracle to the locals. From that time on until the present day that spring bears his name, being called by them "the Abba's spring."

16.2 As they continued on their way together the next day, the elder, who had been convinced by the first miracle, asked the holy one to pray once more for his village to be delivered from ruin, for a swarm of locusts had descended on it and were consuming everything green and every plant. The holy one was won over and, after he had prayed, the swarm of locusts was destroyed.

17 When the holy one arrived at the village in which he was born and from which he came, he found someone from there and said to him, "Come, brother, do me a favor." Then he told him, "Go to one of the residents of this village who is called Christopher and say to him, 'A monk is looking for you and wishes to see you.'" The messenger did this and brought to the saint the man he was looking for. After his brother Christopher had greeted him with the usual reverence for a holy man, the blessed one asked him, "Do you have a mother and a brother?" Christopher, who did not know who was asking him, answered, "My mother is still alive and well. I also had a brother but he's not with us anymore. He abandoned us and ran off secretly. We still don't know about him now, though I very much want to see him and kiss him." The holy one said to him, "If I show him to you, what will you do?" Christopher said in reply to him, "I will be grateful to you, as my benefactor, and I will not leave

οὐκ ἀποστήσομαι." Ταῦτα ἀκούσας ὁ μακάριος Πέτρος, λέγει πρὸς αὐτόν· "Ἐγώ εἰμι ὁ ἀδελφός σου· εἰ οὖν βούλει, ἀκολούθει μοι." Ἐκθαμβηθεὶς δὲ ἐπὶ τῷ λόγῳ ὁ αὐτοῦ ἀδελφός, περιπλακεὶς ἠσπάσατο τὸν ὅσιον, καὶ αὐτῇ τῇ ὥρᾳ ἠκολούθησεν αὐτῷ, μηδενὶ τὸ παράπαν τὰ κατ' αὐτοῦ ἀναθέμενος. Καὶ ἔρχονται οἱ δύο ἐν τῷ προμνημονευθέντι ὄρει καὶ σπηλαίῳ τῷ πλησίον Ἵππου, κἀκεῖ ἀποκείρας τὴν κόμην τῆς κεφαλῆς τοῦ ἀδελφοῦ αὐτοῦ καὶ τὸ ἅγιον ἐνδύσας σχῆμα, Παῦλον ἐπωνόμασεν, ὡς τὰ τοῦ ἀποστόλου Παύλου ἐπιδειξάμενον καὶ σαρκὶ καὶ αἵματι μὴ προσαναθέμενον ὅλως.

18 Ἡ οὖν μήτηρ αὐτοῦ καὶ τοῦτον τὸν υἱὸν ἀποβαλοῦσα καὶ μνήμην τοῦ προτέρου ἀναλαβοῦσα, ἐπὶ τοῖς δυσὶ ὡς ἐπὶ νεκροῖς θρηνοῦσα, λύπῃ τε καὶ πένθει διαβιοῦσα καὶ ἀσθενείᾳ ἐκ τούτου καταπεσοῦσα, μηνύεται παρὰ Θεοῦ τὸν τρόπον καὶ τὸν τόπον ἐν ᾧ ὑπῆρχον οἱ υἱοὶ αὐτῆς καὶ ἀποστέλλει πρέσβεις πρὸς αὐτοὺς καθικετεύουσα καὶ τοιαῦτα ἐπιβοῶσα· "Εἰ ἦν μοι ὑγιὲς τὸ σῶμα, ὦ τέκνα φίλτατα καὶ γλυκύτατα, εἶχον ἂν αὐτὴ παραγενέσθαι πρὸς ὑμᾶς ὡς ὑπόπτερος ἀετὸς ἢ ταλαίπωρος. Ἐπεὶ δὲ νόσῳ ἐκ θλίψεως περιπέπτωκα καὶ πρὸς αὐτὸ ἤδη ὑπάρχω τοῦ τέλους τὸ ἀπαραίτητον, καθικετεύω καὶ δέομαι ἐλθεῖν πρὸς τὴν ὑμᾶς γεννήσασαν καὶ ἀναθρεψαμένην διὰ τὸν Κύριον, ὠδῖνας μητρικάς μου προσμεμνημένοι καὶ τόκου λυπηροῦ καὶ γαλακτοτροφίας καὶ μόχθου τῶν πολλῶν συμφορῶν οὐκ ἐπιλελησμένους, ὅπως θεάσωμαι ὑμᾶς πρὸ τοῦ ἀπελθεῖν, ὅθεν οὐκ ἀναστρέφω." Τοιαύτας ἀγγελίας παρὰ τῆς αὐτῶν τεκούσης δεξάμενος ὁ πανόσιος,

his side for the rest of my life." When the blessed Peter heard this, he said to him, "I'm your brother. *Follow me,* if you want to." His brother was amazed by these words, and embraced and kissed the holy one. And at that very hour he followed him, without telling anyone at all about his actions. The two of them came to the previously mentioned mountain and cave near Hippos, and there the saint cut his brother's hair and dressed him in the saintly habit, naming him Paul, because he demonstrated the behavior of Paul the apostle in not consulting with his *flesh and blood.*

18  Peter's mother, who had now lost this son and still remembered her first one, was mourning both of them as if they were dead. She was living in grief and sorrow and became ill as a result. But after the place where her sons lived and their way of life was disclosed to her by God, she sent messengers to them, imploring them and crying out something like this: "My dear, sweet children, if my body was healthy, wretch that I am, I would visit you like a soaring eagle. But since I have fallen ill from my distress and I am already approaching the inevitable end, I beg and ask you to visit me, the one who gave birth to you and brought you up in the name of the Lord, remembering my birth pains and my anguish in delivery, and not forgetting how I nursed you and my hardship from my many misfortunes. Let me see you before I go to the place from which there is no return." After the most holy one received these messages from the

παραλαβὼν τὸν ἑαυτοῦ ἀδελφὸν Παῦλον καὶ τὸν ἀνωτέρω λεχθέντα Ἰωάννην, πρὸς τὴν ἑαυτοῦ ἐπορεύθη μητέρα. Ἰδοῦσα δὲ αὐτοὺς ἐκείνη καὶ χαρᾶς πληρωθεῖσα, τὴν
νόσον αὐτῆς ἐκλαθομένη καὶ ἀγαλλιαθεῖσα τῷ πνεύματι,
παρεκάλει καὶ αὐτὴ τῷ μοναδικῷ σχήματι περιβαλέσθαι.
Καὶ δὴ τοῦτο ὡς ἐπόθει λαβοῦσα καὶ τὰ κατ' αὐτὴν ἐκκα-
λύψασα πάντα, μετέστη ἡ μακαρία τοῦ σώματος, ἥντινα
καὶ ἐνδόξως κηδεύσαντες πρὸς τὸ ἐπ' Ἵππον ὄρος καὶ
ἄντρον ὑπέστρεψαν, κἀκεῖσε διέμειναν χρόνον οὐκ ὀλίγον
ἀγωνιζόμενοι, ὕδωρ ἔχοντες ὀλίγον ὡς ἀπὸ ἡμίσεος σημείου, ὅπερ πολὺν κόπον παρεῖχε τὴν ἀδελφότητα διὰ τὴν
τοῦ τόπου δυσχέρειαν πρὸς τὴν ἄνοδον.

19.1 Ὁρῶν δὲ τοὺς ὑπ' αὐτὸν ὀλιγωροῦντας ὁ ὅσιος διὰ
τὴν τοῦ ὕδατος χρείαν, τὸν Κύριον καθικέτευσεν, καὶ τῇ
νυκτὶ ἐκείνῃ ὑπὸ τὴν ἐστρωμένην στερεὰν πέτραν ἐκ τῆς
κοίτης αὐτοῦ φλέβα ὕδατος ἐκπηδήσασα, καὶ ὡς ὀξυτόμῳ
δακτύλῳ τὴν πλευρὰν τοῦ ὁσίου πλήξασα, κρουνηδὸν
ἐπορεύετο, ὅπερ καὶ ἕως τοῦ νῦν διαμένει, πολλῶν παθῶν
ἀλεξητήριον πέλον. Τούτου δὲ γεγονότος τοῦ θαύματος
καὶ πανταχοῦ διαφημισθέντος, πολλὰ πλήθη τῶν ἐκεῖσε
πιστῶν προσερχόμενα καὶ παθῶν παντοίων καὶ νόσων
καθαρτήριον ἐπιφερόμενα, ἐδόξαζον τὸν Θεὸν τὸν τοιαύτην χάριν παρασχόντα τῷ ὁσίῳ.

19.2 Ἀνερχομένου ποτὲ τοῦ μακαρίου πατρὸς ἐκ τῶν
τῆς Λυδίας μερῶν πρὸς τὸ μοναστήριον αὐτοῦ τὸ ἐπονο-
μαζόμενον τοῦ Ἁγίου Ζαχαρίου καὶ γενομένου ἐν τοῖς μέρεσι τῆς Δαγούτης, συνήντησαν αὐτῷ ἄφνω ἐπίσκοποι
δύο, καὶ θεωρήσας αὐτοὺς ὡς ἀπὸ τοξοβόλων δύο, λέγει

one who had given birth to them, he took his brother Paul and the aforementioned John with him, and went to his mother. She was filled with joy when she saw them; forgetting her illness and, with her soul rejoicing, she too asked to put on the monastic habit. When she had received it according to her wish, and had confessed everything, that blessed woman departed from her body, which was splendidly buried. After that, they returned to the mountain at Hippos and the cave, and there they remained for a long time, devoted to their ascetic struggles. They had little water, half a mile away, which caused the community much labor, because of the difficulty in getting up to the place.

19.1 When the holy one saw his flock becoming discouraged because of their need for water, he begged the Lord, and that very night a stream of water gushed out from under the hard surface of the rock which served as his bed and poked the holy one's side like a pointed finger. It ran like a spring, and is preserved to the present day, being a protection against many ills. As soon as this miracle happened and news of it spread everywhere, throngs of faithful people from the area came to it, and, after being cleansed of their various ills and diseases, they glorified God, who had conferred such grace on the holy one.

19.2 One time, the blessed father was traveling from the area of Lydia to his monastery which was named after Saint Zechariah. When he had reached the area of Dagouta, two bishops suddenly met him. He saw them half a mile away,

τοῖς μετ' αὐτοῦ οὖσιν ἀδελφοῖς· "Πορεύεσθε, τέκνα, ἐν τῷ τέως." Αὐτὸς δὲ ἐκκλίνας τῆς ὁδοῦ ὡς ὀργυιὰν μίαν, ἔστη ἐκεῖσε· οὐ γὰρ ἠθέλησεν παρὰ τῶν ἐπισκόπων θεαθῆναι διὰ τὸ τὴν αἵρεσιν κατακρατεῖν τῶν παρανόμων Εἰκονο-μάχων. Εὐθέως οὖν οἱ ἐπίσκοποι συνήντησαν τοῖς ἀδελ-φοῖς καὶ ἤρξαντο ἐπερωτᾶν αὐτούς· "Ποῦ ἐστιν ὁ μεθ' ὑμῶν περιπατῶν ἀδελφός; Πέντε γὰρ ἑωράκαμεν ὑμᾶς ἀπὸ μακρόθεν καὶ ἄρτι ὑμεῖς τέσσαρές ἐστε"· ἦν γὰρ ἐκεῖ ὁ τόπος καθαρὸς ἀπὸ παντὸς ἄλσους καὶ δένδρων. Οἱ δὲ ἀδελφοί φησιν πρὸς αὐτούς· "Οὐ γινώσκομεν ἄλλον τινὰ μεθ' ἡμῶν περιπατοῦντα· ἅπαντες γὰρ ὧδέ ἐσμεν." Οἱ δὲ ἐπίσκοποι συντηρήσαντες καὶ ἐρευνήσαντες πολλά, οὐκ ἴδον τὸν ὅσιον Πέτρον, καίπερ ἔγγιστα αὐτῶν ὄντα, ὥστε τοὺς ἵππους αὐτῶν παρὰ μικρὸν ἐγγίζειν, καὶ οὐδεὶς ἐξ αὐτῶν ἑώρακεν αὐτόν. Ἀναχωρησάντων δὲ τῶν αὐτὸν ἐπι-ζητούντων ἀπράκτων, συνῆν ὁ ὅσιος τῇ ἑαυτοῦ συνοδίᾳ περιπατῶν, ἕως οὗ κατέλαβον τὸν ναὸν τοῦ Ἁγίου Ζαχα-ρίου.

20.1 Ἐπὶ πολὺ δὲ ὀχλούμενος ὁ ὅσιος ὑπὸ τῶν ἀσθενῶν καὶ θλιβόμενος, ἀναστὰς ἔρχεται πρὸς τὰ ὄρη τῆς Βιθυνῶν ἐπαρχίας καὶ πρὸς αὐτὴν τοῦ Ὀλύμπου τὴν ὑπορίαν πλη-σίον Προύσης ἀνελθών, ἀντρώδη καὶ λίαν δύσβατον πέ-λουσαν, Δέλη καλουμένην, ἐν ἑνὶ τῶν αὐτῆς ἡσυχάζει σπηλαίων. Ἐν ᾧ καί τις ἀνήρ, κόμης τῇ τύχῃ, Μαυριανὸς τῇ κλήσει, ἐκ Φρυγίας ὁρμώμενος, ἔχων υἱὸν ὡσεὶ χρόνων ἑπτὰ ἐξηραμμένον καὶ ἄλαλον, μαθὼν τὰ περὶ τοῦ ὁσίου, ἤγαγεν αὐτὸν πρὸς αὐτὸν ὀλοφυρόμενος καὶ θρηνῶν καὶ τοὺς τοῦ δικαίου πόδας καταφιλῶν καὶ λέγων· "Ὡς τοῦ

and said to the brothers who were with him, "Go on for a while, my children." He moved a few feet away from the road and stood there, since he did not want to be seen by the bishops because of the heresy of the unlawful Iconoclasts which prevailed at the time. As soon as the bishops met the brothers, they began asking them, "Where is the brother who was walking with you? When we were far away we saw five men walking, but you are now only four." For the place was bare of any woods or trees. The brothers said to them, "We don't know of anyone else walking with us. We're all here." The bishops looked around and investigated at length but did not see the holy Peter, and even though he was so close to them that their horses were almost touching him, none of them saw him. Those who were looking for him left empty-handed and the holy one continued walking with his companions until they reached the church of Saint Zechariah.

20.1 The holy one was greatly troubled and distressed by those who were sick, so he left and went to the mountains in the province of Bithynia. He went up to the foot of Olympos near Prousa, to the place where it is full of caves and hard to walk, called Dele, and he lived in tranquility in one of the caves there. At this point, a man called Maurianos, a count, who came from Phrygia and who had a son, around seven years old, who was disabled and mute, learned about the saint and brought the child to him. Crying and lamenting, and, kissing the righteous one's feet, he said to him,

πανευσπλάγχνου Θεοῦ μιμητής, πάτερ, ἐλέησον τὸν ἐκ
γεννητῆς ἡμιθανῆ μου παῖδα, λῦσον αὐτοῦ τὰς ἐν μέλεσι
καὶ γλώσσῃ πέδας, χαριζόμενος τῇ φύσει τὰ ἴδια, ὁ λύων
πολλοὺς ἐκ σειρῶν ἁμαρτημάτων καὶ τῶν νοσημάτων τῷ
ῥήματι. Ἴδε αὐτὸν παρὰ τοὺς σοὺς πόδας ὥσπέρ τι σκεῦος
ἀνενέργητον καὶ ἀναίσθητον κείμενον, καὶ σπλαγχνισθείς, δεῖξον αὐτόν, θεράπον Χριστοῦ, ὥσπερ ἀναγεννώ-
μενον σήμερον, ὅπως δοξάσω τὸν σὲ δοξάσαντα Κύριον
καὶ τοιαύτῃ χάριτι κατακοσμήσαντι." Ταῦτα ἐκείνου ἐπειπόντος τῷ μακαρίῳ, ἐπιθεὶς ὁ ὅσιος τὴν ἑαυτοῦ χεῖρα τὸν
παῖδα καὶ ἐπευξάμενος, ἀπεκατέστησεν ὑγιῆ.

20.2 Ὁ δὲ μισόκαλος καὶ παμπόνηρος δαίμων, ὁ μηδὲ
κατὰ χοίρων ἐξουσιάζων, τοῦ παιδὸς τοῦ ἐξηραμμένου
ἀπελασθείς, πρὸς τὸν τοῦ ὁσίου πατρὸς ἡμίονον ὡς ἐδόκει
εἰσελθών, ἐν φάραγγι βαθείᾳ ὡς ὀργυιῶν δέκα τῇ προσ-
κειμένῃ τῇ κέλλῃ ἀπέρριψεν αὐτόν, ἀκούσαντι δὲ παρευθὺς τῷ ὁσίῳ τὸ πτῶμα τοῦ ἀλόγου καὶ τῷ ζωοποιῷ τοῦ
σταυροῦ τύπῳ σημειωσαμένῳ τὸν τόπον ἐν ᾧ ἐκρημνίσθη
ὁ ἡμίονος, ἀβλαβὴς διεφυλάχθη μετὰ τῶν ἀμφίων αὐτοῦ.

20.3 Ἐν ἄλλῃ δὲ ἡμέρᾳ καθεζόμενος ἐν τῷ σπηλαίῳ ὁ
διορατικώτατος ἐκεῖνος πατὴρ ἡμῶν Πέτρος, τῷ Θεῷ καὶ
ἑαυτῷ προσαδολεσχῶν, στενάξας καὶ δακρύσας, τῷ ἑαυτοῦ συναγωνιστῇ Ἰωάννῃ προσέφησεν· "Ἰωάννη, μέγας
στῦλος ἔπεσεν καὶ ποιμὴν λογικῶν προβάτων θηριάλωτος
γέγονεν καὶ ἐν πορνείᾳ ἑάλω, οἴμοι, ὁ σωφρονέστατος ὁ
δεῖνα," καὶ ἔκλαιεν μεγάλως. Ὁ δὲ Ἰωάννης τὸ ἀκέραιον
τῆς ῥοπῆς ἀκριβωσάμενος καὶ τὰ λαληθέντα παρὰ τοῦ
ὁσίου ταμιευσάμενος, εὗρεν ὡς ἔφη ὁ μακάριος, καὶ

"Father, as an imitator of the merciful God, you who release many from the chains of sin and illness with a word, take pity on my son, who has been half-dead from birth, and loosen the ties that bind his limbs and tongue, granting what belongs to him by nature. Look at him, lying at your feet like some useless, senseless vessel and, taking pity on him, servant of Christ, show him reborn today, so that I may glorify the Lord who has glorified you and adorned you with such grace." As soon as he said these words to the blessed one, the holy one placed his hand on the child and, saying a prayer, restored his health.

20.2 But the cunning demon, who hates all good things and has no power even over pigs, after he had been expelled from the disabled child, entered into the holy father's mule, it seems, and threw it into the ravine that was near his cell and was about sixty feet deep. As soon as the holy one heard the animal's fall, he made the sign of the life-giving cross over the place where it had plunged over the cliff, and the mule was kept safe along with its trappings.

20.3 Another day, our clairvoyant father Peter was sitting in his cave, conversing with God and his own soul, when he moaned and shed tears, and addressed John, his companion in his struggles, "John, *a great pillar and a shepherd* of rational sheep *has fallen.* Alas, so-and-so, that most chaste man has become food for wild beasts and has been caught in fornication." And he wept intensely. John, who took careful notice of the exact time and kept what the saint had said in his mind, found out that the blessed one had spoken and had

ἀψευδῆ ἐδείχθη τὰ τῆς ὁράσεως. Οὐ μόνον δὲ ἀλλὰ καὶ
τοῖς ὑπ' αὐτὸν μοναχοῖς πολλάκις τὰ κατ' αὐτῶν ἐξεκά-
λυπτεν, ὡς καὶ ἐμοὶ πολλάκις δῆλα τὰ τῆς καρδίας ἐποίησεν.

21 Ἐν μιᾷ γὰρ ἐντολῆς παράβασιν ἐγὼ ἐργασάμενος,
κατ' ἰδίαν καλέσας ὁ θεϊκέλαδος, πρᾴως μοι προεῖπεν καὶ
προσηνῶς· "Διατί μοι, τέκνον, οὐκ ἐκκαλύπτεις τὰ κατασὲ
καὶ τήνδε τὴν τῆς θείας ἐντολῆς θριαμβεύεις παράβασιν;
Ἀνὴρ γάρ," φησίν, "τις ξενοπροσώπως ταῦτά μοι ἐνήχη-
σεν." Καίπερ, ἀδελφοί, Κυρίῳ μόνῳ καὶ ἐμοὶ τῷ πράξαντι
ἐγνωσμένη ἐκείνη ἦν ἡ παράβασις. Ὅτι δὲ τοιοῦτος ὁ
ἀνὴρ ὑπῆρχεν, πρόσεχε· ὁπόταν γάρ τινας ᾔσθετο τῆς ὑπ'
αὐτὸν συνοδίας καὶ ποίμνης ἀναχωρῆσαι βουλομένους,
δαιμονίῳ αὐτοὺς ἢ νόσῳ περιπεσεῖν συνεχώρει, ἐπιστρέ-
φοντας δὲ καὶ τὰ κατ' αὐτῶν ἐξομολογουμένους, παρευθὺ
τῆς νόσου καὶ τῆς δαιμονικῆς μανίας ὁ συμπαθέστατος
ἀπέλυε· τέσσερας γὰρ ἶδον τῶν ἐκ τῆς μονῆς ἡμῶν τοῦτο
παθόντας. Ἀλλ' ἐπὶ τὸ προκείμενον ἐπανίωμεν.

22.1 Καθεζομένου πάλιν τοῦ ὁσίου ἐν τῷ εἰρημένῳ
σπηλαίῳ καὶ ὑπὸ τῶν ἐρχομένων ἐκεῖσε χάριν τῶν ἀσθενειῶν ὀχλουμένου, μὴ φέρων εἰς τέλος τὸν θόρυβον ὁ
φιλήσυχος, ἀναστὰς ἐν Ἀπολλωνίᾳ τῆς Μαυρουσιάδος
εἴτουν Λυδίας κατέρχεται καὶ ἐν ἑνὶ τῶν τοῦ Ἑλλησπόντου
ἡσυχάζει ὀρέων, τὸ παρὰ τὸ πλῆθος τῶν ἰαθέντων ἐκεῖσε
Καλὸν Ὄρος ἐπικληθὲν καὶ ἕως τοῦ νῦν οὕτω καλούμενον. Οἰκήσαντι γὰρ τῷ ὁσίῳ ἐν αὐτῷ, οἱ ἐκεῖσε ἐμφωλεύ-
οντες δαίμονες δίκην πλήθους κοράκων ἀπέπτησαν πρὸς

described truthfully what he had seen in his vision. Not only then, but on many occasions, he revealed to the monks who were under his guidance things about them, as he also frequently made clear to me the matters of my heart.

21 I once did something contrary to an order. That man, who spoke like God, called me to him privately, and mildly and gently made it known to me. "My son, why don't you reveal your actions to me and why you are so proud of this transgression of the divine command? Some other man told me about this." However, my brothers, this transgression was known only to the Lord and to myself who had done it. And that Peter was such a man, just consider this: whenever he sensed that certain members of his community wished to depart from his flock, he permitted them to be caught by a demon or by a disease, but as soon as they repented and confessed about themselves, that most sympathetic man immediately relieved them of their illness and the demonic rage. I witnessed four monks from our monastery experience this. But let us return to our narrative.

22.1 While the holy one was residing in the previously mentioned cave, he was harassed by those who came there because of their illnesses and so, being unable to stand the commotion, the lover of tranquility got up and went to Apollonia in Maurousias, that is, in Lydia, and lived in tranquility on one of the mountains of the Hellespont. It was named the Good Mountain and is still known as such now because of the multitude of those who were cured there. When the holy one started living on this mountain, the demons who lurked there took off like flocks of crows to the

τὰς κώμας χωρήσαντες καὶ εἰς πολλοὺς ἐνεργήσαντες Νεστοριανούς, ὡς ἐπὶ πλεῖστον, καὶ Εἰκονομάχους· οὓς καὶ μαινομένους οἱ σωφρονοῦντες πρὸς τὸν ἅγιον ἀναφέροντες, τὴν ὑγιείαν προεξένουν ἀπαρνουμένους τὴν αἵρεσιν. Εἰς πλῆθος δὲ αὐξανομένης αὐτόθι τῆς ἀδελφότητος, ἐπιτρέπει τοῖς ἀδελφοῖς· προσαρμόσαι κελλία ἐν τῷ αὐτόθι εὐκτηρίῳ ναῷ ἐκ τῆς ἐνούσης τῷ ὄρει ξυλικῆς ὕλης. Οἳ τὸ κελευσθὲν ἀόκνως ἀποπληροῦντες, πεντεκαίδεκα τὸν ἀριθμὸν συναπέρχονται, εἷς ἕκαστος πέλεκυν ἐπιφερόμενος, κοπτόντων δὲ αὐτῶν, συνέβη δένδρον ἀποθραῦσαν ἀώρως, ἐπὶ ἕνα τῶν μοναχῶν καταπεσεῖν Συμεὼν καλούμενον. Τοῦτο οὖν εἰδότες οἱ ἀδελφοὶ γεγονὸς τὸ ἐλεεινόν, μετὰ πολλῆς σπουδῆς τὸν τεθνεῶτα ἐξαγαγόντες τοῦ πτώματος, δακρυρροοῦντες ἅμα καὶ συλλυπούμενοι, ἀνέρχονται, τὴν αἰφνίδιον ἐκείνην συμφορὰν ἐξαγγέλλοντες.

22.2 Τοῦτο ἤδη μεμαθηκὼς παρ' αὐτῶν ὁ ὅσιος Πέτρος, τῇ πρὸς Θεὸν πίστει καὶ ἐλπίδι ἀναπτερούμενος, ἔφησεν· "Ὁ ζωῆς καὶ θανάτου δεσπόζων, Χριστὲ Ἰησοῦ, ᾧ δεδούλευκα καὶ εἰς ὃν ἐκ νεότητος ἤλπισα, μὴ παραχωρήσῃς τοῦτο γενέσθαι εἰς τὴν ἐμὴν εὐτέλειαν." Καὶ λέγει τοῖς ἀδελφοῖς· "Ἄγωμεν ἐντεῦθεν καὶ θεασώμεθα τὸ γεγονός." Κατελθὼν δὲ ὁ ὅσιος καὶ εὑρὼν τεθνεῶτα καὶ ἄπνουν τὸν πρὸ μικροῦ ζῶντα, ἐταράχθη τῷ πνεύματι, δακρύσας δὲ καὶ ἐκ βάθους στενάξας καὶ ἐπιθεὶς χεῖρα τοῦ τεθνεῶτος τῇ κεφαλῇ, ἱερατικὴν εὐχὴν ἐκ τρίτου τῷ ἐν Τριάδι Θεῷ προσανήνεγκεν, μεθ' ἣν καὶ τὸν ζωοποιὸν τοῦ σταυροῦ τύπον ἐπιτελέσας, θαρσαλέᾳ τῇ φωνῇ ἀνεβόησεν· "Ἐν

nearby villages and possessed many people, Nestorians for the most part, and Iconoclasts. Those who were sane, brought these insane people to the saintly one, and they were restored to health after they had denounced their heresy. As the brotherhood there was expanding more and more, Peter allowed the brothers to build cells onto the house of prayer there, using the wood that was abundant on the mountain. They promptly carried out the saint's order and a total of fifteen brothers left together, each of them carrying an ax. But while they were felling the trees, one snapped off unexpectedly and fell upon a monk called Symeon. The brothers who saw this tragic incident take place, moved the dead man out from under the fallen tree with great haste and, weeping and filled with grief, they went up, announcing the sudden accident.

22.2 As soon as he learned this from them, holy Peter, placing all his hope and faith in God, said, "Jesus Christ, you who have the power over life and death, whom I have served and in whom I have hoped from my youth, do not permit this to happen to my humility." Then he said to the brothers, "*Let us go there* and see what happened." The holy one went down, and, finding the one who had been alive a short while ago dead and not breathing, *was disturbed in his soul.* He shed tears and, groaning from the depth of his heart, placed his hand upon the head of the dead man and offered three priestly prayers to the Triune God. He then made the sign of the life-giving cross and in a bold voice called out, "In the

ὀνόματι Ἰησοῦ Χριστοῦ τοῦ ζωοποιοῦντος τὰ πάντα, Συμεών, ἀνάστηθι." Καὶ εὐθὺς ὁ ἄπνους ἀναστάς, αὐτῇ τῇ ὥρᾳ περιεπάτει, ὥστε πάντας τοὺς ὁρῶντας ἐκπλήττεσθαι ἐπὶ τῷ γεγονότι καὶ δοξάζειν τὸν Θεὸν ἐπὶ τῇ παρρησίᾳ τοῦ αὐτοῦ θεράποντος Πέτρου. Ὁ δὲ Συμεὼν ἀποτότε ἔζησεν ἔτη εἴκοσι.

23 Κατ' ἐκεῖνον δὲ τὸν καιρόν, τυπτομένων, δεσμουμένων, ἐξορίᾳ παραπεμπομένων τῶν ἀπειθούντων λογικῶν προβάτων καὶ διδασκάλων τῷ δυσσεβεῖ τοῦ τυράννου Λέοντος δόγματι, συνέβη καί τινα ποιμένα ὀνόματι Ἀθανάσιον ἐν κάστρῳ τινὶ τῶν τῆς Λυδίας μερῶν Πλατεῖαν καλουμένῳ Πέτραν κατακλεισθῆναι. Ὅνπερ θελήσας θεάσασθαι ὁ πατὴρ ἡμῶν Πέτρος, παραλαβὼν τὸν ἑαυτοῦ ἀδελφὸν Παῦλον, διήνυεν τὴν ὁδὸν αὐτοῦ. Καὶ διελθὼν καταπάροδον ἐν ὄρει, εὗρεν εὐκτήριον οἶκον προσπαρακείμενον, ἐν ᾧ καὶ ἀδελφαὶ κατῴκουν, καὶ κατέλυσεν ἐν αὐτῷ.

24.1 Ἡ δὲ τῆς ποίμνης ἐκείνης ὁσιωτάτη ἀμμάς, τὴν ἔλευσιν τοῦ πατρὸς διδαχθεῖσα, μετὰ σφοδροῦ τοῦ δρόμου ἀνῆλθεν διακονήσουσα. Ἐν ᾧ καὶ προσήνεγκαν παρὰ τοὺς πόδας τοῦ ὁσίου οἱ τῆς πλησίον κώμης οἰκήτορες ἄνδρα ἐκ πλείστων χρόνων κατακείμενον, μὴ ποσὶν ἰδίοις βαδίζοντα, μὴ χερσὶν οἰκείαις διακονούμενον, μὴ γλώσσῃ τὰ πρὸς διάλεξιν καθαρεύοντα, ὅνπερ ὁ πατὴρ ἰδών, ἐπηρώτησε λέγων· "Προσκυνεῖς τὴν τοῦ Χριστοῦ εἰκόνα;" Ὁ δὲ νοσῶν φησιν πρὸς τὸν ὅσιον· "Πᾶν ὅπερ κελεύεις μοι ἀναμφιβόλως ποιήσω, τὴν δὲ τῆς τοῦ Χριστοῦ εἰκόνος

name of Jesus Christ who gives life to everything, Symeon, stand up!" Immediately, the one who had stopped breathing stood up and started to walk about right away. All those who saw this were astonished at what had happened and gave glory to God for the great freedom of speech enjoyed by his servant Peter. Symeon lived for another twenty years after that.

23   At that time, when the sheep of the rational flock and their teachers who would not accept the impious doctrine of the tyrant Leo were being beaten, imprisoned, and sent into exile, it so happened that a shepherd called Athanasios was imprisoned in a castle in a region of Lydia called Plateia Petra. Since our father Peter wished to see him, he took his brother Paul with him and set out on the road. As he was passing by on his way, he found a house of prayer nearby, in which sisters were living, and he stayed there.

24.1   The most holy mother of that flock, as soon as she was informed of the father's arrival, came up in great haste to serve him. Meanwhile, the inhabitants of the nearby village brought to the holy one's feet a man who had been bedridden for many years, and was unable either to walk on his feet, or to look after himself with his hands, or to speak clearly with his tongue. When the saint saw him, he asked, "Do you venerate the image of Christ?" The sick man said to the holy one, "I will do whatever you tell me to without any hesitation, but I will never accept the veneration of the

προσκύνησιν ὅλως οὐ παραδέξομαι." Ταῦτα παρ' αὐτοῦ
ἀκούσας ὁ τρισμέγιστος, ὀργισθεὶς κελεύει αὐτὸν ἐκεῖθεν
τὸ τάχος ἐξαιρεθῆναι. Τούτου δὲ γεγονότος καὶ ὥσπερ τι
σκεῦος ἄχρηστον ἐκεῖθεν τοῦ νοσοῦντος ἀποβληθέντος,
ἤρξαντο αὐτὸν ἐπιπλήττειν οἱ συμπαρόντες καὶ οἱ δουλεύ-
οντες αὐτὸν διαγογγύζειν καὶ τοιαῦτα πρὸς αὐτὸν λέγειν·
"Ἐπὰν τῷ θεολέκτῳ καὶ θαυματουργῷ οὐ πείθῃ πατρί, ἵνα
ἀπολαύσῃς τῆς ὑγιείας, ἀφέντες σε νῦν πρὸς τὰ οἰκεῖα πο-
ρευόμεθα." Ὁ δὲ νοσῶν τότε συσχεθεὶς τῇ ἀπορίᾳ, ἤρξατο
δέεσθαι τοῦ πατρὸς μακρόθεν προσερρισμένος λέγων·
"Ἐλέησόν με, πάτερ, τὸν δύστηνον καὶ ἐν πολλοῖς χρόνοις
τῇ ἀπιστίᾳ συζήσαντα· προσκυνῶ τοῦ σαρκωθέντος Θεοῦ
Λόγου τὴν τιμίαν εἰκόνα καὶ τῆς πανάγνου αὐτοῦ μητρός." Ταῦτα αὐτοῦ ἀκηκοὼς ὁ πατὴρ λέγοντος, ἐγκελεύεται τοῖς ὑπηρετοῦσιν αὐτῷ βαστάσαντας ἀγαγεῖν πρὸς
αὐτόν. Ἐλθόντος δὲ καὶ τεθέντος κατὰ πρόσωπον τοῦ μακαρίου καὶ τὴν Χριστοῦ εἰκόνα ἐγγραφῇ προσκυνήσαν-
τος, εὐχῇ ὁ ὅσιος τὰ ἐν γλώσσῃ, χερσί τε καὶ ποσὶ δεσμὰ
διαρρήξας, τὴν ὁλοκληρίαν ἀπέδωκε· ὃν ἐγὼ θεασάμενος
ὑγιῆ καὶ μοναχὸν γεγονότα, ταῦτα ἀκήκοα παρ' αὐτοῦ.
Ἰαθεὶς οὖν, ὡς προγέγραπται, ἀπῆλθεν εἰς τὴν ἑαυτοῦ
οἰκίαν, αἰνῶν καὶ εὐχαριστῶν τῷ Θεῷ καὶ τῷ ὁσίῳ.

24.2 Καί τις ἀνὴρ ἕτερος ἐκεῖσε ὢν τριετίζων κλινήρης
καὶ τὸν πολυχρόνιον ἐκεῖνον παράλυτον ὑγιῆ θεασάμενος,
τοὺς ἑαυτοῦ κελεύει παῖδας τοῦτον ταχέως ἀνακομίσαι
πρὸς τὸν ὅσιον· ἦν γὰρ ὁ ἀνὴρ τῶν εὐπόρων. Καὶ δὴ πρὸς
τὸν τόπον ἐν ᾧ ἦν ὁ ὅσιος ἐγγίζων ὁ παραλελυμένος τοῖς

image of Christ." The thrice great man became irate when he heard this from him and ordered him to be taken away from there as quickly as possible. They did this and the sick man was cast aside there like some useless vessel, for those who were with the man started to castigate him and those who served him started to grumble, and say something like this to him, "Since you won't obey the God-chosen and wonder-working father in order to enjoy your health, we're leaving you now and going home." The invalid realized then that he was in trouble and started to implore the father from a distance, saying vehemently, "Take pity on me, Father. I'm an unhappy man and have lived for many years in my faithlessness. I venerate the precious image of the Word of God who became flesh and that of his most chaste mother." As soon as the father heard him say this, he ordered the servants to pick him up and bring him to him. They came and placed him in front of the blessed man and, after he had venerated the painted image of Christ, the holy one, through his prayer, broke the bonds of his tongue, hands, and feet, and restored him to perfect health. I witnessed him in good health after he had become a monk and heard all these things from him. So, after he had been cured, as I have already said, he returned to his home, praising and thanking God and the holy one.

24.2 Another man there, who had spent three years in his bed, when he saw the one who had been disabled for many years restored to health, ordered his children to bring him urgently to the holy one. And this man was well off. When the man who was disabled in his limbs approached

μέλεσιν, οὐ τὰς τυχούσας δεήσεις καὶ ἱκεσίας τῷ τοῦ
Χριστοῦ θεράποντι προσεκόμιζεν λέγων· "Οἴκτειρόν με
τὸν οἴκτιστον, ὁ πᾶσιν ἐφαπλῶν τοῖς δεομένοις τὸν ἔλεον·
ὑποτὴν στέγην ἐβλήθην τῆς σῆς πρεσβείας, ὦ χριστομί-
μητε, ὅπως διὰ σοῦ ὑγιωθῶ ὁ κατακείμενος." Τοιαῦτα τότε
τῷ παραλύτῳ βοήσαντι, ἐπικαμφθεὶς ὁ ἀοίδιμος κελεύει
αὐτοῦ κατεῖδος ἐξομολογῆσαι τὰ πεπραγμένα, ὁ δὲ νοσῶν
τοῦτο ποιήσας, τῆς ἑαυτοῦ κακοπιστίας ἐνέλιπεν τὸ ἀνό-
μημα, λέγω δὴ τὴν αἴρεσιν. Ποιήσας δὲ ὁ ὅσιος εὐχὴν
ἐπαυτῷ, ἀνενέργητος ἔμεινεν, καὶ δὴ ἀπορούμενος ὁ
τρισόλβιος, ἐπέμενεν ἔτι ὑπὲρ αὐτοῦ τὸν Θεὸν ἐξιλεούμενος, καὶ ὁρᾷ ἐν τῷ σώματι αὐτοῦ θεωρίαν τινὰ φοβερὰν
διὰ τοῦ Πνεύματος ὁ ὅσιος καὶ λέγει πρὸς τὸν ἄνθρωπον·
"Τί ἄτοπον καὶ ἀνεξαγόρευτον κατέλιπες ἁμάρτημα, ἄνθρωπε; Ὁρῶ γάρ τινα φοβερὸν ὄφιν παντί σου ἐνειλημέ-
νον τῷ σώματι καὶ τῶν μελῶν τὰς ἁρμονίας κατέχοντα καὶ
ἰαθῆναί σε μὴ παραχωροῦντα." Ὁ δὲ ταῦτα ἀκηκοὼς γενόμενος ἔμφοβος, ἐξεῖπεν εὐθὺς τῆς ἀσθενείας τὸ αἴτιον
δυσσέβειαν Εἰκονομάχων ὑπάρχειν. Ὅθεν τὸ τῆς τριαδικῆς θεότητος ἐπ' αὐτοῦ ὁμολογήσας ἀμέριστον, ἀσύγ-
χυτόν τε καὶ ἀδιαίρετον, ἀνακηρύξας δὲ τὴν σάρκωσιν
αὐτοῦ καὶ τὴν σεπτὴν εἰκόνα ἀσπάσασθαι καθυποσχόμε-
νος, ἣν καὶ προσκυνήσας, παραυτὰ ἀνέστη καὶ πρὸς τὸν
ἑαυτοῦ οἶκον ἐπορεύθη βαδίζων.

25 Τῇ δὲ ἑξῆς πορευομένῳ τῷ ὁσίῳ πρὸς τὸν ἀνωτέρω
μνημονευθέντα εὐλαβέστατον Ἀθανάσιον σὺν τῷ ἰδίῳ
ἀδελφῷ, ὡς ἐξωρμῶντο, ἀφῆκαν ἐν λήθῃ, ἐν ᾧ ὑπῆρχον
εὐκτηρίῳ, τὸ ἐκ τριχῶν κατεσκευασμένον στιχάριον αὐτοῦ,

the place where the holy one was, he addressed no inconsiderable pleas and supplications to the servant of Christ, saying, "Take pity on me, the most pitiful one, you who extend your mercy to all those in need. I have been put under the roof of your intercession, imitator of Christ, so that I, who am bedridden, may be cured by you." After the disabled man had called out these words, the famous one yielded and ordered him to confess in detail what he had done. The sick man did so, but omitted the sin of his evil faith, I mean his heresy. The holy one said a prayer for him, but he remained unable to move. Not understanding, the thrice-blessed man continued requesting God's mercy on him, and then he saw, through the Spirit, a horrible vision in the man's body. The holy one said to the man, "What terrible and unconfessed sin did you leave out? For I'm seeing a horrible serpent coiling around your whole body controlling the joints of your limbs, and preventing you from being healed." When he heard this, the man became terrified and immediately proclaimed that the cause of his illness was the impiety of the Iconoclasts. After he had confessed to Peter that the threefold divinity is undivided, unconfused, and inseparable, declared the incarnation of Christ, and promised to kiss his hallowed image, which he then venerated, he stood up at once and went home on foot.

25 The next day the saint, together with his brother, went to the previously mentioned most pious, Athanasios, but, as they were leaving, they forgot his hair shirt in the house of prayer where they had stayed. The demons who

ὅθεν οἱ ἐκ τοῦ παραλύτου ὀφιώδεις ἀποχωρήσαντες δαίμονες, μετὰ τὴν ἴασιν τοῦ ἀνδρὸς καὶ τὴν ἀναχώρησιν τοῦ
ὁσίου εἰς τὰς ἐκείνου θεραπαινίδας εἰσοικίσθησαν τὸν
ἀριθμὸν δεκατέσσαρας οὔσας καὶ μαίνεσθαι ταύτας ἐποίουν. Ὅθεν ὁ ἄνθρωπος {εἰς} ἐκείνῳ τῷ ἀφεθέντι στιχαρίῳ
τοῦ ὁσίου ὁμαδὸν τὰς πασχούσας προσενέγκας, ἰάσεως
ἔτυχον αὐθίωρον, δόξαν ἀναπέμπουσαι τῷ Κυρίῳ καὶ τῷ
ὁσίῳ αὐτοῦ θεράποντι Πέτρῳ.

26.1 Τοῦ οὖν κατὰ τῶν εὐσεβῶν διωγμοῦ κατ' ἐκεῖνο
καιροῦ ἐνισχύοντος καὶ τῶν ἁγίων εἰκόνων ἐκπορθουμέ-
νων καὶ τῶν τοῦ διαβόλου ὑπασπιστῶν ἀγωνιζομένων ἐν
τούτῳ, ἄλλοθέν τε καὶ ἀλλαχοῦ περιαγόντων καὶ ἐκλυμαι-
νομένων τοῦ Κυρίου τὸ ποίμνιον, ὑπῆρχέν τις ἐν τοῖς κατὰ
τὴν Ἀσίαν μέρεσιν ἔξαρχος θεοστυγὴς καὶ ἀπάνθρωπος
καλούμενος Λάμαρις, ἔχων εἰς αὐτὸ τοῦτο συνεργούς τινας ἀπανθρώπους. Ὅθεν ἐκ τῆς πρὸς τὸν θεῖον Ἀθανάσιον ἐπισκέψεως ὑποστρέφοντι τῷ ὁσίῳ σὺν τῷ αὐτοῦ
ἀδελφῷ Παύλῳ, ἀπήντησέν τις αὐτῷ καὶ ἤρξατο διαλέγε-
σθαι· "Πόθεν ἐστὲ καὶ ἕως τίνος τὴν ὁδοιπορίαν ποιεῖσθε;
Μὴ τῶν ἀποσχιστῶν εἰκονοσεβαστῶν ἐστε ὑμεῖς;" Ὁ δὲ
ὅσιος τότε πεπαρρησιασμένῃ τῇ ψυχῇ πρὸς αὐτὸν ἀπεκρί-
νατο· "Πᾶς ὁ κατεικόνα Θεοῦ καὶ ὁμοίωσιν ἄνθρωπος, ὁ εἰς
τὴν τοῦ Θεοῦ καὶ Πατρὸς πιστεύων εἰκόνα τὴν ἀπαραλ-
λάκτως ἐν καιροῖς ἰδίοις ὡς οἶδεν ἀσυγχύτως, ἀτρέπτως
ἀνθρωπισθεῖσαν, ὡς δι' αὐτῆς τῆς φθορᾶς ἀπολυτρωθείς,
καὶ σχῆμα ταύτης καὶ πάθος ἐκ πίστεως κατασπάζεται. Ὁ
δὲ μὴ τὴν τοῦ Χριστοῦ προσκυνῶν ἐγγραφῇ εἰκόνα καὶ
σεβόμενος, τοιαύτῃ μορφῇ πρὸς ἡμᾶς τὸν Θεὸν Λόγον οὐ

had come out of the disabled man like snakes, after he had been cured and the holy one had left, took up residence inside his maids, who were fourteen in number, and drove them insane. So the man made them all cover themselves with the holy one's shirt that had been left behind and they were cured that same hour, giving glory to God and his holy servant Peter.

26.1 The persecution against the faithful was intensifying at that time. The holy images were being plundered and the agents of the devil were actively engaged in this, wandering far and wide and destroying the Lord's flock. In the region of Asia there was an exarch called Lamaris, who was cruel and hateful to God and who had some cruel collaborators in this. When the holy one, along with his brother Paul, was returning from his visit to the divine Athanasios, one of them met him and started to question him, "Where are you from? Where are you traveling to? You're not one of those schismatic iconophiles, are you?" The holy one, with a frank and confident spirit, answered him, "Every man who is created *in the image and likeness of God* and believes in the image of God the Father, who became man without undergoing change at the predestined time, as he knows, in an unconfused and immutable way, so that he has been redeemed from corruption through that very image, faithfully venerates its appearance and passion. But someone who does not venerate the painted image of Christ, and respect it, does not believe that the Word of God came to us in this

πιστεύει παραγενόμενον καὶ τῆς τριαδικῆς καὶ ὁμοτίμου
θεότητος ἐκπίπτει πάντῃ ὡς ἀσεβέστατος." Ταῦτα ἀκούσας ἐκεῖνος ὁ ἀλιτήριος, ῥίπτει ἑαυτὸν τάχιστα ἐκ τοῦ
ἵππου, καὶ λαβὼν τοῦ ὁσίου τὴν ῥάβδον, κατὰ τῆς κεφαλῆς
αὐτὸν ἔτυπτεν ἀφειδῶς, αἱμάτων κρουνοὺς ἐκ τῶν πληγῶν
ἀναπέμποντα, καὶ κλασθείσης ἐν τῷ τύπτειν αὐτὸν τῆς
ῥάβδου, ὥσπερ ἐξαπορούμενος τί δεινότερον πράξει εἰς
τὸν θεράποντα τοῦ Θεοῦ, τοῦτον τοῦ κουκουλλίου δραξάμενος καὶ σύρας χαμαί, ἀφειδῶς συνεπάτει. Ταῦτα ὁρῶν ὁ
αὐτοῦ ἀδελφὸς καὶ συνέκδημος Παῦλος, λίθους λαβὼν
βαλεῖν ἠθέλησεν κατ' ἐκείνου τοῦ δυσσεβοῦς καὶ τῶν συναυτῷ. Ὁ δὲ ὅσιος τοῦτον ἐμβριμησάμενος καὶ γραφικὸν
λόγιον προσειπών, "τέκνον, γέγραπται ὅλως μὴ ἀντιστῆναι
τῷ πονηρῷ," τῆς ὁρμῆς ἐκείνης αὐτὸν τῆς θυμώδους κατ-
έπαυσεν.

26.2 Λαβὼν δὲ αὐτοὺς ἐκεῖνος ὁ δυσσεβέστατος, πρὸς
τὸν αὐτοῦ ἀρχηγὸν ἀπήγαγεν Λάμαριν, οὓς ἐν εὐκτηρίῳ
οἴκῳ προσαποκλείσας, φύλακας ἔταξεν ἐν ἀσφαλείᾳ τη-
ρεῖν αὐτούς. Τῇ δὲ ὥρᾳ τῶν ἑωθινῶν ὕμνων, ὡς εἰώθεισαν
οἱ ὅσιοι τὰς εὐχὰς τῷ Κυρίῳ προσαναφέρειν, καὶ τοῦτο
ἐκεῖσε ὑπὸ τῶν ἱερῶν κανόνων κωλυόμενοι ἐπιτελέσαι, "οὐ
δεῖ," λεγόντων, "εἰς ἐκκλησίαν ἀσεβῶν τὸν εὐσεβῆ εἰσιέναι
ἢ προσεύχεσθαι," τῷ ζωοποιῷ τοῦ Χριστοῦ σφραγισάμε-
νοι τύπῳ, διῆλθον τοὺς φύλακας ἀγνοούμενοι καὶ ἐν τῷ
ὑπαίθρῳ τῷ οὐρανοῦ καὶ γῆς δεσπότῃ τὰς εὐχὰς ἀπο-
δόντες, πρὸς ᾧ ἐφρουροῦντο ναῷ ὑπέστρεφον οἱ μακάριοι. Καὶ δὴ ἐν αὐτῷ εἰσιόντων πρὸ τοῦ κλεῖσαι τὴν θύραν,

form, and thus is totally separated from the threefold and equally honored divinity, as a most impious person." As soon as that wicked man heard these words, he swiftly flung himself off his horse and, seizing the saint's staff, struck him mercilessly on the head so that streams of blood gushed from the wounds. And when the staff had been broken by striking him, since he could not think of anything worse to do to the servant of God, the man grasped his cowl and dragged him to the ground, and trampled him mercilessly. When he saw this, Peter's brother and fellow traveler, Paul, wanted to gather stones and throw them at this impious man and his companions. But the holy one grew angry with him and repeated the words of scripture, "My child, it is written that we should *not put up* any *resistance to the evil one,*" and thus put a stop to his angry impulse.

26.2 That most impious man took them off to his commander, Lamaris, who locked them up in a house of prayer and set guards to keep them securely. At the time of the morning service, since the holy ones were accustomed to offer their prayers to God but were prevented from doing so there by the holy canons, which say that "a pious man may not enter a church belonging to impious men or pray there," they crossed themselves with the life-giving sign of Christ, passed the guards undetected, and offered their prayers outside to the master of heaven and earth. Then the blessed ones went back into the chapel in which they were being kept. While they were going in, before they closed the door,

THE LIFE OF SAINT PETER OF ATROA

ἀνέκραξαν οἱ φυλάσσοντες, νομίζοντες τοὺς ὁσίους ἐκπεφευγέναι, καὶ αὐτοὶ πρὸς αὐτοὺς ἔνδοθεν ἐπεβόησαν· "Μὴ
θροεῖσθε, ὦ τέκνα· ἐνταῦθα γάρ ἐσμεν οἱ ἀμφότεροι."

26.3 Τῇ δὲ ἐπαύριον Λάμαρις ἐκεῖνος ὁ δυσσεβέστατος,
διαστήσας ἀπ' ἀλλήλων τοὺς μακαρίους, καὶ τὸν μὲν πατέρα Πέτρον εἰς φρούριον σιδηροδέσμιον θέμενος, τὸν δὲ
αὐτοῦ ἀδελφὸν καὶ συνέκδημον Παῦλον πρὸς ἑαυτὸν
προσκαλεσάμενος, ἤρξατο θωπευτικῶς λέγειν· "Τὸ τῆς
θέας σου ὡραῖον καὶ τὸ καταμφότερα περιδέξιον εἰδώς, ὦ
Παῦλε, ἠβουλήθην, εἰ πεισθῇς μοι, ἐν μιᾷ τῶν μεγίστων
πόλεων ἐπίσκοπόν σε καταστῆσαι." Ὁ δὲ ὅσιος Παῦλος
ὡς ἰὸν ὄφεως τὰς ἐκείνου θωπείας ἐκτιναξάμενος, ἔφησεν·
"Οὐδέν με ὅλως χωρίσει τῆς εὐσεβείας, ὦ δυσσεβέστατε,
οὐ δόξης ἔρως, οὐκ ἀρχῆς ὕψος, οὐ προεδρίας κλέος, οὐδ'
ἄλλο τι τῶν ἐπιγείων καὶ φθαρτῶν, καὶ μάλα εἰδότι ὡς τοῦ
αἰωνίου πυρός ἐστιν κληρονόμος ὁ τῇ ὑμῶν ἀσεβείᾳ πει-
θόμενος καὶ τὴν Χριστοῦ εἰκόνα μὴ σεβαζόμενος." Ταῦτα
ἀκούσας ἐκεῖνος καὶ θυμῷ ὑπερζέσας, κελεύει αὐτὸν τὸ
τάχος ἀποδυθέντα μαστίζεσθαι.

26.4 Τούτου δὲ ἤδη ἀνυομένου ὑπὸ τῶν ἐκείνου ὑπηρετῶν, ἐκ τῆς πλησίον εἱρκτῆς παρακύψας ὁ πατὴρ ἡμῶν
Πέτρος, τοῖς μέλλουσι μαστίζειν αὐτὸν μετὰ πολλοῦ τοῦ
θάρσους ἐβόησεν· "Ἐμοὶ πληγὰς ἐπίθετε ὅσας ἐὰν θέλητε
καὶ ὁποίας βούλεσθε, μηδὲν κατὰ τοῦ νέου τολμήσαντες·
εἰ δὲ τοῖς ἐμοῖς οὐκ ἀνέχεσθε λόγοις, ὁ πάντων ἔκδικος
Κύριος ἐν τῇ νῦν ὥρᾳ φοβερὰ πυρὸς ἐξαποστελεῖ βέλη καὶ
πατάξει ὑμᾶς καιρίᾳ πληγῇ· τὰ γὰρ εἰς ἐμὲ πεπραγμένα

the guards started to shout, believing that the saints had escaped. But they called out to them from inside, "Don't worry, children, we're both here!"

26.3 The next day that most impious Lamaris separated the blessed ones from each other. He locked up father Peter in a prison, bound in irons, but he summoned his brother and fellow traveler, Paul, and started to flatter him, saying, "I've recognized your pleasant appearance and your adaptability to both sides, so I've decided to appoint you bishop in one of the great cities, provided you obey me." The holy Paul shook off his flattery as if it were snake venom and said, "Nothing will separate me from piety, you most impious man, not love of glory, not some high office, not the renown of prestigious rank, and not any other earthly and perishable thing. I am well aware that anyone who follows your impiety and does not venerate the image of Christ will inherit the eternal fire." As soon as he heard this, Lamaris's rage boiled over and he ordered Paul to be quickly undressed and whipped.

26.4 While this was already being carried out by his subordinates, our father Peter peered out of the nearby prison and with great courage shouted at those who were ready to whip him, "Beat me as much as you want and in any way you wish, but don't you dare harm that young man. If you don't do what I say, our Lord, who is the protector of all, will send terrible arrows of fire this very moment and strike you with a fatal blow. I forgive you for the things you've done to me,

συγχωρῶ ὑμῖν, τὰ δὲ κατὰ τοῦ νέου Παύλου οὐ συγχωρη-
θήσεται." Ὁ δὲ κατὰ τὴν ὁδὸν συλλαβὼν τοὺς ὁσίους, δο-
λίᾳ γλώσσῃ ἀποκριθεὶς εἶπεν· "Τὴν παρασοῦ ἐγὼ οὐ χρείαν
ἔχω συγχώρησιν." Καὶ ἅμα σὺν τῷ λόγῳ τοῦ μακαρίου,
ἄγγελος Κυρίου πατάξας τὸν ἀλιτήριον, πληγῇ ἀνιάτῳ
ὑπέβαλεν· αἵματος γὰρ ὀχετοὺς ἐκ τῶν μυκτήρων δια-
πάσης ἡμέρας καὶ τῆς νυκτὸς προχέειν καταδικασθείς,
καίπερ πολλῶν ἰατρικῶν σοφισμάτων περιοδείας ἐκτελε-
σάντων καὶ μηδὲν ὠφελησάντων, τῆς ζωῆς ἀπερράγη ὁ
ἄθλιος. Τοῦτο οἱ συνεταῖροι διῶκται ἑωρακότες, φόβῳ
συσχεθέντες μεγάλῳ, παρευθὺς τοὺς ὁσίους ἀπέλυσαν.
Τῆς δὲ κλασθείσης ῥάβδου τὰ τμήματα οἱ ἐκεῖσε εὑρεθέν-
τες πιστοί, λαβόντες καὶ προσαρμόσαντες, ἐν ἐκκλησίᾳ
ἀπέθεντο πολλῶν δι' αὐτῆς νοσημάτων ἀπολαβόντες τὴν
ἴασιν, καὶ ἐκ τοῦ κουκουλλίου ὡσαύτως τὸ ἀπορραγὲν οἱ
λαβόντες οὐ μετρίως εὐεργετήθησαν· παθῶν γὰρ πολλῶν
ἐκ τούτου τὴν θεραπείαν ἐδέξαντο.

27 Ἀπολυθέντων δὲ ἐκεῖθεν τῶν ὁσίων τούτων ἀνδρῶν
καὶ πρὸς τὴν ἡσυχίαν μετὰ χαρᾶς ἐπιστρεφόντων, ὅτι
ἠξιώθησαν ὅλως ὑπὲρ τοῦ Κυρίου ἀτιμασθῆναι, ἀπήντησεν
αὐτοῖς πένης τίς λεπρὸς ἐλεημοσύνην αἰτούμενος. Εἰδὼς
δὲ αὐτοῦ τὴν νόσον χαλεπωτάτην οὖσαν ὁ ὅσιος καὶ μὴ
ἔχων ἀργύριον ἢ χρυσίον τοῦ δοῦναι αὐτῷ, ὅπερ εἶχεν εἰς
εὐπορίαν δεδώρητο, καθάρας αὐτοῦ δι' εὐχῆς τὴν λέπραν
αὐθημερόν.

28 Καταλαβόντι δὲ αὐτῷ ἐν τῷ προμνημονευθέντι
Καλῷ Ὄρει, προσῆλθεν αὐτῷ τις ποιμὴν λογικῶν προβάτων τῶν κατὰ τὴν Λυδίαν μερῶν, ὀνόματι Πατερμούθιος,

but you will not be forgiven for those against this young man, Paul." The man who had arrested the holy ones on the road answered with his treacherous tongue, "I don't need your forgiveness." And as soon as the blessed one spoke, an angel of the Lord struck that wretched man and afflicted him with an incurable illness, for he was condemned to have streams of blood flow out of his nostrils all day and night. Although they performed procedures from many medical therapies, nothing helped and that miserable man was violently deprived of his life. His fellow persecutors were terrified when they saw this and set the saints free immediately. The faithful people there found the pieces of the broken staff; after they had taken them and pieced them together, they placed them in a church, where many illnesses received a cure through them. In a similar way, those who took hold of the piece that was torn from Peter's cowl benefitted greatly from it, because they received treatment for numerous ills through it.

27 After those holy men were released from there and were returning to their tranquility with joy, *because they had been deemed* fully *worthy of being dishonored for the sake of the* Lord, they met a poor leper who was begging for alms. The saint realized that his disease was very serious and, since he did not have either *silver* or *gold* to give him, he offered him what he had in abundance as a gift, cleansing him from his leprosy that very day through his prayer.

28 As soon as he reached the previously mentioned Good Mountain, a shepherd of the rational sheep of the monastery of Chareus in the region of Lydia, called Pater-

THE LIFE OF SAINT PETER OF ATROA

μονῆς Χαρέως, ὀλοφυρόμενος καὶ θρηνῶν καὶ τοιαῦτα
φθεγγόμενος· "Ἐλέησόν με, πάτερ ἅγιε, τὸν πεπλανημένον καὶ οἴκτιστον, ἐλέησόν με τὸν πολλῶν δακρύων
χρήζοντα καὶ μηδεμίαν εὐποροῦντα σταγόνα, ἐλέησόν με
τὸν ἐν λάκκῳ ἀπωλείας κατολισθήσαντα καὶ ἐπίχαρμα γενόμενον δαιμόνων καὶ γύμνωσιν αἰσθόμενον τῆς παρούσης μοι ἐκ τοῦ βαπτίσματος χάριτος." Ἦν γὰρ οὗτος κρα-
τηθεὶς ὑπὸ τῶν διωκτῶν καὶ τὴν τῆς Χριστοῦ εἰκόνος
προσκύνησιν ἀπαρνησάμενος ἐγγράφως. Ὅνπερ δεξάμενος ὁ πανόσιος οὗτος πατὴρ καὶ διερευνήσας τὰ κατ᾽
αὐτόν, δίδωσιν αὐτῷ εὐλογίαν κανονικὴν καὶ ἀναχωρητικὸν κελλίον τοῦ ἡσυχάζειν, καὶ ἐδέετο ὑπὲρ αὐτοῦ ἀδια-
λείπτως τὸν Κύριον δεχθῆναι αὐτοῦ τὴν μετάνοιαν καὶ
τὴν προτέραν εἰς τοῦτον χάριν ἐπανελθεῖν. Ὅθεν ἐν μιᾷ
νυκτὶ ὀφθαλμοφανῶς ἐπιστάντες τῷ τρισοσίῳ οἱ δαίμονες,
ἔλεγον· "Τί ἡμῖν καὶ σοί, Πέτρε, ὅτι οὕτως ἀνυστάκτως
ἡμᾶς πολεμεῖς, τῶν τόπων ἀποσοβῶν, τῶν ἀνθρώπων ἀποδιώκων καὶ νῦν δὲ ἀπὸ τούτου τοῦ γέροντος; Πάντα σοι
ἤδη παραχωροῦμεν, μόνον τοῦτον ἡμᾶς μὴ ἀποστερήσῃς·
πλεῖστα γὰρ αὐτὸν ἐκ πολλῶν τῶν ἐτῶν προσπαλαίσαν-
τες, μόλις αὐτοῦ περιγενέσθαι ἰσχύσαμεν." Ὁ δὲ ὅσιος
ταῦτα ἀκούων, τὰς χεῖρας ἐξέτεινεν εἰς τὸν οὐρανόν, δεόμενος περὶ τούτου τὸν Κύριον καὶ λέγων· "Ὦ Κύριέ μου
Ἰησοῦ Χριστέ, χάρισαί μοι μετανοοῦσαν τούτου τὴν ψυχὴν
τοῦ γέροντος καὶ σῶσον αὐτήν, ἀνθ᾽ ὧν πρὸς τὴν ἐμὴν
ταπείνωσιν παρεγένετο, ἀποδιώκων ἀπαυτῆς τὰ κατεπαι-
ρόμενα στίφη τῶν δαιμόνων, ὅτι σὺ εἶ μόνος εὔσπλαγχνος
καὶ φιλάνθρωπος καὶ μετανοῶν ἐπικακίαις ἀνθρώπων."

mouthios, came to him, weeping and wailing and saying, "Have mercy on me, saintly father, for I am lost, and truly wretched. Have mercy on me, I am in need of tears, but lack a single drop to shed. Have mercy on me, for I have sunk down into the pit of destruction, become the laughingstock of the demons, and I feel I have been stripped of the grace that was in me from holy baptism." This was because he had been arrested by the persecutors and had denied in writing the veneration of the holy image of Christ. The most holy father received him and, when he had found out all about him, gave him the canonical blessing and a hermit's cell in which to live in tranquility. He begged the Lord continuously to accept his repentance and to give him back his previous grace. Then, one night, the demons appeared to the thrice holy one visibly and said, "Peter, *what have you to do with* us? Why do you fight against us without sleeping, drive us from our homes, throw us out of people, and now do so from this old man? We grant you everything else, but don't deprive us of this one. We've wrestled hard against him for many years, and we've only just managed to overcome him." But when the holy one heard this, he raised his hands to heaven and begged the Lord concerning this man, saying, "Lord Jesus Christ, grant me the repentant soul of this elder and save it, because he took refuge with my humility. Cast out of his soul the arrogant crowd of demons, because you are the only merciful one and you love mankind, *changing your mind concerning the sins* of men." As soon as he had

Τελέσαντος δὲ αὐτοῦ τὴν εὐχὴν καὶ τῷ ζωοποιῷ τοῦ σταυροῦ τύπῳ κατὰ τοῦ πλήθους τῶν δαιμόνων ἐκπέμψαντος,
ἀφανισμῷ ἐκείνους εὐθὺς τοὺς ἐπηρμένους παρέδωκεν.
Διὸ καὶ προσκαλεσάμενος τὸν παραπεσόντα γέροντα ἔφη·
"Πρόσεχε ἐπὶ σεαυτόν, ἀδελφέ, ὅτι πολλὴ κατὰ σοῦ τοῖς
δαίμοσί ἐστιν πικρία, καὶ ὅρα μὴ θρύψῃς σου τὸν τόνον
τῆς ἐγκρατείας καὶ μὴ παύσῃ τρέχων τὴν ὁδὸν ἐνθέως τῆς
ἀληθείας." Ταῦτα εἰπών, πρὸς τὴν ἰδίαν μονὴν ἀπέστειλεν
αὐτόν, πληροφορίαν εἰληφὼς ἐκ Θεοῦ ὁ μακάριος ὅτι
προσεδέχθη αὐτοῦ ἡ μετάνοια καὶ ἡ προενοῦσα εἰς αὐτὸν
χάρις ἐπανῆλθεν τοῦ Πνεύματος.

29 Διηγήσατο ἡμῖν ὁ ἀββᾶς Ματθίας, ὁ καὶ ὕστερον
γεγονὼς ἐπίσκοπος, ὅτι "εἶχον ἐξάδελφον, καὶ ἦν αὐτῷ
τέκνον ἀρρενικὸν περιεχόμενον νόσῳ χαλεπῇ ἐκ γεννή-
σεως αὐτοῦ· ἀπὸ γὰρ τῆς ψόης αὐτοῦ μέχρι τοῦ πληρώματος τῶν ποδῶν αὐτοῦ ὀστοῦν τὸ σύνολον οὐχ ὑπῆρχεν ἐν
αὐτῷ, ἀλλ᾽ ἦν μόνον σάρκες καὶ δέρμα, ὥστε ἐκ τούτου μὴ
δύνασθαι αὐτὸ μήτε κἂν ἐπιτῆς γῆς σύρεσθαι· ἦν δὲ ἐτῶν
ἑπτά. Τοῦτο ἀπενέγκας ὁ πατὴρ αὐτοῦ πρὸς τὸν ὅσιον,
παρεκάλει τῆς ἰάσεως τυχεῖν, ὁ δὲ θεῖος Πέτρος θεασάμενος, αὐτῷ ἔφη· Ὑγιὴς μὲν γενήσεται οὗτος ὁ παῖς ἔτη δύο,
καὶ μετὰ τοῦτο τελευτήσει.᾽ Ποιήσας οὖν εὐχὴν ἐπ᾽ αὐτῷ
ὁ πατὴρ ἡμῶν, μετὰ δύο ἡμέρας ὀστοποιηθέντων τῶν
μελῶν τοῦ παιδός, ὑγιὴς γέγονεν καὶ ἤρξατο περιπατεῖν
καὶ ἐδόξασαν πάντες τὸν Θεόν. Πληρουμένων δὲ τῶν δύο
ἐτῶν, ἐτελεύτησεν καθὼς προεῖπεν ὁ ὅσιος."

30 Ὅμως καὶ ἕτερον ἡμῖν διηγήσατο ὁ αὐτὸς Ματθίας
ὅτι "ἐρχομένου τοῦ ὁσίου πατρὸς καταπάροδον ἐν τοῖς τῆς

completed his prayer, he made the sign of the life-giving cross over the multitude of demons and sent them away, and immediately caused their presumption to vanish. He then summoned the elder who had lapsed and said, "*Take care of yourself,* brother, because the demons are very bitter against you. See that you do not relax the level of your self-control nor stop following the path of God's truth." When he had said this, he sent him back to his monastery. The blessed one was informed by God that that man's repentance had been accepted by him and the grace of the Spirit, which had dwelt in him previously, had returned.

29 We were told this by Abba Matthias, who later became a bishop: "I had a cousin, and he had a boy who was afflicted with a serious illness from birth. For there were no bones at all from the lower part of his back to his feet, which were fully formed, only flesh and skin. As a result, he could not even crawl on the floor. The boy was seven years old. His father brought the boy to the holy one asking for a cure. When the divine Peter saw the boy, he said to the man, 'This boy will be well for two years, but will die after that.' So our father said a prayer for him and after two days the child's limbs were filled with bones, he became healthy, and started walking; and all gave glory to God. But as soon as the two years had passed, the boy died just as the holy one foretold."

30 This same Matthias also told us another tale that: "When the holy father was passing through the region of

Λυδίας μέρεσιν, ἐγένετο αὐτῷ ἐκκλῖναι τοῦ ἀναπαύσασθαι
μικρὸν πλησίον τινὸς μοναστηρίου Σεμνίου καλουμένου
ἀρχαίου ὄντος ἐν τόπῳ ἀλσώδει. Τοῦ δὲ καθηγητοῦ ἡμῶν
συνεσθίοντος τῷ ἡγουμένῳ τῆς μονῆς καὶ ἑτέροις ἀδελφοῖς, ἤμην διακονῶν ἐγὼ ὁ προλεχθεὶς Ματθίας, εἶχον δὲ
ἔλαιον εἰς ἄγγος ὀλιγοστὸν εἰς χρείαν τῆς ὑπηρεσίας.
Τοῦτο δὲ τελειώσαντός μου ἐν τῇ ὑπηρεσίᾳ καὶ διαπο-
ροῦντος περιετέρου, ἀναστὰς εὗρον αὐτὸ πεπληρωμένον
καὶ ἐν τῇ γῇ χεόμενον.

31 "Τοῦ δὲ ὁσίου πατρὸς ἡμῶν τὴν πορείαν ποιουμένου
πρὸς τὸ Καλὸν Ὄρος, παρεκαλοῦμεν αὐτὸν ὅπως ἐξελθοῦσαι αἱ ἀδελφαί, τὰς εὐχὰς αὐτοῦ κομίσωνται. Καὶ δὴ
πεισθεὶς ἡμῖν ἐπένευσεν, καὶ ἐξελθοῦσαι αἱ μοναχαί, ἔστη-
σαν ὡς ἀπὸ τοξοβόλου μήκοθεν. Μία δὲ ἐξ αὐτῶν ἐκ δαιμονικῆς ἐνεργείας ἔπασχε τὴν χεῖρα, τοῦ λοιποῦ σώματος
σωφρονοῦντος, καὶ ἦν θαῦμα ἰδέσθαι· πάσχουσα γὰρ ἡ
χείρ, εἷλκεν ἅπαν τὸ σῶμα τῆς γυναικὸς ὅπου ὥρμησεν,
μᾶλλον δὲ ὅπου ὁ ψυχοφθόρος καὶ πονηρὸς δαίμων ἠβουλήθη. Μὴ ἐνέγκας δὲ ὁ ἀκάθαρτος τὴν τοῦ ἁγίου θέαν,
ἐκταράξας τὴν χεῖρα αὐτῆς, ὥρμησε πρὸς τὸν ὅσιον. Ὡς
δὲ ἴδομεν τὴν ἀδελφὴν δεινῶς πάσχουσαν, ἠρξάμεθα ὁμο-
θυμαδὸν παρακαλεῖν τὸν ἅγιον σπλαγχνισθῆναι ἐπαυτήν.
Ὁ δὲ ἐπιστραφεὶς καὶ τὸ σημεῖον τοῦ ἀχράντου σταυροῦ
πεποιηκώς, λέγει· ''Ἐν τῷ ὀνόματι τοῦ Κυρίου ἡμῶν Ἰησοῦ
Χριστοῦ, οὐκ ἔχεις ἐξουσίαν ἀπὸ τοῦ νῦν, πονηρὸν καὶ
ἀκάθαρτον πνεῦμα, κωλῦσαι αὐτὴν τὸ σύνολον.' Καὶ ἰάθη
ἡ χεὶρ ἀπὸ τῆς ὥρας ἐκείνης, καὶ ἐδοξάσαμεν πάντες τὸν
Θεόν.

Lydia on his way, he made a detour in order to rest near a monastery called Semnion, which was old and in a wooded place. Our teacher was eating with the abbot of the monastery and other monks, while I, the previously mentioned Matthias, was serving. I had very little oil in the container for use in my service and, when I had used it up during my service, I did not know where to get more, but, when I stood up, I found the bottle was full and running onto the floor.

31 "While our holy father was traveling to the Good Mountain, we asked him if the sisters might come out to obtain his blessing. He was persuaded by us and agreed. The sisters came out and stood some distance away. One of them was suffering from a demonically inflicted malady in her hand, but the rest of her body was healthy. It was a remarkable thing to see, for the hand that was suffering was pulling the woman's whole body toward the place where it wanted to go, or, rather, where the spiritually destructive and evil demon wanted. The unclean one who could not stand the sight of the saint, rushed toward the holy one, violently shaking the woman's hand. When we saw the sister suffering so terribly, we began as one to call on the saint to take pity on her. The father turned round, made the sign of the immaculate cross, and said, 'In the name of our Lord Jesus Christ, evil and unclean spirit, you have no power from now on to hinder this woman at all.' And her hand was cured that very hour, and we all gave glory to God.

32 "Πρὸ δὲ χρόνου τινὸς συνέβη κἀμὲ ἐν ἑσπέρᾳ εἰσελθεῖν ἐν τῇ κοίτῃ μου ἀναπαύσασθαι, σκοτίας οὔσης βαθείας, καὶ ἐκτείνας τὰς χεῖράς μου ἐν τῇ στρωμνῇ, φωτὸς μὴ ὑπάρχοντος καὶ μηδὲν θεωροῦντός μου, ἐπελαβόμην ἔχιδνα κατακεκομμένην ἐμεσθεῖσαν ὑπὸ κατουδίου, καὶ ταύτην κατασχόντος μου αἰφνιδίως, αἱ δύο μου χεῖρες κατεψόφησαν ἐκ τοῦ ἰοῦ αὐτῆς καὶ κατήρχετο τὸ αἷμα ἐξ αὐτῶν ἐπὶ πλείστας ἡμέρας, ὥστε μὴ δύνασθαί με μετ᾽ αὐτῶν βεβρωκέναι, εἰ μὴ διὰ μηχανῆς ἑτέρας, ἀλλ᾽ οὐδὲ εἰς διακονίαν τινὰ ἠδυνάμην ἐνεργῆσαι. Εὐθέως οὖν ἐγὼ ὁ τάλας Ματθίας μετὰ τῆς ἰάσεως τῆς ἀδελφῆς προσπεσὼν τῷ ὁσίῳ, ἐδείκνυον αὐτῷ τὸ ἐν ταῖς χερσί μου πάθος, καὶ τὴν αἰτίαν ἐξειπόντος μου αὐτῷ, ὁ χριστομίμητος πατὴρ ἡμῶν ἐμφυσήσας αὐταῖς καὶ τὸ σημεῖον τοῦ σταυροῦ ποιήσας, παραυτίκα ὡς λεπίδες ἐκ τῶν χειρῶν μου πεσοῦσαι, ὑγιὴς γέγονα, εὐχαριστῶν τῷ Θεῷ καὶ τῷ ὁσίῳ πατρὶ ἡμῶν Πέτρῳ."

33 Τούτων οὕτως ἐχόντων, ἐν ἔτει ἑβδόμῳ τοῦ κατὰ τῶν εὐσεβῶν διωγμοῦ, ἑξκαιδεκάτῳ δὲ τῆς τοῦ πατρὸς ἡμῶν Πέτρου ποιμνιαρχίας, τεσσαρακοστῷ δὲ ἑβδόμῳ τῆς πάσης ζωῆς αὐτοῦ, ἐν αὐτῷ τῷ ὄρει καθεζομένῳ, Λέων ὁ τύραννος τῷ θανάτῳ ὑπάγεται καὶ Μιχαήλ τις Ἀμορραῖος τῷ γένει τὸ κράτος ἀντ᾽ αὐτοῦ διαδέχεται, τὴν αἱρετικὴν θραῦσιν εἰς γαλήνην μικρὰν μεταποιήσας, οὐ μὴν δὲ παντελῆ εἰρήνην τῇ ἐκκλησίᾳ τοῦ Χριστοῦ χαρισάμενος, ἔτι ἐκείνων τῶν διωκτῶν ἐπισκόπων τῶν ἐκκλησιαστικῶν θρόνων ἐπικρατούντων.

32 "A short time previously I was going to my bed in the evening to rest, and it was pitch dark. When I stretched out my hand to the mattress—there was no light at all, so I could not see anything—I touched a viper that had been chewed to pieces and thrown up by a kitten. When I unexpectedly took hold of this, both my hands smacked together because of the venom, and blood was running from them for many days, so that I was unable to eat with them, except with some device, and I could not perform any service at all. So, after the healing of the sister, I, the humble Matthias, immediately prostrated myself in front of the holy one, showed him the problem with my hands, and explained the cause to him. Our father, the imitator of Christ, breathed upon them and made the sign of the cross; at once, as though scales fell from my hands, I became well, and I thanked God and our holy father Peter."

33 And so it was that, in the seventh year of the persecution against piety, in the sixteenth year that our father Peter was the chief shepherd, and in the forty-seventh year of his whole life, while he was living on the same mountain, Leo the tyrant went to his death. The rulership passed from him to a certain Michael, whose family came from Amorion. He calmed down *the tempest* of the heresy a bit, but did not grant absolute peace to the church of Christ, since those bishops who had been persecutors retained their ecclesiastical thrones.

34 Ἐν τούτῳ τῷ καιρῷ συγκλητικός τις ὕπατος τῇ
τύχῃ, ἔχων γυναῖκα μαινομένην ἀγρίως ὑπὸ ἀκαθάρτου
δαίμονος, ἐπισκόπους τινὰς τῶν τῆς αἱρέσεως τότε κρα-
τούντων πρὸς τὴν ταύτης ἴασιν αἰτησάμενος καὶ μείνας
ἄπρακτος, ἔσχατον προσέρχεται καὶ αὐτὸς πρὸς τὸν θαυματουργὸν πατέρα Πέτρον σὺν τῇ συζύγῳ, παρά τινων
εὐεργετηθέντων παρ' αὐτοῦ ὁδηγηθείς. Ὅθεν καὶ ὑπὸ τῆς
ἐν τῷ ὁσίῳ θείας τοῦ Πνεύματος χάριτος ἐλεγχθεῖσα μηκόθεν ἡ γυνή, δεινῶς ἔπασχεν ὀνομαστῶς ἐκκαλουμένη
τὸν ὅσιον. Τοῦτο ἑωρακὼς ὁ ταύτης ἀνήρ, καταλαβὼν τὸν
ὅσιον ἡσυχάζοντα, ἤρξατο μεθ' ὅρκων ἐκδυσωπεῖν αὐτὸν
θεραπείας ἀξιῶσαι καὶ ἐλευθερίας τῆς ἐκ δαιμόνων τὴν
κατοφθαλμοὺς αὐτοῦ ἑστῶσαν καὶ βασανιζομένην πικρῶς
σύζυγον αὐτοῦ. Ὅθεν ἐπικαμφθεὶς ὁ ὅσιος ἐκείναις ταῖς
πολλαῖς παρακλήσεσιν, τῷ ζωοποιῷ αὐτὴν τύπῳ τοῦ σταυροῦ σφραγισάμενος, παρευθὺ τοῦ δαίμονος ἐλυτρώσατο.
Τοῦτο τὸ θαῦμα ἰδὼν ὁ ὕπατος, ἤρξατο αὐτοῦ προσπίπτειν
τοῖς ἴχνεσι καὶ τὴν χάριν ὁμολογεῖν τῆς ἰάσεως. Παρεκάλει δὲ αὐτὸν ἔρχεσθαι ἐν τῷ οἴκῳ αὐτοῦ κατὰ πάροδον
εὐλογίας χάριν. Ὅθεν συνθεμένῳ τῷ μακαρίῳ τοῦτο ποιεῖν, ὑποστρέψας ὁ ὕπατος μεταχαρᾶς εἰς τὰ ἴδια, ἡσυχαστικὸν κελλίον ὡς ἀπὸ σημείου ἑνὸς τοῦ οἴκου αὐτοῦ
κατασκευάζει, αὐτόθεν πολλάκις διερχόμενον τὸν ὅσιον
δεξιωσάμενος καὶ πολλὰ παρ' αὐτοῦ εὐεργετηθεὶς ὡς
αὐτὸς διηγήσατο.

35.1 "Ἐν μιᾷ γὰρ συνέβη," λέγων, "ὀλέθριον ἐπεισ-
ελθεῖν συμφορὰν τῇ οἰκίᾳ μου, ὥστε τῷ μηνὶ τῷ ἑνὶ
τριάκοντα πλεῖον ἢ ἔλαττον ψυχὰς ἀποθανεῖν. Κατὰ δὲ

34  At this time a senator, who held the rank of consul, had a wife who had been driven insane by an impure demon. This man had asked some prominent bishops, from among those who adhered to the heresy then, to cure her, but without success. At last he came to the wonder-working father Peter together with his wife, led by some people who had already benefited from him. When she was still a long way off, the woman suffered dreadfully and called upon the holy one by name, due to the divine power of the Spirit residing in the holy one. As soon as he saw this, the woman's husband approached the holy one in his place of tranquility, and started to implore him with oaths to agree to cure and free his wife, who was standing right in front of him and being so terribly tormented by demons. The holy one was moved by his many pleas. He made the sign of the cross over her and immediately released her from the demon. When the consul saw this miracle, he started prostrating himself at the saint's feet, acknowledging the grace of her cure. He asked Peter to visit his house, when he was on his way, in order to bless it. The blessed man agreed to do so and the consul happily returned to his home. He built a small cell suitable for the practice of tranquility about a mile away from his house, in which he welcomed the holy one, who frequently traveled there. And, as he himself related, he received much help from him.

35.1  "Once," he said, "a terrible disaster struck my household since, in just one month, about thirty people died. By

συγκυρίαν ἐκεῖθεν τῷ πατρὶ παροδεύοντι καὶ πρὸς ἡμᾶς
ὡς πολλάκις καταλύσαντι, ἀναγγείλας τὴν συμφορὰν τοῦ
θανατικοῦ τὴν ἐν τῷ οἴκῳ μου, ἐδυσώπουν ἀπελαθῆναι
ταύτην. Ὁ δὲ ὅσιος ἐλθὼν καὶ σταθεὶς μέσον τοῦ οἴκου
μου καὶ πρὸς ἀνατολὴν καὶ δύσιν καὶ ἄρκτον καὶ μεσημ-
βρίαν τὸν ζωοποιὸν τοῦ σταυροῦ τύπον ποιήσας, ἐκείνην
εὐθὺς τὴν συμφορὰν ἀπεσόβησεν.

35.2 "Ἔχοντι δέ μοι κατὰ ταὐτὸ ἐν τῷ οἴκῳ μου τινὰ
νοσοῦντα καὶ κατακείμενον, τὰ κατ' αὐτὸν διαθέμενος ὡς
τὰ ἔσχατα πνέοντι, παραγενέσθαι πρὸς τοῦτον ἐπισκέψεως χάριν τὸν ὅσιον ἐδυσώπησα. Ἐλθὼν δὲ καὶ τῷ νο-
σοῦντι συναλγήσας ὁ συμπαθέστατος, ἐπιτίθησιν αὐτῷ
τὴν χεῖρα καὶ λέγει· Ἀδελφέ, ἰάσεταί σε ὁ Κύριος· ἔγειρε.'
Καὶ ἐνώπιον ἡμῶν πάντων ἀνέστη. Καὶ ἐπέπεσεν φόβος
καὶ ἔκστασις ἐπὶ τοὺς ἐκεῖσε παρόντας καὶ θεωμένους
αὐτόν. Οὐ μόνον δὲ τοῦτο, ἀλλὰ καὶ ἐπὶ ἓν τῶν τέκνων
μου ἐνσκήψασα λέπρα, καθ' ὅλου αὐτοῦ τοῦ σώματος
περιήρχετο. Ὁ δὲ ὅσιος τῆς χειρὸς τοῦ παιδὸς δραξάμενος
καὶ τρίτον αὐτὴν ἐμφυσήσας καὶ σφραγίσας, ἀπέξεσεν
ὅλον τὸ σῶμα σὺν αὐτῇ τῆς λέπρας καὶ ἀπεκατέστησεν
ὑγιῆ ὡς τὸ πρότερον.

36 Εἶχον δὲ καί τινα ἀδελφιδοῦν σώματι δυνατὸν καὶ
ἡλικίᾳ εὐμεγεθέστατον, ὃς πονηρᾷ πληγεὶς ἐνεργείᾳ, λεγεῶνα πνευμάτων ἀκαθάρτων ἔσχεν ἐμφωλευσάντων ἐν
αὐτῷ. Τοῦ δὲ ὁσίου πατρὸς ἡμῶν κατὰ συνήθειαν πρὸς
ἡμᾶς ἐλθόντος καὶ χεῖρα αὐτῷ ἐπιθέντος ὡς ἀσθενοῦντι,
τὴν νόσον εἰς μανίαν ὁ μιαρώτατος τρέψας, τοιαῦτα τῷ
ὁσίῳ ἐπεβόα· Ἔα· τί ἡμῖν καὶ σοί, Πέτρε; Οὐκ ἰσχύεις

chance, the father was passing by and stopped with us as he often did. I told him about the deadly misfortune which had befallen my house and begged him to chase it away. The holy one came and stood in the middle of my house, made the life-giving sign of the cross toward the east, the west, the north, and the south, and immediately drove off that affliction.

35.2 "At that time, I also had in my house a man who was ill and bedridden. I had made the final arrangements for him, as he was breathing his last, so I begged the holy one to go and see him. The most merciful father came and, sympathizing with the sick man's suffering, laid his hand upon him and said, 'Brother, the Lord will cure you. *Stand up!*' And he *stood up* in front of us all. And terror and amazement fell on all those present when they saw him. Not only that, but leprosy had afflicted one of my children, spreading over his whole body. The holy one took the child's hand; three times he breathed upon it and made the sign of the cross, and in this way he cleansed his whole body from the leprosy, restoring the boy to his previous health.

36 "I also had a nephew who was physically strong and in the prime of life, but who was struck by some wicked activity and had *a legion of impure spirits* which had made their lair inside him. When the holy father came to us as usual and put his hand on him, believing that he was ill, that most foul demon transformed the man's illness into a fit of rage and shouted this at the holy one: 'Leave us alone! *What have you*

ἀληθῶς τοῦ πλήθους μου περιγενέσθαι· εἷς γὰρ ἀσθενεῖ
πρὸς λεγεῶνα ἀντιμαχήσασθαι.' Ὅθεν διὰ τῆς τοῦ ὁσίου
προσευχῆς, κατὰ μικρὸν οἱ δαίμονες θρηνοῦντες ὑπεχώ-
ρουν τοῦ μαινομένου. Μήπω δὲ τῶν πολλῶν ἐκείνων ἀπο-
λυτρωθέντος πνευμάτων, ἐμφυλίου πολέμου ὄντος κατ'
ἐκεῖνο καιροῦ, ἁρπάσαντες αὐτὸν οἱ ἐναπομείναντες δαίμονες πλανᾶσθαι ἐποίουν καὶ μαίνεσθαι, καὶ πρὸς τὸν
στρατὸν τοῦ τυράννου Θωμᾶ ἑαυτὸν προσμίξας ὁ νεώτερος, τὴν Πόλιν περιεκαθέζετο. Τοῦ δὲ ὁσίου Πέτρου μὴ
γινώσκοντος τὸν νεώτερον τὸ τί γέγονεν, ἀλλ' ἐν τῇ μονῇ
αὐτοῦ ὑπὲρ τούτου προσευχομένου καὶ τοὺς ἁγίους τοῦ
Χριστοῦ ἰατροὺς καὶ Ἀναργύρους Κοσμᾶν καὶ Δαμιανὸν
προσδεόμενος, διὰ τό, ὡς προλέλεκται, τοῦ θεοστυγοῦς
Θωμᾶ τὸ Βυζάντιον περιστοιχίσαντος, αὐτοῦ τε τοῦ νεω-
τέρου σὺν αὐτοῦ ὄντος καὶ καθεύδοντος, ὁρᾷ τινα ἐκεῖσε
ἐν μιᾷ νυκτὶ φοβερὰν θεωρίαν, ὡς δύο τινὲς ἰατρικὴν
κεκοσμημένοι στολὴν τούτῳ παραστάντες, εἰς τὸν ἕνα
προστὴν αὐτοῦ προσεκαλοῦντο θεραπείαν, δι' ὃ καὶ ὁ εἷς
πρὸς τὸν ἕτερον· 'Γινώσκεις, ἀδελφέ, τίς οὗτός ἐστιν ὁ
νοσῶν;' Ὁ δὲ ἕτερός φησιν· 'Οὐχί.' Εἶτα λέγει πάλιν ὁ
ἄλλος· 'Οὗτός ἐστιν περὶ οὗ ἡμᾶς ἐκδυσωπεῖ καθεκάστην
ὁ θεράπων τοῦ Χριστοῦ Πέτρος.' Ἐκεῖνος δὲ τούτῳ προσ-
βλέψας ἀκριβέστερον, ἔφησεν· 'Οὕτως ἔχει, ἀδελφέ, ἀληθῶς.' Καὶ λέγουσι πρὸς τὸν νεανίαν οἱ ἀμφότεροι· 'Ἄπελθε
πρὸς τὸν θεράποντα τοῦ Χριστοῦ Πέτρον, ὦ τέκνον, καὶ
ἰαθήσῃ· τούτῳ γὰρ ἐδόθη ἐκ τοῦ Πνεύματος ἡ χάρις τοῦ
ἰάσασθαί σε εἰς τέλος.' Ὁ δὲ νεώτερος πρὸς αὐτούς, ὡς
ὅρκοις ἡμᾶς ἐβεβαιοῦτο ὕστερον, ἀντέφησεν· 'Καὶ πῶς

*to do with* us, Peter? You really aren't strong enough to overcome my great numbers, for one person is too weak to fight
against a legion.' Then, through the prayer of the holy one,
the demons gradually started to depart from the insane
man, lamenting as they did so. But he had not yet been relieved from many of those spirits and, during the civil war
which happened at that time, the demons who had remained inside him took hold of him and made him crazy
and wander around. The young man joined the army of the
tyrant Thomas and participated in the siege of the City. The
holy Peter did not know the youngster's whereabouts, but
kept praying for him in his monastery and asked Christ's
holy physicians, the Anargyroi, Kosmas and Damianos, on
his behalf. As previously mentioned, while the God hater
Thomas was besieging Byzantion, the young man, who was
with him, saw a frightful vision one night while he was sleeping. Two men dressed like physicians came to him, urging
each other to cure him. The first one asked the other:
'Brother, do you know who the sick man is?' The other one
answered: 'No, I don't.' Then the first one said again, 'This is
the one about whom Christ's servant Peter is asking us every day.' The other one looked at him more carefully and
said, 'It's true, brother.' Both of them together said to the
young man, 'Go to Peter, the servant of Christ, child, and
you will be cured. For the grace to completely cure you
has been given to him by the Spirit.' The young man, as
he later assured us with oaths, replied, 'But how shall I

ἐγώ, κύριοι, πρὸς ἐκεῖνον παραγένωμαι, τὴν ὁδοιπορίαν
ποιεῖσθαι ὑπὸ τῶν ἐναντίων κωλυόμενος; Εἰ μὴ γὰρ πρὸς
τὴν Πόλιν εἰσέλθω καὶ τὴν κατὰ ἀνατολὰς πόρταν ἐξέλθω,
πρὸς ἐκεῖνον οὐκ ἀπελεύσομαι.᾽ Οἱ δὲ πρὸς τοῦτον εἰρή-
κασιν· Ἀναστὰς τὸ πρωΐ, τῷ προσόντι σοι ἵππῳ ἐπίβηθι,
καὶ πάντα τὰ κατὰ σὲ ἄρας, πρὸς τὸ Βυζάντιον εἴσελθε,
μηδὲν κακὸν τοσύνολον ὑφορώμενος· αὐτὸς γὰρ παρεκε-
λεύσατο ἅπασιν τὴν εἴσοδον καὶ ἔξοδον ἀνενόχλητον
παρασχεῖν σοι.᾽ Διαναστὰς δὲ ἀπὸ τοῦ ὕπνου ὁ νεώτερος
καὶ ἀποπληρώσας τὰ τοῦ χρησμοῦ, ἐπὶ τὴν Πόλιν εἰσῆλθεν,
καὶ ταύτης ἀσκανδαλίστως ἐξῆλθεν. Καὶ καταλαβὼν τὸν
θεράποντα τοῦ Χριστοῦ Πέτρον καὶ τοῖς ποσὶν αὐτοῦ
προσπεσὼν καὶ πάντα διηγησάμενος αὐτῷ τὰ συμβάντα,
ἰάθη ὑπ᾽ αὐτοῦ *ἀπὸ τῆς ὥρας ἐκείνης, καὶ ἐγένετο ὑγιὴς*
δοξάζων τὸν Θεὸν ἐπὶ πάντων τῶν συμπαρόντων."

37  Τοιούτοις καὶ τηλικούτοις χαρίσμασιν ὑπὸ τῆς θείας
χάριτος κατεστεμμένος ὁ ὅσιος καὶ πολλοὺς τῶν παθῶν
λυτρωσάμενος καὶ πνευμάτων ἀκαθάρτων, τοὺς φθονε-
ροὺς ἀνθρώπους οὐ διέδρασεν· τινὲς γὰρ τῶν προγεγραμ-
μένων ἐπισκόπων καὶ ἡγουμένων, τῶν προσθεραπείαν τῆς
τοῦ ὑπατικοῦ συμβίου προσκεκλημένων καὶ τοῦτο τελέσαι
μὴ ἰσχυσάντων, εἰς πονηρὸν ζῆλον τραπέντες, οὐκ ἐν θείᾳ
δυνάμει ταῦτα ποιεῖν τὸν ὅσιον ἐδογμάτιζον, ἀλλ᾽ ἐν τῷ
*Βεελζεβοὺλ ἄρχοντι τῶν δαιμονίων* ἀποτελεῖν ταῦτα. Τοῦτο
ἀκούσας ὁ ὅσιος, τὴν ψυχὴν ταραχθεὶς ὅτι ὅλως δι᾽ αὐτὸν
βλασφημεῖται τὸ θεῖον, ἐδυσώπει τὸν Κύριον οὕτως λέ-
γων· "Ὦ Κύριέ μου Ἰησοῦ Χριστέ, τίς εἰμι ἐγὼ ὁ εὐτελὴς
καὶ ἁμαρτωλὸς καὶ ἀγνωμονέστατος δοῦλός σου, ἵνα δι᾽

reach him, my lords? The enemy will stop me making the journey. Unless I enter the City and exit it through the eastern gate I will not be able to go to him.' They answered him, 'Get up early in the morning, mount the horse you have with you and, taking all your possessions, enter Byzantion, without worrying about anything bad at all, since the holy father himself has already ordered them to allow you to pass into and out of the city without any problem.' The young man woke up and, following the instructions of the vision, entered the City and left it again without encountering any obstacles. He went to Peter, the servant of Christ, fell at his feet, and told him everything that had happened to him. He was cured by him *that very hour* and became healthy, giving glory to God in front of all those who were present."

37 The holy one was adorned with these and similar gifts by the divine grace, but, because he relieved many people of their illnesses and impure spirits, he did not escape the attention of envious people. Some of the previously mentioned bishops and abbots, who had earlier been invited to cure the wife of the consul and had failed to do so, turned to evil envy, and alleged that the holy one did not do these things by divine power but accomplished them in *Beelzebul, the leader of the demons*. When Peter heard this, his soul was disturbed, because the divinity had been slandered entirely because of him, and he implored the Lord, saying, "My Lord Jesus Christ, who am I, your most humble, sinful, and

ἐμὲ βλασφημῆται τὸ ὄνομά σου τὸ ἅγιον; Ἄνες, Δέσποτα, τὰ
κύματά σου καὶ τὴν χάριν ἀνάστειλον, ὁ ἐκ κοιλίας μητρός
μου μὴ παρακούσας μου δεηθέντος σου." Ταῦτα καὶ πλείονα εὐξαμένου τοῦ ἁγίου καὶ πρὸς τοὺς φιλοσκώπτας
ἡγουμένους καὶ ἐπισκόπους ἀπεληλυθότος πρὸς ἀσπασμὸν
καὶ ὑπ' αὐτῶν μὴ προσδεχθέντος τὸ σύνολον, ἀλλ' ὡς
γόητος ὑποπάντων ἀπελασθέντος, ἀναστὰς μετὰ λύπης
πολλῆς, ἀπέρχεται πρὸς τὸν ἐν ἁγίοις ὁμολογητὴν Θεόδωρον ἡγούμενον τῶν Στουδίου, εἰς ἐξορίαν ὄντα σὺν
λοιποῖς πατράσι πρὸς τὰ Κρησκεντίου καθήμενον, καὶ
δῆλα ποιεῖ αὐτῷ μετὰ δακρύων τὰ κατ' αὐτοῦ ὑπὸ τῶν κα-
κοζήλων καὶ φθονερῶν ἀνθρώπων θρυλλούμενα. Ὁ δὲ
ὁμολογητὴς τοῦ Χριστοῦ Θεόδωρος ταῦτα ἀκούσας παρὰ
τοῦ μακαρίου Πέτρου, λέγει αὐτῷ· "Βούλομαί σε, ἀδελφέ,
τῇ φύσει ὡς ἐπὶ Κυρίου ἀνυποστόλως ἐξειπεῖν μοι τὰ κατὰ
σέ, ὅπως γνοὺς διακρινῶ τί σου ὑπάρχει τὸ κάθισμα." Ὁ
δὲ ὅσιος πατὴρ ἡμῶν Πέτρος ἀφιλενδείκτως τὰ ἐκ παιδὸς
αὐτοῦ καὶ μέχρι τοῦ νῦν ἐξεῖπεν καὶ μὴ βουλόμενος, ὅτι
"ἔστιν μοι πάτερ ἤδη πρὸς τοῖς λοιποῖς, ἔτος ὀκτωκαι-
δέκατον ἀφοῦ ἄρτου καὶ οἴνου καὶ τυροῦ καὶ ἐλαίου ἐνε-
κρατευσάμην, μόνοις λαχάνοις καὶ ὀσπρίοις ἀρκούμενος,
τεσσαρακονθήμερον ἐκτελῶν τὴν νηστείαν, ἔσθ' ὅτε καὶ
αὐτοῦ τοῦ ὕδατος πολλάκις ἀποτῶν Θεοφανείων μέχρι
τοῦ Πάσχα ἀσκητικῶς ἀπεχόμενος, μονοχίτων ὤν, σιδη-
ροφόρος τε καὶ ἀπέδιλος, τῆς τριαδικῆς θεότητος λάτρης,
καὶ τοῦ ἑνὸς αὐτῆς ἐξ ἁγίας Παρθένου Μαρίας ἀσυγχύτως, ἀτρέπτως σεσαρκωμένου ἱεροθύτης πιστότατος, καὶ
τῆς αὐτοῦ εἰκόνος σεβαστῆς ποθεινότατος." Ἀκούσας οὖν

ungrateful servant, that your *holy name should be slandered because of* me? *Let loose* your waves, Master, and hold back your grace, you who have not disregarded my supplications to you from the time I was in my mother's womb." The saint said these and many more prayers, and then went to those mocking abbots and bishops in order to greet them. But when he was not received at all by them and instead was driven away by all of them as a sorcerer, he got up in great distress, and went to Theodore, the confessor among the saints, the abbot of Stoudios, who was in exile with some other fathers and living in the area of Kreskentios. In tears, Peter made known to him what those jealous and envious men were saying about him. The confessor of Christ, Theodore, heard these things from the blessed Peter, then said to him, "My brother, I want you to tell me all about yourself in detail, frankly, as you would to the Lord, so that, knowing this, I may determine your situation." Our holy father Peter, modestly recounted to him everything, from the time of his childhood until the present, and reluctantly added, "My father, in addition to everything else, this is the eighteenth year that I have refrained from bread, wine, cheese, and oil. I am satisfied only with vegetables and pulses. I observe the forty-day fasts, and there are times when I abstain ascetically even from water itself on many occasions in the period from Epiphany until Easter. I have only one tunic, I wear irons, and I have no shoes. I am a worshipper of the triune divinity, and I am a most faithful priest of that one person of the Trinity, who took flesh from the holy Virgin Mary without suffering any confusion or change. And I am a most ardent venerator of his image." When he had heard these and

ταῦτα καὶ τὰ τούτων πλείονα καὶ μειζότερα ὁ διακριτικώτατος ἐκεῖνος καὶ μέγας ὁμολογητὴς Θεόδωρος, τοῖς
αὐτοῦ ὑπηρέταις κελεύει τράπεζαν αὐτῷ παραθεῖναι πλου-
σίαν καὶ πάντων αὐτῶν μεταλαβεῖν τὸν ὅσιον κατηνάγκα-
σεν, πέδιλά τε περιβαλὼν τοῖς ποσὶν αὐτοῦ, ἐπενδύτῃ τινὶ
τὸ ἐκ τριχῶν αὐτοῦ περικαλύπτει στιχάριον, οὑτωσὶ γράψας κοινῇ πρὸς τοὺς καταυτοῦ γλωσσαλγήσαντας.

38 "Ἔδει μὲν ὑμᾶς εἰδότας ὦ φίλοι τὰ τῶν θείων
γραφῶν πνευματόφθεγκτα λόγια, μὴ ἀκονᾶν τὴν γλῶσσαν
κατὰ τοῦ πλάσαντος· ὁ ἁγιάζων γὰρ καὶ οἱ ἁγιαζόμενοι
ἐξενὸς πάντες. Ἐπεὶ δὲ ἢ ἀγνοίᾳ περικρατούμενοι, ἢ φθόνῳ
περινυττόμενοι, τὸν τοῦ Χριστοῦ ἄξιον θεράποντα οὐ
προσδέχεσθε Πέτρον, τὴν θείαν χεῖρα ὡσπάλαι αὐτοῦ διὰ
τῶν ἀποστόλων καὶ διὰ τούτου ἐκτείνοντος ἐν σημείοις καὶ
τέρασι καὶ ποικίλαις δυνάμεσιν, γόην αὐτὸν καὶ δυσσεβῆ
ὑποπτεύετε, τὸ τῆς ζωῆς αὐτοῦ ἀνεπίληπτον μὴ γινώσκον-
τες—ἡμεῖς γὰρ πάντα αὐτοῦ τὰ κατὰ πίστιν καὶ τὸν βίον
διερευνήσαντες, οὐδαμοῦ αὐτὸν σφαλλόμενον εὕραμεν,
μᾶλλον μὲν οὖν καὶ πολλοὺς τοὺς ἐν τοῖς καθημᾶς χρόνοις ἀσκητὰς ὑπερβαίνοντα· ὅνπερ οἱ πιστῶς ἀδελφοὶ
προσδεχόμενοι τῶν ἁγίων λειτουργοὶ καὶ τῶν εὐαγγε-
λικῶν λογίων ἐρευνηταὶ ἀκριβέστατοι καὶ τῆς ἐκκλησίας
Χριστοῦ κανονικοὶ πέλουσιν ἱερώτατοι, οἱ δὲ τὰ ἐγκελευ-
όμενα παρ' ἡμῶν τῶν εὐτελῶν μὴ δεχόμενοι τὴν θεόφθεγ-
κτον εὐαγγελικὴν ῥῆσιν τὴν λέγουσαν φανερώτατα, 'ὁ
πιστεύων εἰς ἐμὲ τὰ σημεῖα ἃ ἐγὼ ποιῶ κἀκεῖνος ποιήσει καὶ
μείζονα τούτων ποιήσει,' μὴ προσδεχόμενοι, ὡς ἀπαιδευ-
σίας ζήλῳ καὶ ἀσεβείας λόγῳ κρατούμενοι, ἀποστολικῇ

even greater and more important things, that most perceptive and great confessor, Theodore, ordered his servants to
serve him a sumptuous meal, and he forced the holy one to
eat some of everything. He put shoes on his feet, covered
his hair shirt with a coat, and then wrote as follows to all
those who had slandered Peter:

38 "My friends, you should be aware of the words of the
holy scriptures that were inspired by the Spirit, not to
sharpen your tongue against your creator, *for the one who
sanctifies and those who are sanctified all have one origin.*
Whether you are in the grip of ignorance or incited by envy,
you do not receive Peter, the worthy servant of Christ, who
extends his hand through him as he did in the past through
the apostles *with signs and wonders and* various *mighty works,*
and you suspect that he is a sorcerer and an impious man.
This is because you do not know the irreproachable quality
of his life. I have, however, examined everything concerning
his faith and his life, and have found no fault in him, rather,
indeed, that he even surpasses many ascetics of our times.
Those brethren, therefore, who receive him with confidence are servants of the saints, most diligent inquirers of
the words of the gospel, and legitimate priests of the church
of Christ; but those who do not accept the orders of my
humble self, since they do not accept the word of the gospel
uttered by God that most clearly states, '*He who believes
in me will also do the* signs *that I do, and will do greater ones
than these,*' and as they are in the grip of ignorance in their
jealously and impiety in their speech, are placed under

ψήφῳ, καὶ πατρικῷ κανόνι τῷ ἀναθέματι ὑποβάλλονται."
Τοῦτο τὸ γράμμα δεξάμενοι οἱ συνειδήσει πονηρᾷ κατὰ
τοῦ ὁσίου ὑπερεχόμενοι, διηλλάγησαν τούτῳ καὶ μὴ βου-
λόμενοι.

39.1 Περὶ τῆς τοῦ κατακλείστου Ζαχαρίου ἀπολυτρώσεως

Ὑποστρέψαντι δὲ ἐκεῖθεν τῷ μακαρίῳ πρὸς τῷ ἐν τῷ
Καλῷ Ὄρει ἡσυχαστικῷ αὐτοῦ κελλίῳ, ὅθεν ἐξώρμητο,
ἄνθρωπός τις νοτάριος ἐν τοῖς καταλυδίαν μέρεσιν ἔχων
τὴν κατοικίαν Ζαχαρίας καλούμενος πρὸς τὸν τοῦ ἐμφυλίου ἐκείνου πολέμου τύραννον Θωμᾶν ἀπελθών, τούτῳ
προσοικειώθη τὰ μέγιστα. Ὃν καί τις τῶν τοῦ Βυζαντίου
στρατηγέτης καὶ ἀνταγωνιστὴς κατασχών, ἐν μιᾷ τῶν
περιτετειχισμένων τῆς θαλάσσης νήσων, Φύγελα καλουμένην φρούριον, σιδηροδέσμιον θέμενος, στρατιώτας ἐν-
όπλους χιλίους τὸν ἀριθμὸν εἰς τήρησιν αὐτοῦ ἀσφαλῆ
ἐγκατέταξεν. Τοῦτο ἡ αὐτοῦ μεμαθηκυῖα ὁμόζυγος, τὸν
χιτῶνα ἑαυτῆς περιρρήξασα, ἔρχεται ἐν τῷ Καλῷ Ὄρει
πρὸς τοῦτον τὸν μέγα μετὰ Θεὸν ἀντιλήπτορα ὅσιον Πέτρον πικρῶς θρηνοῦσα καὶ μακρόθεν βοῶσα· 'Ἐλέησον,
ἅγιε τοῦ Θεοῦ, τὸν κατάκλειστον σύζυγόν μου καὶ τοῦ
θανάτου ἐξάρπασον. Χάρισαι αὐτῷ τὴν ζωὴν παρελπίδας
διὰ τῆς σῆς πρὸς Θεὸν πεπαρρησιασμένης προσευχῆς καὶ
δεήσεως, ὅτι οὐ χρείαν ἔχουσιν οἱ ἰσχύοντες ἰατροῦ, ἀλλ' οἱ
κακῶς ἔχοντες. Μὴ ἀποστραφῇς, πάτερ, τοῖς θέλουσιν ἡμῖν
δανείσασθαι παρασοῦ τῶν πρεσβειῶν σου τὸ τάλαντον, μὴ
κενὴν τῆς αἰτήσεως ἀπολύσῃς με δέομαι τὴν χάριν παρὰ

anathema according to the apostolic decision and the canon of the fathers." When they received this letter, those who had a bad opinion of the holy one were reconciled with him, albeit unwillingly.

### 39.1 On the liberation of the prisoner Zechariah

The blessed one returned from there to his hesychastic cell on the Good Mountain, from where he had set out. Now there was a man, a notary called Zechariah who lived in the region of Lydia, who went off with the tyrant Thomas to that civil war, and became very close to him. But one of the generals and opponents from Byzantion arrested this Zechariah and ordered one thousand armed soldiers to keep him securely, bound in iron chains, on one of the islands surrounded by the sea, in a prison called Phygela. When his wife learned this, she tore her tunic, and came to the Good Mountain to holy Peter, that great helper with God. Crying bitterly, she called out from a distance, "Saint of God, have mercy on my husband who is imprisoned and save him from death. Grant him his life, against all hope, through the prayer and supplication which you are able to offer with freedom to God; *for the healthy do not need a physician, only those who are ill.* Do not turn away from those of us who wish to borrow from you the gift of your intercessions. Please do not let me leave empty-handed, you who have received the

Χριστοῦ εἰληφὼς τῶν θαυμάτων." Ὁ δὲ ὅσιος δηλοῖ αὐτῇ, "ἄπελθε" λέγων "ὦ γύναι εἰς τὴν οἰκίαν σου τὰ κατὰ σὲ φροντίζουσα καὶ μηδεμίαν μέριμναν ἔχουσα περὶ τούτου." Ἡ δὲ τῇ κελεύσει πιστωθεῖσα τοῦ μακαρίου, χαίρουσα ἅμα τε καὶ ἐλπίζουσα ἀπεχώρει ἐκεῖθεν. Ὡς δὲ εἰώθει ὁ ὅσιος διὰ πάσης νυκτὸς ἀγρυπνεῖν καὶ προσεύχεσθαι (οὕτω γὰρ ἦν αὐτῷ σύνηθες ἐν πάσῃ αὐτοῦ τῇ ἐν ἀσκήσει ζωῇ, ἀπὸ ἑσπέρας εὐθὺς τὸ δαυϊτικὸν ἀποστηθίζειν ψαλτήριον, τὸν μεσονύκτιον εἶτα ἐπιτελεῖν κανόνα, εἶθ' οὕτως ἀποπληροῦν τὸν ἑωθινὸν καὶ τότε μικρὸν ἀναπαύλης μεταλαγχάνειν), οὕτως ποιοῦντος καὶ κατ' αὐτὴν τὴν νύκτα καὶ ὑπὲρ τοῦ κατακλείστου ἐκδυσωποῦντος τὸν Κύριον, ἀποστέλλεται ἄγγελος οὐρανόθεν, τὰς μὲν θύρας τῆς φυλακῆς αὐτομάτως ἀνοίγων, τὰ δὲ τοῦ κατακλείστου σιδηρᾶ δεσμὰ ἀλύτως λύων καὶ ὁδηγῶν πρὸς σωτηρίαν αὐτὸν καὶ ζωήν. Ὅθεν καὶ ἀνθρωποειδῶς ὁραθεὶς αὐτῷ, μέσῳ τῶν ἐκεῖσε ὄντων φυλάκων ἐχειραγώγει, καὶ πρός τι μικρὸν ἀναβιβάσας πλοιάριον, ἐπὶ τὴν χέρσον ἐξήγαγεν, ἔνθα οἱ δεύτεροι διενυκτέρευον φύλακες, προσειπὼν αὐτῷ· "Πορεύου ἐν εἰρήνῃ πρὸς τὰ οἰκεῖά σου, χάριν ὁμολογῶν τῷ τοῦ Χριστοῦ θεράποντι Πέτρῳ δι' ὃν καὶ τῶν δεινῶν ἀπολύεσαι." Ὁ δὲ πρὸς ἐκεῖνον τὸν ξένον ὁδηγὸν ἀγαλλιώμενος ἔφησεν· "Τίς εἶ κύριε ἀνάγγειλόν μοι." Ὁ δέ, "ἄπιθι τὸ τάχος" φησίν "τὰ κατ' ἐμὲ μὴ ἐρευνώμενος ἄνθρωπε." Καὶ ταῦτα εἰπών, ἀφανὴς γέγονεν ἀπαυτοῦ. Τούτου δὲ ἀπὸ τῆς παραλίου ἀνύοντος τὴν πρὸς τὰ οἰκεῖα ὁδὸν αὐτοῦ, οἱ ἐπὶ τῆς ξηρᾶς δευτερεύοντες φύλακες, γνόντες

grace of miracles from Christ." The holy one answered her, "Go home, woman," he said, "and take care of your affairs, and don't worry about this." As she trusted the blessed one's order, she left there, elated and full of hope. It was the holy one's custom to be vigilant and pray all night (for it was his habit during his whole ascetic life to recite by heart the Psalter of David as soon as it was evening, then to perform the midnight service, then to complete the office of vespers, and then take a little rest). While he was doing this that night, and begging the Lord on behalf of the prisoner, an angel was sent from heaven, who opened the doors of the prison of their own accord, loosed the prisoner's iron fetters, and led him to safety and life. The angel, who looked like a man to Zechariah, led him by the hand between the guards who were there, put him aboard a small boat, and took him to the mainland, where the second set of guards were passing the night. He said to him, "Go home in peace, and be grateful to the servant of Christ, Peter, by whom you have been released from these terrible things." Zechariah, who was full of joy, said to his strange guide, "Tell me who you are, sir." But the angel said, "Go away quickly, and don't ask about me." After he had said this, the angel disappeared. While Zechariah was making his way from the beach to the road to his home, the second set of guards on dry land,

ἐκπεφευγέναι τὸν δέσμιον, οὐ μικρῷ συσχεθέντες θορύβῳ, διεταράττοντο, ἄλλος ἄλλοθεν ξιφήρεις περιερχόμενοι. Αὐτὸς δὲ διὰ μέσου αὐτῶν διελθὼν καὶ αὐτὰς διαδράσας αὐτῶν τὰς χεῖρας, πρὸς τὰ ἴδια ἦλθεν, καὶ πρὸς τὸν αὐτὸν θεράποντα τοῦ Χριστοῦ Πέτρον, δοξάζων καὶ αἰνῶν τὸν Θεὸν τὸν ῥυσάμενον αὐτὸν δι᾽ εὐχῶν αὐτοῦ τῆς δεινῆς καταδίκης.

39.2 Περὶ τῆς ἀναρρύσεως ἐξ αἰχμαλωσίας τοῦ δομεστίκου Βενιαμὶν

Ἄλλος δέ τις Βενιαμὶν τῇ κλήσει, γνώριμος τούτῳ τῷ πατρὶ ὑπάρχων, στρατιωτικὴν ἐμπεπιστευμένος ἀρχήν, ἐν μιᾷ πολέμου παρεμβολῇ μετὰ καὶ ἄλλων τινῶν ὑπὸ τῶν Ἀγαρινῶν συλληφθεὶς ἐπὶ ἓν τῶν κάστρων εἰρχθῆναι ὑπ᾽ αὐτῶν κατεπείγετο. Εἰς νοῦν δὲ λαβὼν τὸν ὅσιον πατέρα καὶ τοῦτον προσκαλεσάμενος, ἐδεήθη μετὰ δακρύων. Ὅθεν τῶν συστρατιωτῶν, καὶ συναιχμαλώτων αὐτοῦ πάντων ἐκ τῶν ἵππων κατενεχθέντων, καὶ δεσμίων ἐλαυνομένων, αὐτὸς μόνος κατελείφθη ἐπιβαίνων καὶ ἄδετος. Καταμικρὸν δὲ τὴν πρὸς τὸ κάστρον πορείαν ποιούντων τῶν τε κρατηθέντων καὶ τῶν κρατησάντων, ὁ Βενιαμὶν λιποθυμήσας ὄπισθεν ἠκολούθει, καὶ ἦλθεν αὐτῷ φωνὴ λέγουσα· "Βενιαμὶν ἐπίστρεφε εἰς τὰ ὀπίσω καὶ διασώζου." Ὁ δὲ ταύτης τῆς φωνῆς ἐπακούσας ὧδε κἀκεῖσε περιεβλέπετο, καὶ μηδένα ὁρῶν, πλάνον ἐκείνην τὴν φωνὴν ὑπενόει. Καὶ ἦλθεν αὐτῷ πάλιν ἡ αὐτὴ φωνή, "ὑπόστρεφε, ὑπόστρεφε" λέγουσα "Βενιαμὶν μὴ πτοούμενος." Ὁ δὲ πά-

realized that the prisoner had escaped, fell into a great commotion, and were confused. They went around the area, one here, another there, with their swords drawn, but that man passed right between them and escaped their clutches. He went to his home and to Peter the servant of Christ, glorifying and praising God, who had saved him from this terrible sentence through Peter's prayers.

39.2 On the liberation from captivity of the *domestikos,* Benjamin

Another man, called Benjamin, who was acquainted with the father, had been entrusted with a military command. During a skirmish in the war, he was captured, together with some others, by the Hagarenes and was being taken quickly by them to one of their castles to be held captive. But he brought the holy father to mind and, calling on him, tearfully asked for his help. Then, while all his fellow soldiers and fellow captives had been taken from their horses and were being driven off as prisoners, he alone was left on his horse and free. While both captors and captives were slowly making their way toward the castle, Benjamin, who was feeling faint, was following them, when a voice came to him saying, "Benjamin, turn back and save yourself!" As soon as he heard this voice, he looked around here and there, but did not see anything and thought that the voice was a delusion. But the same voice came to him again, "Go back," it said, "go back, Benjamin, don't be scared." When he heard the

λιν ἀκροασάμενος τῆς φωνῆς, καὶ γνοὺς θείαν ἐκείνην
τὴν πρόσκλησιν ὑπάρχειν, καὶ τῆς τοῦ ἐπικληθέντος παρ'
αὐτοῦ ὁσίου Πέτρου πρεσβείας καὶ χάριτος εἰς τὴν ἐκείνου
ἐπιφανείσης βοήθειαν, θαρρήσας εὐθὺς τῇ ψυχῇ ὁ Βενιαμὶν ἀπεχώρει τῶν ἐναντίων καὶ εἰς τὰ οἰκεῖα ἑαυτοῦ
ἐπανῆλθε σῳζόμενος, Κυρίῳ εὐχαριστηρίους ἀναπέμπων
φωνὰς καὶ τῷ πανοσίῳ αὐτοῦ θεράποντι Πέτρῳ.

39.3 Περὶ τῆς τοῦ σπαθαρίου ἀνασώσεως ἐξ ἐχθρῶν πολεμίων

Ἕτερος συγκλητικὸς ὡς αὐτὸς ἡμῖν ἐκεῖνος προσδιηγή-
σατο, γνώριμος καὶ αὐτὸς πέλων τῷ τρισοσίῳ, ἐν παρεμβολῇ πολέμου ἡττημένος καὶ φεύγων ὑπὸ τῶν διωκτῶν
συνείχετο κατὰ μικρὸν ἐλαυνόμενος, ὡς δὲ αὐτοῦ ἤδη
πλησίον γεγόνασιν οἱ πολέμιοι, ὥσπερ ἐξαπορούμενος μὴ
ἁλοὺς τῶν ἐχθρῶν ὑποχείριος γένηται, τοῦ ἵππου αὐτοῦ
τελείως ἐξατονήσαντος, τὸν ὅσιον ἐπικαλεσάμενος Πέτρον, ὡς ὑπόπτερος ὤφθη τοῖς ἐναντίοις, τοῦ ἵππου τῇ
αἰτήσει δυναμωθέντος. Ὅθεν μοι φησίν "ἀποδιδράσκοντι
τὸ ἑξῆς, καὶ εἰς ἑτέρους ἱππεῖς καταπάροδον ὀκτὼ τὸν
ἀριθμὸν προστυχόντι τῶν ἐναντίων, καὶ πάλιν ἐξαπορή-
σαντι καὶ ἐπικαλεσαμένῳ τὸν ὅσιον ἐκ μέσου αὐτῶν εἷλκεν
καὶ ὡς ἐκ θήρας τῶν ὀδόντων αὐτῶν, ἀλώβητόν με καὶ
ἀβλαβῆ διεσώσατο."

voice again, he realized that it was a divine message, in fact the manifestation of the help from the intercession and grace of that holy Peter, whom he had invoked. So, immediately filled with confidence, Benjamin got away from the enemies and returned home safe, addressing words of gratitude to the Lord and to his most holy servant Peter.

39.3 On the deliverance of the *spatharios* from wartime enemies

Another senator, as he himself told me, who was also an acquaintance of the thrice holy one, was defeated during a skirmish in the war. As he was fleeing, he was being hard pressed by his pursuers and close to being struck, but when his enemies were already near him, and just as he was sure he would be caught and fall into his opponents' hands since his horse was completely exhausted, he called on the assistance of holy Peter. Immediately it appeared to his enemies that he had wings, because the horse regained its strength through his prayer. He said to me, "While I was making my escape, I met eight other enemy horsemen on the way, and I was in despair once more, but after calling on the holy one's assistance, he drew me out from among them and kept me safe and unharmed as if from the teeth of their trap."

40 Περὶ τῆς ἐν ὥραις κεραυνῶν καὶ ζάλης παραδόξως σω-
θείσης νηὸς

"Καὶ ἄλλος δέ μοι" φησίν "τις ἀξιοπιστότατος μοναχὸς διηγήσατο, ὅτιπερ ἐν καιρῷ χειμερίῳ ἐν βαθείᾳ νυκτὶ ἐν
ὥρᾳ κεραυνῶν μοι κατὰ τὴν θάλασσαν πλέοντι, καὶ τὰς
τῆς ζωῆς ἐλπίδας δι᾽ ἐκείνης τῆς ζάλης ἀποβάλλοντι,
καὶ πρὸς τὴν τοῦ ὁσίου εὐθὺς ἀντιληπτικὴν προστασίαν
καταφυγόντι, ἅμα αὐτὸν ἐξαιτήσασθαι καὶ λόγῳ προσ-
δεηθῆναί με, παμφαεστάτη τίς γέγονεν ἀστραπή, χεῖρα
λαμπρὰν κατὰ τὴν μέσην ταύτης ἐμφέρουσα, ἣ καὶ ὑπεισ-
δύσασα ὅλη τῷ πλοίῳ, γαλήνην βαθεῖαν ἐξαίφνης τῷ κλύ-
δωνι ἐποίησεν, καὶ ἡμᾶς παραδόξως ἐρρύσατο.᾽"

41.1 Περὶ τῆς τοῦ γυναικείου σεμνείου, ἐξ ἐμφυλίων ἐθνῶν
σωτηρίας καὶ ἀβλαβείας

Ἐν δὲ τοῖς καταλυδίαν μέρεσι γυναικείου ὄντος σεμνείου
τοῦ πάλαι προγεγραμμένου, κατεντολήν τε τοῦ πατρὸς
ἡμῶν Πέτρου διαζῶντος, ἐν ἡμέραις συγχύσεως ἐμφυλίου
πολέμου τε καὶ διαρπαγῆς, ἐπέστη αὐτῷ συμμορία τῶν
ἐναντίων, τὰ κατὰ ψυχὴν καὶ σῶμα αὐτῶν βουλομένη
αἰχμαλωτίσαι. Καὶ εὑρόντες αὐτὰς οἱ πολέμιοι κατὰ τὸ
εἰωθὸς τὸν ἑωθινὸν κανόνα ἐπιτελούσας, προσέμενον τὴν
τελείωσιν, καὶ δὴ ἐκεῖναι τοῦτο θεώμεναι, μετὰ τὸ τέλος
τῷ παντοδυνάμῳ Θεῷ καὶ τῷ αὐτοῦ θεράποντι Πέτρῳ
μετὰ πολλῆς τῆς πίστεως καθικέτευον. Καὶ εἶδον αὐτὸν
ἔμπροσθεν τοῦ θυσιαστηρίου ἀορασίᾳ ἱστάμενον, τὰς
χεῖρας ἐκτεταμένον, καὶ σὺν αὐταῖς διαυτὰς ἐκδυσωποῦντα

40 On the miraculous saving of a ship during a thunderstorm

He also said, "Another most trustworthy monk told me, 'I was on a boat at sea in winter, at dead of night, during a thunderstorm, and had lost all hopes of surviving because of this storm. But I immediately took refuge in the protective patronage of the holy one, and as soon as I asked him and said a word in prayer, there was a dazzling flash of lightning, and a shining hand appeared in the middle of it which slipped entirely into the boat and suddenly created a deep calm in the waves, miraculously saving us.'"

41.1 On how the nunnery was kept safe and unharmed from foreigners in the civil war

In the region of Lydia, there was a convent of women, which we mentioned previously, living under our father Peter's guidance. In the days of unrest and plundering during the civil war, a group of the enemy came to it, wishing to take the nuns captive in both body and soul. As these hostile men found them performing their usual morning service, they waited for its conclusion, and the nuns, seeing this, at the end implored God and his servant Peter with great faith. And they saw him standing in front of the altar, invisible to the others, stretching out his hands and entreating the Lord

τὸν Κύριον, καίπερ ἐν τοῖς κατὰ τὸν Ὄλυμπον μέρεσιν τοῦ ὁσίου τότε σωματικῶς ἡσυχάζοντος. Δι᾽ οὗ καὶ καταπάντα ἐκεῖναι ἀβλαβεῖς ἐτηρήθησαν θείᾳ δυνάμει ἐκεῖθεν τῶν αἰχμαλωτισόντων ἀπελασθέντων, ὥστε μετὰ τὸ αὐτόθεν αὐτοὺς ἀπράκτους ἀποχωρῆσαι, διερωτᾶν αὐτοὺς καὶ ἀμηχανεῖσθαι τὸ τῆς βουλῆς αὐτῶν ἄπρακτον, καὶ παρ᾽ ἑαυτῶν βεβαιοῦσθαι τὴν ἀπορίαν, ὡς "ἀνήρ τις φοβερός" λεγόντων "ἐπιστὰς ἡμῖν, ἀστραπηφόρον ἐπιφερόμενος μάχαιραν, ἐκείνης θᾶττον ἀπήλασεν ἡμᾶς τῆς μονῆς, μὴ δὲ τὸ βραχὺ ἐκεῖθεν συγχωρήσας λαβεῖν."

41.2 Περὶ τῆς εἰς τὸν ὁμολογητὴν Θεόδωρον τὸν Στουδιώτην ἀφίξεως πάλιν

Κρατοῦντος δὲ Μιχαὴλ ἔτι τὸ σκῆπτρον, καὶ τὴν αἱρετικὴν ὡς προέφην καταστείλαντος θραῦσιν, οὐ μήν τε εὐσταθίᾳ τὴν ἐκκλησίαν στηρίξαντος, ἀπέρχεται πάλιν ὁ μέγας οὗτος πατὴρ ἡμῶν ἐκ τοῦ Καλοῦ Ὄρους πρὸς τὸν ἀνωτέρω μνημονευθέντα Θεόδωρον τὸν Στουδιώτην τοῦτον ἐπισκεψόμενος. Ὃς χαριέντως αὐτὸν προσδεξάμενος καὶ φιλοφρόνως δεξιωσάμενος, ἠγαλλιᾶτο τῷ πνεύματι. Ὅθεν αὐτῷ ὁ πατὴρ ἀνακοινοῦται πάντα τὰ κατ᾽ αὐτὸν βουλευσάμενος καὶ τὰ περὶ τῆς ἀδελφότητος ἐξειπών, ὡς οὐ φέρει τὸν κόπον ἔτι ἄλλοθεν ἀλλαχοῦ περιάγουσα, καὶ τὴν βλάβην τὴν διὰ χρείαν περ τοῦ σώματος, καὶ παραινεῖται ἅπαντας συναθροῖσαι τοὺς περὶ αὐτὸν κατὰ συστήματα ἕκαστον, μηδενὸς τέως ὑπάρχοντος τοῦ διώκοντος.

with them, although at the time the holy one was living in tranquility in the region of Olympos. Thanks to him they were preserved totally unharmed, because the men who were going to capture them were driven away from there by the divine power. And, as a result, after they had left in a hurry and empty handed, they asked themselves and were unable to explain why their plan had not worked, but they themselves settled their puzzlement, for they said, "a terrifying man confronted us, carrying a flashing sword and swiftly chased us from that monastery, not letting us take even some little thing from there."

41.2 On his subsequent visit to the confessor Theodore the Studite

While Michael was holding the scepter, and had reduced the plague of the heresy, as I said before, albeit not restoring the health of the church, this great father left the Good Mountain again in order to meet with the previously mentioned Theodore the Studite. Theodore received him happily and entertained him hospitably, rejoicing in his spirit. Then, after our father had updated him on everything concerning himself, and received his advice, he also explained to him the situation of his brotherhood, how they could not bear the burden of still wandering about from one place to another and the harm from their physical privations. Theodore advised him to gather them all around him, each in their group, since there was no longer any persecutor.

42 Περὶ τῆς ἐν Ὀλύμπῳ ἐκεῖθεν ἀναστροφῆς αὐτοῦ καὶ περὶ τοῦ ἀποπνιγέντος ἐν τῇ πηγῇ ὄφεως διοράσεως

Δι' ὃ καὶ καταλαβὼν ἐκεῖθεν τὴν ἐν Ὀλύμπῳ μονὴν αὐτοῦ ἐν ἑσπέρᾳ βαθείᾳ καὶ ἐν τῷ ἀποσημείου ἑνὸς ἐκείνης ὄντι ἀντρώδει εὐκτηρίῳ καὶ ἡσυχαστικῷ καταλύσας κελλίῳ, ὑπὸ τῶν ἐκεῖσε ἡσυχαζόντων ὑποτακτικῶν αὐτοῦ χριστο-φρόνως ἐδεξιοῦτο. Τοῦ δὲ τὴν διακονίαν τῆς χρείας ἐμπε-πιστευμένου ἀδελφοῦ κατὰ τὴν κοινοβιακὴν παράδοσιν εὐχὴν αἰτουμένου παρ' αὐτοῦ πρὸς τὸ ὕδωρ ἀντλῆσαι ἐκ τῆς πλησίον πηγῆς, ὅθεν αὐτοὶ ἑκάστοτε ἔπινον, θεωρη-τικῶς αὐτὸν ἐκείνης ὁ διορατικώτατος καὶ ἅπαξ καὶ δὶς ἀπεκώλυσεν, πρὸς τὴν μήκοθεν πέμπων. Τοῦ δὲ ἀδελφοῦ μετὰ κόπου τῇ ἑσπέρᾳ τὴν τοῦ ὕδατος κομιδὴν ἐκτελέσαν-τος, καὶ τῆς ὑπομονῆς αὐτοῦ δοκιμὴν εἶναι τοῦτο ὑπονο-ήσαντος, τὸ αἴτιον ἐξεῖπεν πᾶσιν ὁ μέγας ἀριδηλότατα, ὡς "ὄφις" λέγων "παμμεγεθέστατος σήμερον εἰς τὴν πλησίον ἀπεπνίγη πηγὴν τῇ συνεργείᾳ τοῦ πονηροῦ φαρμάξαι τινὰ πιόντα βουληθέντος τοῦ λυμεῶνος, ἀλλ' ἐκπέπτωκεν τῆς ἐλπίδος ὁ πανσκόλιος καὶ πολύμορφος ὄφις." Ταῦτα τῶν ἐκεῖσε ἀκηκοότων, καὶ πιστωθέντων τὸν λόγον διὰ τῆς ὄψεως, δόξαν Κυρίῳ προσέφερον καὶ τὴν διόρασιν τοῦ πατρὸς ἀπεθαύμαζον, πίστιν ἐπὶ πίστει πρὸς τουτονί, καὶ πληροφορίαν ἐπὶ πληροφορίᾳ προσθέμενοι.

42  On his return to Olympos and his vision concerning the snake that had drowned in the spring

From there, he reached his monastery on Olympos late in the evening and when he went to stay in the cave of prayer and tranquility that was one mile away from it, he was welcomed like one who carries Christ within himself by his subordinates who were living in tranquility there. The brother who was entrusted with the task of serving the community's needs, following the coenobitic order, asked his permission to draw water from the nearby spring, from which they always drank. But our most discerning father, perceptively prohibited him from doing so once and then twice, sending him to the one that was further away. The brother, who completed the provision of the water with great labor in the evening, thought that this was a test of his endurance, but the great one revealed the reason for this to them all, with great clarity. "An enormous snake drowned in the nearby spring today through the machinations of the evil one," he said. "The destroyer wanted to poison someone who drank from it, but that most cunning and many shaped serpent had his hopes dashed." All those present heard this and, after they had confirmed what he said with their eyes, gave glory to the Lord and wondered at the father's insight, adding faith to their faith and confidence to their confidence in him.

43 Περὶ τῆς ἐν τῇ μονῇ τοῦ Ἁγίου Ζαχαρίου τῶν ἀδελφῶν συναθροίσεως, καὶ προβολῆς οἰκονομικῆς τοῦ αὐτοῦ ἀδελφοῦ Παύλου

Τῇ οὖν ἑξῆς, τοὺς ἄλλοθι ἀλλαχοῦ περιιόντας ὑποτακτικοὺς αὐτοῦ ὡς βεβούλητο, ἐν τῇ προρρηθείσῃ συναθροίζει μονῇ τοῦ ἁγίου καὶ ἐνδόξου προφήτου Ζαχαρίου, ἐνῷ καὶ ἦσαν σεσυνηγμένοι τὸ πρότερον, καταστήσας αὐτοῖς οἰκονόμον καὶ φροντιστὴν τῶν πρὸς τὴν χρείαν Παῦλον τὸν αὐτοῦ ἀδελφὸν πάνυ σπουδαῖον καὶ ἐνάρετον ὄντα ὁμολογητήν τε καὶ κατὰ πάντα θεάρεστον. Ὃς καὶ εὐσεβῶς τὰ τῆς μονῆς διοικῶν, ἀνελλιπῆ τῶν πρὸς τὴν χρείαν ἐπιτηδείων αὐτὴν ἐτήρει, τοῦ πατρὸς ἤδη Πέτρου ἐν τῷ ἀπὸ σημείου ἑνὸς ἡσυχαστικῷ κελλίῳ καὶ ἀντρώδει εὐκτηρίῳ τῆς ὑπερενδόξου Θεοτόκου καθεζομένου.

44 Περὶ τῆς ὑποδοχῆς τῆς ἑαυτοῦ ἀδελφῆς καὶ τῶν ταύτης τέκνων

Ἐνῷ καιρῷ δέχεται τὴν αὐτοῦ ἀδελφὴν σὺν τῷ ταύτης συζύγῳ καὶ τοῖς παισὶν αὐτῶν τεσσάρων ὄντων ἀρρενικῶν καὶ δύο θηλείων, καὶ τὰς μὲν θηλείας ἐν γυναικείῳ εὐθὺς κατατάξας σεμνείῳ, τοὺς δὲ ἄρρενας τῇ αὐτοῦ κατηρίθμησεν συνοδείᾳ, τοῦ ἑνὸς ἐξαυτῶν καὶ μείζονος παιδὸς προδήλως ἐν τῷ κόσμῳ ὑπολειφθέντος, διὰ τὸ φθαρῆναι αὐτοῦ παρά τινων κοσμοφρόνων ἀνδρῶν τὴν διάνοιαν, ὃν καὶ μεταχρόνον ἀποστείλας ὁ ὅσιος πατὴρ καὶ ποιμὴν ἐξηῦρεν ἔτι ἀμφίβολον ἔχοντα τὴν διάνοιαν. Οὕτως δὲ αὐτῷ ἀστατοῦντι τοῖς λογισμοῖς κατὰ τὴν ὁδὸν καὶ πρὸς

43 On the gathering of the brothers in the monastery of Saint Zechariah and the election of his brother Paul as steward

The next day, as he had wished, he called together all his subordinates, who were dispersed here and there, in the previously mentioned monastery of the holy and glorious prophet Zechariah, in which they had formerly been gathered. He appointed his brother Paul as steward and manager of all their needs, since he was a very serious and virtuous man, a confessor, pleasing to God in all respects. He piously took care of the affairs of the monastery, and made sure it lacked nothing that was needed, since our father Peter was already installed in the hesychastic cell, the cave church of the most glorious Theotokos, that was one mile away from the monastery.

44 On the reception of his sister and her children

At that time, he received his sister with her husband and their children, four males and two females. He immediately installed the females in a nunnery, while the males he numbered among his own community. One of those children, the oldest, was left behind in the world to start with, since his mind had been corrupted by some worldly-minded men, but, sometime afterward, the holy father and shepherd sent an invitation to him but found him still harboring doubts in his mind. So the man still had mixed thoughts during the

τὴν μονὴν πλησιάσαντι ἐπεισέρχεται νόσος χαλεπωτάτη, ὥστε μὴ ἰσχύειν βαδίζειν ὅλως, τῶν ποδῶν σογχωθέντων, ἀλλ᾽ ἐπικτήνους ἐπικαθήμενον πρὸς τὸν ὅσιον πατέρα καταλαβεῖν. Ἐλθόντα δὲ καὶ προσδεχθέντα καὶ ἐν ἡμέραις πολλαῖς τῇ αὐτῇ συνεχόμενον νόσῳ αὐτὸν θεώμενος ὁ μακάριος, ἐπιτρέπει κατεῖδος τὰ αὐτοῦ πρακτέα ἐξαγορεῦσαι. Αὐτοῦ δὲ τοῦτο τελέσαντος, φησὶν ἔτι πρὸς αὐτὸν ὁ ἀοίδιμος· "Εἰ ἰάσεταί σε τέκνον, ὁ Θεός μου καὶ Κύριος πρὸς τὸν κόσμον πάλιν ἐπαναστρέψεις;" τοῦτο γὰρ ᾔδει αὐτῷ ὁ διορατικώτατος καταδιάνοιαν μελετώμενον. Ὁ δὲ "οὔ" φησιν προσεῖπεν "πάτερ θεόσοφε." Ταῦτα ἐκείνῳ ὁμολογήσαντι ἐπιθεὶς ὁ ποιμὴν χεῖρα, τὸ τάχος τὴν ὁλοκληρίαν τῆς ἰάσεως ἀπέδοτο.

45 Περὶ Θεοφυλάκτου τοῦ τὰ νεῦρα τῆς χειρὸς αὐτοῦ ἐκκόψαντος

Θεοφύλακτος δέ τις ἀπὸ τῆς κώμης Πρεβετοῦ, τέμνων ξύλον τῷ σκεπάρνῳ συνέβη δῶσαι τῇ χειρὶ αὐτοῦ πλησίον τῆς παλάμης, καὶ ἐκκόψαι τὴν καλουμένην φλέβα βασιλικὴν σὺν τῶν νεύρων. Τοῦ δὲ αἵματος σφοδρῶς κατερχομένου καὶ ἀθυμίᾳ βληθέντος διὰ τὴν πολλὴν ῥύσιν τοῦ αἵματος, συνδραμόντων τινῶν καὶ βοτάνας ἐπιθέντων, μόλις ἔστη ἡ τοῦ αἵματος ῥύσις, ἡ δὲ χεὶρ αὐτοῦ πάντως ἀνενέργητος ἔμεινεν· στραφέντων γὰρ τῶν δακτύλων καὶ τῇ παλάμῃ κολληθέντων, οὐδαμῶς ἴσχυεν κρατῆσαι τὸ οἱονδήποτε. Ἔρχεται οὖν πρὸς τὸν ὅσιον, καὶ ποιήσας αὐτῷ εὐχὴν παραυτὰ τῶν δακτύλων αὐτοῦ ἁπλωθέντων ὑγιὴς ἐγένετο.

journey, and, as soon as he approached the monastery, a terrible illness fell on him so that he was unable to walk at all, since his feet were swollen, and he reached the holy father riding on a pack animal. After he had arrived and been received, when the blessed one saw that he continued to be affected by the illness for many days, he urged him to confess his actions in detail. After he had finished doing so, the celebrated one said to him once more, "If my Lord God cures you, my child, are you going to go back to the world?" For that most perceptive man knew that he was thinking about this in his mind. But he said, "No, my divinely wise father." After he had made this commitment, the shepherd laid his hand on him and swiftly restored him to complete health.

### 45  On Theophylaktos, who cut the tendons of his hand

A certain Theophylaktos from the town of Prevetos, while cutting wood with an ax, hit his hand near his palm by accident, and cut the so-called royal vein together with the tendons. The blood was running down profusely and the man was falling into despair because of the copious flow of blood when some people came to his assistance. After they had put some herbs on his wound, the bleeding stopped, though with difficulty, but his hand remained totally useless, for his fingers were twisted and stuck to his palm, and he was unable to hold anything. Then he came to the holy one and, when he had said a prayer for him, the man stretched out his fingers immediately, and became well.

46 Περὶ τῆς ἀνακαινίσεως τοῦ ναοῦ τοῦ Ἁγίου Ζαχαρίου, καὶ περὶ τῆς σωτηρίας τοῦ ἀποβληθέντος ἀδελφοῦ ἐν τῷ φάραγγι

Εἰδὼς δὲ εἰς πλῆθος αὔξουσαν τὴν αὐτοῦ συνοδείαν ὁ παμμακάριστος, τὸν ναὸν τοῦ Ἁγίου Ζαχαρίου ἠβουλήθη περιπλατῦναι μικρὸν ὄντα καὶ μὴ ἰσχύοντα τοὺς ἐπὶ τῆς μονῆς αὐτοῦ ἐπὶ <τὴν ψαλμῳδίαν> χωρεῖν ἀδελφούς. Ὅθεν ἐκείνην εἰσπέρας ἄγων τὴν βουλήν, τοῖς ἀδελφοῖς κελεύει ξύλα τεμεῖν καὶ λίθους πρὸς μίαν τῶν φαράγγων ἀθροῖσαι εἰς τὸ ἀσβεστοποιῆσαι. Τῶν δὲ τὸ κελευσθὲν ἀόκνως ἀποπληρούντων τοῦ πατρὸς ἐκεῖσε παρόντος καὶ τῶν ξύλων ἄνωθεν πρὸς τὴν φάραγγα ῥιπτουμένων εἰς ἣν τὰς καμίνους οἱ τεχνίται ἐποίουν, συνέβη μιᾶς παμμεγεθεστάτης σχίζης κυλιομένης, ἑνὸς τῶν κυλιόντων ἱματίου περικρατῆσαι Θεοδούλου καλουμένου, καὶ τοῦτον συγκαταφέρειν ἐπὶ τὴν φάραγγα. Τούτου δὲ γεγονότος καὶ βοησάντων τῶν ἀδελφῶν, ὁ πατὴρ εὐθὺς ἐπιδραμὼν πρὸς τὴν φάραγγα καὶ τὸν ζωοποιὸν τοῦ σταυροῦ τύπον ποιήσας, ἀβλαβῆ τὸν ἀδελφὸν διετήρησεν καὶ πᾶσιν ἐπέπεσεν φόβος καὶ ἔκστασις τοῖς ἐκεῖσε παροῦσι καὶ θεωμένοις ἐπὶ τῷ θαύματι καὶ ἐδόξαζον τὸν Θεόν.

47 Περὶ τῆς ἀθροίσεως τῶν κατὰ τὸν Ῥύνδακα διεσπαρμένων ἀδελφῶν ἐν τῇ τοῦ Ἁγίου Πορφυρίου μονῇ

Ἐκεῖθεν ἀναστὰς ὁ ὅσιος ἐπὶ τὸν Ῥύνδακα ἔρχεται· εἶχεν γὰρ καὶ ἐν αὐτῷ μοναστήριον τοῦ Ἁγίου Πορφυρίου ὀνομαζόμενον, καὶ ἀδελφοὺς αὐτόθι διεσπαρμένους. Οὓς καὶ

46 On the renovation of the church of Saint Zechariah, and the saving of the brother who had been thrown into the ravine

The most blessed one, seeing that his community was growing in numbers, wanted to expand the church of Saint Zechariah, which was small and could no longer hold the brothers of the monastery for their psalmody. When this plan was put into action, he ordered the brothers to cut wood and gather stones near one of the ravines, in order to prepare quicklime. When they were unhesitatingly carrying out their father's order and he was also present, the wood was being thrown from high up toward the ravine to where the workmen were constructing the kilns. But one gigantic log, which was being rolled down, caught by accident on the tunic of one of those who were rolling it, called Theodoulos, and swept him along as far as the ravine. As soon as this happened, the brothers shouted for help and the father immediately rushed to the ravine. He made the sign of the life-giving cross and kept the brother safe. Terror and amazement seized all who were present and saw the miracle, and they gave glory to God.

47 On the gathering of the brethren who were dispersed in the area of the Rhyndakos to the monastery of Saint Porphyrios

The saint left there and went to the Rhyndakos, because he had a monastery there, named for Saint Porphyrios, and there were brothers who had been dispersed there. He

συναθροίσας κατὰ τὴν ἐπιδοθεῖσαν ὑπὸ τῶν πατέρων βουλὴν ἐν τῇ προλεχθείσῃ τοῦ Ἁγίου Πορφυρίου μονῇ, αὐτὸς ἀπὸ σημείου ἑνὸς ἐν τόπῳ σπανυδρίῳ ἀναχωρητικὸν κελλίον κατασκευάζει, ἐν αὐτῷ ἡσυχάζων ὡς εἴθιστο. Ἐνῷ καί τινα ἀδελφὸν συνέβη Ἁδριανὸν καλούμενον νόσῳ βαρείᾳ περιπεσεῖν, ἐνῇ καὶ μετολίγον τελειοῦται τοῦ πατρὸς ἤδη ἐκεῖθεν ἀπολειφθέντος δι' ἐπίσκεψιν ἀδελφῶν τῶν πλησίον καὶ σύνεγγυς οἰκονομικῶς δύο ὑπηρετῶν αὐτοῦ Βαρνάβα φημὶ καὶ Φιλοθέου μετὰ τοῦ νοσοῦντος καταλειφθέντων. Τοῦ δὲ Ἁδριανοῦ περὶ τὸ τέλος ἐγγίσαντος καὶ θελήσαντος τινὰ ἐξαγορεῦσαι τῶν κατ' αὐτὸν καὶ μὴ δυνηθέντος διὰ τὸ μὴ παρεῖναι τὸν ὅσιον, μετὰ λύπης μετέστη καὶ ἀπεβίω. Τοῦτο ἀκηκοὼς ὁ πανάγαστος καὶ δρομαίως τὸ αὐτοῦ κελλίον καταλαβὼν εὗρεν τὸν νοσοῦντα ἀδελφὸν ἐκλείψαντα καὶ προκείμενον. Μαθὼν δὲ καὶ παρὰ τῶν ἰδίων διακόνων τὰ κατ' αὐτόν, ὡς τοῦ σώματος ἐχωρίσθη περιλυπούμενος, παραστὰς τῇ κλίνῃ ἔνθα ἀνέκειτο ὁ ἀδελφὸς τεθνηκώς, εὐχὴν ὑπὲρ αὐτοῦ ποιήσας ἔκραξεν· "Ἐν τῷ ὀνόματι Ἰησοῦ Χριστοῦ τοῦ Υἱοῦ τοῦ Θεοῦ Ἁδριανὲ πρόσχες μοι." Ὁ δὲ νεκρὸς καὶ ἄπνους ἀναβλέψας τοὺς ὀφθαλμούς, ὁρᾷ τὸν ὅσιον καί φησιν· "Οὐδέποτέ σε ὦ πάτερ ὡς ψιλὸν ὁρᾶν λελόγισμαι ἄνθρωπον, ἀλλ' ὡς οὐράνιον ἄγγελον, καὶ ὡς ἐκ Θεοῦ οὕτως ἐν ὅλῃ μου τῇ ζωῇ ἐδεξάμην τὰ ὑπὸ σοῦ μοι λεγόμενα ἢ προσφερόμενα πράγματά τε καὶ ῥήματα. Δι' ὃ σοι καὶ νῦν τὴν τῶν ἐμῶν παραπτωμάτων ἐξαγορεύσω ὑστέρησιν, τὰ λοιπά σοι κατεῖδος προαπαγγείλας, ὅπως καὶ τούτων σὺν τῶν προτέρων τὴν λύσιν παρὰ σοῦ κομισάμενος, λύπης ἐκτὸς τῆς

gathered them all in the previously mentioned monastery of Saint Porphyrios according to the advice given him by the fathers, while he himself built a hermit's cell one mile away from the monastery in a place which had no water, and lived a life of tranquility there according to his habit. A brother, who was called Adrianos, fell sick with a serious illness at this place, and died from it a short time afterward while the father was away from there because he was visiting the brothers who were close nearby. Prudently, he had left two servants with the patient, I mean Barnabas and Philotheos, to take care of him. When Adrianos was close to the end, he wanted to confess certain things concerning himself, but was unable to do so, because the holy one was not there. So he departed this life full of grief and died. As soon as he heard, the most admirable one hurried back to his cell, but he found the brother who had been ill already lying dead. After he learned from his servants how Adrianos had been separated from his body, full of grief, he stood by the bed on which the brother was lying dead and, saying a prayer for him, called out, "Adrianos, in the name of Jesus Christ, the Son of God, look at me." The man who was dead and not breathing opened his eyes, and, looked at the saint, and said, "Father, I have never thought of looking at you as a mere human being, but as a heavenly angel, and so, all my life I have accepted your words addressed to me or your actions concerning me as though they came from God. For this reason I am going to confess the more recent of my sins to you now, having revealed the rest in detail to you in the past, so that, when I have also received remission from you for them, along with the earlier ones, I may leave this life without

παρούσης ἐξέλθω ζωῆς." Καὶ ἐξειπὼν ὡς ἤθελεν ὁ ἀδελφὸς
Ἀδριανὸς τὰ ἐλλείμματα τῆς ζωῆς τῷ ὁσίῳ πατρί, τῆς
παρούσης ζωῆς ἀπελύθη, τοιαῦτα τοῦ πατρὸς πρὸς αὐτὸν
εἰρηκότος· "Πορεύου ἐν εἰρήνη ὦ τέκνον τὸν πρὸς ζωὴν
ὕπνον ὑπνώσας, μηδὲ μίαν φροντίδα ποιούμενος περὶ τῶν
πάλαι καὶ νῦν ἐξαγορευθέντων μοι ἐγκλημάτων σου. Ὁ
Κύριος συγχωρήσει σοι." Καὶ θᾶττον σὺν τῷ λόγῳ ὑπνώσας τοῦ σώματος ἐξεδήμησεν.

48 Περὶ τῆς τῶν ἐμοὶ μελετωμένων λογισμῶν φανερώ-
σεως

Ἄλλοτε δὲ τούτῳ τῷ μεγάλῳ πατρὶ συνδειπνοῦντί μοι, λόγου κινηθέντος κατὰ τὸ δεῖπνον ὡς πλῆθος Ἰσμαηλιτῶν
κατὰ τῆς Ῥωμαϊκῆς βεβούληται ἐξελθεῖν χώρας καὶ ταύτην αἰχμαλωτίσαι, τοιοῦτος ἐμοὶ λογισμὸς ἐπῆλθεν ἐσθί-
οντι, ὡς "εἰ τοῦτο γένηται ὡς φασίν, ποῦ πορεύσομαι ἢ
ποῦ ἐγὼ ὁ τάλας διασωθήσομαι; Ἐν ὄρει ἀνίσχυρός εἰμι
ἀνελθεῖν διὰ τὸ τῆς πεζοπορίας ἀσύνηθες. Ἐπιβὰς ἐν κτή-
νει; Ἀλλ᾽ οὐ τὰ πρὸς τὴν χρείαν ἐκείνου τὲ καὶ ἐμοῦ εὐπο-
ρήσω. Τί πράξω, πόθεν καὶ ποῦ ἀπελεύσομαι, οὐχ εὑρίσκω.
Ὅμως τὸν ὅσιον πατέρα καθικετεύσας πρὸς τὴν βασιλεύουσαν καταδράμω τῶν πόλεων, καὶ τῶν αἰχμαλωτιζόντων
διασωθεὶς μετὰ τὴν θραῦσιν πρὸς τὸν ὅσιον πατέρα παρα-
γενοῦμαι." Ἔτι δέ μου τὰ τοιάδε διαλογιζομένου καθ᾽ ἑαυτόν, ὁ μέγας εὐθὺς τότε πρὸς τοὺς συνδείπνους ἀδελφοὺς
χαριέστατα ἔφησεν· "Ὁ ἀββᾶς Σάβας ἤδη καταλιπεῖν
ἡμᾶς βούλεται καὶ πρὸς τὰ ἴδια ἀπελθεῖν." Ἐμοῦ δὲ τοῦτο

sorrow." Our brother Adrianos confessed the deficiencies of his life to the holy father as he wanted, and departed from this life, after the father had said this to him: "Go in peace, my child, and sleep the sleep that leads to life, with no concern about your past and present sins, which you have confessed to me. The Lord will forgive you." Adrianos fell asleep as soon as he heard that word, and departed from his body.

## 48   On the revelation of my secret thoughts

Another time, while I was dining with this great father, word went round at dinner that a multitude of Ishmaelites were planning to raid the Roman territory and take it captive. While I was eating, the following thought came to me: "If this happens, as they say, where shall I go? Where shall I, wretch that I am, take refuge? I don't have the strength to climb a mountain, for I'm unaccustomed to walking. Shall I mount a pack animal? But then I won't be able to provide both for it and for me. I don't know what to do or where to go. All the same, I'll ask the holy father, and then rush off to the queen of cities; and so, after escaping from the slavers, I may return to the holy father when the slaughter is over." Immediately, while I was still debating these things with myself, the great father very kindly addressed the brothers who were having dinner, and said, "Abba Sabas is already thinking of abandoning us and going home." While I was

ψευδῶς ἐπὶ πάντων ἀρνησαμένου, κατεῖδος μοι ἐξεῖπεν ἅπαντα τὰ μεμεριμνημένα.

49 Περὶ τῆς τῶν καταλυδίαν μερῶν διεσπαρμένων ἀδελ-φῶν ἐν τῇ Βαλέων μονῇ συναθροίσεως, καὶ περὶ τοῦ πλη-θυνθέντος ἑνὸς ἄρτου

Οὐ μετὰ πολλὰς δὲ ἡμέρας, πρὸς τὸ Καλὸν Ὄρος τὸ κατὰ τὴν Λυδίαν καὶ τοὺς ἐκεῖσε διεσπαρμένους ὑποτακτικοὺς αὐτοῦ καταλαμβάνει, κἀκείνους συναθροίσων ἐν τῇ ἀπο-σημείων δύο οὔσῃ μονῇ τῶν ἐκεῖσε ὄντων ἡσυχαστικῶν αὐτοῦ κελλίων Βαλέᾳ καλουμένῃ, αὐτὸς καταλύων κατη-συχίαν. Ἐνῇ παραγενομένων τινῶν πρὸς αὐτὸν δι᾽ εὐχὴν μετὰ πίστεως, κελεύει τοῖς ὑπηρετοῦσι αὐτῷ ἀδελφοῖς πρὸς τὴν τῶν παραγεγονότων αὐτῷ ὑποδοχὴν ἀριστο-ποιῆσαι. Οἱ δὲ εἶπον· "Ἄρτους πάτερ οὐκ ἔχομεν πρὸς αὐτάρκειαν, εἰ μὴ ἕνα σμικρὸν καὶ οἶνον ὀλίγον ἐν τῷ ἀγγείῳ, πρὸς πεντεκαίδεκα δαιτυμόνας μὴ ἐξαρκοῦντα." Ὁ δέ φησιν· "Ὁ ἐκ πέντε ἄρτων πέντε χιλιάδας εἰς κόρον θρέψας Χριστὸς ὁ Θεὸς ἡμῶν, αὐτὸς καὶ ἐφ᾽ ἡμῖν σπλαγ-χνισθήσεται· δι᾽ ὃ παράθετε τούτοις φαγεῖν." Φαγόντων δὲ πάντων ἐξεκείνου καὶ ἐμπλησθέντων, δύο ἄρτων ἐγκατε-λείφθησαν κλάσματα.

50.1 Περὶ τοῦ πληθυνθέντος σίτου ἐν τῇ μονῇ Βαλέων

Μέλλοντι δὲ τῷ πατρὶ πρὸς τὴν ἐν Ὀλύμπῳ αὖθις μονὴν αὐτοῦ τὴν πορείαν ποιεῖσθαι, καὶ εἰς τὴν αὐτόθι τῶν Βα-λέων μονὴν αὐτοῦ κατεληλυθότι, ὑπὸ τῶν ἐκεῖσε ὄντων ὁ

falsely denying this to them all, he revealed all my thoughts to me in detail.

### 49 On the gathering of the brethren who were scattered in the area of Lydia at the monastery of Baleoi, and on the multiplication of a loaf

A few days later he went to the Good Mountain in Lydia and his subordinates who were scattered there, in order to gather them in the monastery of Baleoi, which was two miles away from his hesychastic cells, while he himself would continue to lead a life of tranquility. When some people came in faith to that monastery for his blessings, Peter ordered the brothers who served him to prepare a meal in order to welcome those who had come to him. But they said, "Father, we don't have enough bread, just one little loaf and a bit of wine in the jar, and those aren't sufficient for fifteen guests." He said, "Christ, our God, who fed five thousand people with five loaves until they were satisfied, will take pity on us. So, serve them this to eat." And, after everyone ate and was full, there were pieces of two loaves of bread left over.

### 50.1 On the grain that was multiplied in the monastery of Baleoi

The father was about to make the journey to his monastery on Olympos again but, after he had gone down to his monastery of Baleoi in that region, the holy one was troubled by

ὅσιος ἐθλίβετο μὴ ἔχειν σῖτον λεγόντων πρὸς τὴν τοῦ ὅλου ἔτους διάρκειαν. Ὁ δὲ λέγει· "Ἄγωμεν ἀδελφοὶ τοῦ σίτου τὸ ποσὸν ἐρευνήσωμεν." Καὶ εἰς τὸν σιτοβολῶνα ἐλθόντες ἐναρχῇ τοῦ Μαΐου μηνός, εὗρεν ἐν αὐτῷ ὡσεὶ μοδίους ἓξ τὸν ἀριθμὸν καὶ οὐ περαιτέρω, ἤσθιον δὲ τῷ μηνὶ τριάκοντα μοδίους οἱ ἀδελφοί. Καὶ πεσόντες αὐτοῦ παρὰ τοὺς πόδας, τὰ πρὸς τὴν χρείαν αὐτῶν προνοήσασθαι παρεκάλουν. Λαβὼν δὲ αὐτὸς ἣν κατεῖχεν ἐν χερσὶ βακτηρίαν ἐπὶ τοῦ σίτου προσήρεισεν τοῖς ἀδελφοῖς προειπών· "Μὴ φοβεῖσθε ὦ τέκνα, μηδὲ μέριμναν ποιεῖσθε τῶν ἐδωδίμων, *ἀλλὰ τὴν μένουσαν μάλιστα βρῶσιν εἰς ζωὴν αἰώνιον θησαυρίζετε·* τοῦ γὰρ Κυρίου μου συνεργοῦντος, ἕως τοῦ νέου σίτου, οὐκ ἐκλείψει ἐκ τούτου πάντων ὑμῶν ἐσθιόντων καὶ πάντων καθεκάστην κορεννυμένων." Ὅπερ καὶ γέγονεν. Ὁ γὰρ τὴν διακονίαν τοῦ ἀρτοκοπίου πεπιστευμένος ἀδελφὸς ὅρκοις ἡμᾶς πολλάκις ἐπληροφόρει ὅτι "ἐρχόμενος καὶ λαμβάνων ἐξ αὐτοῦ τέσσαρας μοδίους κατὰ περίοδον, δύο μόνους κατελίμπανον, καὶ πάλιν τὸ αὐτὸ πλήρης εὑρίσκων, ἄλλους ἐλάμβανον τέσσαρεις, καὶ οὕτως τὸ μικρὸν ἐκεῖνο θινίον, ἕως τοῦ νέου σίτου διήρκεσεν ἡμῖν κατὰ τὴν πρόρρησιν τοῦ πατρὸς ἡμῶν Πέτρου."

## 50.2 Περὶ τῆς θαυματοποιοῦ ῥάβδου

Οὐ μόνον δέ, ἀλλὰ καὶ ἄλλα θαύματα πλεῖστα, διὰ ταύτης ἐγεγόνει τῆς ῥάβδου· ὁπόταν γάρ τις αὐτῶν τὰς τῶν μελῶν αὐτοῦ ἁρμονίας ἐπόνει, ταύτην ἐπιθεὶς ἑαυτῷ, ἀπεκαθίστατο ὑγιὴς ὡς τὸ πάλαι.

those who lived there, who said that they did not have enough grain for the whole year. He said to them, "Brothers, let's go see how much grain is left." They went to the granary at the beginning of May and Peter found around six *modioi* in it and no more, while the brothers consumed thirty *modioi* each month. They fell at his feet asking him to take care of their needs. The holy one took his staff in his hands and thrust it into the grain, making the following prophecy to the brothers, "Don't be afraid, children. Have no concern about food, *but* treasure especially *the imperishable nourishment that endures forever.* With the help of my Lord you will not be short of food until the new crop, and all of you will eat and all will be satisfied every day." This did indeed happen, for the brother entrusted with the service of the bakery repeatedly assured us with oaths that, "I would regularly come and retrieve four *modioi* from the granary, leaving only two behind, but afterward I would find it full and would retrieve another four. So that little heap supplied us with nourishment until the new crop, according to our father Peter's prediction."

## 50.2 On the wonder-working staff

Not only this one, but many other miracles were performed through that staff. For, whenever anyone felt pain in his joints, he would put it on himself and would be restored to his previous health.

51 Περὶ τοῦ πενταετοῦς ἰαθέντος ἐξηραμμένου παιδὸς
τοῦ πρωτονοταρίου Βάρδα

Ἐκεῖθεν ὁ ὅσιος ὡς ἐβούλετο πρὸς τὴν ἐν Ὀλύμπῳ καταλαμβάνει μονὴν αὐτοῦ καὶ ἐν τῷ ἀπὸ σημείου ἑνὸς σπηλαίῳ καὶ εὐκτηρίῳ ἐφησυχάζει ὡς εἴθιστο. Ἐνῇ συγκλητική τις πλησίον χωρίον ἔχουσα καὶ ἐν αὐτῷ διατρίβουσα
τρέφουσα υἱὸν ὡσεὶ χρόνων πέντε, νόσῳ λεπτῇ ἐκ μήτρας
κατακρατούμενον παρ' ἰατρῶν ἁπάντων ἀπεγνωσμένον,
τὰ περὶ τοῦ ὁσίου μεμαθηκυῖα πρέσβεις ἀποστέλλει πρὸς
αὐτὸν τοιαῦτα καθικετεύουσα· "Εἰ καὶ πάσης ἁμαρτίας
ὑπάρχω πεπληρωμένη ἡ τάλαινα ὦ τρισόσιε, ἀλλὰ πίστει
μεγίστῃ τῇ πρὸς Θεὸν καὶ σὲ τὸν θεράποντα αὐτοῦ δια-
πυρὸς συνέχομαι, πόθον τε οὐ μικρὸν ἔχω τὴν σὴν ἁγιωσύνην θεάσασθαι καὶ τῶν τιμίων εὐχῶν σου καταπολαῦσαι.
Δι' ὃ εἰ μέν ἐστίν σου θελητὸν καὶ Θεῷ φίλον, ἕως σου τὸ
τάχος παραγενέσθαι με κέλευσον, καὶ μὴ ἀπαξιώσῃς με
γύναιον οὖσαν. Μνήσθητι ἅγιε τοῦ Θεοῦ, ὅτι καὶ Χριστὸς
ὁ Θεὸς ἡμῶν κατελθὼν ἐπὶ τῆς γῆς τοῦ σῶσαι τὸ γένος
τῶν ἀνθρώπων οὐκ ἀπώσατο ἡμῶν τὴν φύσιν, ὅπως κἀγὼ
καταξιουμένη προσκυνῆσαι τὰ σὰ τίμια ἴχνη, μετὰ πάντων
τῶν εὐεργετηθέντων ὑπὸ σοῦ τὸν σὲ δοξάσαντα Κύριον
ἀπευχαριστήσω." Ταῦτα παρὰ τῶν φορολόγων ἀκηκοὼς ὁ
ἀοίδιμος ὁ μηδ' ὅλως θέλων ποτὲ ψυχὴν λυπῆσαι ἐπικαμφθεὶς ἐκέλευσεν αὐτὴν παραγενέσθαι, ἡ δὲ ταχέως ἐλθοῦσα, ἐν τῷ ναῷ τῆς παναχράντου Δεσποίνης ἡμῶν
Θεοτόκου τῷ ἀπέναντι τῆς μονῆς αὐτοῦ (ὄρος γὰρ ἦν

51  On the healing of the disabled five-year-old child of the
*protonotarios* Bardas

From there, the holy one went off to his monastery on
Olympos, as he wanted, and was living in tranquility in the
cave and chapel that was one mile away, as he usually did.
The wife of a senator, who had land nearby, was there at the
time while she looked after her son, who was about five
years old, since he had been critically underweight since
birth and all the physicians had lost hope for him. As soon
as she learned about the holy one, she sent representatives
to him, imploring him with these words, "Even though I am
a wretched woman, filled with every sin, I possess great and
fervent faith in God and in you, his servant, thrice holy one.
I have a great desire to see your holiness and avail myself of
your precious prayers. Therefore, if you so wish and it is
agreeable to God, tell me to come quickly to you and do
not refuse because I am a woman. Remember, saint of God,
that even Christ our God who came down to earth in order
to save the human race, did not reject our nature. So may I,
after being permitted to fall at your precious feet, express
my gratitude to the Lord who has glorified you, together
with all those who have been helped by you." After the celebrated one, who never wanted to cause grief to any soul,
heard this from the messengers he was moved to pity, and
ordered her to come to him. She quickly arrived at the
church of our most pure Lady, the Theotokos, which lies
opposite his monastery (for it was a rule established by

τοιοῦτος παραυτοῦ δεδομένος μὴ εἰσελθεῖν γυναῖκα ἔνδον τῆς μονῆς), λαβὼν ὁ ὅσιος μεταυτοῦ Φιλόθεον καὶ Βαρνάβαν τοὺς ἀξιομνημονεύτους ὑπηρέτας αὐτοῦ, ἔτι τε καί τινα ἕτερον ἐπίσκοπον Κύπριον τῷ γένει καὶ τῇ ἀρχῇ Ἰωάννην καλούμενον, ὃς καὶ τῷ ὁσίῳ πατρὶ ταπεινοφρονῶν ὑπετάττετο πρὸς πᾶσαν διακονίαν τοῖς κατὰ τὴν μονὴν ἐπιτηδεύων. Οὕσπερ ἰδοῦσα ἡ πιστοτάτη ἐκείνη συγκλητική, καὶ μετὰ πολλῆς προσυπαντήσασα πίστεως, ῥίπτει ἑαυτὴν παρὰ τοὺς πόδας τοῦ ὁσίου, κλαίουσα καὶ τοιαῦτα καθικετεύουσα οἷά ἐστιν εἰκὸς ἔθος τοῖς θλιβομένοις λέγειν· "Παιδίον μοι ἐστὶν πενταετὲς ὦ πανόσιε, καὶ ἐκ τοῦ πλήθους τῶν ἐγκλημάτων μου τῇ πασῶν βαρυτάτῃ περιπέπτωκε νόσῳ, ὀστέοις μόνοις καὶ νεύροις περικρατούμενον, σαρκῶν δὲ χωρὶς ὑπάρχον ἀπογεννήσεως. Ὅπερ ὡς συμπαθὴς ἰατρὸς καὶ φιλόψυχος διὰ τὸν Κύριον ἴασαι· οὐ φέρω γὰρ ἔτι ὁρᾶν εἰς τέλος τὴν τούτου νεκροζωΐαν ἡ οἴκτιστος." Οὕτως αὐτῆς ἐκδυσωπούσης τὸν ὅσιον τὸν υἱὸν μεταχεῖρας φερούσης, καὶ ὀχετοὺς δακρύων ἀποπεμπούσης, σπλαγχνισθεὶς ὁ τρισόσιος, ἐπιθεὶς τῷ παιδὶ χεῖρα ἀπεκατέστησεν ὑγιῆ, καὶ τῇ ἑαυτοῦ ἀπέδωκεν μητρὶ φήσας· "Ἴδε ἔχεις τὸν υἱόν σου ὑγιαίνοντα. Πορεύου χαίρουσα καὶ δοξάζουσα Κύριον τὸν ποιήσαντα μετασοῦ μεγαλεῖα." Ἡ δὲ τὸν ἀσθενῆ καὶ νενεκρωμένον παραμικρὸν ἐρρωμένον ἀπολαβοῦσα, ἠγαλλιάσατο πανοικεὶ τῇ ἑξῆς πρὸς τὰ ἴδια πορευθεῖσα· ἐν γὰρ τῇ πόλει Νικαέων τῆς Βιθυνῶν ἐπαρχίας ἐποιεῖτο τὴν οἴκησιν.

him that a woman should not enter the monastery). The holy one took with him those distinguished servants of his, Philotheos and Barnabas, as well as another man, a bishop called John who hailed from and held office on Cyprus, who had made himself subordinate to the holy father because of his humility, and performed every kind of service for those in the monastery. As soon as the senator's faithful wife saw them, she went to meet them with great faith; throwing herself at the holy one's feet, and weeping and imploring in the way people in distress usually do, she said, "I have a child who is five years old, most holy one, and because of the multitude of my sins he contracted the gravest possible disease. He is only skin and bones, and has had no flesh since his birth. As a compassionate and tenderhearted physician for the sake of the Lord, cure him! For I, most pitiful woman that I am, cannot bear to see him like a living corpse anymore." In this way she pleaded with the holy one, while carrying her son in her hands and weeping streams of tears. The thrice holy one took pity on her, laid his hand on the child and restored his health. He gave him back to his mother, saying, "See, you have a healthy son. Go on your way happily and giving glory to the Lord, who has done great things for you." The woman took back her healthy son, who had been ill and near death, and shared her happiness with all her relatives. The next day she took the road to her home, for she lived in the city of Nicaea in Bithynia.

52 Περὶ τῆς τοῦ αὐτοῦ Βάρδα οἰκειώσεως, καὶ ἐνενηκον-
ταημέρου ζωῆς αὐτοῦ προσθήκης, προοράσεώς τε καὶ πε-
ρατώσεως

Καταλαβούσης δὲ λοιπὸν αὐτῆς ἐν αὐτῇ ὡς βεβούλητο, ὁ
τοῦ ἰαθέντος παιδὸς πατὴρ καὶ ταύτης τῆς γυναικὸς τῆς
προλεχθείσης ὁμόζυγος, τὸ ἐπὶ τῷ παιδὶ γεγονὸς ἐκπλητ-
τόμενος θαῦμα, τὸν τοῦτο τὸ παράδοξον ποιήσαντα
πιστῶς ἠθέλησεν θεάσασθαι ὅσιον καὶ ἐμφορηθῆναι αὐτοῦ
τῶν εὐχῶν. Ὅθεν δρομαίως, ἐν τῷ πλησίον τῆς μονῆς προ-
αστείῳ αὐτοῦ καταλαβὼν νόσῳ παραυτὰ περιπέπτωκεν,
καὶ τὰς τῆς ζωῆς ἐλπίδας ἀπώλεσεν. Ὅθεν πρεσβείας πρὸς
τὸν ὅσιον ἀποστέλλει τὸ τάχος, "μὴ ὀκνήσῃς" λέγων "πάτερ, ἕως τῆς ἐμῆς εὐτελείας καὶ ἀσθενείας παραγενέσθαι,
ὁ πάσης ἐντολῆς εὐαγγελικῆς πληρωτὴς καὶ ἐμὲ τὸν νοσοῦντα ἐπισκεψόμενος, τὸν ψυχὴν καὶ σῶμα καθηλκωμέ-
νον ὑπάρχοντα. Ἤδη γὰρ ἐκλείπω τῆς συγγενείας μου,
καὶ πρὸς τὴν <. . .>." Ὁ δὲ μὴ δὲ κεραίαν μίαν τῶν τοῦ Θεοῦ
ἐντολῶν παρερχόμενος, πρὸς ἐπίσκεψιν τοῦ ἀσθενοῦντος
ἐπορεύθη, συμπαραλαβὼν Βαρνάβαν καὶ Πέτρον τινὰ
διορατικώτατον μαθητὴν αὐτοῦ, ὃς καὶ ἠξιώθη, καιροῦ
καλοῦντος, γενέσθαι ἐπίσκοπος, καὶ καταλαβόντες τὸν
ἀσθενῆ, τοῖς προϋπαντήσασιν αὐτῷ ὑπηρέταις ἐκείνου
ἐπηρώτα περιτούτου πῶς ἔχει. Οἱ δέ φησιν· "Ἑβδόμη
παρῆλθεν ἡμέρα ἤδη, ἀφ' ἧς οὐδόλως, πάτερ, ἀφύπνωσεν
ἤ τινος ἀπεγεύσατο. Ἡ δὲ σὴ ἔνθεος παρουσία ὑπνῶσαι
νῦν αὐτὸν πεποίηκεν." Ἐγνώσθη δὲ τοῖς ἀδελφοῖς, ὡς
ἠκριβώσαντο τὴν ὥραν, ὅτι ἡ παρὰ τοῦ πατρὸς γεγονυῖα

146

52   On Bardas's acquaintance with Peter, and his prediction
and its fulfillment of the addition of ninety days to his life

After she had reached her home as she wished, the father of
the child that had been cured, who was the previously mentioned woman's husband, was amazed by the miracle that
had happened to his child and, filled with faith, wanted to
see the holy one who had performed this wonder and avail
himself of his prayers. So he rushed to his estate near the
monastery, but immediately came down with an illness, and
lost hope of surviving. So he quickly sent representatives to
the saint. "Do not delay, father, you who fulfill all evangelical
laws," they said, "but come to me, who am both worthless
and sick, and look after me, who am ill and whose body and
soul are full of wounds. I am already departing from my relatives and toward <. . .>." The one who did not overlook even
*one iota* of God's commandments went to look after the sick
man, taking with him Barnabas and Peter, a disciple of his
who was clairvoyant and was deemed worthy of becoming a
bishop at the appropriate time. As soon as they reached the
sick man, the holy one asked his servants who met them
how he was. They answered, "It's already been seven days
since he last slept or ate anything. But your divine presence
has made him sleep now." The brothers realized, as they had
checked the time, that the prayer the father had said when

εὐχὴ μελλόντων ὁδεύειν ἀπὸ τῆς αὐτοῦ ποίμνης, τούτου
αἰτία τοῦ ὕπνου καθέστηκεν· ἦν γὰρ ὁ ὅσιος δέησιν ὑπὲρ
αὐτοῦ προσενέγκας. Μεμαθηκὼς οὖν τότε ὑπνοῦντα τὸν
ἀσθενῆ ὁ πανάγαστος, μικρὸν διαστὰς τῇ νυκτὶ ἐκείνῃ
ὑπὸ τὸ αἴθριον ἔμεινεν, τῇ δὲ ἐπαύριον εἰσιὼν πρὸς τὸν
νοσοῦντα τοῦτον ἐπισκεψόμενος, ἰδὼν αὐτὸν ὁ νοσῶν,
ἐξαιτεῖται τὴν ἴασιν λέγων οὕτως· "Ὁ πᾶσαν τοῦ ἐχθροῦ
διὰ τῆς ἐν σοὶ τοῦ Πνεύματος ἐνεργείας ὀλοθρεύων κα-
κίαν πᾶσάν τε νόσον καὶ πᾶσαν μαλακίαν ἐκ τῶν ἀνθρώπων ἀποδιώκων, καὶ εἰς ἐμὲ τὸν ταπεινὸν ἐπικάμφθητι,
δεόμενος περιεμοῦ τὸν φιλάνθρωπον Κύριον, ἵνα μοι δω-
ρήσηται κἂν τριάκοντα ἡμερῶν διωρίαν, ὅπως τοῦ νῦν
ἀναστὰς καὶ τὰ κατ' ἐμὲ εὐσεβῶς διοικήσας, τῆς παρούσης
ζωῆς ἀπολυθῶ." Ὁ δὲ τοῦ Χριστοῦ πιστὸς θεράπων φησὶν
πρὸς αὐτόν· "Εἰ ἔργα ἄξια, ὦ ἄνερ, ἐπιδείξῃ τῆς μετανοίας
ἐξαγορεύσας τὰ κατασὲ καὶ καρποὺς βλαστήσεις ἐνθέους
λυθεὶς τῆς νόσου, τὸν ζωῆς καὶ θανάτου δεσπόζοντα Κύριον δυσωπήσωμεν δωρήσασθαί σοι ἀπὸ τοῦ νῦν ἐνενήκοντα ἡμερῶν προθεσμίαν. Δι' ὃ ἐν ὀνόματι Ἰησοῦ Χριστοῦ τῆς ἐλπίδος ἡμῶν ἀναστὰς ὑγίαινε, καὶ τὰ κατὰ σὲ
εὐσεβῶς, ὡς ἀπηγγείλω, διοίκησον, παρασκευαζόμενος,
ὡς ἔφημεν, πρὸς τὴν ἔξοδον τελειουμένων τῶν ἐνενήκοντα ἡμερῶν." Καὶ ἅμα σὺν τῷ λόγῳ τοῦ μακαρίου ὑγιωθεὶς ὁ νοσῶν, ἀνέστη καὶ πρὸς τὸν οἶκον αὐτοῦ ἀπῆλθεν,
ἔκτοτε τὰ τῆς μελλούσης ζωῆς φροντίζων, μετανοῶν ἐπι-
μελῶς, χήραις ἐπαρκῶν, ὀρφανοῖς εὐποιῶν, τοῖς πένησι τὰ
ἑαυτοῦ μεταδιδοὺς ἐν ἁπλότητι, δούλοις καταγράφων ἐλευ-
θερίαν, τοὺς χάρτας τῶν δανειστῶν αὐτοῦ διασχίζων.

they were about to leave his flock was the reason for that slumber, for the holy one had made an entreaty for his sake. When he learned, then, that the sick man was asleep, this most admirable man stood a little apart and spent that night in the open air. The next day he went in to the man who was ill to take care of him. As soon as the sick man saw him, he asked him for his healing, saying, "You, who destroy every evil of the enemy through the energy of the Spirit which is in you, who chase away *every illness and disease* from men, take pity also on my humble self and pray to the benevolent Lord concerning me, that he may give me at least a period of thirty days in order that I may be released from this present life after I have got up now and piously arranged my personal affairs." The faithful servant of Christ said to him, "If you demonstrate actions worthy of your repentance after you have confessed your sins, and produce divine fruits after you have been relieved from your illness, we shall ask the Lord, who rules over life and death, to give you a respite of ninety more days from now. Therefore, in the name of Jesus Christ, our hope, stand up and be well. Arrange your affairs piously, as you have promised, and prepare yourself, as we have said, for your departure at the end of the ninety days." And, as soon as the blessed man spoke, the sick man was well; he stood up and went off to his home. From that time on he began taking care of things to do with the future life, repenting diligently, *helping widows,* doing good for orphans, *generously distributing* his wealth to the poor, and tearing up the documents of his creditors.

53 Οὕτως ποιοῦντι, τῆς παρελπίδα νόσου καὶ τοῦ θανάτου ἀναρπασθεὶς καὶ ζωὴν ἐμπρόθεσμον δι' εὐχῶν τοῦ ὁσίου πατρὸς ἡμῶν Πέτρου ἀπειληφώς, τῇ ὀγδοηκοστῇ ἡμέρᾳ ἐπεισῆλθεν αὐτῷ νόσος οὐκ ἀνεκτή. Εἰδὼς δὲ τὴν προθεσμίαν τῷ λόγῳ τοῦ μακαρίου συντρέχουσαν, δηλοῖ τῷ ὁσίῳ τὸ δρᾶμα ὡς ἀγνοοῦντι. Ὁ δὲ ὅσιος Πέτρος ἀντεπιστέλλει αὐτῷ τοιαῦτα· "Ἡμεῖς μὲν ἁμαρτωλοὶ και ταπεινοὶ κατὰ πάντα ὄντες, ὦ τέκνον, ἀφιέναι ἁμαρτίας ἐπιτῆς γῆς οὐκ ἰσχύομεν, διὰ δὲ τὴν θεόλεκτον καὶ παναγίαν φωνὴν ἐκείνην τὴν πρὸς τοὺς ἀποστόλους μετὰ τὴν ἀνάστασιν γενομένην καὶ μέχρι συντελείας συντηρουμένην τὴν λέγουσαν, Λάβετε Πνεῦμα Ἅγιον· ἄν τινων ἀφῆτε τὰς ἁμαρτίας, ἀφίενται αὐτοῖς, ἄν τινων κρατεῖτε, κεκράτηνται,' εἰς ἐκείνην θαρροῦντες γράφομεν· Ἀφέωνταί σου αἱ ἁμαρτίαι· πορεύου οὖν ἐν εἰρήνῃ, τὸν τίμιον ὕπνον ὑπνώσας, καὶ μηδεμίαν ἔχε φροντίδα περὶ τῶν ἐξομολογηθέντων ἐγκλημάτων σου, πάντων ἤδη παρὰ Θεοῦ λαβὼν τὴν συγχώρησιν." Τοῦτο τὸ γράμμα ὁ ἀσθενὴς δεξάμενος καὶ τὰ ἐν αὐτῷ γεγραμμένα γνούς, εἶπεν· "Δόξα σοι, Κύριε Ἰησοῦ Χριστὲ ὁ Θεὸς ἡμῶν, ὁ μόνος ἅγιος καὶ ἁμαρτίας ἐλεύθερος, ὁ καταξιώσας με ταύτης ἀκοῦσαι τῆς μακαρίας φωνῆς." Καὶ ταῦτα εἰπών, ἀφῆκεν εὐθὺς τὸ πνεῦμα τῇ ἐνενηκοστῇ ἡμέρᾳ κατὰ τὴν πρόρρησιν τοῦ ὁσιωτάτου πατρός.

54 Ἀπάρας οὖν πάλιν, κατῆλθεν ἐν τῷ μοναστηρίῳ τῶν Βαλαίων καὶ ἐν τῷ εἶναι αὐτὸν ἐκεῖ συνέβη ἀσθενείᾳ περιπεσεῖν Βαρνάβαν τὸν ὑπουργὸν αὐτοῦ, καὶ μεταχρόνον ὀλίγον ἀποκινήσας τῶν ἐκεῖσε ὁ ὅσιος Πέτρος, πρὸς τὴν ἐν Ὀλύμπῳ μονὴν αὐτοῦ ἀπαίρει. Ἦν δὲ ἀκολουθῶν αὐτῷ

53 This he did, after he had been saved unexpectedly from his disease and death and had obtained a limited life span through the prayers of our holy father Peter, until, on the eightieth day, he was overtaken by an unbearable illness. Realizing that this was in accordance with the date set by the blessed one's word, he let the holy one know of this turn of events as if he were ignorant of it. Holy Peter wrote back to him as follows: "My child, as I am a sinner and humble in all respects, I am unable to forgive sins on this earth, but having confidence in that most holy word spoken by God to the apostles after his resurrection, which is valid until the end, and which says, '*Receive the Holy Spirit. If you forgive the sins of any, they are forgiven; if you retain the sins of any, they are retained*,' I say to you, *your sins are forgiven*. Go in peace, then, sleep that dear sleep, and give no thought to the sins you have confessed, since you have already been forgiven for them all by God." The sick man received this letter and, when he read what was written in it, said, "Glory to you, Lord Jesus Christ, our God, you who are alone holy and free from sin, and who has deemed me worthy of hearing this blessed voice." And after he had said this, he gave up his spirit on the nineteenth day, in accordance with the prediction of the most holy father.

54 Peter left again and went down to the monastery of Baleoi. During his stay there his servant Barnabas happened to be afflicted with an illness, but a short time later the holy one moved from there and left for his monastery on Olympos. Barnabas was following him, but was debilitated

ὁ αὐτὸς Βαρνάβας, καὶ ἀτονίᾳ ἐλήφθη διὰ τὸ πολλὰ ἐκ-
δαπανηθῆναι τὴν σάρκα αὐτοῦ ἀπὸ τῆς ἀσθενείας. Ὁδοι-
πορησάντων δὲ ἡμερῶν δύο ὁδοιπορίαν καὶ ἐκκλινάντων
μεῖναι ἐν τόπῳ ἀοικήτῳ, ἦλθεν εἰς νοῦν τῷ αὐτῷ Βαρνάβᾳ
οὕτως, ὅτι "ἐὰν ἔπιον εἰς τὸ βαυκάλιον τοῦ ὁσίου, ὑγιωθεῖν εἶχον." Καὶ ἅμα τῷ ἐνθυμηθῆναι αὐτὸν τοῦτο, εὐθέως
ὁ θεοφόρος πατὴρ ἡμῶν τῷ διορατικῷ πνεύματι γνοὺς
τὸν λογισμὸν αὐτοῦ, προσκαλεσάμενος Φιλόθεον τὸν ἕτερον ὑπουργὸν αὐτοῦ, λέγει· "Δὸς πιεῖν οἶνον ἄκρατον τὸν
ἀββᾶν Βαρνάβα ἐν τῷ ἐμῷ βαυκαλίῳ." Καὶ εὐθέως δεξάμενος καὶ πιὼν ὁ ἀββᾶς, ἱδρῶτι περιχεθείς, αὐτῇ τῇ ὥρᾳ
ὑγιὴς γέγονεν.

55 Ἄλλοτε καθεζομένου τοῦ μεγάλου τούτου πατρὸς
εἰς τὸ ἡσυχαστικὸν κελλίον τῆς ἐν Ὀλύμπῳ μονῆς αὐτοῦ,
συνέβη τινὰς ἀδελφοὺς παραγενέσθαι τοῦ παρ' αὐτοῦ
εὐλογηθῆναι. Οὓς καὶ μετὰ πολλῆς χαρᾶς ὁ πατὴρ δεξάμενος, κελεύει ἐμοὶ τῷ ἐλαχίστῳ Σάβᾳ τράπεζαν παραθεῖναι, μὴ ἔχοντι ταύτης πλουσίως τὰ ἐπιτήδεια, εἰ μὴ
βραχὺν ἄρτον καὶ ὀλίγον οἶνον εἰς ἄγγος ὡς λιτρῶν τριῶν,
δώδεκα ὑπαρχόντων τῶν ἀδελφῶν. Παραθέντος μου δὲ
τράπεζαν ἐκ τοῦ εὑρεθέντος ὡς ἐκελεύσθην καὶ πάντων
ἐναυτῇ καθεσθέντων σὺν τῷ πατρί, ἔφαγον πάντες ἐκ τοῦ
ἑνὸς ἄρτου εἰς κόρον καὶ ἐνεπλήσθησαν. Κελευσθεὶς δὲ
καὶ οἶνον δοῦναι πιεῖν αὐτοῖς, ἐκ τοῦ ὀλιγοστοῦ ἐκείνου
ἄγγους προσμίαν δέδωκα, μὴ καταλείψας ἑναυτῷ ὡς ἐπὶ
Κυρίου εἰ μὴ ποτήριον οἴνου. Ὁ δὲ ὅσιος λέγει μοι· "Δὸς
ἡμᾶς πιεῖν." Ἐγὼ δέ φημι πρὸς αὐτόν· "Οὐκ ἔχομεν, πάτερ,
εἰ μὴ ἓν ποτήριον τὸ καταλειφθὲν εἰς τὸ ἄγγος." Ὁ δὲ τῆς

because of his extreme physical exhaustion due to his illness. After they had traveled for two days on their journey and had turned off to stay in an uninhabited place, the thought came to Barnabas: "If I drink from the holy one's flask, I may be cured." At the same time as he was thinking this, our God-bearing father became aware of his thought through his perceptive spirit and, calling his other servant, Philotheos, he said, "Give Abba Barnabas unmixed wine to drink in my flask." And as soon as the abba received and drank it, he sweated profusely and was cured that very hour.

55 Another time, when this great father was living in his hesychastic cell at his monastery on Olympos, some brothers came to him to obtain his blessing. Our father welcomed them with great joy and ordered me, the most humble Sabas, to set the table for them. But I did not have very much that was necessary for this except a small amount of bread and a little wine, around three liters in a jar, and there were twelve brothers. I set the table for them with what I could find, as I had been ordered; then they all sat at the table with the father and they all ate from that single loaf of bread, until they were satisfied and had enough. After I was also ordered to give them wine to drink and I had served them once from that tiny little jar, as the Lord is my witness, there was only one glassful left inside it. But the holy one said to me, "Give us more to drink." I answered him, "Father, we have no more than a glassful left in the jar." But that supplier

ἀγάπης πληρωτὴς εὔελπις γενόμενος, λέγει· "Ὁ ἐκ τοῦ μὴ
ὄντος ἡμᾶς παραγαγὼν Κύριος καὶ *κατ᾿ εἰκόνα καὶ ὁμοίωσιν αὐτοῦ κτίσας καὶ πάντα δι᾿ ἡμᾶς τὰ ἐν τῷ κόσμῳ δημι-
ουργήσας*, ὁ λόγῳ μόνῳ τὸ ὕδωρ εἰς οἶνον μεταποιήσας, τὸ
ὀλίγον οὐ πληθύνει πρὸς τὴν χρείαν ἡμῶν τῶν δούλων
αὐτοῦ; Ἔχου λοιπὸν τῆς διακονίας σου, τέκνον, καὶ δίδου
πιεῖν τοῖς ἀδελφοῖς ὡς ἐκέλευσα." Ἐμοῦ δὲ ἐξεκείνου ἀρξα-
μένου τοῖς ἀδελφοῖς ἐπιδίδειν, ἔπιον πάντες καὶ ηὐφράν-
θησαν, καὶ ἡμῖν ἐκ τούτου ὑπελείφθη εἰς τὴν ἑξῆς.

56 Ἐν δὲ τῇ αὐτῇ τραπέζῃ καὶ ἑστιάσει καὶ ἕτερον
θαῦμα πεποίηκεν ὁ θεοφόρος οὗτος καὶ μέγας ἀνήρ. Τοῦ
γὰρ πολλάκις μνημονευθέντος ἐπισκόπου Ἰωάννου, πλησίον τοῦ πατρὸς ἐπιτῆς τραπέζης καθεζομένου καὶ τῶν
παρακειμένων ἐσθίοντος, εἷς τῶν ἐκείνου ἔπεσεν ὀδόντων,
ὃν ἐπὶ τῆς χειρὸς δεξάμενος ὁ αὐτὸς Ἰωάννης, τῷ πατρὶ
ἐπιδεικνύων μετὰ δακρύων ἔφησεν· "Οἴμοι, πάτερ, ὅτι
ἐγγίζω πρὸς τὸ τέλος τοῦ θανάτου, τῶν μελῶν μου πιπτόν-
των." Ὁ δὲ πανόλβιος πρὸς αὐτόν· "Τί τοῦτο, πάτερ Ἰωάννη, ὃ λέγεις ἐκπεπτωκέναι;" Ὁ δὲ δείκνυσιν αὐτῷ ἐπιτῆς
χειρὸς τὸν ὀδόντα, ὁ δὲ ὅσιος λέγει αὐτῷ· "Θές, ὦ πάτερ,
αὐτὸν εἰς τὸν τόπον ὅπου ὑπῆρχεν." Τοῦ δὲ Ἰωάννου ἐνω-
δύνως ἀποκριθέντος· "Καὶ πόθεν μοι τοῦτο, πάτερ, ἁμαρτωλῷ μοι ὄντι;" Ὁ θαυμάσιος πατὴρ ἡμῶν ἄρας τὸν ἐκ-
πεπτωκότα ὀδόντα ἐκ τῆς χειρὸς τοῦ ἐπισκόπου, τέθηκεν
αὐτὸν ἐν ᾧ ὑπῆρχεν τόπῳ τὸ πρότερον, καὶ τῇ τοῦ ὁσίου
εὐχῇ ῥιζωθείς, ἐγένετο ὑγιὴς ὡς τὸ πρίν. Ζήσας οὖν ὁ
ἐπίσκοπος ἔκτοτε ἔτη ἕνδεκα καὶ μετ᾿ αὐτοῦ ἐσθίων τοῦ

of love, was hopeful and said, "Will the Lord who brought us from nonexistence into being, created us *in his image and likeness,* produced everything in the world for our sake, and who by his word alone transformed the *water into wine,* not increase that little bit for the sake of us, his servants? So carry on with your duty, child, and give the brothers to drink as I ordered." When I started serving wine to the brothers from that moment, they all drank and were happy, and there was even some of it left for us for the next day.

56  At that same table and meal, that great, divinely inspired man performed another miracle. For Bishop John, who has been mentioned many times before, was sitting near the father at the table and, while he was eating from what had been set there, one of his teeth fell out. John took the tooth in his hand and tearfully showed it to the father. "Oh dear, father," he said, "because I'm coming to the end of my life, parts of me are falling off." The most blessed one said to him, "What is it, father John, that you say fell off?" When John showed him the tooth in his hand, the holy one said to him, "Put it back where it was, father." John, replied sadly, "*How can I,* a sinner, *do that,* father?" Then our wonderful father took the tooth that had fallen out from the bishop's hand and put it back in its original place himself; and through the holy one's prayer it took root and became healthy as before. The bishop lived for eleven more years,

ὀδόντος, οὐδέποτε ἐσαλεύθη οὔτε ἤλγησεν τὸ σύνολον·
ἦν γὰρ ὁ ἐπίσκοπος ὡς ἐτῶν ἐνενήκοντα.

57 Κουράτωρ τις ὀνόματι Εὐστάθιος, τῶν Θρᾳκησίων
ὁρμώμενος, ἦν δουλεύων πρωτοσπαθάριόν τινα ὀνόματι
Σταυράκιον. Οὗτος ὁ Εὐστάθιος παρεγένετο πρὸς τὸν
ὅσιον πατέρα ἡμῶν ἐν τῇ μονῇ τοῦ Ἁγίου Ζαχαρίου εὐλογηθῆναι παρ' αὐτοῦ. Ἐλθόντος δὲ καὶ εὐλογηθέντος,
ἐξῆλθεν τοῦ πορευθῆναι ἐν τοῖς προαστείοις οἷς ἐπεπί-
στευτο παρὰ τοῦ πρωτοσπαθαρίου. Λέγει οὖν ὁ ὅσιος
πατὴρ ἡμῶν Βαρνάβᾳ τῷ ὑπουργῷ αὐτοῦ· "Κάλεσόν μοι
ὧδε τὸν κουράτορα." Φωνήσας δὲ αὐτόν, εἰσῆλθεν μόνος,
καὶ λέγει αὐτῷ ὁ τὸ προφητικὸν ἔχων χάρισμα· "Πορευθεὶς εἰπὲ τῷ σῷ αὐθέντῃ· 'Φύλαξον σεαυτὸν τὰς πέντε ἡμέρας ταύτας· κίνδυνος γάρ σοι μέγας ἐπεισέρχεται.'" Πεσὼν
οὖν ὁ κουράτωρ εἰς τοὺς πόδας τοῦ ὁσίου, ἐδέετο αὐτοῦ
ἀποκαλύψαι αὐτῷ τὰ περιτοῦ κινδύνου. Ὁ δὲ ὅσιος οὐδὲν
πλέον ἠθέλησεν ἐκφάναι αὐτῷ, ἀλλ' ἢ τοῦτο μόνον· "Συντόμως πορεύθητι, τέκνον, καὶ εἰπὲ αὐτῷ ἃ λέγω σοι." Ἦν
γὰρ ὁ αὐτὸς πρωτοσπαθάριος παρὰ τοῦ βασιλέως ἐν ὑποψίᾳ πολλῇ ὡσότι ἐπίβουλος αὐτοῦ ἐστιν καὶ ἐζήτει ἀφορ-
μὴν τοῦ ἀποκτεῖναι αὐτόν. Ἀπελθὼν οὖν ὁ κουράτωρ ἐν
τῇ Πόλει, ἰδὼν αὐτὸν ὁ κύριος αὐτοῦ, λέγει θαμβηθείς· "Τί
οὕτως ἐτάχυνας τοῦ ὑποστρέψαι;" Ὁ δὲ διηγήσατο αὐτῷ
ὅτι "τάδε μοι λελάληκεν ὁ ὅσιος Πέτρος μηνῦσαί σοι." Ὁ
δὲ ἀκούσας ταῦτα, φόβῳ συσχεθεὶς λέγει· "Ἐγὼ ἀπέλθω
πρὸς τὸν ὅσιον καὶ ἀκριβῶς ἴδω τί ἄρα ἔσται τοῦτο." Καὶ
τοῦτο βουλόμενος ποιῆσαι ὁ πρωτοσπαθάριος, τῇ ἐπαύριον κατέλαβον πρὸς αὐτὸν οἱ τοῦ βασιλέως ὑπηρέται

THE LIFE OF SAINT PETER OF ATROA

eating with that very tooth, which never again came loose or
hurt him at all. For the bishop was about ninety.

57 A *kourator* called Eustathios, from the Thrakesion,
was serving a *protospatharios* called Staurakios. Eustathios
came to our holy father who was in the monastery of Saint
Zechariah, to obtain his blessing. After he had come and
had his blessing, he went out to go to the estates which had
been entrusted to him by the *protospatharios.* Then our holy
father said to his servant Barnabas, "Call the *kourator* to me
here." He called him and the *kourator* came in alone. The
one who had the gift of prophecy said to him, "When you
go, say to your lord, 'Take care of yourself for the next five
days, because a great danger is approaching you.'" The *kourator* fell at the holy one's feet and begged him to reveal the
danger to him. But the holy one was not willing to reveal
anything more to him, only this, "Go quickly, my child, and
tell him what I said to you." For this *protospatharios* was under grave suspicion by the emperor of plotting against him,
and he was looking for a pretext to kill him. So the *kourator*
went to Constantinople, and when his lord saw him he said
in surprise, "Why have you returned so soon?" The *kourator*
answered him, "Holy Peter has told me to let you know
this." As soon as the *protospatharios* heard these things, he
was seized with fear and said, "I shall go to the holy one myself and learn exactly what this is." Although this was what
the *protospatharios* wanted to do, the next day the emperor's

λέγοντες αὐτῷ· "Κελεύει σοι δι' ἡμῶν ὁ βασιλεὺς τάδε· εἰ θέλεις ζῆσαι, γενοῦ μοναχός. Εἰ δὲ τοῦτο οὐ βούλῃ, ἐν τῇ ὥρᾳ ταύτῃ στερεῖσαι τῆς ζωῆς σου." Ὁ δὲ ταχέως ἀποθριξάμενος, γέγονεν μοναχὸς καὶ ἀφέθη τοῦ ζῆν. Τότε ἔγνωσαν οἱ ἀκούσαντες ὅτι περὶ τούτου προεῖπεν ὁ προβλεπτικώτατος οὗτος πατὴρ ἡμῶν.

58 Συνέβη οὖν κἀμοί, ἀδελφοί, νόσῳ ποτὲ χαλεπωτάτῃ περιπεσεῖν, ῥιγίῳ τε πολλῷ καὶ πυρετῷ καθ' ἑκάστην ἐκδαπανᾶσθαι. Ἐν τούτῳ δέ μοι τῷ πάθει χρονίζοντι καὶ μὴ κατὰ νοῦν τὸν πατέρα καὶ ἰατρὸν καταλαμβάνοντι ἐκ τῶν πλείστων μου καὶ χαλεπῶν ἀνομημάτων, ἐν μιᾷ φησιν πρὸς μὲ οἱ συνδιάκονοί μου καὶ συμμόναχοι· "Ἰατρὸν μέγα, ἀδελφέ, ἔχομεν ἐνθάδε, καὶ σὺ νοσεῖς; Πρόσελθε τῷ πατρὶ ἡμῶν ὡς οἱ πολλοὶ καὶ πλησθῇς τῆς ὑγείας." Ταῦτα ἀκούσας ἐγώ, αὔθωρον προσδραμὼν τῷ ὁσίῳ, προσέπεσα πρὸς τοῖς ποσὶν αὐτοῦ παρακαλῶν καὶ λέγων· "Ἐλέησόν με, πάτερ, τὸν δοῦλόν σου, καὶ τῆς συνεχούσης με ἀσθενείας ἀπάλλαξον· οὐ φέρω γὰρ ἔτι τοῦ δυσμενοῦς ῥίγους τὴν καθημέραν πάροδον." Ὁ δέ μοι πράως καὶ προσηνῶς εἶπεν· "Τί, τέκνον, οὕτως εἰστέλος ἐλιποθύμησας; Ἄπιθι μὴ φοβούμενος αὐτοῦ τέως τὴν ἐνόχλησιν σήμερον." Καὶ διέμεινα ἐν τῇ ἡμέρᾳ ἐκείνῃ καθὼς εἴρηκεν ὁ πατὴρ ἀνενόχλητος. Τῇ δὲ ἐπαύριον πάλιν αὐτῷ τῷ πάθει περιέπεσα. Τότε θεασάμενος ὁ ταλαίπωρος ἐγὼ ὅτι τῷ τοῦ πανοσίου βουλήματι ἡ νόσος οὐκ ἀντιτάσσεται, ἀπελθών, ῥίπτω ἐμαυτὸν παρὰ τοὺς πόδας αὐτοῦ, δεόμενος καὶ λέγων· "Οὐχ ὑποφέρω, πάτερ ὅσιε, τὴν νόσον ταύτην, ἀλλ'

servants came to him and said, "This is what the emperor is ordering you, through us: if you want to live, become a monk; if you don't want to do this, you'll lose your life this very moment." He cut his hair immediately, and became a monk, and so his life was spared. Then those who heard this realized that it was this that our father, who was so gifted with foresight, had foretold.

58 Brothers, it so happened that I was once afflicted by a grave illness, and I was exhausted by shivering and fever every day. Even after I had been sick in this way for some time I did not think of going to our father, the physician, because of my numerous and horrible sins. One day my fellow servants and fellow monks said to me, "Brother, although we have a great physician here, are you still sick? Go to our father like all the others, and you will regain your health." As soon as I heard these words, I immediately rushed to the saint and, prostrating myself at his feet, I begged him, and said, "Father, have mercy on me, your servant, and relieve me from the disease I have; because I can no longer bear this terrible shivering every day." He answered me, calmly and gently, "My child, why have you become so fainthearted? Go away, and do not be afraid of this annoyance today." And I remained undisturbed the whole day, as the father had said; but the next day I was afflicted by the same condition again. Then I, wretch that I am, realized that the illness could not resist the will of the most holy one, and I went and fell at his feet, and begged him, saying, "I can't bear this

ἐκλείπω ἤδη καὶ ἀπολύομαι τῆς ζωῆς." Ὁ δὲ ὅσιος ἀποκριθείς, λέγει μοι· "Δυνάμει τοῦ Κυρίου μου Ἰησοῦ Χριστοῦ,
οὐκ ἔχει ἀπὸ τοῦ νῦν ἐξουσίαν πλησιάσαι σοι." Καὶ ἰάθην
ἐγὼ ὁ ἄθλιος ἀπ' ἐκείνης τῆς ἡμέρας καὶ ὥρας.

59  Τοῦ οὖν ἀδελφοῦ τοῦ πατρὸς ἡμῶν Παύλου καὶ τῆς
μονῆς οἰκονόμου συνήθως ποτὲ εἰς διακονίαν πορευομένου ἐν πιστῷ τέ τινι καὶ εὐσεβεῖ οἰκήτορι καταλύσαντος,
παρακαλοῦσιν αὐτὸν τοῦ δι' ἑαυτοῦ ὑπὲρ αὐτῶν καθικε-
τεῦσαι τὸν ὅσιον αὐτοῦ ἀδελφὸν Πέτρον παιδίον αὐτοῖς
ἐκ τῆς τοῦ θανάτου ἐπιδρομῆς ἀτεκνοῦντας χαρίσασθαι·
ἦν γὰρ ὁ ἀνὴρ μετὰ τῆς συζύγου αὐτοῦ τρισκαίδεκα τέκνα
ποιήσας, καὶ πάντα ἐκεῖνα ἐτελειώθησαν ἄωρα. Εἶτα ἐπαγ-
γειλάμενος ὁ ὅσιος καὶ πιστὸς οἰκονόμος Παῦλος τοῦ
ἀναγγεῖλαι τὸν ὅσιον τὸ συμβαῖνον, ἀνέκαμψεν, καὶ τὴν
μετὰ πίστεως αἴτησιν τοῦ ἀνδρὸς τῷ πατρὶ ἀναγγείλαν-
τος, ἐπένευσεν εὐθὺς ὁ σημειοφόρος δοῦναι ζωῆς σπέρμα
τῷ δυσωπήσαντι. Καὶ προσευξάμενος ἐξ ὅλης ψυχῆς τῷ
Δεσπότῃ, μεθ' ἡμέρας ὀλίγας συνέλαβεν ἡ γυνή, καὶ ἔτε-
κεν ἄρσεν, ὅπερ διαφυγὸν τὴν τοῦ θανάτου πεῖραν, ἀν-
δρυνθὲν δῶρον προσηνέχθη Κυρίῳ, καὶ ἐν τῇ τοῦ πατρὸς
μονῇ δοκιμώτατος γέγονεν μοναχός.

60  Κατεκεῖνον δὲ τὸν χρόνον ἀνῆλθέν τις ἀνὴρ
Κοσμᾶς ὀνόματι, πλησιόχωρος τοῦ Καλοῦ Ὄρους, προσ-
τοῦτον τὸν θαυμαστὸν καὶ μέγαν Πέτρον, φέρων υἱὸν
πνεῦμα κωφὸν καὶ ἄλαλον ἔχοντα, πιστῶς κραυγάζων
ταῦτα· "Ὁ ἔργῳ, πάτερ, μιμητὴς ὑπάρχων τοῦ Κυρίου σου,
παρ' αὐτοῦ τε τοῖς ἴσοις κατεστεμμένος χαρίσμασιν καὶ

illness, holy father, I'm already failing and departing this life." In reply the holy one said to me, "By the power of my Lord Jesus Christ this illness has no hold over you anymore," and I, miserable one that I am, was cured at that very day and moment.

59 Our father's brother, Paul, who was steward of the monastery, was once traveling on a service, as usual, and stayed in a faithful and pious household. These people asked him to beg his holy brother Peter on their behalf to be given a child, since they had been left childless by death's assault; for the man and his wife had had thirteen children, all of whom had died prematurely. Then, after the holy and faithful steward Paul promised to tell the holy one what had happened, he went back and, when he told the father about that man's request, which had been made with faith, the wonderworker agreed to give a seed of life to the one who had asked for it. He prayed to the Master with his whole heart and a few days later the woman became pregnant and gave birth to a boy, who, since he escaped death's attempt, was offered as a gift to the Lord after he came of age, and became a most respected monk in the father's monastery.

60 At that time a man named Kosmas, who lived near the Good Mountain, went up to that admirable and great father Peter, bringing his son, who had *a dumb and mute spirit*. In faith he cried out, "Father, since you are an imitator of the Lord in your deeds, are invested by him with the same

πολλοὺς λύσας ἐκ νόσων καὶ πνευμάτων ἀκαθάρτων, καὶ
τανῦν ἐφ᾽ ἡμᾶς σπλαγχνισθείς, ἐπικάμφθητι· οὗτος γὰρ ὃν
βλέπεις οἴκτιστον υἱόν μου τοιούτῳ πονηροτάτῳ πνεύματι
ἐκ παιδὸς ἐνεργεῖται, ὥστε εἰς κρημνὸν αὐτὸν καὶ εἰς πῦρ
καὶ εἰς ὕδωρ ἀπορρίπτειν καὶ ἄθεσμα κράζειν, καὶ ἤγαγον
αὐτὸν πρὸς τὴν σὴν ὁσιότητα ἐλεηθῆναι καὶ τῇ ἁγίᾳ σου
μονῇ καταταγῆναι." Ταῦτα εἰπών, ἐκεῖσε αὐτὸν καταλείψας εἰς τὰ ἴδια ᾤχετο, τοῦ δὲ δαιμονῶντος παιδὸς ἐν τῇ
μονῇ καταλειφθέντος τοῦ ὁσίου καὶ πρὸς χρόνον ὑπὸ τοῦ
ἀκαθάρτου ἐκείνου καὶ κωφοῦ πνεύματος ἐνοχλουμένου,
προσῆλθον τινὲς τῆς ἀδελφότητος τῷ πατρὶ περὶ αὐτοῦ
ἱκετεύοντες καὶ βοῶντες· "Τῶν ἐμφορηθέντων τῆς παρὰ
Θεοῦ σοι δεδομένης χάριτος τῶν ἰάσεων, πάτερ, ἐμπέπλη-
σται ἡ σύμπασα γῆ, ἄλλοθεν ἀλλαχοῦ καθεκάστην προσ-
ερχομένων, καὶ τούτων ἁπάντων ἐξιωμένων, οὗτος ἕως
τίνος ὁ δοῦλός σου ὑπὸ τῆς μανίας τοῦ πονηροῦ καὶ κωφοῦ πνεύματος τυραννηθήσεται, τῆς παρὰ σοῦ βοηθείας
καὶ ἀντιλήψεως ἀμοιρῶν;" Ὁ δὲ μακάριος πρὸς αὐτούς·
"Παύσατε, τέκνα· οὐ γὰρ οἴδατε τί αἰτεῖσθε, τὸ παρὸν ὑμεῖς
καὶ οὐ τὸ μέλλον βλέποντες· εἰ γὰρ οὗτος ταχέως τοῦ ἀκαθάρτου πνεύματος ἀπολυτρωθῇ, εἰς τὸν κόσμον θᾶττον
ἐπανελεύσεται, καὶ τὰ ἔσχατα αὐτοῦ χείρονα τῶν πρώτων
γενήσεται." Ταῦτα παρὰ τοῦ πατρὸς ἀκηκοότες οἱ ἀδελφοί, ἡσύχασαν. Ὁ δὲ ὅσιος ποιμήν, ὅτε τὴν τῶν πονηρῶν
λογισμῶν τοῦ δαιμονῶντος παρὰ Θεοῦ ἀπεκαλύφθη καθαίρεσιν, βέβαιόν τε καὶ ἡδρασμένον αὐτὸν πρὸς πᾶσαν
ἐντολὴν ἐγνώρισεν, τότε καὶ τοῦ δαίμονος, ἔλυσεν, καὶ τῇ
αὐτοῦ συνοδίᾳ συνηρίθμησεν.

THE LIFE OF SAINT PETER OF ATROA

gifts as his, and have relieved many people from diseases and unclean spirits, take pity on us now and be merciful. For my most pitiful son, whom you see, has been possessed by a most malevolent spirit since childhood; it even throws him over cliffs, and *into fire and water,* and makes him scream inarticulately. I've brought him to your holiness to receive your mercy and to join your holy monastery." After he had said this, he left his son there and went off home. So the possessed boy was left in the holy one's monastery. As he was troubled by that impure and deaf spirit from time to time, some members of the brotherhood went to the father; they begged him on his behalf and cried out, "The whole world is full of people who have benefitted from the God-given grace of your healings; every day, people come to you from here and there and all of them are healed. How long is this servant of yours going to be tortured by the frenzy of the malevolent and deaf spirit, with no benefit from your help and protection?" The blessed one replied to them, "Silence, children, for *you do not know what you are asking.* You're only looking at the present, not the future. If he is quickly relieved from the impure spirit, he will soon go back to the world and his *last state will be worse than* his *first.*" As soon as the brothers heard these words from the father, they calmed down. And when the holy shepherd was informed by God that the malevolent thoughts of the possessed boy had been purged, and was sure that he was reliable and ready to perform every order, at that point he freed him from the demon and numbered him in his community.

61 Κἀκεῖθεν διαβάντος τοῦ πνευματοφόρου πατρὸς ἡμῶν ἐπὶ τὸν Ἅγιον Πορφύριον πρὸς ἐπίσκεψιν τῶν ἐκεῖσε ὄντων ἀδελφῶν, ἣν ξενιζόμενος ἐν συνηθείᾳ κατὰ πάρ-οδον παρά τινι τῶν οἰκούντων τοὔνομα Κωνσταντίνῳ πρὸς τὰ μέρη τοῦ Πετζικᾶ, ἐν κώμῃ Πηγαδίᾳ, πλησίον δὲ αὐτοῦ ἦν βαλανεῖον συμπτωθὲν ἀπὸ ἐτῶν πλείστων, καὶ κατῴκουν ἐν αὐτῷ δαιμόνια ἀκάθαρτα. Ποιήσας δὲ ἑαυτῷ οἶκον ὁ προρρηθεὶς Κωνσταντῖνος, οὐκ ἔων οἱ ἐν αὐτῷ δαίμονες καταμεῖναί τινα, τῶν δὲ μενόντων τὰ μὲν στό-ματα ἔστρεφον, τὰ δὲ μέλη ἐξήραινον, ἑτέρους δὲ παρά-φρονας ἐποίουν. Προσπεσὼν οὖν τῷ ὁσίῳ ὁ αὐτὸς Κων-σταντῖνος καὶ τὴν αἰτίαν ἐξειπών, ἐπέτρεψεν Βαρνάβᾳ τῷ ὑπουργῷ αὐτοῦ φιλοκαλῆσαι ἐκεῖνον τὸν οἶκον, καὶ ἀπελθὼν ὁ ὅσιος ἔμεινεν ἐν αὐτῷ. Τῶν δὲ πονηρῶν πνευ-μάτων ἀνακραζόντων καὶ πολλὰ δυσφημούντων, ἀπηλά-θησαν διὰ τῶν εὐχῶν τοῦ ἁγίου, καὶ ἔκτοτε ἐγένετο ὁ οἶκος ἐκεῖνος ἀνάπαυσις μεγάλη πᾶσιν τοῖς οἰκοῦσιν ἐν αὐτῷ μέχρι τῆς σήμερον.

62 Πρωΐας δὲ καταλαβούσης τῇ ἡμέρᾳ ἐκείνῃ, ὁ διορα-τικώτατος νοῦς καὶ πατὴρ ἡμῶν, θεασάμενος χώραν ἄσπο-ρον οὖσαν τοῦ αὐτοῦ Κωνσταντίνου, "πῶς οὐκ ἔσπειρας, ἀδελφέ," ἠρώτα, "ἐν τῷ τόπῳ τούτῳ;" Ἦν γὰρ λοιπὸν ὁ καιρὸς τοῦ σπόρου. Ὁ δὲ ἀποκριθεὶς λέγει αὐτῷ· "Τριετὴς χρόνος ἐστίν, τίμιε πάτερ, ὅτι πλῆθος τῶν μυσαρῶν λυμαί-νεται τὴν χώραν ταύτην, καὶ οὐκ ἀφίουσιν ἡμᾶς θερίσαι, καὶ ἠθυμήσαμεν πάνυ καὶ διατοῦτο σπεῖραι αὐτὸ οὐ βου-λόμεθα." Ὁ δὲ κατὰ ἀλήθειαν ἄνθρωπος τοῦ Θεοῦ λέγει πρὸς αὐτόν· "Κύριος ὁ Θεὸς ἡμῶν, ὁ διὰ σπλάγχνα ἐλέους

61 When our spiritually inspired father left there and went to Saint Porphyrios in order to visit the brothers who lived there, he was accommodated on his journey as usual by a man named Konstantinos who lived in the area of Petzikas in a village called Pegadia. There was a bath nearby, which had collapsed many years previously and impure demons were living in it. The previously mentioned Konstantinos had built a house for himself, but the demons would not let anyone live in it, because they twisted the mouths and paralyzed the limbs of those who stayed there, and drove others crazy. So when this Konstantinos prostrated himself before the holy one, and revealed the affair, Peter told his servant Barnabas to look after that house and the holy man went and stayed there. The unclean spirits started to shriek and swear a lot, but they were driven away through the prayers of the saint and, from that time on until today, that house has become a great comfort to all its inhabitants.

62 In the morning of that same day, that most observant mind who was our father, saw that a plot of land belonging to this same Konstantinos had been left unsown. "Why did you not seed that place, brother?" he asked. For it was sowing season then. Konstantinos answered and said to him, "For three years, honored father, a mass of foul pests has ruined this field; they've stopped us reaping and we've become very dispirited and don't want to seed it." Peter, who was truly a man of God, said to him, "Our Lord God, who takes pity upon the race of men *because of his mercy,* will make this

οἰκτείρων τὸ γένος τῶν ἀνθρώπων, ἀφανῆ ποιήσει τὴν ὀργὴν ταύτην ἀφ' ἡμῶν· πορευθεὶς οὖν σπεῖρε ταύτην, μηδὲν δεδοικώς." Καὶ εὐθέως ἠλεήθη πᾶσα ἡ χώρα ἐκείνη ἐκ τῆς λύμης ταύτης.

63 Τῷ οὖν πεντηκοστῷ καὶ ὀγδόῳ ἔτει τῆς ἐν σαρκὶ ζωῆς τοῦ πατρὸς ἡμῶν Πέτρου, Μιχαὴλ ὁ κρατῶν τὰ σκῆπτρα τῆς βασιλείας Ῥωμαίων, νοσήσας σφοδρῶς, ὑπεξῆλθεν τοῦ βίου, καὶ κρατεῖ ἀντ' αὐτοῦ τὴν βασιλείαν Θεόφιλος ὁ υἱὸς αὐτοῦ, Ἰωάννῃ τινὶ προστοιχειωθεὶς Εἰκονομάχῳ καὶ δυσσεβεῖ, τῷ καὶ τὸν πάλαι ἐπὶ Λέοντος κατὰ τῶν εὐσεβῶν γενόμενον μέγαν διωγμὸν ἐνεργήσαντι, ὥστε μάλιστα τότε παρρησίαν ἐπειλημμένος <αὐτὸς> καὶ οἱ αὐτοῦ, τῷ τετάρτῳ ἔτει τῆς βασιλείας Θεοφίλου, τῆς αὐτῶν μανίας κατήρχοντο καὶ κατὰ τῶν εὐσεβούντων ἄνομα διεπράττοντο αἰκίζοντες, διώκοντες, ἐξορίζοντες· οὐ γὰρ ἔφερεν ὁ τούτων πατὴρ καὶ μισόκαλος διάβολος εἰς τέλος ὁρᾶν τῆς Χριστοῦ μορφῆς καὶ τῆς παναγίας αὐτοῦ μητρὸς τὴν προσκύνησιν. Ὅθεν ἐγείρει ὡς ὑπασπιστὴν αὐτοῦ καὶ ἔκδικον τὸν τὴν Προυσαέων χώραν κρατοῦντα ψευδεπίσκοπον Λέοντα, τὸ θεοσύλλεκτον ποίμνιον διασπαρακότα τοῦ πατρός. Τοῦτο οὖν μεμαθηκὼς ὁ πανόσιος Πέτρος, συναθροίζει εὐθὺς τὴν ἀδελφότητα, καὶ φησίν· "Ὁ ἀεὶ πολεμῶν τὴν ἐκκλησίαν διάβολος καὶ ἀεὶ ὑπὸ τῆς ἀκαταλήπτου δυνάμεως τοῦ Κυρίου ἡμῶν Ἰησοῦ Χριστοῦ ἀορασίᾳ καταβαλλόμενος, καὶ τανῦν τὸν ψευδώνυμόν τε καὶ ψευδεπίσκοπον ἤγειρεν καθ' ἡμῶν, τῆς ποίμνης ἡμᾶς τῆς ἰδίας ἀποδιῶξαι. Ἀλλ' ἐπὶ τούτῳ μὴ λυπηθῆτε, τέκνα, χαίρετε δὲ καὶ μάλα εἰδότες ὡς

visitation of his wrath vanish. So go and seed the field and don't be afraid of anything." And that field was immediately spared from that destruction.

63 In the fifty-eighth year of our father Peter's life in the flesh, Michael, who held the scepter of the empire of the Romans, fell seriously ill and departed this life. His son, Theophilos, took control of the empire instead of him. He had been previously taught by one John, an impious Iconoclast who had instigated a great persecution against the pious under Leo. Thus he and his followers, made particular use of their freedom of speech at the time and, in the fourth year of Theophilos's reign, began their previous frenzy again and were acting unjustly against the pious, maltreating, persecuting, and exiling them. For their father, the devil, who hates what is good, simply could not bear to see veneration of the form of Christ and of his all-holy mother. He thus incited the pseudo-bishop of the region of Prousa, Leo, as his supporter and representative, to disperse our father's flock. As soon as the most holy Peter learned this, he immediately gathered the whole community, and said, "The devil, who is always fighting the church but is always cast down by the unfathomable power of our Lord Jesus Christ because of his blindness, has now incited the falsely named false bishop against us in order to eject us from our own fold. But do not despair over this, my children, but be happy, since you know

οἱ θέλοντες εὐσεβῶς ζῆν ἐν Χριστῷ Ἰησοῦ διωχθήσονται. Ὅθεν καὶ νῦν ὡς πάλαι καὶ πολλάκις ἀναδύο ἢ τρεῖς συσταθέντες ἀδιαιρέτως, ἐν ἡσυχαστικοῖς τόποις προσδιατρίψωμεν, ὅπως ἀντὶ ἑνὸς εἰς πολλὰ διαιρεθέντες συστήματα, πολυπλασίως πλήξωμεν τὸν ἐχθρὸν ἡμῶν. Φεύγετε οὖν τὰς φιλίας καὶ συντυχίας τῶν ἀκαθάρτων αἱρετικῶν καὶ τὰς κοσμικὰς συνεστίας καὶ καλοκαγαθίας σὺν ταῖς παροικίαις ἀποδιδράσκετε." Ταῦτα καὶ πλείονα τούτων νουθετήσας καὶ στηρίξας τὴν ἀδελφότητα ὁ πατὴρ καὶ ἐπευξάμενος, πρὸς τὴν ἡσυχίαν ἀπέλυσεν. Ὁ δὲ διώκτης ἐκεῖνος καὶ ψευδεπίσκοπος ἐλθὼν καὶ μηδένα εἰς τὴν μονὴν εὑρηκώς, ὑπεχώρησεν ἐκεῖθεν, κρῖμα καὶ αἰσχύνην ἐνδεδυμένος.

64.1 Φθάσαντι δὲ τῷ ὁσίῳ ἐν τῇ κατὰ τὸν Ῥύνδακα τοῦ ἁγίου Πορφυρίου μονῇ αὐτοῦ καὶ πρὸς αὐτὸ τὸ κοινόβιον ἐν μιᾷ διὰ τὴν ἱερατικὴν λειτουργίαν καταλαβόντος, ταύτην ἤδη ἐπιτελοῦντος καὶ τοῖς ἐκεῖσε παροῦσιν τοῦ κυριακοῦ καὶ ζωοποιοῦ αἵματος μεταδιδοῦντος, συνέβη καὶ τὸν πολλάκις μνημονευθέντα ὕπατον ἐκεῖσε παρεῖναι καὶ λειτουργεῖσθαι. Ὃς καὶ χάριν τοῦ μεταλαβεῖν εἰσήει πρὸς τὸν ὅσιον. Ὡς οὖν εἶδεν ὁ ἱερώτατος τὸν αὐτὸν ὑπατικὸν τινὰ προφανῶς ἀδικήσαντα καὶ τὸν Θεὸν λυπήσαντα, βαστάζων ἤδη τὸ ποτήριον, τοῦτον ἀφῆκεν ἀκοινώνητον, μὴ μεταδοὺς αὐτῷ τῶν ἁγιασμάτων. Μετὰ δὲ τὴν τῆς φρικτῆς ἐκείνης καὶ ἱερᾶς θυσίας τελείωσιν, τὸν ὑπατικὸν προσκαλεσάμενος ἐν τῷ κειμηλιαρχείῳ, τὰ πρέποντα ἐνουθέτησεν. Τοῦ δὲ τὸ σφάλμα ὁμολογήσαντος καὶ διορθοῦσθαι

very well that those who wish to live piously in Christ Jesus will be persecuted. Now, then, as we have done repeatedly in the past, let us live in quiet places, gathered indivisibly in groups of *two or three,* so that, by dividing ourselves into many groups instead of one, we may attack our enemy many times over. So avoid meeting the impure heretics and socializing with them and keep away from public gatherings and entertainments with their congregations." The father gave the brotherhood these and many more instructions and words of support; then, after he had blessed them, he let them go into solitude. And when that persecutor and false bishop came and found no one in the monastery, he left there, covered in guilt and shame.

64.1 One day, after the holy one had arrived at his monastery of Saint Porphyrios in the area of the Rhyndakos, he went down to the main community to carry out his priestly duty. While he was performing the service and distributing the life-giving blood of the Lord to those who were present, that consul who has been mentioned many times before happened to be there and to attend the liturgy. And he went to the holy one in order to receive communion. But as soon as the most holy one realized that the consul had clearly wronged somebody and had displeased God, although he was already holding the cup, he sent him away without receiving communion, refusing to share the holy sacraments with him. After the holy and awe-inspiring sacrifice was completed, he summoned the consul to him in the sacristy and gave him some proper advice. The man confessed his sin and agreed to set things to rights and so the saint

συνθεμένου, δοὺς αὐτῷ ἐπιτίμια προσμετάνοιαν, μεθ᾽ ἡμέρας ἑπτὰ καὶ τῶν ἁγιασμάτων ἠξίωσεν.

64.2 Οὐ μεταπολλὰς δὲ ἡμέρας ἐγένετο τὸν αὐτὸν ὑπατικὸν ὑπό τινων συκοφαντηθέντα τῷ βασιλεῖ Θεοφίλῳ,
διαβληθῆναι ὡς ἐκείνῳ ἐπιβουλεύοντι. Ταῦτα ἀκούσας
ὁ ὑπατικός, φοβηθεὶς τὴν τοῦ βασιλέως ἀγανάκτησιν,
τῆς βασιλευούσης τῶν πόλεων ἐξελθὼν καὶ ἀποδράσας,
ἐκρύβη εἰς τόπον τινά. Τοῦτο ἀκούσας ὁ βασιλεύς, εἰς
ἔρευναν εὐθὺς καὶ καταδρομὴν ἀπέστειλεν τοῦ ὑπατικοῦ.
Τούτου δὲ κρυβηθέντος διὰ τὸν φόβον, εὑρών τις αὐτὸν
τῶν κατασάρκα ἰδιαζόντων, ἔφη αὐτῷ. "῞Εως πότε," φησίν,
"ὦ φίλε, ἐκ τόπου εἰς τόπον ἀποδιδράσκεις πλανώμενος,
τοῦτο σαφῶς ἐπιστάμενος ὡς οὐκ ἐκφεύξει τὰς τοῦ βασιλέως χεῖρας; Ἰδοὺ γὰρ πολὺ πλῆθος στρατιωτῶν ἐξῆλθεν
εἰς ἀναζήτησίν σου. Νῦν οὖν ἄκουσόν μου συμβουλεύ-
οντός σοι καὶ ἑκουσίως σεαυτὸν ταῖς αὐτοῦ χερσὶ καὶ τῇ
αὐτοῦ εὐσπλαγχνίᾳ ἐπίρριψον, μήποτε τῶν παρ᾽ αὐτοῦ
ἀπεσταλμένων καὶ ἐρευνούντων, καὶ μὴ βουλόμενον,
αὐτοῦ ταῖς χερσὶ παραδώσουσι. Διό, εἰ βούλῃ, αὐτὸς ἐγὼ
μετὰ σοῦ πορεύσομαι καὶ ἐξαγορεύσω τῷ βασιλεῖ ὡς ἑκουσίως ἐλήλυθεν πρὸς τὰς χεῖράς σου, Δέσποτα, καὶ πρὸς
τὴν σὴν θεομίμητον φιλανθρωπίαν κατέδραμεν.᾽"

64.3 Τοῦτον οὖν οὕτως πληροφορῶν ὁ ψευδὴς ἐκεῖνος
καὶ δολιόφρων γαμβρὸς αὐτοῦ, τῷ βασιλεῖ λάθρα ἐμήνυσεν διὰ γράμματος γράψας τοιαῦτα· "Τὸν τοῦ Θεοῦ ἀντί-
παλον καὶ τῆς σῆς βασιλείας ἐχθρὸν ὑπατικόν, ὦ ἄναξ
φιλευσεβέστατε, κατασχών, πρὸς τὸ σὸν γαλήνιον καὶ
πανίερον κράτος ἄγω δεδεμένον ὁ δοῦλός σου." Καὶ ἀπο-

imposed penance on him for his repentance and, after seven days, he considered him fit to receive the holy sacraments.

64.2  Not long after, this same consul was falsely accused to the emperor Theophilos by some people, who claimed that he was conspiring against him. When the consul heard this, he was afraid of the emperor's rage, so he left the queen of cities and escaped, and went into hiding somewhere. When the emperor heard this, he immediately sent people out to search for the consul and track him down. And while he was hiding in fear, one of his relatives found him and spoke to him. "My friend," he said, "how long are you going to wander about from one place to another, trying to run away, when you know very well that you're not going to escape the emperor's grasp? Look, a whole host of soldiers are out searching for you. So, now, listen to my advice and hand yourself over voluntarily to the emperor and throw yourself on his mercy, so that those who have been sent by him and are searching for you, may not hand you over to him involuntarily. If you want, I'll come with you and testify to the emperor that 'This man has handed himself over of his own free will, Master, and has taken refuge in your godlike mercy.'"

64.3  Although he gave him these assurances, that lying and conniving brother-in-law of his, secretly informed the emperor in a letter, in which he wrote the following: "Most revered monarch, I, your servant, have arrested the consul, that opponent of God and enemy of your rule, and am bringing him as a prisoner to your serene and most holy majesty."

κινήσας τὸν ὑπατικὸν ἀπὸ τοῦ τόπου ὁ προδότης καὶ δυσ-
μενέστατος, ἐν μιᾷ τῶν μονῶν δήσας αὐτὸν ὁ δόλιος,
πρὸς τὸν βασιλέα προσέφερεν. Ταῦτα ἀκηκοὼς ὁ πατὴρ
ἡμῶν Πέτρος, τὸ συμβὰν αὐτῷ θλιβερὸν καὶ ἔμφοβον
δραματούργημα μὴ ἐνέγκας, κατέδραμεν ὀπίσω αὐτοῦ·
καὶ δὴ φθάσας αὐτοὺς ἐν μιᾷ τῶν μονῶν καταλύσαντας,
εὑρίσκει τὸν ὑπατικὸν πενθοῦντα ὡς τὰς τῆς ζωῆς ἀπο-
λελωκότα ἐλπίδας. Ὃς τότε τὸν ὅσιον πατέρα ἡμῶν θεασάμενος, ἥψατο τῶν ποδῶν αὐτοῦ καταφιλῶν αὐτοὺς καὶ
τοῖς δάκρυσι βρέχων καὶ λέγων· "Πολλῶν καὶ μεγάλων
εὐεργεσιῶν κατακαιροὺς ἀπολαύσας ὁ τάλας ἐγὼ διὰ τῶν
σῶν τιμίων, πάτερ, εὐχῶν, καὶ νῦν πίστει καθικετεύω καὶ
δέομαι, εἴ τίς σοί ἐστιν πρὸς Θεὸν παρρησία, ἀντιλαβέ-
σθαι μου τῆς εὐτελείας καὶ τῆς θανατηφόρου συκοφαν-
τίας ἐκσπᾶσαί με· ἐλπίζω γάρ, πάτερ, ὅτι ἢ μαχαίρῃ τὴν
κεφαλήν μου ἀποτμηθήσομαι ἢ τοὺς ὀφθαλμούς μου ἀδίκως ἀποστερηθήσομαι." Ὁ δὲ ὅσιος πατὴρ ἡμῶν Πέτρος
φησὶν πρὸς αὐτόν· "Μὴ φοβοῦ ὅλως, ὦ φίλτατε, ἀγωγὴν
τὴν πρὸς θάνατον ἢ ἐκτομήν τινος τῶν μελῶν ἢ τῶν ὀμμάτων σου τὴν στέρησιν, ζημίαν δὲ ὑπομείνῃς καὶ ἀφαίρεσιν
χρημάτων ἐκ τῆς ἐνούσης σοι περιουσίας." Καὶ ταῦτα
εἰπών, ἐπιστραφεὶς πρὸς ἐκεῖνον τὸν δολίως τούτῳ συμ-
πορευόμενον ὁ πατήρ, λέγει· "Τούτου μέν, ὦ σύ, τοῦ κατὰ
ἀνθρώπους ἀπελπισμένου γενήσεται ἀντιλήπτωρ ὁ Κύριος. Ὁ δὲ κατ' αὐτοῦ συρράπτεις σκολιοβούλως, κατὰ
σαυτοῦ ἐργάσῃ καὶ μὴ βουλόμενος, κατὰ τὸ ἐν τῇ Σοφίᾳ
Σολομῶντος ἀδόμενον, 'ὁ ὀρύσσων βόθρον τῷ πλησίῳ
αὐτοῦ ἐμπεσεῖται εἰς αὐτόν,'" ὅπερ καὶ γέγονεν. Τοῦ γὰρ

After this traitor and most bitter enemy had made the consul leave that place, the deceitful man tied him up in some monastery and started taking him to the emperor. As soon as our father Peter heard about what had happened to the consul and the horrible and frightening twist to the plot, he could not bear it, and followed close behind him. When he reached them in some monastery where they were staying, he found the consul in mourning, because he had given up hope of surviving. Then, as soon as he saw our holy father, he clasped his feet, kissing them and sprinkling them with his tears, and he said, "Father, I have enjoyed many great benefactions at various times, wretch that I am, through your precious prayers. Now I beg and implore you in faith, if you have any freedom to speak with God, take care of my humility and get me out of this lethal slander, for I am expecting that they will either cut off my head with a sword, father, or unjustly deprive me of my eyes." Our holy father Peter said to him, "Have no fear at all, my dearest friend, that they'll put you to death, cut off one of your limbs, or deprive you of your eyes. You'll receive a fine and the confiscation of money from your surplus wealth." When he had said this, the father turned to that treacherous traveling companion who was with the consul, and said to him, "As for you, the Lord will be the protector of this man, who has no hope, according to the judgment of men; but, what you have deceitfully concocted against him, you will have actually done to yourself, without meaning to, according to what is sung in the Wisdom of Solomon, '*Whoever digs a pit for his neighbor will fall into it.*'" Which is indeed what happened.

ὑπατικοῦ ἀπελθόντος πρὸς τὸν βασιλέα, τῆς κατὰ τῶν μελῶν λώβης καὶ θανάτου διασωθείς, χρημάτων μόνον ὑπήνεγκεν ζημίαν. Αὐτὸς δὲ ὁ τούτῳ σκολιοφρόνως συμπορευσάμενος γαμβρὸς αὐτοῦ οὐ ταῖς τυχούσαις μάστιξιν παρατοῦ βασιλέως καθυπεβλήθη κατὰ τὸν λόγον τοῦ ὁσίου πατρός.

65 Ἐκεῖθεν οὖν ἀναστρέψας ὁ ὅσιος πρὸς τὴν τοῦ Ἁγίου Πορφυρίου μονήν, καιροῦ καλοῦντος, νυγεὶς τὴν ψυχὴν ὑπὸ τῆς θείας τοῦ Πνεύματος χάριτος, ἐπὶ τὰ μέρη τῆς Βιθυνῶν ἐπαρχίας ἐξώρμησεν καὶ πρός τινα μέγαν ἡσυχαστήν, Ἰάκωβον προσαγορευόμενον, ἐπίσκοπον Ἐγχελίου γεγονότα τῆς κατὰ Μακεδονίαν ἐν ἡμέραις τοῦ ἐν Ἁγίοις Ταρασίου καὶ ταύτην παραιτησάμενον διὰ τὸ εἰς ἄκρον αὐτὸν εἶναι φιλόθεον καὶ φιλήσυχον, τοῦτον ἐπισκεψόμενος ἄνεισιν. Καταλαβὼν δὲ τὸν τόπον ἔνθα ἐκεῖνος ὁ ἡσυχαστὴς ἐκαθέζετο, πίπτει αὐτοῦ πρὸς τοὺς πόδας ὁ ὅσιος Πέτρος, καὶ ᾐτεῖτο παρ' αὐτοῦ εὐλογηθῆναι. Αὐτὸς δὲ θεωρητικώτατος ὢν καὶ τὴν ἐν τῷ ὁσίῳ πατρὶ Πέτρῳ τοῦ Πνεύματος χάριν εἰσβλέψας, εἰς ἄκρον αὐτὸν ἐπεπόθησεν εἰπών· "Αὐτὸς ἡμῖν, πάτερ, τοῖς χρήζουσιν τὴν εὐλογίαν σου δώρησαι· ἀποτοῦ νῦν γὰρ ἐν πάσῃ τῇ ζωῇ μου οὐκ ἀποστήσομαί σου τῆς συνδιαίτης." Ὁ δὲ ὅσιος πατὴρ ἡμῶν Πέτρος ταπεινοφρόνως ἐκείνῳ προσαπεκρίνατο· "Εὔχομαι τῷ Θεῷ καὶ Δεσπότῃ μου, ὅτι ὅλως ἠξίωσέν με τῆς θέας σου τὸν ἀνάξιον. Εἰ δὲ καὶ τῆς συνδιαίτης σου τεύξομαι, μεγάλως εὐχαριστήσω αὐτῷ καὶ ὑπερδοξάσω."

For, when the consul went to the emperor, he escaped death and the mutilation of his limbs and only received a monetary fine; but his deceitful brother-in-law who accompanied him on his journey was subjected to a severe flogging by the emperor, in accordance with the holy father's prediction.

65  The holy one returned from there to the monastery of Saint Porphyrios. But when circumstances dictated it and incited by the grace of the divine Spirit in his heart, he set out for the region of Bithynia. He went to visit a great hesychast, called Jacob, who had been bishop of Anchialos in Macedonia in the days of Saint Tarasios but had resigned from his bishopric because of his great love of God and his desire to lead a solitary life. As soon as he reached the place where that hesychast was living, holy Peter fell at his feet, and asked for his blessing. But the hesychast, who was a contemplative man, and recognized the grace of the Spirit in the holy father Peter was filled with the utmost desire for him and said, "It is you yourself, father, who must give your blessing to me who needs it. For from now until the end of my life I will not leave your company." Our holy father Peter humbly answered him, "I thank my Lord and Master that, although I am unworthy, he has deemed me worthy of seeing you; and if I do keep your company, I will give him great thanks and glorify him."

66 Ὑποστρέφοντος οὖν τοῦ τρισοσίου πατρὸς ἡμῶν Πέτρου ἐκ τοῦ ἡσυχαστοῦ Ἰακώβου μετὰ τῶν συναυτῷ ἀδελφῶν ἐν τῇ τοῦ Ἁγίου Πορφυρίου μονῇ, ἔτι τῆς αἱρέσεως κατακρατούσης, καταλαβόντες τὴν λίμνην τῆς Ἀπολλωνιάδος, συνήντησεν αὐτοῖς ὁ ἐπίσκοπος τοῦ αὐτοῦ τόπου. Μὴ ἐχόντων οὖν δι' ἑτέρας ὁδοῦ διελθεῖν διὰ τὴν λίμνην καὶ τὸ πάγος καὶ τὸ παρακείμενον ὄρος, μὴ θέλων θεαθῆναι ὑπ' αὐτοῦ ὁ ὅσιος, ποιήσας τὸ σωτήριον ὅπλον τοῦ ἀχράντου σταυροῦ, οὐχ ὡράθη παρὰ τοῦ ἐπισκόπου ἐκείνου. Ἀπελθόντος δὲ καὶ ἐπιστραφέντος, λέγει πρὸς τοὺς συναυτῷ ὁ ἐπίσκοπος· "Οὐχὶ ἓξ μονάζοντας ἑωράκαμεν; Ποῦ οὖν ὁ μετ' αὐτῶν γέρων;" Τοῦτο ἀκούσαντες οἱ ἀδελφοί, ἐθαύμασαν τὴν χάριν τοῦ Θεοῦ τὴν δοθεῖσαν τῷ θεράποντι αὐτοῦ.

67 Ποιουμένῳ δέ, ὡς προέφην, τῷ μεγάλῳ πατρὶ τὴν πρὸς τὸν μέγαν ἡσυχαστὴν Ἰάκωβον πορείαν, γυνή τις προσαιτὶς τούτῳ ὑπαντήσασα, κωφόν τε καὶ ἄλαλον παιδίον συμπεριάγουσα, ἐλεημοσύνην ᾔτει βοῶσα· "Δώρησαι ἡμῖν, ὦ πάτερ, τοῖς αἰτοῦσι τὸν ἔλεον· οἴκτειρον τὴν πτωχείαν καὶ ἀλογίαν τοῦ κωφοῦ καὶ ἀλάλου παιδίου μου καὶ χάρισαι ἡμῖν τὰ προσδύναμιν." Ὁ δὲ ὅσιος λέγει· "Συγχώρησον ἡμῖν, ὦ γύναι, μὴ ἔχουσιν ἀργύριον ἢ χρυσίον τοῦ παρασχεῖν σοι." Ἡ δὲ γυνὴ πλέον ἐπέμενεν κράζουσα. Ὁ δὲ σπλαγχνισθεὶς ἐπ' αὐτῇ καὶ δακρύσας ἔφη· "Ὁ Θεός, γύναι, ἐλεήσει καὶ ἰάσεται τὸ τέκνον σου." Καὶ ἅμα σὺν τῷ λόγῳ τοῦ μακαρίου ἤρξατο εὐθὺς τοῦ λαλεῖν τὸ παιδίον καὶ ἐξέστη αὐτοῦ ἡ μήτηρ διαποροῦσα, ὅτι "πῶς ἄρα διέρρηξεν τῷ λόγῳ τὰ δεσμὰ τῆς γλώττης τοῦ τέκνου μου;

66  While our thrice holy father was returning from Jacob the hesychast to the monastery of Saint Porphyrios, along with the brothers who were with him, the heresy was still dominant. When they reached Lake Apollonias, the bishop of that place encountered them. Since they had no other way to go, because of the lake, the ice, and the mountain that lay there, and because the holy one did not want to be noticed by the bishop, he made the lifesaving sign of the immaculate cross and was not visible to that bishop. But after he had passed, the bishop turned round and said to his companions, "Didn't we see six monks? So where is the elder who was with them?" When the brothers heard this, they were amazed by the grace of God that had been given to his servant.

67  While the great father was making his journey to the great hesychast Jacob, as I said before, a beggar woman met him. She was carrying a deaf and mute child with her and asked for alms, calling out, "Father, have mercy on us who are seeking it; pity the poverty and dumbness of my deaf and speechless child and give us whatever you can." The holy one said, "I'm sorry, lady, I have *neither gold nor silver* for you." But the woman continued to call out even more. Peter took pity on her and said with tears, "May God have mercy, lady, and cure your child." As soon as the blessed one had uttered these words, the child immediately started to speak and his mother who was amazed, asked in astonishment, "How did he manage to break the bonds of my child's tongue

Ἄγγελον αὐτὸν εἴπω; Ἀλλὰ κατεμὲ ἄνθρωπός μοι ὡράθη. Ἄνθρωπον; Ἀλλ' ὑπὲρ ἄνθρωπον ἐστὶν τὸ πραχθέν." Καὶ ἐδόξαζεν ἡ γυνὴ διαπαντὸς τὸν Θεόν. Τοῦ γὰρ ἁγίου τότε διανύοντος τὴν ὁδὸν καὶ πρὸς τὸ πλησίον ὑπάρχον μοναστήριον τοῦ ἡσυχαστοῦ ἐκείνου Ἰακώβου προσαναπαύσαντος, τοῦ Ἁγίου Κηρύκου ὀνομαζόμενον (ἦν γὰρ ἑσπέρα), καὶ ἡ γυνὴ ἅμα σὺν τῷ ἰαθέντι ἐπέστη παιδὶ τοῖς ἐκεῖσε τὸ θαῦμα ἀνακηρύττουσα καὶ ἡμεῖς δὲ αὐτήκοοι γεγόναμεν καὶ αὐτόπται τοῦ θαύματος.

68 Ἔτι δὲ τοῦ πατρὸς πρὸς τὸν ἡσυχαστὴν ἐκεῖνον καὶ μέγαν Ἰάκωβον ὄντος, ἐπίσκοπος τίς τῆς χώρας τῶν Βουκελλαρίων, ἐπισκοπῆς Πλουσιάδος, Παῦλος καλούμενος, αὐτοῦ πλησίον ὑπάρχων διὰ τῆς εἰς Χριστὸν ὁμολογίας ἐξόριστος καὶ τῇ τῆς αὐτοῦ εἰκόνος προσκυνήσει, σὺν Κλήμεντι τινὶ ὁσιωτάτῳ ποιμένι, φιλοθέῳ καὶ φιλολόγῳ, νόσῳ δεινοτάτῃ κατακλιθεὶς καὶ ὀκτωκαίδεκα διαρκέσας ἡμέρας ἄσιτος καὶ ἄϋπνος ἐκ τοῦ διακαοῦς πυρετοῦ, ἀκηκοὼς περὶ τοῦ ὁσίου Πέτρου ὅτι πρὸς τὸν μέγαν τοῦτον Ἰάκωβον παρεγένετο, λιτὰς οὐ τὰς τυχούσας αὐτῷ καὶ δεήσεις ἀπέστειλεν, τῆς παρ' αὐτοῦ τυχεῖν ὀμειρόμενος ἐπισκέψεως. Παραγενομένου οὖν τοῦ πατρὸς Πέτρου πρὸς τὸν νοσοῦντα Παῦλον, ἀναγκάζεται παρ' αὐτοῦ ὁ ἀοίδιμος τῇ ἑαυτοῦ κεφαλῇ ἱερατικὴν εὐχὴν ποιῆσαι. Ὁ δὲ ὅσιος Πέτρος λέγει· "Οὐκ ἔξεστιν τὴν ταπεινήν μου χεῖρα καὶ ἁμαρτωλὴν ὡς πρεσβυτέρου ἐπέχουσαν βαθμὸν εἰς ἐπισκόπου κάραν ἐπιτεθῆναι· τὸ ἔλαττον γὰρ ὑπὸ τοῦ κρείττονος εὐλογεῖται." Εἰδὼς δὲ αὐτοῦ ὁ νοσῶν ἱεράρχης τὴν καλλίστην ἐκείνην καὶ ταπεινόφρονα ἔνστασιν, λέγει

with his word? Shall I call him an angel? But he looks like a human being to me. Is he a man? But what he did is super-human." And the woman went on giving glory to God con-tinuously, for when the saint completed his journey and rested (because it was evening) at the nearby monastery of the hesychast Jacob, which was named after Saint Kerykos, the woman was also there along with the child who had been cured, and she told those who were there about the miracle. I heard about the miracle with my own ears and saw it with my own eyes.

68 While the father was still with that great hesychast Jacob, a bishop from the area of Boukellarioi, the bishop of Plousias, named Paul, was in exile nearby because of his con-fession of Christ and his veneration of his icon. With him was a most holy shepherd, Clemens, who was both highly educated and a lover of God. This Paul became bedridden after contracting a most serious illness and spent eighteen days without food or sleep because of his high fever. As soon as he heard that holy Peter had come to visit that great Ja-cob, he sent him profound appeals and entreaties out of his longing for a visit from him. So father Peter came to Paul, who was ill, and that man of blessed memory was asked forcefully by the bishop to say a priestly prayer over his head. But the holy Peter said, "As someone who holds the rank of priest, I am not permitted to lay my humble and sin-ful hand on the head of a bishop, for *it is the inferior that is blessed by the superior.*" When the sick bishop understood his excellent and humble objection, he said to him, "You have

αὐτῷ· "Εὐλογίαν ἔχεις, ὦ πάτερ, τὴν αἴτησίν μου πληρῶσαι καὶ εὐλογῆσαί με." Τοῦτο οὖν ποιήσας καὶ μὴ βουλόμενος ὁ πατὴρ ἡμῶν Πέτρος, ὑπεχώρησεν ἐξ αὐτοῦ εἰς ἕτερον κελλίον. Οἱ δὲ ὑπηρέται τοῦ ἐπισκόπου παρέθηκαν αὐτῷ τράπεζαν πρὸς τὸ γεύσασθαι. Ὁ δὲ ὅσιος ἑκάστῳ τῶν βρωμάτων τῶν παρατιθεμένων αὐτῷ εὐλογῶν καὶ μεταλαμβάνων ἐξ αὐτοῦ μίαν ἢ δεύτερον, τολοιπὸν τὸν ἀσθενοῦντα ἀπέστελλεν, κἀκεῖνος ὅλον ἤσθιεν τὸ παρ' αὐτοῦ πεμπόμενον. Καὶ ἐξέστημεν πάντες οἱ συμπαραγενόμενοι, ὅτιπερ ὀκτωκαιδεκάτην ἔχων ἡμέραν μὴ βεβρωκὼς τὸ παράπαν, διὰ τῆς εὐλογίας τοῦ ὁσίου ἤσθιεν ἀνενδοιάστως. Ὅθεν ἀναστὰς πάλιν ἐκ τῆς τραπέζης ὁ ὅσιος, ποιήσας εὐχὴν πάλιν ἐπ' αὐτῷ δυσωπηθείς, ἅμα τῷ τελέσαι, ἀναστὰς ὁ ἐπίσκοπος ἀπὸ τῆς κλίνης, ἤρξατο περιπατεῖν ἀκωλύτως, καὶ μέχρι πολλοῦ συνώδευσεν τῷ ὁσίῳ, καὶ ὑπέστρεψεν εἰς τὸ κελλίον αὐτοῦ εὐλογῶν τὸν Θεὸν καὶ εὐχαριστῶν τὸν ἀοίδιμον πατέρα Πέτρον.

69 Ἀπάρας δὲ ὁ ὅσιος ὅθεν ἐξώρμητο, καταλαμβάνει τὸν ὅσιον καὶ μέγαν ἡσυχαστὴν Ἰάκωβον, καὶ συμπαραλαβὼν αὐτόν, ἐπὶ τὴν αὐτοῦ μονὴν τὴν καλουμένην τοῦ Ἁγίου Πορφυρίου ἀπέρχεται καὶ ἐν τῷ ἀποσημείου ἑνὸς ἡσυχαστικῷ αὐτοῦ κελλίῳ σὺν τῷ θαυμασίῳ καὶ φιλερήμῳ Ἰακώβῳ ἀποκαθίσταται, ἀγγελικῶς ὡς εἰπεῖν ἐν αὐτῷ διάγοντες καὶ ἀλλήλοις συνδιαιτώμενοι, καὶ ὡς ἵπποι συναμιλλώμενοι, εἰς τὸν ἕνα πρὸς θεῖον καὶ οὐράνιον δρόμον διήγειρον, ἕως εἰς αὐτὰ ἤδη ἔφθασαν οὐρανοῦ τὰ βασίλεια.

my blessing, father, to fulfill my wish and bless me." After our father Peter had done this, albeit unwillingly, he left him and went into another cell. The servants of the bishop served him with a meal to eat. The holy one took and blessed all the food they served him with and then, after eating two or three bites, sent what was left to the sick man; and he ate all that was sent to him by Peter. All of us who were present were amazed, since although he had not eaten anything at all for eighteen days, he now ate everything without any hesitation through the holy one's blessing. When the holy one got up again from the table, he again said a prayer for him because he was sorry for him. As soon as he had completed this, the bishop rose from his bed and began to walk about without any problem. He accompanied the saint for a long way and then returned to his cell, blessing God and thanking our father Peter of blessed memory.

69 The holy one left this place and went back to where he had come from, where he caught up with the great and holy hesychast, Jacob. He took him with him and went off to his monastery named for Saint Porphyrios; and he stayed there with the wonderful lover of solitude Jacob in the hesychastic cell that was one mile away from the monastery. They lived in it like angels, so to speak, and spent their time there struggling together like horses, each urging the other on the divine and heavenly road, until they reached the heavenly kingdoms together.

70 Μετὰ δὲ τὴν χρονικὴν αὐτῶν καὶ ἀπαράκλητον ἐκείνην ἄσκησιν, ἐπιτὸ καταλυδίαν Καλὸν Ὄρος σὺν τῷ ἡσυχαστῇ Ἰακώβῳ ὁ πατὴρ ἡμῶν Πέτρος ἔρχεται φωτίσαι πολλῶν τὰ κατὰ Θεὸν διαβήματα. Ἐν ᾧ καί τις ἀδελφὸς εἰς παράβασιν καταπεσὼν ἐντολῆς, ἐλεπρώθη· ἀποσταλεὶς γὰρ αὐτὸς ἐν μιᾷ παρὰ τοῦ πατρὸς εἰς διακονίαν, θερμῶν βλυζόντων κατὰ τὴν ὁδόν, ἐπιτρέπεται παρὰ τοῦ πατρὸς τοῦ μὴ ἐκεῖσε διαβαίνων εἰσιέναι, ἢ προσεγγίσαι. Αὐτὸς δὲ τοῦ ὁσίου παρακούσας τὸ ἐπίταγμα, εἰσελθὼν ἐν τοῖς θερμοῖς ἀπελούσατο, καὶ χρόνου <οὐ> πολλοῦ παρελθόντος, λέπρα ἀνέβη ἐπὶ ὅλον τὸ σῶμα αὐτοῦ. Τοῦ δὲ ὁσίου Πέτρου τὴν νόσον μὲν ἰδόντος καὶ τὸ αἴτιον μὴ μαθόντος, ἐπιθεὶς τῷ λεπρῷ χεῖρα καὶ ἐλαίῳ ἁγίῳ ἐπιχρίσας, ἀνενέργητος ἔμεινεν. Καί φησιν πρὸς αὐτὸν ὁ ὅσιος· "Τί τὸ ἐν σοὶ ἁμάρτημα, τέκνον, ὅτι οὐκ ἐκκαλύπτεις με; Οὐκ ἔστι γὰρ λυθῆναι τῆς ἐν σώματι νόσου δυνατὸν ὅλως, πταίσματα ἀνεξαγόρευτα ἔχοντα καὶ λελεπρωμένον τὰ κατὰ ψυχήν." Ὁ δὲ λεπρὸς μὴ συνειδέναι ἕτερόν τι ἐβεβαιοῦτο ἀνεξαγόρευτον, μὴ ἐρχομένης εἰς νοῦν τῆς περὶ τῶν θερμῶν παρακοῆς τοῦ ὁσίου πατρός. Ἐπὶ πολὺ δὲ τοῦ μακαρίου ὑπὲρ τοῦ λεπροῦ ἐκδυσωποῦντος τὸν Κύριον, ἐν μιᾷ ἡμέρᾳ ἐνείδει παιδαρίου μικροῦ αἰσχροῦ τε καὶ δυσώδους καὶ τὴν ἐσθῆτα διαρερηγμένου, καταμικρὸν ὁ τῆς παραβάσεως αἴτιος δαίμων ἡσυχάζοντι τῷ ὁσίῳ ἐπιστὰς λέγει· "Τί ἐμοὶ καὶ σοί, ὦ κακόγηρε, ὅτι βιάζει τοῦ ἐκδιῶξαί με; Τοῦτο γὰρ αὐτῷ παρεμοῦ ἐνηργήθη διὰ τὸ τῆς ἐντολῆς σου παραβῆναι καὶ λούσασθαι ἐν τοῖς θερμοῖς κατὰ τὴν ὁδόν." Ταῦτα ἀκούσας ὁ ὅσιος παρὰ τοῦ δυσαχθοῦς δαίμονος,

70 After they had completed that long and unrelenting ascetic struggle, our father Peter, together with Jacob the hesychast, went to the Good Mountain of Lydia in order to illuminate many in the ways of God. At that time a brother, who had fallen by disobeying an order, contracted leprosy. For one day he had been sent by the father to perform a task. But the father had warned him neither to get into the hot springs that bubbled up near the road, nor go near them, as he passed by. But he disobeyed the holy one's order and got into the hot spring and washed himself. Not long after, leprosy took possession of his whole body. When holy Peter saw the disease, without knowing its cause, he put his hand on the leper and anointed him with holy oil, but to no avail. The holy one said to him, "What sin of yours, child, have you not revealed to me? For you can't possibly be relieved of your physical illness if you have faults which you have not confessed, and you have leprosy in your soul." The leper assured him that he was not aware of any unconfessed sins on his conscience; his disobedience to the holy father in the hot springs did not come to his mind. For a long time, the blessed one kept asking the Lord for the sake of the leper until one day, while he was living in spiritual tranquility, the demon who was responsible for that transgression appeared to the holy one in the form of a small, ugly, and foul-smelling child with torn clothes. The demon said, "*What have you to do with me,* you evil old man? Why are you trying so hard to get rid of me? I did this to him because he disregarded your order and washed himself in the hot springs while he was on his way." As soon as the holy one heard this from the nasty

προσκαλεσάμενος τὸν λελεπρωμένον, λέγει αὐτῷ· "Διατί
μοι, τέκνον, ἕως ἄρτι τὰ κατὰ σὲ οὐκ ἐξήγγειλας; Διὰ γὰρ
τὸ παραβῆναί σε τινὰ ἐντολὴν τοῦτό σοι γέγονεν, καθὼς
ὁ ἀπατήσας σε δαίμων τῆς παραβάσεως ἐλεγχόμενος εἴρηκεν." Ταῦτα ἀκούσας ὁ ἀδελφὸς καὶ τὸ σφάλμα κατανοή-
σας καὶ ἐξομολογησάμενος, αὔθωρον ὑγιώθη, τὴν χεῖρα
αὐτῷ ἐπιθέντος τοῦ μακαρίου.

71 Ἐμοῦ δὲ ἐκεῖσε, ἀδελφοί, ἐν μιᾷ τὸν κῆπον καλλιερ-
γήσαντος καὶ σπεῖραι μέλλοντος σπέρμα ἐν τῷ ἀνύδρῳ
τόπῳ ἐκείνῳ καὶ εὐχὴν ἤδη αἰτουμένου παρὰ τοῦ ὁσίου
σπεῖραι, ὁ μακάριος λέγει μοι· "Ἔκδεξαι, τέκνον." Προσ-
μείναντος δέ μου μικρόν, ἐλθὼν ὁ πατὴρ καὶ τὰ σπέρματα
πάντα ἀνάμιξ ποιήσας, ταῖς οἰκείαις χερσὶν αὐτοῦ ἔσπει-
ρεν. Καὶ μετὰ τὸ πάντα ἀποσπεῖραι τὰ σπέρματα, εὐθὺς ὡς
ἐπὶ Κυρίου νεφέλη μικρὰ ἐλθοῦσα καὶ στᾶσα μόνον ἐπάνω
τῶν σπερμάτων, ἐπέβρεξεν, πανταχοῦ τότε καθαρεύοντος
τοῦ ἀέρος.

72 Καθεζομένου δέ μου πάλιν ἄλλοτε ἐν κρυφῇ ἐπὶ τὸ
τῆς διακονίας κελλίον μεμονωμένου, ἐγένετο τὸν πατέρα
ἐκ τῆς ἑαυτοῦ κέλλης καταβάντα, εἰσελθεῖν ἐν αὐτῷ. Ἑτέρου δέ τινος ἐκεῖσε μὴ συμπαρόντος μοι, τῇ ῥάβδῳ αὐτοῦ
ἤρξατο τύπτειν ὅνπερ ἐκεῖσε παρόντα προστετύχηκε δαί-
μονα καὶ λέγειν· "Ἔξελθε ἐκεῖθεν, πονηρὸν καὶ ἀκάθαρτον
πνεῦμα, εἰς τὸ ἡτοιμασμένον πῦρ." Καὶ τοῦτο ἐγὼ θεασάμενος, ἐθαμβήθην τὸ διορατικὸν τοῦ ὁσίου πατρός, ὅτι
ἐγὼ τινὰ οὐχ᾽ ἑώρακα καθεζόμενος ἐν τῷ κελλίῳ.

73 Ἐν τούτῳ δὲ τῷ χρόνῳ παρεγένετο μοναχὸς τίς
πρὸς τὸν ὅσιον, Εὐθύμιος προσαγορευόμενος, ἐκ χώρας

demon, he summoned the leper and said to him, "My child, why have you not yet confessed to me what you did? This happened to you because you disobeyed an order, as the demon who deceived you revealed to me after I interrogated him." When the brother heard this, he realized his mistake, and confessed it; he was healed that very hour, after the blessed one laid his hand on him.

71 When I was there, brothers, I was taking care of the garden one day. I was ready to sow seeds in that waterless place and had already asked for the holy one's blessing to sow them. But the blessed one said to me, "Wait a bit, child." So I stayed there for a short while, until the father came, mixed all the seeds together and sowed them with his own hands. After he had sowed all the seeds, immediately, as God is my witness, a little cloud came and stopped only above those seeds, and it rained, although the sky was clear everywhere else at the time.

72 Another time, while I was living there in secret, I was alone in the cell where I performed my service, when the father came down from his own cell and entered mine. There was no one else there with me, but the father started to beat the demon who happened to be there with his staff, and say, "Go away from here, evil and unclean spirit, into the eternal *fire prepared* for you." When I witnessed this, I was astonished by the holy father's perceptiveness, since I had not seen anyone, although I was living in the cell.

73 At that time, a monk visited the holy one. He was called Euthymios and came from the region of Asia, from

Ἀσίας μητροπόλεως Σμύρνης καὶ τῆς ἐκεῖσε μονῆς Πρινα-
βάριος ἡγούμενος καὶ πρεσβύτερος, ἔχων μεθ᾽ ἑαυτοῦ
κοσμικοὺς δύο. Οἳ τούτῳ ὁμογνωμονήσαντες, τῆς πρὸς
τὸν ὅσιον χάριν εὐχῆς συνηκολούθησαν. Ὁ δὲ ἱερὸς Εὐθύμιος αὐτός μοι ἐκεῖνος ἐξηγήσατο ὅτιπερ "ἀδελφὲ Σάβα,
ἐκ πολλοῦ ἤμην τὰ περὶ τοῦ πατρὸς ἐνηχούμενος καὶ
ἀκούων, οὐ μὴν δὲ αὐτὸν ἐθεασάμην, ἀλλ᾽ εἶχον ἤδη ἔτος
πεντεκαιδέκατον εἰς τὴν παρεμοῦ ἀναφερομένην θυσίαν
τῆς λειτουργίας ἐκ πίστεως αὐτῷ προσμεμνημένος. Ὅτε
δὲ ἦλθον πρὸς τοῦτον τὸν ἄγγελον ἐν ἀνθρώποις, πανευ-
χαρίστους φωνὰς τῷ Θεῷ ἐνώπιον αὐτοῦ ἀνέπεμψα, ὅτι
ὅλως ἠξιώθην θεατὴς γενέσθαι τοῦ ἐκ πολλοῦ πεποθημέ-
νου μοι πατρός. Ὁ δὲ ὅσιος αὐτός μοι προσεῖπεν χαριεστά-
τως· Μνησθείη σοι Κύριος, πάτερ Εὐθύμιε, ὡς κατηνύγης
μνείαν ἐμοῦ ποιεῖσθαι τοῦ ταπεινοῦ εἰς τὴν θείαν καὶ ἀναί-
μακτον καὶ ἱερὰν λειτουργίαν σου.᾽ Τοῦτο οὖν ἀκηκοὼς
ἐγὼ τὸ μυστήριον ὅπερ ἔπραττον, καὶ οὐδενὶ ἄλλῳ ἐθάρ-
ρησα ποτὲ καὶ τοῦ ὀνόματός μου τὴν κλῆσιν, ἐξέστην
ἔκστασιν μεγάλην ἐπεκείνῃ ὄντως τοῦ ὁσίου τῇ διοράσει.
Οὐ μόνον δέ, ἀλλὰ καὶ τοῖς συνοδεύουσί μοι δύο κοσμι-
κοῖς τὰ κατὰ τὴν ὁδὸν ἐξεῖπεν μελετώμενα· τοῦ μὲν γὰρ
ἑνὸς γυναικὶ συνεζευγμένου, τοῦ δὲ ἑτέρου γυναῖκα μὴ
ἔχοντος, ὁδευόντων ἡμῶν, ἔφην ἐγὼ πρὸς τὸν μὴ ἔχοντα
γυναῖκα· Τί ἄρα βούλει σύ, ἀδελφέ, ἀπερχομένων ἡμῶν
πρὸς τὸν ἅγιον; Γίνῃ μοναχὸς καὶ ἀποτάσσῃ πράγμασι
βιωτικοῖς;᾽ Ὁ δὲ τῇ γυναικὶ συνεζευγμένος προεκείνου μοι
ἀπεκρίθη, ἐκ τοῦ θησαυροῦ τῆς καρδίας αὐτοῦ ὑλικήν τινα
καὶ ἐπιβλαβῆ βουλὴν ἐρευξάμενος καὶ εἰπών· Μᾶλλον μὲν

the bishopric of Smyrna, and he was the abbot of the monastery of Prinabaris and was a priest. He was accompanied by two laymen who shared his views and had followed him to the holy one in order to obtain his blessing. That holy Euthymios himself told me the following: "Brother Sabas, I had been aware of and heard about the father for a long time, but I had never seen him, although, I had already been commemorating his name during the liturgy for the past fifteen years because of my confidence in him. When I came to this angel among men, I addressed words of deep gratitude to God in front of him, because I had been deemed worthy of meeting the father whom I had long desired to see. The holy one most graciously told me, 'May the Lord remember you, Father Euthymios, because you were moved to make mention of me, humble as I am, during your divine, bloodless, and holy liturgy.' When I heard him say what I had done in secret and had never confided to anyone else, and even my own name, I was really amazed by the holy one's perception. Not only that, but he also revealed to the two laymen accompanying me what had been in their minds during the journey. One of them was married to a woman, while the other did not have a wife. While we were traveling, I said to the one who had no wife, 'Brother, what do you want from the saint we're going to see? Will you become a monk, and give up everyday life?' But the one who was married to a wife gave me an answer before him. Blurting out a worldly and harmful plan from *the treasury of his heart,* he said

οὖν, ὦ φίλε, γενοῦ τοποτηρητὴς καὶ οὐ μοναχός· ἄξιος
γὰρ ἦν πρὸς τὴν τοιαύτην ἀξίαν. Εἶτα ἀνελθὼν καὶ αὐτὸς
συνεμοὶ πρὸς τὸν ὅσιον, ἔφην αὐτὸς ἐγὼ τῷ πατρί· Εὖξαι,
πάτερ, τὸν δεῖνα, ὅπως γένηται μοναχὸς καὶ τῷ Θεῷ
ἀμερίμνως δουλεύσῃ.᾽ Ὁ δὲ ὅσιος Πέτρος λέγει πρόσμε·
Οὗτος, ἀδελφέ, τοποτηρητὴς ἐν τῇ χώρᾳ βούλεται κατα-
στῆναι, καθὼς ὁ συνοδοιπόρος αὐτῷ, καὶ φροντιστὴς ἐπιγείων καὶ οὐ μοναχός.᾽ Ταῦτα ἀκούσας ὁ κοσμικὸς παρὰ
τοῦ πατρός, ἔντρομος γέγονεν καὶ ἠλλοιώθη αὐτοῦ τὸ
πρόσωπον τῇ ἐκστάσει, ὅτι οὕτως φανερὰ γέγονεν διὰ τῆς
ὁράσεως τοῦ πατρὸς τὰ ὑπ᾽ αὐτῶν μεριμνώμενα."

74 Οὐ μόνον δὲ τοῦτο, ἀλλὰ καὶ οἷς τεθαρρήκει πατράσι καὶ ἀδελφοῖς ὁ ἅγιος ἔλεγεν ταπεινοφρονῶν πρὸς
αὐτοὺς ὅτι "πιστεύσατε, ἀδελφοὶ καὶ πατέρες, ἐμοὶ τῷ
ἁμαρτωλῷ καὶ ταπεινῷ Πέτρῳ, ὅτι χάριτι Χριστοῦ τοῦ φι-
λανθρώπου προβλέπω ὑμῶν τὰ πρακτέα καὶ μὴ βουλόμενος, ὡς οὐδὲ ὑμεῖς ἕκαστος ἑαυτὸν συγγινώσκετε. Καὶ
εἰ <μὴ> εἰς μισθὸν ἦν ὑμῖν τὸ ἀκούσιον, τοῖς πᾶσι πάντα
ἐξέλεγον. Ὅταν δέ τινα ὁρῶ ἐν ἀμελείᾳ διάγοντα καὶ
σκληρότητι, τούτῳ φανερῶ, τοῦ Πνεύματος τοῦ ἁγίου
ἐπιτρέποντος." Καὶ οὐ πάντοτε ἐποίει ταῦτα ὁ ὅσιος, οὐδὲ
πᾶσιν ἁπλῶς ἐπέλεγεν. Καὶ τοῦτο δῆλόν ἐστιν, ἀδελφοί,
καταμφότερα, ἀφ᾽ ὧν πολλάκις πολλοῖς τὰ αὐτῶν ἐξεκά-
λυπτεν καὶ ἀπ᾽ αὐτῆς ἐκείνης τῆς θείας δυνάμεως καθέκα-
στον ἀλλοιουμένης. Εἰ γάρ τις ἡμῶν ἐκ τῶν πονηρῶν λογισμῶν καθαριεύων ἐτύγχανεν, ἑώρα τὸν αὐτοῦ χαρακτῆρα
ὁ ὅσιος φωτοειδῆ καὶ ὑπέρλαμπρον, χαριεντῆ καὶ ἡδύτα-
τον· εἰ δὲ πάλιν τίς ἠσχολεῖτο τοῖς ἐναντίοις νοήμασιν,

'My friend, you'd be better off becoming a *topoteretes*, not a monk.' For he had the honor of such a position. Then, when this man also went up with me to the holy one, I said to the father myself, 'Father, pray that so-and-so may become a monk and may serve God without any worries.' But holy Peter said to me, 'My brother, this man wants to be made a *topoteretes* in the region, like his fellow traveler, and take care of worldly things, not to be a monk.' As soon as the layman heard this from the father, he started trembling and his face was contorted with amazement, since what he had been thinking to himself was thus revealed through the father's vision."

74  And this was not all. The saint used to say humbly to those fathers and brothers in whom he confided, "Brothers and fathers, believe me, sinful and humble Peter, that, by the grace of the benevolent Christ, I foresee your actions, even if I do not want to, in a way in which not even each of you himself may be aware. And if my involuntary insight is beneficial to you, I reveal everything to everybody. But whenever I see somebody living carelessly and obdurately, I reveal this to him, with the permission of the Holy Spirit." The holy one did not always do this, nor did he reveal these things indiscriminately to all. Brothers, this is evident from two things: from the way he often revealed things to many people concerning something about them, and from the way that divine power transformed itself in regard to each person. For if one of us was free from evil thoughts, the holy one would see his face luminous and shining brightly, graceful and very pleasant; but if, again, someone was occupied by the opposite ideas, he used to perceive him as dark and

ζοφώδη καὶ ἀκάθαρτον ἔβλεπεν αὐτόν, φοβερώτατόν τε καὶ δυσαχθέστατον, καὶ αὐτὸς δὲ ἐν τρόμῳ ἠτένιζεν εἰς τὴν ὄψιν τοῦ ὁσίου.

75 Τῷ οὖν ἑβδόμῳ ἔτει Θεοφίλου τῆς βασιλείας, ἑξη-κοστῷ δὲ καὶ τρίτῳ χρόνῳ τῆς ἐν σαρκὶ ζωῆς τοῦ τρισμά-καρος, πρὸς τὸ ἐν Ῥύνδακι κοινόβιον αὐτοῦ μετὰ τοῦ ἡσυ-χαστοῦ Ἰακώβου διὰ τὸν ἐπικρατοῦντα διωγμὸν ἐν τοῖς κατὰ τὴν Λυδίαν μέρεσιν ὑποστρέψαντος καὶ ἐν τοῖς τῆς τοῦ Ἁγίου Πορφυρίου μονῆς ἡσυχαστικοῖς αὐτοῦ κελλίοις καταπαύσαντος, ὁ τὴν διακονίαν τότε πεπιστευμένος ἀδελφὸς περὶ τῆς κατασύναξιν αὐτοῦ ἐκκλησιαστικῆς ἀπολείψεως ἀσχάλλων καὶ λυπούμενος, τῷ ὁσίῳ πατρὶ λέ-γει· "Θλίβομαι, πάτερ ἅγιε, ὑπὸ τῶν λογισμῶν, ὅτι οὐ συν-έρχομαι τοῖς ἀδελφοῖς εἰς τὴν ψαλμῳδίαν, προστὴν τῶν κτηνῶν καὶ ἡμιόνων ὑπηρεσίαν ἐνασχολούμενος." Ὁ δὲ μακάριος φησὶν πρὸς αὐτόν· "Πίστευσόν μοι, τέκνον, ὡς οὐδέποτε ἀπέλιπες ἡμῶν τῆς συνάξεως· ὅτε γὰρ τοὺς ἐξέ-θους ἐπιτελῶ ὕμνους μου πρὸς τὸν Θεόν, τοὺς ἐν τῇ δια-κονίᾳ ὑπάρχοντας ἀδελφοὺς καὶ δι' αὐτὴν τῶν συνάξεων ἀπολειπομένους, πάντας ὁρῶ ἑστῶτας κατοφθαλμούς μου καὶ τὴν σύναξιν μεθημῶν ποιοῦντας."

76 Προσῆλθεν τῷ μακαρίῳ τίς κοσμικὸς πτωχός, τοὔ-νομα Ἀμπέλης, ἐκ κώμης καλουμένης Σοφοῦ, ὡσότι ἡ λίμνη ἐπλησίαζεν αὐτοῖς ἡ ἐπιλεγομένη Ἀπολλωνιάς, καὶ ὅτε πλημμύρα τοῦ ὕδατος γένηται ἐξ ἐπιρροίας τοῦ χει-μῶνος, εἰσέρχεται ἐν τοῖς οἴκοις αὐτῶν. Ὅτε δὲ ἐθεάσατο τὸ ὕδωρ ὁ λεχθεὶς Ἀμπέλης φθάσαν ἐν τῷ οἴκῳ αὐτοῦ καὶ ἐπιπλεῖον πληθυνόμενον καὶ αὐξάνον, ἀναστὰς

unclean, frightening and very unpleasant; and that person would also gaze in fear at the holy one's face.

75  In the seventh year of the reign of Theophilos, in the sixty-third year of the life in the flesh of the thrice blessed one, he returned, together with the hesychast Jacob, to the monastery at the Rhyndakos because of the persecution that was prevalent in the region of Lydia. And when they stopped at his hesychastic cells near the monastery of Saint Porphyrios, the brother who had been entrusted with serving them and who was upset and sad because he was missing the church service, said to the holy father, "Saintly father, I'm troubled by my thoughts because I'm not with the brothers when they're singing the psalms since I'm occupied with looking after the animals and the mules." The blessed one said to him, "Believe me, child, you have never missed the service that *I* say; for when I am performing my usual hymns to God, I see all the brothers, who are occupied with their duties and who are thus missing the common prayers, standing in my sight and participating in the service with me."

76  A poor layman, whose name was Ampelis, from the village called Sophos, came to the blessed one, because the lake known as Apollonias was near them and, whenever the water flooded due to the winter rains, it came into their houses. When the previously mentioned Ampelis saw the water reaching his house and rising more and more, he got

σπουδαίως, ἦλθεν πρὸς τὸν θαυματουργὸν πατέρα Πέτρον, καὶ πεσὼν παρὰ τοὺς πόδας αὐτοῦ, ἐδυσώπει αὐτὸν εὔξασθαι διωχθῆναι τὸ ὕδωρ ἐκ τοῦ οἴκου αὐτοῦ. Ὁ δὲ ταπεινόφρων Πέτρος, ποιήσας σταυρὸν ἐκ ξύλου κεδρίνου καὶ τοῦτον δεδωκὼς αὐτῷ, ἔφη· "Ἀπελθὼν στῆσον αὐτὸν ἔμπροσθεν τοῦ ὕδατος καὶ τὸ θέλημα τοῦ Θεοῦ γινέσθω." Καὶ τοῦτο ποιήσας ὁ ἀνήρ, ἀναστὰς τῷ πρωΐ, ἐθεάσατο τὸ ὕδωρ ἀπέχον ἐκ τοῦ οἴκου αὐτοῦ ὡς ἀπόημισυ σημείου, καίπερ τὸ ὕδωρ κατὰ τὴν ἡμέραν ἐκείνην ἐπιπλεῖον ἦν αὐξάνον, καὶ ἐδόξασεν τὸν Θεὸν σὺν παντὶ τῷ οἴκῳ αὐτοῦ τῷ δόντι ἐξουσίαν τοιαύτην τῷ αὐτοῦ θεράποντι Πέτρῳ.

77.1 Τινὶ δὲ νοταρίῳ γνωρίμῳ ὑπάρχοντι τῷ πατρί, ὀνόματι Νικοστράτῳ, πάθος κρυπτὸν κατὰ τὸ ἐντὸς μέρος τοῦ φάρυγγος γενηθέν, ἔμελλεν αὐτὸν ἀποπνίγειν. Εἰς ἰατροὺς δὲ τότε ἐκεῖνος ἐμπείρους καταδραμὼν καὶ παραπάντων ἀπογνωσθείς, ἀναστὰς ἔρχεται πρὸς τὸν ὅσιον, τοῦ φθέγγεσθαι καὶ ἀποπνεῖν μόγις ἰσχύων. Ἐλθὼν δέ, προσπίπτει τῷ ὁσίῳ λέγων· "Ἐλέησόν με, τὸν πολλῶν παρὰ σοῦ δωρεῶν ἀπολαύσαντα, καὶ νῦν ἄφωνον ἐκ τοῦ συνέχοντος ὑπάρχοντα πάθους." Ὁ δὲ ὅσιος τὴν αἴτησιν αὐτοῦ προσδεξάμενος καὶ τῇ χειρὶ αὐτοῦ τὸ πάθος τῷ ζωοποιῷ τύπῳ τοῦ σταυροῦ σφραγισάμενος, οἷά τινι χειρουργίᾳ πνευματικῇ καὶ ἀοράτῳ χρησάμενος, παρευθὺ τὸ ὑγρὸν τοῦ πάθους ἐκένωσεν καὶ ὑγιῆ τὸν ἄνθρωπον ἀπέστειλεν εἰς τὰ ἴδια, αἰνοῦντα καὶ εὐλογοῦντα τὸν Κύριον ἐπὶ τῷ γεγονότι θαύματι παραδόξως εἰς αὐτόν.

77.2 Μεθ' ἡμέρας δέ τινας ὁ αὐτὸς νοτάριος Νικόστρατος ἐπὶ τοῦτον τὸν μέγαν θεράποντα τοῦ Κυρίου δρομαίως

up quickly and came to the wonder-working father, Peter. He fell at his feet, and begged him to pray, so as to send the water away from his house. The most humble Peter made a cross from cedar wood, and gave it to him saying, "Go and set it up in front of the water, and may God's will be done!" The man did this and, when he got up in the morning, he saw the water about half a mile away from his house, even though there was much more water that day. And *he gave glory* with his whole family *to God, who gave such power* to his servant Peter.

77.1 An acquaintance of the saint, a notary called Nikostratos, suffered from a mysterious disease in his pharynx, which threatened to suffocate him. After he had gone to experienced physicians but had been given up by all of them, he got up and came to the holy one, barely able to speak or even breathe. When he arrived, he prostrated himself in front of the holy one and said, "Have mercy on me, who have already received many gifts from you, now that I've lost my voice because of the disease from which I'm suffering." The holy one accepted his plea and made the life-giving sign of the cross with his hand on the affected part. Immediately, as if he had performed some spiritual and invisible surgical operation, he drained the fluid of the disease and sent the man home, healthy, praising and blessing the Lord for the wonder that had miraculously happened to him.

77.2 After a few days, the same notary Nikostratos came running to this great servant of the Lord, and told him,

ἦλθεν ἀπαγγέλλων αὐτῷ ὡσότι "τὶς τῶν προσόντων μοι
εἰς ὑπηρεσίαν οἰκείων τινὰ τῶν πραγμάτων μου συλήσας
ἀπέφυγεν. Ἀλλ᾽ εὖξαι πρὸς Κύριον, ὦ πάτερ, ὅπως ἐγ-
κρατὴς γένηται παρά τινων." Ὁ δὲ μέγας πατὴρ ἡμῶν ἔφη
αὐτῷ· "Μὴ ἀθύμει, ἀδελφέ, ἐν τούτῳ περιλυπούμενος, καὶ
μὴ θυμομάχει ἀλόγως κατὰ τοῦ κλέψαντος, ἀλλ᾽ ἔστω ὁ
θυμός σου κατὰ μόνου τοῦ ὄφεως τοῦ ἀρχεκάκου ἐχθροῦ,
τοῦ τῶν κακῶν σπορέως καὶ συνεργοῦ· δυνάμει γὰρ τοῦ
Κυρίου Ἰησοῦ Χριστοῦ ὁ συλαγωγήσας σε, τέκνον, μετὰ
πέμπτην ἡμέραν παρά τινων ἀνθρώπων δεδεμένος ἐλεύσε-
ται μετὰ καὶ τῶν πραγμάτων ὧν ἐσύλησεν. Ἀλλ᾽ ὅρα,
μηδὲν πονηρὸν κατ᾽ αὐτοῦ ποιήσῃς, μὴ δεσμὸν μὴ μάστι-
γας, μνημονεύων τοῦ λέγοντος *μὴ ἀποδοῦναι κακὸν ἀντὶ
κακοῦ*." Ταύτην οὖν ἐκεῖνος ἀκηκοὼς ἐκ τοῦ πατρὸς τὴν
πρόρρησιν, ἐπορεύθη εἰς τὸν οἶκον αὐτοῦ ἐκτὸς λύπης καὶ
φροντίδος. Μετὰ δὲ πέμπτην ἡμέραν, ὡς ἡ προφητικὴ
ἀνάρρησις τοῦ πατρὸς πεφώνηται, ἦλθόν τινες φέροντες
δέσμιον τὸν κλέπτην σὺν τοῖς κλαπεῖσιν ἀπαραλείπτως.

78 Ἄλλος δέ τις μοναχὸς τοῦ αὐτόθι κοινοβίου, Ζηνό-
βιος προσαγορευόμενος, φαγεδαινικὸν πάθος κατὰ τοῦ
βραχίονος ἀνενέγκας, τὸ πλεῖστον ὡς ἐδόκει μέρος αὐτοῦ
κατανέμεσθαι, τῷ θεοδωρήτῳ τούτῳ ἰατρῷ καὶ μεγάλῳ
πατρὶ προσδραμών, εὐχῇ τὸ τάχος τὴν ἴασιν ἀπεδέξατο.

79 Περὶ Μηνᾶ <καὶ> τῆς τῶν δαιμόνων πρὸς αὐτὸν
σπουδῆς

Οὐ μόνον δὲ ἀλλὰ καί τις ἕτερος φυγὰς τοῦ κόσμου μετα-
νάστης γενόμενος, καὶ πρὸς τοῦτον τὸν τοῦ Θεοῦ παρα-

"One of my people, who serves in my house, has stolen some of my property and run away. Pray to the Lord, father, that he'll be arrested by somebody." But our great father said to him. "My brother, don't despair and be sorry about this, and don't be unreasonably angry with the thief. Just be angry with the serpent, the enemy who is the origin of evil, the sower and accomplice of evil things. For by the power of our Lord Jesus Christ, my child, the man who robbed you will be brought to you as a prisoner in five days' time by some people, together with the things he stole from you. But watch out! Don't do anything bad to him: don't imprison him, don't whip him, and keep in mind the one who said one should *not repay anyone evil for evil*." As soon as he heard the father's prediction, Nikostratos went home relieved from his sorrow and worry. After five days, just as the father's prophetic proclamation had announced, some people came, bringing the thief as a prisoner together with everything that had been stolen.

78 Another monk of the monastery there, who was called Zenobios, had a cancer on his arm which seemed to be spreading to the greater part of it; he rushed to this God-given physician and great father, and through his prayer he was quickly restored to health.

79 On Menas and the demons' fixation on him

Not only this, but another fugitive from the world, who had become a vagrant, came to this man of God and wanted to

γενόμενος ἄνθρωπον, παρ' αὐτῷ ἠθέλησεν ἀποτάξασθαι. Ὅνπερ δεξάμενος περιχαρῶς ὁ πανόσιος, ταῖς θείαις καὶ ψυχωφελέσι διδασκαλίαις ἐνῆγεν καταμικρὸν πρὸς τὴν ἐν ἀσκήσει τοῦ μονήρους βίου τελείωσιν θεοέραστον καὶ ἐργασίαν τῶν θεοποιῶν ὄντως ἐντολῶν χριστομίμητον. Ὁ δὲ μισόκαλος καὶ παμπόνηρος δαίμων ὁ ἀεὶ φθονῶν ἡμῶν τῆς σωτηρίας, οὐ ταῖς τυχούσαις θροήσεσι, νύκτωρ τε καὶ μεθ' ἡμέραν αὐτὸν ἐφόβει καθεύδειν μέλλοντα ἐπὶ τῆς στρωμνῆς, ποτὲ μὲν ὑὸς δίκην τὰ πρὸς τῇ κεφαλῇ αὐτοῦ κείμενα ἀνορύττων, ποτὲ δὲ δρακοντιαῖον σύριγμα ἐπηχῶν, τοῦ πρὸς σωτηρίαν διὰ τούτων οἰόμενος αὐτὸν ἀποπαῦσαι σκοποῦ καὶ εἰς τὸν κόσμον ἐπανελθεῖν. Ἀλλ' ἐψεύσθη τῆς ἐλπίδος ὁ πολυένεδρος. Τοιαῦτα γὰρ καὶ τοσαῦτα ὡς ἔφην κατ' αὐτοῦ σκολιευσαμένου τοῦ δράκοντος, φόβῳ συσχεθεὶς αὐτὸς οὐ μικρῷ, εὐθὺς ἀνέδραμεν πρὸς τὸν ὅσιον πίστει αὐτῷ ἀναθεὶς τὰ συμβάντα. Ὁ δὲ ταῦτα μεμαθηκώς, σφραγίσας αὐτοῦ τὴν κεφαλὴν τῷ ζωοποιῷ τοῦ σταυροῦ τύπῳ λέγει· "Ὁ φοβερὸς ἐν ἰσχύι Χριστὸς Ἰησοῦς ὁ Θεὸς ἡμῶν, ὁ ἄξας δράκοντα ἐν ἀγκίστρῳ θεότητος κατὰ τὸν Ἰώβ, τὸν σκολιευόμενον κατὰ σοῦ τέκνον ὄφιν ἀποσοβήσῃ, τὸν μὴ δὲ καταχοίρων ἐξουσιάζοντα." Καὶ ἅμα σὺν τῷ λόγῳ τοῦ πανοσίου, τῆς πονηρᾶς ἐκείνης ἐνεργείας καὶ θροήσεως ἀπολυτρωθείς, γέγονεν αὐτοῦ μοναχὸς ὡς ἐβούλετο. Ὡς δὲ ἐκείρατο τὴν κόμην τῆς κεφαλῆς αὐτοῦ, πάλιν κατὰ τὸ σύνηθες ἐπίστανται αὐτῷ οἱ παμπόνηροι δαίμονες καθευδήσαντι ἐπὶ τῆς κλίνης αὐτοῦ, καὶ ἔτι ἐγρηγορότος αὐτοῦ, εἰς τὸν ἕνα προετρέπετο ψηλαφᾶν εἰ ὅλως ἀπεκάρθη, καὶ τοῦτο ποιήσας, λέγει τῷ

renounce the world with him. The most holy man happily received him and, with his divine and spiritually edifying teachings, gradually led him to the perfection beloved by God in the struggle of the monastic life, and to the engagement in imitation of Christ with the truly deifying commandments. But the demon, who hates good and is completely evil, who always envies our salvation, used to frighten him, terrorizing him night and day, and, when he was going to sleep in his bed, he would sometimes root up the ground near his head like a hog, or at other times he would hiss like a serpent, thinking that through these actions he would put a stop to Menas's efforts at saving himself and make him return to the world. But that most devious one was mistaken in his hopes. For when the serpent did all the things I have mentioned, according to his crooked plans, the man was seized with great fear and immediately rushed to the holy one, and faithfully reported to him what had happened to him. As soon as he learned these things, Peter sealed the man's head with the life-giving sign of the cross and said, "May our God, Jesus Christ, who is fearsome in his might, who draws out *the serpent* with the *fishhook* of divinity according to Job, scare away the snake that is writhing deviously against you, since he has no power even over pigs." As soon as the all-holy one said this, the man was set free from that evil activity and terrorization and he became a monk, as he wished. But after he had cut the hair of his head, the most wicked demons came to him again as usual when he lay down to sleep on his bed and, while he was still awake, one demon urged the other to touch him in order to see if his head was completely shaven. When it had done this it said

ἑτέρῳ· "ἔχομεν κακὰ ἔτη, τοῦτος ἐκουρεύσατο καὶ ἀπέδρα-
σεν ἡμᾶς." Καὶ ἔκτοτε οὐκέτι ἑώρακεν αὐτούς.

80 Περὶ τῆς τελευταίας νόσου τοῦ ὁσίου

Ἐν αὐτῷ δὲ τῷ χρόνῳ καὶ τόπῳ τῷ πλησίον ὄντι τῆς τοῦ
Ἁγίου Πορφυρίου μονῆς ἐν οἷς ὁ μέγας οὗτος κατησυχίαν
διέτριβεν, νόσῳ συσχεθεὶς βαρυτάτῃ ἔμελλεν ἐκλείπειν ὡς
πᾶσιν ἡμῖν τοῖς παροῦσιν ἐδόκει. Ἀλλ᾽ οὖν ὡς ἄλλου τινὸς
ὁ πατὴρ μεμαλακισμένου καὶ πάσχοντος διακείμενος καὶ
ὡς ἱμάτιον τὴν νόσον ἀπορριψάμενος, πρὸς τὸν ἐν ἁγίοις
πατέρα ἀπῆρεν Ἰωαννίκιον, ἐν τοῖς κατ᾽ Ὀλύμπου τότε
ὄρεσιν ἡσυχάζοντι· τοσαύτη γὰρ ὑπῆρχεν ἐν τοῖς δυσὶ
τούτοις πατράσιν θεοχαρίτως σύμπνοια, ὡς ἕνα ὁρᾶσθαι
τρόπον ἐν ἀμφοτέροις θειότατον, καὶ τοὺς δύο ἕνα ἄνθρωπον νοεῖν θεοσύνδετον καταλλήλων πίστει καὶ πόθῳ καὶ
χάριτι. Τούτου οὖν γεγονότος καὶ ὡς ἑκούσιον φορτίον
τοῦ πατρὸς τὴν νόσον ἀποβαλόντος, ἔκστασις ἐπέπεσεν
ἡμῖν οὐ μικρὰ τοῖς οὖσιν αὐτόθι καὶ θεωμένοις, ὡς λέγειν
"διὰ τῆς πρὸς Θεὸν παρρησίας αὐτοῦ ὁ πατὴρ ἕως θέλῃ
ἐν σαρκὶ περιέσεται, καὶ ὡς ἂν θέλῃ καὶ ὅτε τοῦ βίου ἀπο-
λυθήσεται." Τότε γὰρ ἀνελθὼν καὶ τῆς συνεστίας τοῦ
πατρὸς ὁ μέγας Πέτρος ἀπολαύσας καὶ ὁμιλίας, ἐν εὐκτηρίῳ τοῦ ἁγίου ἱεράρχου Νικολάου ἄνωθεν ὄντι τῆς Βα-
λέου μονῆς, ἐπί τινας ἡμέρας ἐφησυχάζει τοῦ ποθουμένου
πατρὸς ὡς ἐφίλει τὸ καθεκάστην κατατρυφῶν.

to the other, "We're in big trouble, he's cut his hair and escaped us." And he did not see them from then on.

80  On the final illness of the holy one

At that same time and place, near the monastery of Saint Porphyrios, while this great man was living in spiritual tranquility, he fell seriously ill and was near death, as it seemed to all of us who were there. However, our father behaved as if it was someone else who was weakened by illness and suffering. Throwing off his illness as if it were a garment, he left for our saintly father Ioannikios, who was living in spiritual tranquility in the mountains near Olympos at the time. There was such harmony between these two fathers, by the grace of God, that they gave the impression of having one and the same divine behavior, and might be thought to be one and the same person, united by God through their confidence in each other, their mutual love, and their grace. When this happened and our father set aside his illness as if it were a voluntary burden, all of us who were there and witnessed these events were completely astonished, so that we said, "Because of his ability to speak freely with God, the Father will stay in his body as long as he wants, and will be released from life, as and when he wants." Then, after the great Peter had gone up and enjoyed the company and conversation of that father, he stayed for a few days in spiritual tranquility in the chapel of the holy hierarch Nicholas, which was above the monastery of Baleoi, delighting every day in the company of Father Ioannikios, whom he loved so much.

81 Ὅτι δὲ τοιοῦτος ὑπῆρχεν ἀδελφοί, ὁ μέγας οὗτος θαυματουργὸς καὶ πατὴρ ἡμῶν Πέτρος, ἀκούσατέ τινα φοβερὰν ἀγγελίαν τοῦ ὁσίου πατρὸς Ἰωαννικίου μετά τινα χρόνον τῆς τελειώσεως τοῦ πατρὸς πρός με τὸν εὐτελῆ καὶ πανελάχιστον μυστικῶς γεναμένην λέγοντος, ὅτιπερ "ἐν αὐτῇ τῇ ἡμέρᾳ καὶ ὥρᾳ τῶν ἑωθινῶν ὕμνων, ἐνῇ ὁ πατὴρ Πέτρος τετελείωτο τέκνον Σάβα προσευχομένου μου γεγονὼς ἐν ἐκστάσει, εἶδον ὡς ἐν τῷ τοῦ ἱεράρχου Νικολάου ναῷ σὺν τῷ τρισοσίῳ πατρὶ Πέτρῳ παρήμην. Καὶ ἰδού" φησίν "ὄρος περικαλλὲς καὶ τερπνότατον, οὗ ἡ κορυφὴ τὰς οὐρανίους ὑπερῆρεν ἁψίδας. Ὑπὸ πόδας δὲ τούτου ἄμφω ἡμῶν ἱσταμένων καὶ συλλαλούντων, δύο τινὲς ἡμῖν ἄνδρες ἀστραπηφόροι ἄνωθεν ἐπιστάντες, χεῖρα αὐτοῦ κατασχόντες πρὸς ἑκάτερα, σὺν ἐκείνῳ ἀνέβαινον ὅθεν κατῆλθον. Ὅσον δέ μου αὐτὸς τῇ ἀναβάσει διΐστατο, τοσοῦτον λοιπὸν τῇ θείᾳ δόξῃ κατηγλαΐζετο, καὶ ὅσον τοῖς ἐμοῖς σωματικοῖς ὀφθαλμοῖς ἀπεκρύπτετο, μᾶλλον αὐτὸς καὶ μᾶλλον κατελαμπρύνετο. Καὶ τὸ πνεῦμά μου ταχθείη μετὰ τοῦ πνεύματος αὐτοῦ." Ταῦτα, ἀδελφοί, ὡς ἐπὶ Κυρίου, παρὰ τοῦ ἁγίου στόματος τοῦ πατρὸς Ἰωαννικίου ἀκηκοὼς εἰς ὑμῶν ὑπήκοον καὶ ὠφέλειαν γέγραφα.

82 Ἐν ταύταις γὰρ ταῖς ἡμέραις, ἐν τῷ τοῦ ἱεράρχου Νικολάου ναῷ ὡς ἔφην τοῦ ὁσίου οἰκοῦντος, ἡ ἔνθεος καὶ δεδοξασμένη διόρασις τοῦ πατρὸς Ἰωαννικίου ἡ εἰς αὐτὸν ἐγεγόνει αὐτόχρημα ὡς ἐθεάθη, ἐν τῇ ἔκπαλαι προοραθείσῃ τούτῳ ἡμέρᾳ τῆς ἑαυτοῦ πρὸς Χριστὸν ἀναλύσεως δῆλον ὅτι μικρὸν προμαλακισθέντος. Ὅτι δὲ ἐκ πλείστων

81 That this great wonder-worker, our father Peter, was indeed such a man, my brothers, you may learn from a frightful declaration that the holy father Ioannikios secretly made to me, humble and most unworthy as I am, a short time after our father's death. He said, "Sabas, my child, on the very day our father Peter died, at the time of morning hymns while I was praying, I fell into a trance, and I saw that I was in the church of the hierarch Nicholas together with the thrice-holy father Peter. Lo and behold," he said, "there was a very beautiful and most delightful mountain there, the peak of which reached above the vaults of heaven. We were standing at its foot and talking to each other when two men, flashing like lightning, appeared above us; each of them took Peter by the hand and started going up with him to where they had come down. The further he went from me in his ascent, the more resplendent he became with the divine glory, and the more he vanished from my corporeal eyes, the more splendid he grew. May my spirit be with his spirit." As the Lord is my witness, my brothers, these are the things I heard from the saintly mouth of our father Ioannikios and I wrote them down for you to hear and profit from them.

82 For in the days during which the holy man was living in the church of the hierarch Nicholas, as I mentioned, Father Ioannikios's divine and glorious vision concerning him was fulfilled, exactly as it had appeared to him, on the day of his departure to Christ that had been foreseen by him, that is to say when he had been weakened by illness a short time

THE LIFE OF SAINT PETER OF ATROA

χρόνων ἦν τῷ πατρὶ Πέτρῳ ἐγνωσμένη ἡ ἡμέρα τῆς τελευ-
τῆς αὐτοῦ, τοῦτο πᾶσιν ἡμῖν τοῖς εὖ εἰδόσιν οὐκ ἄδηλον,
καὶ τοῖς νοῦν ἔχουσι λογικὸν οὐκ ἀβέβαιον. Κατὰ μίαν
γὰρ ὡς εἰπεῖν ἀδελφοὶ τοῦ ὅλου ἔτους περίοδον πανεόρτιον ὄντως καὶ πάνδημον ὁ πατὴρ ἦγε ταύτην ἡμέραν
τοῖς παροῦσι δαιτυμόσιν αὐτόχειρ καὶ φαιδρὸς διάκονος
ἐνορώμενος, καὶ τοῦτο οὐκ ἂν ἐνδοιάσειέν τις τῶν εὖ φρο-
νούντων τῶν παραυτοῦ τελεσθεισῶν θεοσημειῶν προμυη-
θεὶς τὰ ἀπόρρητα.

83  Τότε γὰρ τότε ἡ προοραθεῖσα αὐτῷ ἐπιστᾶσα ἡμέρα,
ἐνῇ ἡ τοῦ Κυρίου ἡμῶν Ἰησοῦ Χριστοῦ καὶ Θεοῦ τελεῖται
περιτομὴ τῆς σαρκὸς καὶ τοῦ ἱεράρχου κοίμησις Βασιλείου
τῶν παραυτῷ ἀδελφῶν τῆς ἑορτῆς τὸν κανόνα τελούντων
καὶ ἀπὸ τούτοις ἐν κλίνῃ κεκλιμένος συνεμελῴδει. Εἶτα
τοῦ τέλους ὡς ᾔσθετο προσεγγίσαντος, τοῖς ἐκεῖσε ὑμνοῦ-
σιν ἀδελφοῖς προσεφώνησεν. Τῶν δὲ τὸ τάχος κύκλῳ τῆς
στρωμνῆς περιστάντων τοῦ μακαρίου, ποτνιωμένων, λυ-
πουμένων, καὶ δακρυόντων, ἀνοίξας τὸ στόμα, ἤρξατο
αὐτοὺς νουθετεῖν ὁ πνευματοκίνητος καὶ λέγειν· "Τεκνία,
ὁ καιρὸς τῆς ἐμῆς ἤδη ἐφέστηκεν ἀναλύσεως, καὶ ἡ ὥρα
πάρεστι τῷ δεδωκότι Θεῷ ἀποδοῦναι τὴν παραθήκην.
Νῦν οὖν ἀκούσατέ μου τοὺς λόγους, καὶ ἐνωτίσασθέ μου
συμβουλὴν καὶ τοῦ δρόμου μηδ' ὅλως τοῦ πνευματικοῦ
ἀποπαύσησθε, ἵνα τῶν στεφάνων τῶν οὐρανίων καταπο-
λαύσητε. Ἐὰν γὰρ καὶ ἀθλῇ τίς, οὐ στεφανοῦται, ἐὰν μὴ
νομίμως ἀθλήσῃ' προεκπεφώνηται. Ἀγνεύσατε σώματι ἀπὸ
τοῦ τῶν παθῶν μιασμοῦ διϊστάμενοι, ὅπως μετὰ ἀγγέλων
ἁγίων ἀξίως κατασκηνώσητε· οἱ γὰρ τῶν γηΐνων ἄκρως τε

before; because it is clear to all of us who have a good grasp and it is quite certain to those who have a rational mind, that the day of his death was known to Father Peter for a long time. For, so as to tell you my brothers, on only one day in the whole year did the father hold a truly great and popular festival, and on that day would be seen happily serving those who were present with his own hands. No well-disposed person who had been previously initiated into the mysteries of the divine miracles performed by him would doubt this.

83 For then indeed the day foreseen by him arrived; it was the day on which the circumcision in the flesh of our Lord Jesus Christ and God is celebrated and the dormition of the hierarch Basil. Despite being bedridden, when the brothers who were with him performed the canon of the feast, he sang along with them. Then, when he felt the end approaching, he called the brothers who were singing there. After they had quickly formed a circle around the blessed one's bed, full of sorrow, grief, and tears, that man who was moved by the Spirit, opened his mouth and started to admonish them, saying, "My children, *the day of my departure has come already* and the time for giving back the deposit that was entrusted to me by God is here. Listen to my words now, heed my advice, and never cease walking the road of the Spirit, so that you may enjoy the celestial crown. For, *'If someone competes, he is not crowned unless he competes according to the rules,'* as has already been said. Keep your bodies pure by distancing yourselves from the pollution of the passions, so that you may dwell worthily with the holy angels;

καὶ ἀπροσπαθῶς ἐξαπτόμενοι, ὡς τῇ ἐλπίδι τῶν θείων ἀναπτερούμενοι, ναοποιοῦνται τῷ Πνεύματι, τῆς στάσεως ἐκείνης τῶν δεξιῶν ἀξιούμενοι. Μισήσατε πᾶσαν ἡδονὴν βίου, καὶ γαστρὸς κόρον ἐξουθενήσατε, ἵνα τῆς θείας καὶ ὄντως ἡδονῆς τῶν νοερῶν ἐπιτύχητε· οὐδὲν γὰρ τοῦ Χριστοῦ κάλλους καὶ τῶν ἀγαθῶν ἐκείνων ἡδονικώτερον, ἅπερ καὶ ἀϊδίως καταπολαύουσιν οἱ τούτων ἐνθέως καταφρονήσαντες. Τὴν πίστιν ὑμῶν ἀκράδαντον συντηρήσατε, μὴ δόντες ἑαυτοῖς τοῖς ἐχθροῖς δαίμοσιν εἰς ἐπίχαρμα· ἐν οὐδενὶ γὰρ οὕτως ὁ ἐχθρὸς ἡμῶν διάβολος ἐνευφραίνεται, ὡς ἐπὶ τῇ τῆς πίστεως ἡμῶν παρεκτροπῇ τὲ καὶ ἀποπτώσει. Τοῖς τὴν Χριστοῦ εἰκόνα δυσφημοῦσιν αἱρετικοῖς καὶ πᾶσι μηδὲ 'χαίρειν' λέγετε. Τὸ δὲ τούτοις συνδιαιτᾶσθαι περιττόν μοι καὶ λέγειν· ὁ γὰρ τοῖς τοῦ βασιλέως φιλιάζων ἐχθροῖς πολλῶν γίνεται τιμωριῶν ὡς ἴστε παρὰ τοῦ βασιλέως μέτοχος. Τῇ ἐλπίδι τῶν ἀποκειμένων ἀγαθῶν βεβαιούμενοι, τὸν ὑπὲρ Χριστοῦ διωγμὸν ἐν χαρᾷ καταδέξασθε, πᾶσάν τε κάκωσιν καὶ θλίψιν δι' αὐτὸν ὑπομείνατε, ἵνα καὶ ὑμεῖς ὦ τέκνα θεομακάριστοι γενήσεσθε· 'Μακάριοι' γὰρ φησὶν ὁ Κύριος 'οἱ δεδιωγμένοι ἕνεκεν δικαιοσύνης ὅτι αὐτῶν ἐστιν ἡ βασιλεία τῶν οὐρανῶν.' Τῇ τελείᾳ πρὸς Θεὸν καὶ ἑαυτοὺς ἀγάπῃ συνδεδεμένοι, ἰδιοποιείσθω ἕκαστος ὑμῶν τὰ τοῦ πλησίον κατὰ τὸν λέγοντα, 'τίς ἀσθενεῖ καὶ οὐκ ἀσθενῶ; Τίς σκανδαλίζεται, καὶ οὐκ ἐγὼ πυροῦμαι;' Ὁ γὰρ οὕτως ἐν παντὶ εὐσεβεῖ ἀδελφῷ διακείμενος εὐφραίνει Χριστὸν τὸν Θεὸν ἡμῶν, τὸν τῆς αὐτοῦ ἐκκλησίας κεφαλὴν ὄντα καὶ ἀναδεχόμενον τὰ ἡμέτερα. Τῷ Κυρίῳ μετεμὲ ἐσομένῳ πατρὶ εὐλαβῶς πειθαρχήσατε, μηδὲν ὅλως τῶν

for those who only superficially and dispassionately associate themselves with earthly things because they are given wings by the hope of holy things make themselves a temple for the Spirit and are deemed worthy of that position *on the right-hand side.* Hate all life's pleasure and disregard the fullness of the belly in order that you may attain the divine and true pleasure of the intelligible beings, since nothing is more pleasurable than the beauty of Christ and the good things which those who divinely hold the earthly pleasures in contempt enjoy eternally. Keep your faith unshaken, do not surrender yourselves to the hostile demons as an object of malignant joy, for our enemy, the devil, enjoys nothing more than our turning aside and falling away from faith. *Do not say 'welcome'* to those heretics who abuse the image of Christ, or to any others. There is no need for me to say anything about eating with them, for anyone who fraternizes with the king's enemies becomes, as you know, a partner in many punishments from the king. Assured *by the hope of those good things reserved for you,* gladly accept persecution for the sake of Christ, and endure every torture and grief for his sake, in order that you too, my children, may be blessed by God, for the Lord says, *'Blessed are those who are persecuted for righteousness's sake, for theirs is the kingdom of heaven.'* United with each other in *the perfect love* of God and each other, each of you must manage the affairs of your fellows according to the one who says, *'who is weak and I am not weak? Who is made to stumble, and I am not indignant?'* For someone who behaves with all piety toward his brother in this way, pleases *Christ* our God, who is *the head of his church,* and takes upon himself all our affairs. Be piously obedient to the one who will succeed me as your father in the Lord, not neglecting any of his

ἑαυτοῦ ἐντολῶν παραλιπόντες. Ὁποῖος δ' ἂν εἴη τοῦτος, γνωριῶ καὶ ἐπεύξομαι προτοῦ με τῶν ἐνθένδε ἀπολυθῆναι· ὑμῖν γὰρ τοῦτον ψηφίσασθαι ἐπιτρέπεται."

84.1 Ταῦτα παρὰ τοῦ πατρὸς ἀκηκοότες οἱ ἀδελφοί, καὶ ὡς μέλλει ἤδη τοῦ σώματος ἀπανίστασθαι, λύπης καὶ δακρύων πεπληρωμένοι ἄπορον τοῦ πατρὸς ἐκείνην τὴν προτροπὴν ἐγκατέλιπον, τὴν τίς ἄρα μετ' αὐτὸν ποιμαίνειν ἐκείνους προχειρισθήσεται. Ὁ δὲ πατὴρ πάλιν, "παύσατε" φησίν "τέκνα τοῦ περὶ ἐμὲ θρήνου καὶ δότε ὧδέ μοι ἀξίως τὸν κυβερνήσοντα." Οἱ δὲ ἔτι δακρυρροοῦντες καὶ συλλυπούμενοι ἔφησαν· "Ἡμῖν τανῦν μὴ γένοιτο χωρισθῆναί σου πάτερ τῆς γλυκυτάτης θέας ὁμιλίας τε ψυχωφελοῦς καὶ συνδιαίτης, εἰ δὲ οὕτω Θεῷ φίλον ὑπάρχει, μετατεθῆναί σε νυνὶ τῶν τῇδε, τὸν τῆς μονῆς οἰκονόμον καὶ σὸν ἀδελφὸν Παῦλον ἡμῶν ἐγχείρισον τὴν κυβέρνησιν· ὡς σοὶ γὰρ τούτῳ ὑποταγησόμεθα, πάτερ ἅγιε, αὐτὸν ἐν σοὶ καὶ σὲ ἐν αὐτῷ ὁρῶντες καὶ προσβλέποντες." Ταῦτα παρ' αὐτῶν ἀκηκοὼς ὁ πατὴρ φωνήσας ἵστησιν εἰς μέσον τὸν αὐτοῦ ἀδελφὸν Παῦλον καὶ λέγει· "Ἐγὼ μὲν τέκνον τοῦ Κυρίου μου εὐδοκήσαντος, σήμερον τῆς σωματικῆς ταύτης φυλακῆς ὑπεξέρχομαι, καὶ ὡς γῆ πρὸς τὴν γῆν ἐπανέρχομαι. Σὺ δὲ ὡς ἦς ἐν πάσῃ σου τῇ ζωῇ οἰκονομῶν τοῖς ἀδελφοῖς τὰ τοῦ σώματος, καὶ ἀπὸ τοῦ νῦν τὰ κρείττω τούτους οἰκονόμει καὶ τελεώτερα, ποιμαίνων ἐνθέως, ἐνάγων ὁσίως, καὶ εἰς πᾶσαν τρίβον ἁγιωσύνης καθοδηγῶν, τὸ χωλὸν ἀνορθώσων, ἐπιστρέφων τὸ πεπλανημένον, τὸ νοσοῦν ὑγειάζων, διαβαστάζων τὸ ἀσθενές, ἵνα οὕτως βιῶν καὶ οὕτως ποιῶν παρὰ τοῦ ἀρχιποίμενος Χριστοῦ εἰς τὴν

commands. I shall learn who that may be, and I shall pray
for him before I depart from this life, since his election is
left to you."

84.1 When they heard these words from the father and
that he was already about to depart from his body, the brothers, who were filled with grief and tears, left unheeded the
father's admonition concerning who would be chosen to
shepherd them after him. Our father said again, "Stop
mourning me, children, and tell me who is to be your worthy
governor." Still shedding tears and grieving, they said, "Father, may we not be separated from your most sweet sight,
your spiritually helpful speech and communion with you.
But if it pleases God for you to depart from this world now,
entrust our governance to the steward of the monastery,
your brother Paul. We shall subject ourselves to him as we
did to you, saintly father, seeing and considering him in you
and you in him." When he had heard this from them, the father called his brother Paul, stood him in the middle, and
said, "My child, with my Lord's approval, I am today escaping from this mortal prison and, *being earth,* I am returning *to
the earth.* But you who have managed the material affairs of
the brothers your whole life, must from now on manage
what is more important and sublime for them, shepherding
them with divine inspiration, guiding them in a holy way,
leading them in all the ways of holiness, raising up the one
who is lame, bringing back *the one who has gone astray,* curing
the one who is ill, and *supporting the one who is feeble,* so that,
by living like this and acting like this, you may be welcomed
by Christ, the arch-shepherd, into the heavenly city above,

ἄνω δεχθείης πόλιν τὴν νοητὴν Ἰερουσαλήμ, τὴν ἀκατά-
λυτον ζωήν, τὴν οὐράνιον βασιλείαν ὥσπερ τι πολύχουν
καὶ ἱερὸν ἀκροθίνιον."

84.2 Ὁ δὲ ὅσιος Παῦλος, πένθος ἐπὶ πένθει καὶ
κλαυθμὸν ἐπὶ κλαυθμῷ συνάψας, ὠδύρετο, τὸν χωρισμὸν
τοῦ πατρὸς καὶ τὸ ἐπιτεθὲν αὐτῷ βάρος τῆς ποιμαντικῆς
ἀξίας συναισθανόμενος. Ὅθεν καὶ τοῦ πατρὸς Πέτρου τῇ
κλίνῃ τότε προσκυλινδούμενος ἔλεγεν· "Ἀνάξιον ὄντα με
πάτερ ἅγιε καὶ τῆς συνομιλίας τῶν ἀδελφῶν, μὴ συγχω-
ρήσῃς με πιστευθῆναι τῆς ποιμνιαρχίας τοὺς οἴακας· τῶν
ἀξίων γὰρ αἱ ἀξίαι, τοῖς ἁγίοις τὰ ἅγια, τοῖς μεγίστοις τὰ
μέγιστα δικαίως προχειρισθήσεται, οὐ τοῖς κατεμὲ δὲ ἀμυ-
ήτοις καὶ ἐναγέσι τὰ ὁσιώτατα." Ὁ δὲ πατὴρ "ἐπίσχες"
λέγει "μικρὸν ὦ τέκνον τοῦ θρήνου, παῦσαι τὲ τῆς ἀντι-
λογίας τῆς πολυρρημοσύνης τῆς ἀνωφελοῦς, ὁ καιρὸς
γάρ μοι ἐπέστη καὶ κατεπείγει με, ἔχου τὲ τῆς διακονίας
σου τοῦ λοιποῦ, ἥν σοι τὸ Πνεῦμα τὸ Ἅγιον ἐνεχείρισεν,
διὰ τῆς τῶν ἀδελφῶν σήμερον ψήφου καὶ προχειρήσεως."
Ταῦτα οὖν ἀκούσας ὁ πατὴρ Παῦλος ἡσύχασεν, καὶ σιγῆς
γενομένης βαθείας, ἦρεν ὁ πατὴρ πρὸς οὐρανὸν τὰς χεῖρας, καὶ ἤρξατο αὐτοὺς εὐλογεῖν οὕτως λέγων.

85.1 Εὐχή

"Ὁ Θεὸς ὁ μέγας, ὁ φοβερός, ὁ μόνος δυνάστης καὶ
ἀγαθός, ὁ ἐκ τοῦ μὴ ὄντος εἰς τὸ εἶναι τὰ πάντα παραγαγὼν τά τε ὁρατὰ καὶ τὰ ἀόρατα, ὁ τὴν ἡμετέραν
πτωχείαν, διὰ τοῦ μονογενοῦς σου Υἱοῦ καὶ Θεοῦ

the intelligible Jerusalem, the eternal life, the kingdom of heaven, as a prolific and holy perfect exemplar."

84.2 The holy Paul redoubled his mourning and crying, bemoaning the separation from the father and feeling the weight of the shepherd's office which had been placed upon him. So, then, prostrating himself at Father Peter's bed, he said, "Saintly father, I am unworthy even of conversation with the brothers, so do not entrust me with the helm in ruling the flock. Worthy offices are held by those who are worthy of them, *holy things* belong *to those who are holy,* and great things are properly assigned to great men; so the most holy matters should not be assigned to those, like me, who are uninitiated and impure." The father said, "Hold back your mourning for a while, child, stop your objecting, and your useless chattering, for my time has come, and is urgently pressing on me. Hold the office from now on which the Holy Spirit has assigned to you through the vote and choice of the brothers today." When he heard this, Father Paul fell quiet and in a deep silence, Father Peter raised his hands to heaven and started blessing them, saying this:

85.1 His prayer

"Great God, you who are fearsome, the only ruler who is good, who has brought everything, visible and invisible, into being from nothing, who visited us in our poverty through your only begotten Son and God, our

Κυρίου δὲ ἡμῶν Ἰησοῦ Χριστοῦ ἐπισκεψάμενος τοῦ
ἐκ πλάνης ἡμᾶς ἀνακαλέσασθαι τῇ συνεργείᾳ τοῦ
Πνεύματος, ἑνώσας τε τοῖς οὐρανίοις τὰ ἐπίγεια, καὶ
αὖ πάλιν τοῖς ἐπὶ γῆς τὰ οὐράνια, καὶ *μίαν ποίμνην
κατασκευάσας ἀμφότερα,* σοὶ παρατίθημι τὴν περὶ
ἐμὲ ποίμνην διὰ σὲ συνελθοῦσαν ἐκ τῶν περάτων.
Τήρησον αὐτὴν *ἐκ τοῦ πονηροῦ.* Στήριξον ταύτην ἐν
τῇ στερρᾷ σου ὁμολογίᾳ τῆς πίστεως. Κράτυνον αὐτὴν κατεχθρῶν ἀοράτων. Ἐκ πάσης ἐπιβουλῆς δυσ-
μενῶν ἀλώβητον αὐτὴν διαφύλαξον. Οὐ μόνον δὲ
ἀλλὰ καὶ τοῖς αἰτοῦσίν σε πᾶσι δι' ἐμοῦ τοῦ ἀναξίου
σου δούλου Κύριε τὰ ἀγαθὰ αἰτήματα δίδου, ἐν
θλίψεσι προασπίζων, ἐν ἀνάγκαις προϊστάμενος, ἐν
περιστάσει περιφρουρῶν, ὅτι σὺ εἶ *ὁ βασιλεὺς τῆς
εἰρήνης,* καὶ παντὸς ἀγαθοῦ αἴτιος καὶ χορηγὸς ἀνε-
πίφθονος, καὶ σοὶ τὴν τρισάγιον ἀναπέμπομεν δόξαν
σὺν ταῖς ἁγίαις σου πάσαις καὶ ἀσωμάτοις δυνάμεσιν
εἰς τοὺς αἰῶνας, ἀμήν."

85.2  Οὕτως εὐξάμενος ὁ πατήρ, καὶ πάντας ἐπευλογήσας λέγει· "Βάλετε θυμίαμα τέκνα καὶ ἐκτενῶς συνεμοὶ
προσεύξασθε." Εὐχομένων δὲ αὐτῶν φησὶν ὁ πατήρ· "Τέκνα σώζεσθε, ἔρρωσθε ἐν Κυρίῳ ᾧ παρεθέμην ὑμᾶς," καὶ
ἐκτείνας πρὸς οὐρανὸν τὰς χεῖρας παρέδωκεν τὸ πνεῦμα.
Τότε οὖν οἱ ἀδελφοὶ μετὰ κηρῶν καὶ λαμπάδων ὑμνῳδίας
καὶ εὐωδίας, τὸ τίμιον καὶ ἅγιον αὐτοῦ κηδεύσαντες λείψανον ἐν γλωσσοκόμῳ κατέθεντο, καὶ αὐτὸ ἐπὶ τοῦ τόπου
ἄχρι ἐνιαυτοῦ διεφύλαττον, πολλῶν θεοσημειῶν ἐξαυτοῦ
πηγαζόντων διὰ τῆς χάριτος.

Lord Jesus Christ, in order to recall us with the collaboration of the Spirit, uniting the earthly with the heavenly, and again the heavenly with those on earth, creating *one flock* from both, I am entrusting to you the flock which has been gathered around me by you from the ends of the earth. Protect it *from the evil one.* Support it in firm confession of your faith. Fortify it against invisible enemies. Keep it safe from every plot of the adversaries. Not only this, but also grant, Lord, the good requests of all those who request you for anything through me your unworthy servant, shielding them in affliction, protecting them in need, guarding them in adversity, because you are *the king of peace,* the cause of all good things, and the unstinting provider, and to you we offer the thrice-holy glory together with all your saintly and incorporeal powers unto the ages, amen."

85.2 After the father had prayed in this way, he blessed them all and said, "Burn incense, children, and pray fervently with me." While they were praying, the father said to them, "Farewell, children. Be strong in the Lord, to whom I have entrusted you." He raised his hands up to heaven and *relinquished his spirit.* Then the brethren, carrying candles and torches, singing and burning aromatic incense, conducted his funeral; they placed his venerable and saintly remains in a coffin, and kept it in that place for a whole year, and many miracles flowed from it through grace.

86.1 Ἕως ὧδε ὑπάρχει ἀδελφοί, τὰ τῆς ἐν σαρκὶ ζωῆς
τοῦ πατρὸς Πέτρου ἀγωνίσματά τε καὶ θαύματα. Τὰ δὲ
μετὰ ταῦτα ὁποῖα, ἰδίως ἡμῖν τοῖς πιστοῖς καὶ εὐγνώμοσιν
ἐκθησόμεθα, ὅπως γνῶτε τὴν τοῦ Θεοῦ ἐν τῷ πατρὶ ἀφθο-
νόβρυτον δωρεὰν ἐνταῦθά τε καὶ μετέπειτα, ἀμεταμέλητον
ὑπάρχουσαν ἀποστολικῶς, καὶ γνόντες ἀναπέμψητε δόξαν
τῷ τρισαγίῳ καὶ τρισυποστάτῳ Θεῷ ἡμῶν, τῷ Πατρὶ καὶ
τῷ Υἱῷ καὶ τῷ Ἁγίῳ Πνεύματι, νῦν καὶ ἀεὶ καὶ εἰς τοὺς
αἰῶνας τῶν αἰώνων, ἀμήν.

86.2 Ἐπεὶ οὖν λοιπὸν Θεοῦ τοῦ ἀγαθοῦ χάριτι τῶν ἐν τῇ
ζωῇ τοῦ πατρὸς ἡμῶν Πέτρου θαυμάτων τῆς ἐξηγήσεως
τὸ πέρας πτωχολογοῦντες ἐθέμεθα, ἐπὶ τῶν μετὰ τὴν κοίμησιν αὐτοῦ τὸν λόγον οἱ εὐτελεῖς ὡς ὑπεσχόμεθα τρέψω-
μεν τὴν ἐν αὐτῷ δεικνύντες τοῖς πιστοῖς τοῦ Θεοῦ δωρεὰν
ἀνεπίφθονον, τὰ τοιάδε ὅλως καὶ μεταστάντος ἐνεργεῖν
οὐκ ἐλλείπουσαν, τῶν τε Εἰκονομάχων αἱρεσιωτῶν τὰ στό-
ματα ἀποφράττοντες, ἐπιμαρτυροῦντα ἡμῶν τῇ πίστει τὸν
Θεὸν τῇ τῆς θαυματουργικῆς χειρὸς ἐκτάσει ἀποστολικῶς
ἐνσημαίνοντες, καὶ ἐκ τῶν πολλῶν θαυμάτων ὀλίγα τοῖς
ἀγνοοῦσιν ἐγγράφοντες.

87 Τῇ οὖν πρώτῃ τοῦ Ἰαννουαρίου μηνὸς ὡς προγέγραπται τοῦ ὁσίου καὶ θαυματουργοῦ πατρὸς ἡμῶν
Πέτρου τοῦ σώματος ἐκδημήσαντος, καὶ πρὸς τὸν ποθούμενον Κύριον Ἰησοῦν Χριστὸν ἐνδημήσαντος, καὶ αὐτῷ
φιλικῶς πρόσωπον πρὸς πρόσωπον ὁμιλήσαντος τῇ πεντεκαιδεκάτῃ ἰνδικτιῶνι ἡμέρα Δευτέρᾳ τῷ ἑξακισχιλιοστῷ
τριακοσιοστῷ τεσσαρακοστῷ πέμπτῳ ἔτει ἀπὸ τῆς τοῦ

86.1 This is the final point, brothers, of the struggles and miracles of Father Peter's earthly life. What came afterward we are going to expound separately for those of you who are faithful and loyal, so that you may know the gift of God which flowed abundantly in the father, and which is *irrevocable,* to put it apostolically, both here and later, and so that learning it, you may give glory to our thrice-holy and tri-hypostatic God, the Father, the Son and the Holy Spirit, now and forever, amen.

86.2 Since, then, by the grace of the good God we have reached the end of our poorly worded description of our father Peter's miracles when he was alive, I will turn my discourse to those after his dormition as I, wretch that I am, promised; firstly demonstrating to the faithful the abundant gift of God which was in him, which never ceased working such miracles even after his death, miracles which shut the mouths of the Iconoclast heretics and bore witness to our the faith; secondly, drawing attention to God by the extension of Peter's miracle-working hand, to put it apostolically; and thirdly, writing down a few of his many miracles for those who are ignorant of them.

87 As has been written above, our holy and wonder-working father Peter departed from his body on the first day of the month of January and went to the Lord Jesus Christ, whom he so loved, and spoke to him *face-to-face* as a friend. This was in the fifteenth indiction, on a Monday, in the year 6345 from the creation of the world; and he was sixty-three

κόσμου συστάσεως ἑξηκοστῷ δὲ καὶ τρίτῳ τῆς πάσης ζωῆς
αὐτοῦ, καὶ ἐν τῷ προλεχθέντι ναῷ τοῦ ἁγίου ἱεράρχου
Νικολάου κατακειμένου, πλήθη αὐτόθι τῶν ἀσθενούντων,
οἶάπερ ἔλαφοι διψῶσαι ἐν ὕδατι τῆς ὑγείας, συνέρρεον, καὶ
συνέτρεχον ὡς τὴν ἔρημον τάχα δείκνυσθαι πόλιν καὶ τὴν
ὄχλων ποτὲ σπανίζουσαν πολυάνθρωπον.

88 Ὅτε καί τινες δύο γυναῖκες χεῖρας καὶ πόδας καὶ
ἅπαν ἐξηρθρωμέναι μέλος φοράδην ἀνακομισθεῖσαι, ἐκ
τῆς ὑπεράνω τοῦ γλωσσοκόμου αὐτοῦ καιομένης κανδήλας ἀλιφεῖσαι τὸ σῶμα τὴν ὑγείαν ἀπολαβοῦσαι, αἳ τρισὶν
ἔτεσιν πρὸς τὴν ἑαυτῶν τε καὶ ἄλλων ἐργασίαν καὶ ὑπηρεσίαν ἀκίνητοι διαμένουσαι αὐτοβαδεῖς ἀπήεσαν εἰς τὰ
ἴδια, Κυρίῳ καὶ τῷ αὐτοῦ θεράποντι εὐχαριστηρίους φωνὰς ἀναπέμπουσαι.

89 Μοναχὸς δέ τις τῆς ὑπὸ τοῦ ἁγίου πατρὸς συστά-
σης μονῆς καὶ τῇ αὐτοῦ πρὸς Θεὸν ἱκεσίᾳ συντηρουμένης
καὶ ὑπὸ Παύλου τοῦ αὐτοῦ ἀδελφοῦ τότε ἰθυνομένης Βαρ-
θολομαῖος καλούμενος καθ᾽ ὅλον τὸ σῶμα φυσηθεὶς καὶ
ἀλγῶν τὸν δεξιὸν αὐτοῦ πόδα οὐκ ἀνεκτῶς, βίᾳ καὶ μόλις
ἀναδραμὼν πρὸς τὸν ὅσιον παρὰ τῶν τῷ ἁγίῳ λειψάνῳ
προσκαθημένων ὁσίων καὶ ἐναρέτων ἀνδρῶν Βαρνάβα
καὶ Φιλοθέου, λουσθεὶς τὸ σῶμα καὶ ἀλειφθεὶς ἐκείνῳ τῷ
ἁγιαστικῷ τῆς λαμπάδος ἐλαίῳ, αὐθημερὸν αὐτοῦ ἐκομί-
σατο τὴν ὑγείαν, αὐτόχειρ διάκονος ὀφθεὶς τοῖς ἀδελφοῖς
καὶ ἀνάλγητος. Αὐτοῦ δὲ εὐχαρίστως διημερεύσας, καὶ
συμμετασχὼν αὐτοῖς τῶν παρατεθέντων βρωμάτων εὐ-
διακρίτως (οὐκ ἦν γὰρ λαβὼν τὴν θεοκρίτως παρ᾽ αὐτῶν
δεδομένην μετὰ τὴν ἀλοιφὴν ἑπταήμερον ἐντολὴν τοῦ μὴ

years old. While he was lying in the previously mentioned church of the saintly hierarch Nicholas, crowds of sick people, like *deer thirsting* for the water of health, flowed and hurried together there, so that the desert practically resembled a city and that once desolate place was now crowded.

88  At that time, two women whose hands, feet, and all their limbs were completely dislocated, were brought there on a litter. After they had anointed their bodies from the lamp that burned above his coffin, their health was restored. These women had remained unable to work and serve themselves or others for three years, but then they returned to their homes walking by themselves and giving shouts of thanks to the Lord and to his servant.

89  There was a monk, called Bartholomaios, from the monastery founded by our father, which is maintained through his supplication to God and was then directed by his brother Paul. The monk, whose whole body had become swollen and who had unbearable pains in his right foot, came up with great difficulty to the holy one, but, when his body had been washed and anointed with that most holy oil from the lamp by those holy and virtuous men, Barnabas and Philotheos, who were looking after the saintly relic, he was restored to health the same day and was seen by the brothers taking care of himself with his own hands, without pain. He spent the whole day there giving thanks and shared the food that was served by them through their good judgment (for since they sympathized with him, they did not apply the rule that had been established by them with divine

παρεκτὸς ἄρτου καὶ ὀσπρίου μεταλαμβάνειν καὶ ὕδατος τὸν χριόμενον, συμπαθησάντων αὐτῷ), νυκτὸς ἤδη κατα- λαβούσης καὶ ἀφυπνῶν, ὁρᾷ τινα ἄνδρα ἐμπληκτικὸν ἐν ὁράματι ἀφειδῶς αὐτὸν τύπτοντα, ὡς οὐκ ἐντολῆς τῆς κατασυνήθειαν φύλακα καὶ ἀνεξαγόρευτον περὶ τὸν βίον ὑπάρχοντα, καὶ τῆς ταχείας αὐτοῦ ἐκ τοῦ σώματος ἐξόδου τὸν χρόνον ἀποκαλύπτοντα· ὃς τότε ἐκ τῶν καθύπνους ἐταστικῶν γενομένων βοῶν αὐτοῦ διυπνήσας τοὺς συν- υπνοῦντας, ὑπ᾽ αὐτῶν δὲ κἀκεῖνος διυπνισθεὶς ἀλγόπληξ ὅλως εὑρέθη καὶ σύντρομος καὶ κῆρυξ τῶν ὁραθέντων πολύθαμβος. Ἀλειφθεὶς δὲ εἶτα μετὰ ταῦτα τὸ σῶμα καὶ τὰς ἐκ τῶν πληγῶν αὐτῷ προσγινομένας ἀλγηδόνας ἐξια- θεὶς ἐπιπεσὼν τῇ τιμίᾳ τοῦ ἁγίου τῶν λειψάνων σορῷ, καὶ εὐξάμενος πρὸς τὴν μονὴν κάτεισιν, τῷ πατρὶ Παύλῳ ἐξαγγείλας τὰ πεπραγμένα, καὶ τὴν ἑαυτοῦ σωματικὴν ὑγείαν καὶ μετὰ μικρὸν ἐκδημίαν τοῖς πᾶσιν ὡς ἀπεκα- λύφθη ἀνακηρύξας. Ὅθεν καὶ μετὰ δεκάτην ἡμέραν ὡς προεώρακεν τελευτᾷ ὑγιωθεὶς τὸ σῶμα ἐν τῷ ἐλαίῳ, τὴν δὲ ψυχὴν ὄντως ἐξαγορεύσει καὶ προσοχῇ καὶ τὸ ὅλον εἰπεῖν, τῇ τοῦ χριστομιμήτου πατρὸς ποιμαντικῇ προνοίᾳ καὶ προσευχῇ ἐλεηθεὶς καταμφότερα.

90 Ὑπό τινος δέ τις δριμυτάτου ῥεύματος τὴν δεξιὰν χεῖρα ἐξηραμμένος, μετὰ ἐννενηκοστὴν ἡμέραν παραγε- νόμενος, ὡς μόνον τοῦ ἁγίου ἐλαίου ἠλείψατο, τὴν κατα- φύσιν ὑγείαν ἀπολαβών, ἐργάτης ὤφθη τῶν συμφερόντων πολύμοχθος καὶ ἄγγελος τῆς θεοχαριτώτου σωτηρίας ἑαυτοῦ μεγαλόφωνος.

judgment that, for a week after the anointment, the person who had been anointed should not eat or drink anything except for bread, pulses, and water). When night had already fallen and he was asleep, Bartholomaios had a dream in which he saw an impressive man beating him mercilessly, because he had not kept the usual rule and he had not made confession concerning his life; the man also revealed the time of his departure from his body, which was near. Bartholomaios woke up those who were sleeping nearby, since he was shouting because of the tortures happening in his sleep, and, when he had been woken up by them, they discovered he was wracked with pain and trembling and he gave them an astonished account of what he had seen. Afterward, when his body had been anointed with oil and the pains of his beating were cured, he fell upon the precious coffin of the saint's relics and, after he had prayed, went back to the monastery. There he told Father Paul what had happened, and announced to everybody that his body had been cured and that he was soon to depart from this life, as had been revealed to him. And so, ten days later, just as he had foreseen, he died, his body cured by the oil, and his soul truly cured by his confession, his attention, and to sum up, having received mercy in both respects through the pastoral care and the prayers of our Christ-imitating father.

90  A man, who had his right hand paralyzed by a very painful flux, arrived there after ninety days and, as soon as he was anointed with the holy oil, was restored to his natural health. He proved himself a hardworking laborer in useful things, as well as a vocal messenger of his salvation by the grace of God.

THE LIFE OF SAINT PETER OF ATROA

91 Ἕτεροι δέ τινες δύο, φθαρτικὸν ἐν ἑαυτοῖς αἰσθόμε-
νοι γενόμενον νόσημα, ὃ "μυῖαν" τινὲς ὀνομάζειν φιλοῦσιν,
ὡς μόνον τὰς φλυκταίνας ἐν τῷ ἐλαίῳ ἐπέχρισαν, παραυτὰ
τῶν ὑμένων ῥαγέντων καὶ τοῦ ἀλγηδότηρος ἐκκενωθέν-
τος ὑγροῦ, τοῦ πάθους καὶ τοῦ ἄλγους ἠλευθερώθησαν.

92 Παιδὸς δέ τινος φαγεδαινικὸν ἔρψαν ἐν τῇ κεφαλῇ
πάθος ὃ πολλοὶ καλοῦσιν "ἀσφάλακα" τὸ περὶ τὴν κεφαλὴν ἅπαν σαρκῶδες πυῶσαν εἰς ἅπαξ κατεδαπάνησεν.
Ὅπερ εἰδὼς ὁ τούτου πατὴρ πλείσταις ἰατρικαῖς πάλαι
ἐπιμελείαις, κατὰ τοῦ πάθους ἀγωνισάμενος ἀνωφελῆ καὶ
ἀνήνυτα, καὶ ὑπὸ τῶν πατρῴων ἔτι σπλάγχνων πολυβού-
λως περινυττόμενος ἀνατρέχει πρὸς τοῦτο λοιπὸν πιστῶς
τὸ ἀδαπάνητον ἰατρεῖον, ταῖς χερσὶν αὐτοῦ ἐπιφερόμενος
ἔλαιον, καὶ σκευάσας λαμπάδα, κἀκεῖσε διανυκτερεύσας
λίαν πρωῒ τοῦ ἐλαίου λαβὼν τὸ ἀπόκαυμα, ἐπορεύθη πρὸς
τὰ οἰκεῖα, ὡς δὲ φθάσας ἤλειψεν ἐκ τούτου εὐελπίστως τὸν
παῖδα, τὸν βιβρώσκοντα εὐθὺς ἑρπηστῆρα νεκρώσας, καὶ
τῷ παιδὶ ἀποδόμενος τὴν ὑγείαν, δόξαν πιστῶς ἀναπέμπει
Κυρίῳ σὺν δάκρυσιν τῷ ἐν πυρὶ δροσίζοντι, καὶ ἐν ὕδατι
φλέγοντι καὶ ἐν ἐλαίου χρίσματι θᾶττον τὰς νόσους ἐξ-
αφανίζοντι.

93 Ταύτης τῆς φήμης πανταχοῦ ἐξηχηθείσης, ἕτερός
τις ἔχων τὸ αὐτὸ πάθος πρὸς αὐτὸ τὸ σφυρὸν καὶ τοῦ
ποδὸς τὸν ἀστράγαλον, ὡς μικροῦ δεῖν ὑπάρχων ἀκίνητος,
καὶ αὐτὸς ὡσαύτως ἔλαιον ἀποστείλας εἰς τὴν τῆς ἁγίας
κανδήλας ἁφὴν μετευχῆς καὶ πίστεως ἀπολαβὼν τὸ κατά-
λειμμα ἀλειψάμενος ὑγιώθη, αὐτοβαδὴς εὐχάριστος τῷ

218

91 Two other men, who felt they had a deadly disease in them, which people like to call the "fly," when they simply rubbed their pustules with the oil, the skin of these was immediately broken, the fluid that was causing the pain drained out, and they were relieved from their suffering and pain.

92 A cancerous tumor, which many people call "blind mole rat," was slowly spreading on the head of a child; as it was filling all the flesh of his head with pus, it was completely destroying it. When he saw this, the boy's father had earlier fought against the disease with many medical treatments, but with no benefit and to no result. So, driven desperately by his paternal love, he rushed with faith to this inexhaustible hospital. He brought oil, prepared a lamp, and spent the night there. Early in the morning he took the remains of the oil that had been burned with him and went home. As soon as he arrived, he confidently anointed the child with this and killed the creeping tumor that was consuming him. After he had restored the boy to health, he gave glory, in faith and with tears, to the Lord who makes dew in fire, fire in water, and illnesses disappear swiftly through anointment with oil.

93 After this news had spread far and wide, another man, who was suffering from the same thing in his heel and ankle and was almost unable to move, similarly sent oil for lighting the holy lamp. He took the remaining oil with him with prayer and faith, and was cured after he anointed himself.

θαυματουργῷ καὶ πατρὶ Πέτρῳ παραγενόμενος, καὶ τῶν αὐτοῦ θείων λειψάνων προσκυνητὴς πολυέραστος.

94 Ἑνὶ οὖν τῶν προσκαθημένων αὐτῷ, καὶ ἀνωτέρω μνημονευθέντων εὐλαβῶν καὶ πανοσίων ἀνδρῶν Βαρνάβα καὶ Φιλοθέου ἐπισυχνῷ ὁ ἅγιος ἐνεφάνιζεν ἀγωνίζεσθαι αὐτὸν προτρεπόμενος. "Τὸ γὰρ τέλος ἐγγίζει σου" φησίν "ὦ τέκνον Φιλόθεε καὶ σπεῦδε ὥσπερ ἱκέτευσας, συνεῖναί μοι, ὡς ἐν τῇ τῆς σαρκὸς ζωῇ καὶ μετὰ τὴν ἐκ τοῦ σώματος ἔξοδον." Ὅθεν μετὰ τὸ τῶν ὀπτασιῶν πέρας, καὶ κατ᾽ αὐτὴν τὴν πρώτην τοῦ ἔτους περίοδον τῆς τοῦ πατρὸς πρὸς Θεὸν μεταβάσεως, μετέστη καὶ οὗτος τῆς σαρκὸς ὁ ἀείμνηστος, τῆς πατρικῆς ἐντολῆς οὐδαμῶς ποτε παραχαράξας τὸ γνώρισμα ἢ ἑαυτῷ ὅλως πιστεύσας, ἀλλ᾽ ὡς Θεῷ τῷ Θεοῦ ὁσίῳ θεράποντι ὑποκείμενος καὶ ταῖς ἐκείνου προσταγαῖς ἀληθῶς εἰπεῖν ζῶν καὶ κινούμενος, ὁ καὶ μεταστὰς σὺν αὐτῷ ἀξίως, ὡς πιστὸς διάκονος διαινιττόμενος· ἦν γὰρ αὐτῷ ἔτι ὢν ἐν σώματι ὡς ἔφην ὁ ἅγιος ὑποσχόμενος, ὡς "εἰ εὑρήσω" φήσας "τέκνον πρὸς τὸν Κύριον παρρησίαν, προσλήψομαί σε ταχέως προσεμαυτόν." Τοιαύτη γάρ ἐστιν ἀδελφοὶ τῶν ἁγίων ἡ δόξα καὶ παρρησία πρὸς Χριστὸν ὃν ἐπόθησαν, ὡς δύνασθαι προστιθέναι καὶ περικόπτειν τῆς ἐπικήρου ζωῆς τὰ μέτρα τοῖς πιστεύουσιν ἀληθῶς ἢ προσπταίουσιν. Οἱ γὰρ ὅλῳ Θεῷ ὅλον τὸ σαρκὸς ὑποτάξαντες, <φρόνημα> καὶ πνεύματι ἐν ταύτῃ πολιτευσάμενοι ὡς ἀπελεύθεροι ὄντες Κυρίου ἡμῖν τοῖς ἐν γῇ θεοπτικῶς ἐμφανίζουσι πρὸς ἀρετὴν ἐπαλείφοντες, πρὸς θυμηδίαν ἐκ πολυτρόπων θλίψεων ἐπανάγοντες, καὶ

In gratitude, he went to the wonder-working father Peter, walking by himself, and became a loving venerator of his divine relics.

94  The saint appeared frequently to one of his two caretakers, who were mentioned above, those pious and most holy men, Barnabas and Philotheos, urging him to continue his ascetic struggles. "Philotheos, my child," he said, "the end of your life is approaching. Strive, then, as you have asked, so that you may be with me after the departure from your body, just as you were during your life in the flesh." After the end of these visions, in the first part of the year after our father's departure to God, that man of blessed memory also departed from his flesh. He never once defiled the spirit of the father's commandments, nor trusted himself at all, but subjected himself to the servant of God as if he were God himself, so that it is true to say, *he lived and moved* according to his orders. Philotheos also hinted that, after his death, he would be worthy to be with Peter as a faithful servant, for when he was still alive and with him, as he used to say, the saint had promised him, "If I may speak freely to the Lord, my child, I will quickly summon you to me." Such, brothers, is the glory and the freedom of the saints to speak with Christ, whom they loved so much, that they are able to increase or cut short the length of the mortal life of those who truly believe or who stumble. For those who subjected all *thought of the flesh* completely to God and conducted themselves according to the Spirit in this life, being *freedmen of the Lord,* appear to us who live on earth through divine visions, urging us to be virtuous, restoring our happiness in the midst of all sorts of afflictions, and leading us through

πρὸς σωτηρίαν ἐκ ψυχολέθρου ζωῆς πρεσβευτικῶς ἀνα-
σώζοντες.

95 Τοῦ οὖν λειψάνου ἔτι τοῦ πανοσίου πατρὸς ἡμῶν
Πέτρου ἐν τῷ προμνημονευθέντι εὐκτηρίῳ τοῦ ἁγίου
ἱεράρχου Νικολάου ὑπάρχοντος, τῆς πρώτης ἐτησίου
αὐτοῦ μνήμης φθασάσης τῆς πρὸς Θεὸν μεταστάσεως, οἱ
κατὰ τὴν μονὴν αὐτοῦ μέλλοντες ἑορτάζειν πνευματικῶς
τε καὶ μεταδοτικῶς ὡς τῇ προσευχῇ ἀεὶ τὴν ἐλεημοσύνην
ζευγνύντες τὰ πρὸς τὴν ἑορτὴν ἡτοίμαζον ἐπιτήδεια. Ἀλλ᾿
ὁ βάσκανος καὶ ἐχθρὸς τῆς ζωῆς ἡμῶν δαίμων ὁ ἀεὶ τοῖς
καλοῖς ἐνεδρεύων, θλίψεως ἀντιχαρᾶς πληρῶσαι καὶ τα-
ραχῆς τοὺς ἑορτάσαντας βουληθείς, τῶν ἀδελφῶν ἐν τῷ
ἀρτοκοπείῳ τοὺς ἄρτους πεπτόντων τῆς τῶν πτωχῶν διαδόσεως, τὴν ὅλην στέγην καταυτῶν ἐπέρριψεν, ὡς δοκεῖν
τοὺς ἔξωθεν κατασυντυχίαν ὑπολειφθέντας τῶν ἀδελφῶν,
ὁμαδὸν τοὺς ἀρτοποιοῦντας τεθνάναι καὶ ἕνα τάφον αὐτοῖς γεγενῆσθαι τὸν οἶκον. Ἀλλ᾿ ἡ τοῖς πιστοῖς μὴ βρα-
δύνουσα χάρις, καὶ ἐγγὺς τοῖς διὰ Κύριον κοπιῶσιν
ὑπάρχουσα, ἀπορρήτως ὑπὲρ ἐλπίδας τοὺς ἐκείνῳ τότε
καταληφθέντας τῷ πτώματι ἀβλαβεῖς τε ἀσπίλους καὶ
ἀσινεῖς τῇ ἀοράτῳ ἐπιστασίᾳ καὶ βοηθείᾳ τοῦ πατρὸς διετήρησεν, καὶ θάμβους μεγίστου μνήμην τοῖς ἐν ταῖς
μετέπειτα γενεαῖς πιστεύουσι καταλέλοιπεν.

96 Οὐ μόνον δέ, ἀλλὰ καὶ αὐτῆς τῆς μνήμης ἤδη τοῦ
πατρὸς τῇ ἐπαύριον ἐπιστάσης, μετὰ τὴν πρὸς Θεὸν
νυκτερινὴν εὐχαριστίαν καὶ αἴνεσιν οἱ ἐν τῇ μονῇ τὴν εἰς
τοὺς δεομένους ὡς ἔφημεν ἱλαρὰν καὶ πρόθυμον μετάδο-
σιν ἐργαζόμενοι, ἐπαυτὰ τὰ πρόθυρα τῆς μονῆς μετὰ τοῦ

their intercession to salvation from the life which destroys our souls.

95 While the relics of our most holy father Peter were still lying in the church of the holy hierarch Nicholas that was mentioned above, the time arrived for the first commemoration of his departure to God. The monks of his monastery who were going to celebrate both spiritually and charitably, because they always combined almsgiving with prayer, were making preparations for the festival. However, the demon, who is jealous and hostile to our life and who always ambushes good men, wanted to fill the celebrants with affliction and turmoil instead of joy, so, when the brothers were baking the bread for distribution to the poor, he threw down the whole roof on top of them. It appeared to those of the brothers who happened to be outside that all those who were making the bread had been killed and that the building had become their common grave. But the grace which never delays in coming to the faithful and is always near those who toil much for the sake of the Lord, mysteriously, against all hope kept those who were caught in that collapse unharmed, undamaged, and unhurt through the father's invisible protection and help, leaving a memory of an extraordinary miracle for the faithful in future generations.

96 Not only that, but, when the day after the feast of our father had already arrived and after they had completed their nocturnal thanksgivings and praises of God, those in the monastery, together with their shepherd Paul, the

ποιμένος αὐτῶν Παύλου τοῦ ἀδελφοῦ τοῦ ἁγίου καὶ οἷά
τις Χριστοῦ μελισσὼν τὸ τῆς ἐλεημοσύνης κηρόπλαστον
μελικήριον, ὁ μὲν προσῄει τῷ πατρὶ ἔνδοθεν σὺν τοῖς ἐπι-
τηδείοις τῆς διαδόσεως, ὁ δὲ ἀπῄει δρόμῳ τὸ ἐλλεῖπον
αὐτῇ κομισόμενος. Ὅτε καὶ συνέβη λείψαντος οἴνου ἕνα
τῶν ἀδελφῶν παρὰ τοῦ πατρὸς πρὸς τοῦτο ἀποσταλέντα,
σὺν δυσὶ κενωθεῖσιν ἀγγείοις ἀναμετρητῶν δύο χωροῦσιν
μὴ εὑρηκέναι αὐτόθι τὸν κελλαρίτην, μικρὸν ἤδη πρὸς
ἄλλην διακονίαν ἐκνεύσαντα τὴν κλεῖδα τοῦ οἴνου ἐπιφε-
ρόμενον. Ἅπερ καὶ θεὶς παρὰ τῇ θύρᾳ ὁ ἀδελφός, ἀνεζήτει
δρομαίως αὐτόν, ἑτέρων τάχα αὐτοῦ κατόπιν τὸ αὐτὸ ἐπι-
ταχυνόντων. Βραδύνοντος δὲ καὶ οὕτως ἐπιπλεῖστον τοῦ
οἰνοφόρου, αὐτὸς ὁ πατὴρ Παῦλος πάρεισιν ἐπισπεύδων
τοῦ οἴνου τὴν ἐπικόμισιν, καὶ εὑρηκὼς κείμενα τὰ τεθέντα
δύο κενὰ ἀγγεῖα παρὰ τῇ θύρᾳ τοῦ οἴνου πεπληρωμένα
τοῖς προλαβοῦσιν αὐτόθι ἀδελφοῖς διὰ τὴν βραδυτῆτα
ἐπέπληξεν, "ἵνα τί" λέγων "τοῦ οἴνου τῶν ἀγγείων μεμε-
στωμένων, τάχιον ταῦτα πρὸς τὴν διάδοσιν οὐκ ἠνέγκατε,
ἀλλ᾽ ἐστήκατε ὧδε μάτην ἀργοῦντες;" Οἱ δὲ διεβεβαι-
οῦντο ἐξομολογούμενοι τῷ πατρὶ ὡς "τοῦ ἀδελφοῦ ταῦτα
κεκενωμένα ἐνέγκαντος, καὶ πρὸς τὴν ἀναζήτησιν πορευθέντος τοῦ κελλαρί<τ>ου, ἡμεῖς ὅλως πάτερ οὐκ ἀπέστη-
μεν ἐκ τῶν τῇδε, καὶ πόθεν ταῦτα πλήρη τοῦ οἴνου ηὑρέθη
ἐξαποροῦμεν." Ταῦτα παρ᾽ αὐτῶν ἀκηκοὼς ὁ πατὴρ θάμβους ὅλος καὶ ἐκπλήξεως γέμων, πρὸς τὴν ἐνεργουμένην
τότε διάδοσιν σὺν τοῖς ἀδελφοῖς ἐγένετο προθυμότερος,
τῷ ἐκ τοῦ μὴ ὄντος εἰς τὸ εἶναι παραδοξοποιῷ Θεῷ τὰ

brother of the saint, engaged in the joyful and eager distribution of alms to those who were begging at the monastery
gate. The waxy honeycomb of their almsgiving was like
some beehive of Christ: one of them would come to the father from inside with what was needed for the almsgiving,
while another would leave at a run, in order to bring what
was lacking for it. So when there happened to be a shortage
of wine, one of the brothers was sent for it by the father
with two empty containers which held two *metretai*. But he
did not find the cellarer there, because he had left a short
while before on another task, taking the key for the wine
with him. After the brother had placed the containers by
the door, he rushed off to look for him, but some others
came soon after him in order to hurry things up. As the man
who was to carry the wine was very late, Father Paul himself
arrived there to expedite the transportation of the wine.
When he found the two empty containers that had been assigned to the brother placed by the door and already filled
with wine, the father told off the two brothers who had arrived earlier for their slowness. "If the containers were full
of wine," he said, "why didn't you bring them more quickly
to the almsgiving, instead of standing around here idly to no
good purpose?" The brothers assured the father, declaring
to him that, "After the brother brought the empty containers and went in search of the cellarer, we never left here,
father, and have no idea how they've now come to be filled
with wine." As soon as he heard them say this, the father
was astonished and filled with amazement and, along with
the brothers, became more eager for the distribution of
alms which was already underway. He gave thanks both to
the wonder-working God, who brought everything from

THE LIFE OF SAINT PETER OF ATROA

πάντα παραγαγόντι ἐξ ἰγμάδος τὲ οἴνου τὰ ἀγγεῖα πληρώσαντι, εὐχαριστῶν καὶ τῷ θαυματουργῷ πατρὶ Πέτρῳ, δι’ οὗ τὰ τοιάδε παρὰ τῆς τοῦ Πνεύματος χάριτος ἐνεργεῖται καὶ εἰς ἀεὶ ἀφθόνως τοῖς πιστεύουσι βλύζει.

97 Μετὰ οὖν τὴν πρώτην τοῦ ὁσίου πατρὸς ἡμῶν Πέτρου ἐτήσιον μνήμην ὀγδόῳ μηνὶ ἐννεακαιδεκάτῃ Αὐγούστου, ἀπὸ τοῦ εὐκτηρίου τοῦ ἁγίου ἐνδόξου καὶ ἱεράρχου Νικολάου σὺν τῷ γλωσσοκόμῳ αὐτὸν ἀναλαβόντες οἱ μοναχοὶ ἅμα τῷ πατρὶ αὐτῶν Παύλῳ μετῳδῆς καὶ λαμπάδων καὶ εὐωδίας κυκλοῦντες αὐτὸ σεραφικῶς ὡς Θεοῦ θρόνον, πρὸς τὴν μονὴν ἀπεκόμισαν, καὶ πρὸς αὐτὸ τὸ ἀγωνιστικὸν αὐτοῦ σπήλαιον, ὃ αὐτὸς ἑαυτῷ λατομήσας θυσίας τε καθαρὰς ἐν αὐτῷ προσενέγκας πολλοῖς ἱδρῶσι καὶ δάκρυσι κατεπίανεν, πρὸς αὐτό τε τὸ βόρειον μέρος τοῦ ἐκεῖσε ἀντρώδους εὐκτηρίου ναοῦ τῆς Παναγίας Θεοτόκου λαξεύσαντες κατατέθηκαν πλακίον αὐτὸ μαρμάρου ἐπικαλύψαντες. Ἀλλ’ ἡ τῆς θείας χάριτος δωρεά τε καὶ δύναμις ὡς οὖσα ἀμεταμέλητος περικαλύμματί τινι ὑλικῷ οὐ διείργεται, ἢ βασκανίᾳ δυσσεβῶν περιτρέπεται. Τότε γὰρ τότε μετὰ τὴν αὐτόθι τοῦ πανοσίου λειψάνου κατάθεσιν, πηγὴ μύρου ἰαματώδης ἐκ τῆς σοροῦ ἀναβλύσασα, ψυχὰς ἅμα τῶν ἐκεῖσε παρόντων καὶ σώματα κατεμύρισεν, πλείστους ἐκ παθῶν καὶ νοσημάτων ῥυσάμενον, καὶ εἰσέτι καὶ νῦν θεοφανῶς, οὐκ ἀεννάως ἀλλὰ κατὰ καιροὺς βλύζει τοὺς προσιόντας ἀπολυτρούμενον.

98 Ἐγένετο γάρ με ἐν μιᾷ αὐτόθι διὰ τὴν τοῦ πανοσίου μνήμην παραγενέσθαι, ὅτε καὶ ἀσπασάμενος τὴν τὸ θεῖον ἐκεῖνο καὶ πανίερον σκῆνος περικαλύπτουσαν πλάκα

nonbeing to being, for filling the containers from a drop of wine, and to our wonder-working father Peter, through whom such things are produced by the grace of the Spirit and always gush out in abundance for the faithful.

97 In the eighth month after the first commemoration of the memory of our holy father, on the nineteenth of August, the monks, together with their father Paul, took him in his coffin from the chapel of the glorious saint and hierarch Nicholas and brought him to the monastery, singing, carrying torches and burning incense, surrounding it like the seraphim around the throne of God. There they brought him to the cave of his struggles, which he himself had quarried out, offering pure sacrifices in it and enriching it through much sweat and tears. After they had chiseled out the north part of the cave chapel of the Most Holy Theotokos, they laid him there, covering the place with a marble slab. But since the gift and power of divine grace are irrevocable, they are neither obstructed by a material covering, nor are they diverted by the jealousy of the impious one. For at the very moment of the deposition of that most holy relic there, a healing spring of myrrh spouted from the coffin, anointing the souls and bodies of those who were present there, relieving many from afflictions and diseases; and it still flows with divine radiance even now, not constantly but periodically, redeeming those who approach it.

98 For on one occasion, when I was there for the commemoration of the all-holy one's memory, I kissed the slab which covered that divine and most holy resting place, but

ἰσχνὴν τέως καὶ ἄνικμον ἐνυπάρχουσαν ὡς ἄλλου Σιλωὰμ
ἐκδέχεσθαι τὴν ἀνάβλυσιν. Ὅθεν κατὰ τὸν ὄρθρον πλήθους παρόντος καὶ τοῦ θαυμαστοῦ αὐτοῦ βίου ἀναγινω-
σκομένου εἰς ἐπήκοον πάντων, τὸ ἰαματῶδες ἐκεῖνο ἔβλυ-
σεν νάμα, οὗ καὶ τὸ πλῆθος τὴν παρουσίαν αἰσθόμενον,
μυρίσαι ἑαυτῶν τὰ πρόσωπα θερμῶς, ἅπαν ἐκεῖσε συνέρρεον καὶ συνέτρεχον. Μεθ' ὧν κἀγὼ ἐφ' ἑνὶ τοῖν ποδοῖν
ἐσχηκὼς τραῦμα, ἀλειψάμενος ὑγιώθην· καὶ λαβών <...>
99 Μοναχοὶ δέ τινες δύο ἐλθόντες, τὸν ἑαυτῶν ἀδελφὸν
ὡς ἐτῶν ὑπάρχοντα δώδεκα, ἐπὶ τῶν ὤμων βαστάζοντες,
χεῖρας καὶ πόδας πρὸς τὰ καταφύσιν πλεονεκτήματα ἀνενέργητον ἔχοντα, γλώσσῃ δὲ μόνῃ καὶ τῇ εἰσροῇ τοῦ ἀε-
ρίου πνεύματος καὶ ἀπορροῇ ὅτι ζῇ γινωσκόμενον πιστῶς
πρὸς τὸν ἅγιον προσιόντες, καὶ πρὸς αὐτὴν αὐτὸν τὴν
ἁγίαν σορὸν ὥσπερ τι σκεῦος ἄχρηστον ἀποθέμενοι τῇ
πρὸς Θεὸν καὶ τὸν ἅγιον δεήσει διενυκτέρευον, καὶ λίαν
πρωῒ τῷ ἁγιαστικῷ ἐλαίῳ, ἀλείψαντες αὐτόν, ἐξ αὐτοῦ τὲ
λαβόντες ἐν ἀγγείῳ, ὡς πληροφορίαν εἰληφότες διὰ τῆς
πίστεως τῆς τοῦ παιδὸς ἐσομένης ὑγείας ἄραντες αὐτὸν
ἀπήεσαν πρὸς τὰ ἴδια. Ὅθεν καὶ ἐπὶ τρεῖς ἡμέρας ἐκ τοῦ
μετὰ χεῖρας αὐτοῖς εἰληφότες ἐλαίου <καὶ> αὐτὸν ἐπαλεί-
ψαντες, ὑγιῆ τοῦτον καὶ ὁλόκληρον ἔσχον, πάντα τὸν
κόσμον ἀποταξάμενον καὶ σὺν αὐτοῖς μοναχικῶς καὶ ἀπε-
ρισπάστως, προσεδρεύσας τῷ Κυρίῳ καὶ εὐχαριστήσας,
ὡς διὰ νόσου σωματικῆς οἰκονομικῶς εἰς τὴν κατὰ ψυχὴν
καὶ σῶμα ὑγείαν διὰ τοῦ ἁγίου πατρὸς Πέτρου παραδόξως
αὐτὸν εἰσελάσαντα.

it was dry, without any moisture on it, like another Siloam waiting for its flow. And so, at the morning service, when there was a crowd there, and his wonderful life was being read in the hearing of all, that healing stream started flowing. Sensing its presence, the whole crowd flowed and ran together there in order to fervently anoint their faces from it. Alongside them, I too anointed a wound I had on one of my feet and was healed, and taking <. . .>

99 Two monks came, carrying on their shoulders their twelve-year-old brother, who had lost all natural function in his hands and his feet; only his tongue, and his inhalation and exhalation of air gave an indication that he was alive. The monks approached the saint with faith and placed the boy near the saint's holy coffin like some useless vessel. After they had passed the whole night there, making their pleas to God and the saint, they anointed the boy with the sanctifying oil early in the morning and then, taking some of it in a small jar, as their faith had given them confidence that the boy was going to be well, they picked him up and went back home. So, after they had continued anointing him for three days with the oil they had brought with them, he was completely cured. The boy renounced the world and, along with his brothers, devoted himself to the Lord as a monk, without distraction. And he gave thanks that miraculously, through the holy father, Peter, he had come to spiritual and physical health as the result of a physical illness.

100 Καὶ ἕτερος δέ τις μοναχός, τῆς κατὰ τὴν Δαγοῦταν μονῆς προσαγορευομένης Ἵππου τὸ αὐτὸ κατὰ νῶτον ἐκβαλὼν πάθος παλαιστιαῖον μονότρητον καὶ πολύϋγρον κατὰ τὸν τράχηλον δὲ τὸ αὐτὸ πλατύτερον καὶ πολύτρητον, πιστῶς ἀνελθὼν πρὸς τὸν ἅγιον ἐπὶ τρεῖς ἡμέρας ἀλειψάμενος τοῦ ἐλαίου, ὑγίανεν τὰ ἀμφότερα τῆς παθούσης αὐτοῦ σαρκὸς δέρεως δίκην πολυτρήτου ἀποπεσούσης.

101 Οὐ μόνον δὲ ἀνθρώποις χρήσιμόν ἐστιν ἀδελφοί, τὸ ὑγιαστικὸν τοῦτο καὶ θεοχαρίτωτον ἔλαιον, ἀλλὰ καὶ κτήνεσιν ὄντως εὐεργετικὸν λίαν ὡς δηλωθήσεται. Μοναχὸς γάρ τις ἔχων ὑφ᾽ ἑαυτὸν μαθητὰς δύο, ὠνησάμενος ἔκ τινος πρὸς ἀροτρίωσιν βοῦν, εἰς τὴν ἑαυτοῦ ἀπῆρεν μονήν. Ὡς δὲ ὁμοῦ τότε κατὰ πάροδον ἤγοντο, πρὸς ἀνάπαυλαν μικρὸν καταλύσαντες, ὁρῶσιν τὸ τοῦ βοὸς κέρας εἰς ἅπαν κατερραγμένον, μόνου κρατοῦντος αὐτὸ καὶ περιισχύοντος τοῦ περιέχοντος δέρματος, ὅπερ ἦν ὁ πωλήσας θυμῷ πολλῷ ὑπερζέσας λίθῳ συντρίψας. Ὅθεν θᾶττον βουλεύονται τῷ ἰδίῳ αὐτὸν ἀποδοῦναι δεσπότῃ. Μεταβουλεύονται δὲ καὶ λέγουσι πρὸς ἑαυτοὺς εὐσυνείδητα· "Μὴ ἀποδώμεθα τὸν βοῦν, ὦ πάτερ, διὰ τὴν τοῦ κέρατος αὐτοῦ συντριβήν, ἀλλ᾽ ἐκ τοῦ πολυθαυμάστου καὶ ῥωστικοῦ ἐλαίου τοῦ ἁγίου πατρὸς Πέτρου ἀλείψωμεν αὐτὸν καὶ παραυτὰ ἐλπίζομεν ἑδρασθήσεται εἰς τὴν κατὰ φύσιν ἐπανῆξαν ὑγείαν εὐχαῖς αὐτοῦ." Ὅθεν τὸ κατεαγὸς καὶ ἀρίζωτον τοῦ βοὸς κέρας ἐκεῖνο ἐν τῷ τοῦ ἁγίου πατρὸς ἐλαίῳ ἀλείψαντες πεπηγὸς εἰς ἅπαξ καὶ στερεὸν καὶ ἀσάλευτον εὗρον ἀεὶ κατὰ τὴν χρείαν δεσμούμενον.

100 Another monk, from the monastery called Hippos at Dagouta, had the same disease on his back. It was the width of a palm, with just one opening and full of pus and he had the same thing on his neck, but broader and full of openings. He went up to the saint filled with faith, and, after he had anointed himself for three days with the oil, both carbuncles were cured, with his diseased flesh falling away like a piece of leather full of holes.

101 This healing oil, full of divine grace, is not only useful for people, brothers, it is also very effective on animals, as I will now demonstrate. For a monk, who had two disciples under his guidance, bought an ox from somebody for plowing, and brought it to his monastery. When they were leading it on the way together and had stopped for a little rest, they noticed that the ox's horn was completely broken and only the skin that enveloped it was holding and supporting it, since the man who sold it had broken it with a stone in a fit of rage. They immediately decided to return it to its master, but then changed their minds, saying to themselves sensibly, "Let's not give back the ox, father, just because its horn is broken, but let's anoint it with the amazing and powerful oil of the holy father Peter and hope that it will be immediately set in its natural place and return to health through his prayers." So, when they anointed the ox's broken and uprooted horn with the holy father's oil, they saw that it was immediately fixed, and they found it strong and dependable, always capable of serving their needs.

102 Γυνὴ δέ τις ἐκ χρόνων πνεῦμα πονηρὸν καὶ ἀκάθαρτον ἔχουσα καὶ δεινῶς ὑπ' αὐτοῦ ἀεὶ βασανιζομένη,
μάλιστα δὲ κατὰ τὸν Αὔγουστον μῆνα, ὅτε ἠγριωμένη ὅλη
καὶ πάρετος περὶ κρημνοὺς καὶ ὄρη ἐπλανᾶτο καὶ βάραθρα
Ὀλυμπιακὰ ὑπὸ τῶν ἐνεργούντων αὐτῇ δαιμόνων, ἄβρω-
τος, ἄποτος ἐλαυνομένη καὶ ἄϋπνος, παραγενομένη Θεοῦ
προνοίᾳ ἄκουσα πρὸς τὸν ἅγιον, ὡς ὑπ' αὐτοῦ τοῦ πολυ-
σπλάγχνου προσκληθεῖσα καὶ ἀχθεῖσα παρὰ τῆς χάριτος
παρὰ τῇ ἁγίᾳ καὶ παθοκτόνῳ σορῷ στερεῶς ἐξετάζεται,
ἐκπίνει τε τὴν ἁγίαν αὐτοῦ κανδήλαν εὐθέως ἐλεγχομένη
καὶ ἁγιάζεται, πᾶσαν τὴν τῶν πονηρῶν δαιμόνων ἐνέργειαν ἐξεμέσασα, καὶ ἐκτότε εἰσαεὶ σωφρονήσασα.

103 Τοῦ δὲ πολλάκις μνημονευθέντος ἀοιδίμου καὶ
πανοσίου ποιμένος Παύλου, ἀδελφοῦ τοῦ ἁγίου πατρὸς
ἡμῶν καὶ θαυματουργοῦ Πέτρου, ἐπὶ χρόνους ἑπτὰ τὸ ἐν
Κυρίῳ ἑαυτοῦ ποιμάναντος ποίμνιον ἐν ὁσιότητι καὶ δικαιο-
σύνῃ, ἀπροσπαθῶς ἅμα καὶ ἀνυστάκτως καὶ δίκην φωστῆ-
ρος ταῖς ἀρεταῖς ἐναστράψαντος, καὶ ὑπὸ τοῦ τηνικαῦτα
εὐσεβοῦς πατριάρχου καὶ θεόφρονος Μεθοδίου, καὶ τοῦ
κατακαιροὺς ἱεράρχου Ἰγνατίου Νικομηδείας, εἰς τὴν τῆς
ἱεραρχικῆς λυχνίας ἀνάβασιν προτραπέντος, οὐκ ἐπεδίδου
ἑαυτὸν ὁ ταπεινόφρων ἐν τούτῳ ὑπ' αὐτῶν βιαζόμενος, τὸ
ὑπὲρ πολλῶν ἀπολογήσασθαι τῷ Θεῷ φοβερὸν ὄντως καὶ
φρικτὸν ἐννοούμενος. Ἐνιστάμενος δὲ ἔτι πρὸς τὸ αὐτὸ ὁ
ὅσιος κραταιότερον, δεσμεῖται δεσμῷ ἐντολῆς παρὰ τοῦ
προλεχθέντος Νικομηδείας, τοῦ παραγενέσθαι αὐτὸν καὶ
ἥξειν πρὸς τὴν χειροτονίαν ἐπὶ τὴν Κωνσταντινούπολιν

102 A woman had an evil and impure spirit for many years and was always being tormented by it, but particularly during the month of August, when she would wander, completely out of control and distraught, around the crags and mountains and chasms of Olympos, due to the demons that possessed her. Driven without food, drink, or sleep, she came to the saint unwillingly, by the providence of God, as if summoned by the merciful one himself and guided by his grace. Near to the holy coffin that destroyed illness she was severely tormented but, when she drank from his holy lamp, she was immediately tested and purified, vomiting all the evil demons' energy, and from then on she always behaved appropriately.

103 Paul, the renowned and most holy brother of our saintly and wonder-working father, Peter, who has been mentioned many times before, shepherded the flock entrusted to him by the Lord for seven years in a *most holy and righteous way,* dispassionately and, at the same time, vigilantly, shining like a star with his virtues. Even when he was encouraged by the pious and godly minded patriarch at the time, Methodios, as well as by Ignatios, the current metropolitan of Nikomedeia, in ascending to the lampstand of the priesthood, that humble man did not yield to them in this, despite being pressured by them, for he thought it truly terrifying and frightening to render to God an account on behalf of many people. When this holy man resisted this more forcefully, he was bound with a spiritual oath by the previously mentioned metropolitan of Nikomedeia to go to him and then move on to Constantinople for his ordination,

καὶ μὴ βουλόμενον. Τοιαύτην οὖν ὁ πατὴρ Παῦλος δεξάμενος ἐπιτίμησιν, ποτνιώμενος καὶ δακρυρροῶν ἀνατρέχει
εὐθὺς πρὸς τὸν ἅγιον, πίπτει τὲ αὐτοῦ παρὰ τῇ σορῷ διὰ
πάσης ἡμέρας καὶ τῆς νυκτὸς ἱλεούμενος· ᾧ δὴ καὶ μικρὸν
ὁ ἅγιος ἀφυπνώσαντί φησιν ἐπιφανεὶς χαριέστατα· "Ὦ
ἀδελφὲ καὶ σύμψυχε Παῦλε, διὰ τί οὕτως σεαυτὸν τῷ πένθει καὶ τῇ λύπῃ καταβαπτίζῃ; Χριστὸς ἤδη ἐπισκοπήν σου
ποιεῖται· μὴ ἄσχαλλε." Διυπνισθεὶς δὲ τότε ὁ πατὴρ Παῦλος καὶ μὴ νοήσας τὸ βάθος τοῦ ἁγίου τῆς ὁμιλίας, εὐδο-
κίαν ὑπέβαλεν εἶναι Θεοῦ τὴν ἐπ᾽ αὐτοῦ θρυλλουμένην
χειροτονίαν, δι᾽ ὃ ἀσπασάμενος τὸ τελευταῖον τὸν ἅγιον
πρὸς τὴν μονὴν αὐτοῦ κάτεισι τὴν ὅρασιν ἐκείνην πᾶσι
τοῦ πατρὸς ἐξηγούμενος. Ταύτῃ δὲ αὐτῷ ἡ πρὸς τὸν ἅγιον
παράκλησις γέγονεν καὶ ἐμφάνεια ἡμέρᾳ τετάρτῃ Αὐγούστου τεσσαρεσκαιδεκάτῃ, καὶ τῇ ἐπαύριον θερμῶς καὶ
λαμπρῶς τὴν κοίμησιν ἐπιτελέσας τῆς θεομήτορος, τῇ
ἑξκαιδεκάτῃ τοῦ μηνὸς ἡμέρᾳ ἕκτῃ πρὸς τὴν ἐπιτροπὴν
ἀπέβλεψεν τοῦ δεσμήσαντος. Τῇ οὖν ἑπτακαιδεκάτῃ τοῦ
Αὐγούστου ἡμέρᾳ ἑβδόμῃ τῆς δὲ ὁδοιπορίας δευτέρᾳ
κατὰ Νίκαιαν φθάσας, ῥίγει σφοδροτάτῳ καὶ πυρετῷ λα-
βροτάτῳ πρὸς ἑσπέραν κατασχεθείς, τῇ ἑβδόμῃ ἡμέρᾳ
ὀγδόῃ τῆς ἀνακλήσεως καὶ δεκάτῃ τῆς ὀπτασίας, εἰκάδι
δὲ καὶ ἕκτῃ Αὐγούστου, "ἡ τῆς τοῦ Κυρίου Ἰησοῦ Χριστοῦ
ἐπισκοπῆς" ἀπόφασις κατέλαβεν αὐτὸν ὡς ἑώρακεν, καὶ
μετέστη τοῦ σώματος ὁ μακάριος Παῦλος. Τότε οἱ συν-
οδεύοντες αὐτῷ μοναχοί, μετὰ ὕμνων καὶ λαμπάδων ἐν
γλωσσοκόμῳ συστείλαντες αὐτόν, πρὸς τὴν μονὴν ἀνεκό-
μισαν, καὶ πρὸς τὸ ἀνατολικὸν μέρος ἔξωθεν τοῦ ναοῦ, τοῦ

even though he did not want to. After Father Paul received this rebuke, full of grief and shedding tears, he immediately hurried to the saint and prostrated himself beside the coffin, imploring him for a whole day and night. As soon as he fell asleep, the saint appeared to him and said very kindly, "Paul, my brother and soul mate, why are you immersed in such sorrow and grief? Christ is taking care of you now; don't worry." Our father Paul woke up and, not realizing the spiritual depth of the saint's speech, assumed that God was favoring his proposed ordination. So, he kissed the saint for the last time and went down to his monastery, describing to everyone this vision of our father. His appeal to the saint and the vision took place on the fourth day of the week, August the fourteenth. The next day he celebrated the feast of the Dormition of the Mother of God, fervently and splendidly, and on the sixteenth of the month, on the sixth day of the week, he set about the assignment of the man who had bound him by oath. On the seventh day of the week, the seventeenth of August, and the second day after starting his journey, he reached Nicaea. There he developed severe tremors and a very high fever in the evening. On the seventh day there, which was the eighth day after he followed the summons and the tenth after his vision, on the twenty-sixth of August, the promised "taking care by Christ our Lord" arrived for him, as he had seen, and the blessed Paul departed from his body. Then the monks who were accompanying him enclosed him in a coffin with hymn singing and torches, and brought him back to the monastery. They buried him outside the eastern part of the church of the holy and

ἁγίου καὶ ἐνδόξου προφήτου Ζαχαρίου κατέθεντο σημεῖα
πολλοῖς καὶ ἰάσεις παθῶν χορηγοῦντα διὰ τοῦ Πνεύματος,
τὸν αὐτοῦ ἀνεψιὸν Ἰάκωβον διάδοχον τῆς μονῆς καταλεί-
ψαντα.

104 Ἀπὸ οὖν τῆς μονῆς τοῦ ἁγίου πατρὸς ἡμῶν Πέτρου, συνέβη μοναχῷ τινι καλουμένῳ Ἀνδρέᾳ, φαγεδαινικὸν ἐκβράσαι πάθος ἐν ἑνὶ τῶν μελῶν αὐτοῦ συνωνυ-
μοῦν καὶ ὁμοιοτροποῦν τῷ γηφάγῳ ἐκείνῳ καὶ ἑρπηστῆρι
ἀσφάλακι. Ὃς καὶ ἀνιὼν χλιαρῶς πρὸς τὸν ἅγιον, καὶ τῇ
τοῦ ἁγίου ἐλαίου ἀλοιφῇ μὴ ἀπαλλαγηθεὶς αὐθημερὸν τοῦ
νοσήματος, πρὸς θεραπείαν ἰατρῶν ἑαυτοῦ τὴν διάνοιαν
ἔτρεψεν, κρείττονα ταύτην κακῶς τῆς τοῦ ἁγίου ὑπολα-
βὼν καὶ ταχινὴν εἰς ἐξίασιν. Δοὺς δὲ αὐτὸν χερσὶν ἰατρῶν,
καὶ τέχναις ὡς ὑπενόησεν, μᾶλλον ηὔξησεν τὸ τραῦμα πυ-
ορροοῦν εἰσέτι καὶ πλατυνόμενον. Ἐπὶ τρία δὲ ἔτη τούτῳ
τῷ πάθει κατατρυχόμενος ὁ ἀδελφὸς ἀνωφελῆ καὶ ἀνήνυτα εἰς ἑαυτὸν ἐλθών, καὶ λογισάμενος τῆς ἀνιάτου
παραμονῆς τοῦ ἕλκους αὐτοῦ τὸν δι' ἀπιστίας γεγονότα
παραλογισμὸν τοῦ πατρὸς αἴτιον εἶναι, ἔρχεται δρόμῳ
πρὸς τὸν τῆς μονῆς πατέρα Ἰάκωβον ἀδελφιδῆν καὶ διάδοχον Παύλου τὴν ἑαυτοῦ θερμῶς θριαμβεύων ἀγνωμο-
σύνην, καὶ δυσωπῶν συνικέτην αὐτὸν γενέσθαι πρὸς τὸν
πατέρα, συγγνωμονῆσαι αὐτῷ ἀφρόνως ἀγνωμονήσαντι,
καὶ ἰάσασθαι αὐτὸν τοῦ πάθους εἰς τέλος ἐξαπορήσαντα.
Εἴξας οὖν τότε ὁ συμπαθέστατος ποιμὴν Ἰάκωβος τῇ
παρακλήσει τοῦ ἀδελφοῦ καὶ εὐξάμενος, ἀλείψας τὲ αὖθις
αὐτὸν τῷ θεολαμπεῖ καὶ ἁγίῳ ἐλαίῳ τὴν ὑγείαν ὁμοῦ καὶ
σωτηρίαν ἀπέδοτο, τὴν πολυχρόνιον αὐτοῦ δι' ἀπιστίαν

glorious prophet Zechariah, and he keeps performing miracles for many people and healings from afflictions through the Spirit; and he left his nephew Jacob as his successor in the monastery.

104 It so happened that a cancerous tumor developed on one of the limbs of a monk called Andrew, from the monastery of our saintly father Peter; this tumor had the same name and a similar character to the blind mole rat which eats and crawls in the earth. He approached the saint with lukewarm faith, and since he was not relieved from that disease on the same day by his anointment with the holy oil, he turned his mind to treatment by physicians, wrongly believing this would be better and faster at healing than that of the saint. He gave himself over to the physicians' hands and arts, as he had decided, but his wound became worse, still suppurating and spreading. After the brother had been afflicted by this disease for three years without benefit and to no result, he came to his senses and realized that it was his distrust of the father due to his faithlessness which was the cause of the persistent refusal of his sore to heal. He thus came running to Jacob, the father of the monastery, who was the nephew and successor of Paul, fervently proclaiming his ingratitude, and begging him to become his fellow suppliant in winning over Father Peter to forgive him for having been so foolishly skeptical of him, and to finally cure his disease, since he was in despair. The most compassionate shepherd Jacob yielded to the brother's plea: he prayed, anointed him once more with that divinely enlightened and holy oil and gave him back his health and his salvation at the same time. Andrew forgot the long affliction he had endured because

κάκωσιν ἐκλαθόμενον, καὶ σὺν τοῖς ἀδελφοῖς προθύμως
τὰ κατὰ τὴν μονὴν ἐργαζόμενον.

105.1 Πολλὰ οὖν καὶ μέγιστα ἐν τοῖς νοσοῦσι πράττων
ὁ ὅσιος πατὴρ ἡμῶν Πέτρος τερατουργήματά τε καὶ θαύματα διὰ τῆς τοῦ ἁγίου αὐτοῦ ἐλαίου ἐπιχρίσεως λέγω, ἢ
πόσεως ἢ ῥαντίσματος, καὶ παῖδάς τινας ἐκ λοιμικοῦ νοσήματος τῆς ἐκβράσεως τὰς κόρας τῶν ὀμμάτων ἀμαυρω-
θέντας ἐπιχρίσει μόνῃ τὸ πρότερον φῶς αὐτοῖς ἐχαρίσατο,
τῶν πρὸς τὰς κόρας αὐτῶν φλυκταίνων γενομένων τὰ ἴχνη
ἐπαφεὶς παραδόξως, πάντων τῶν θεωμένων εἰς ἔκστασιν,
καὶ τοῦ ἐνεργήσαντος Θεοῦ δι' αὐτοῦ εὐχαριστίαν καὶ
αἴνεσιν.

105.2 Καὶ ἕτερον δὲ παιδίον ἐκ τοῦ σύνεγγυς τῆς μονῆς
χωρίου Κακάλου τῇ αὐτῇ συσχεθὲν νόσῳ, καὶ πρὸς αὐτὴν
ἤδη τὴν κόρην τοῦ ἑνὸς τῶν ὀμμάτων ἐκβράσαντος, τοῦ
ἄλλου σώματος αὐτοῦ μετὰ τὴν ὑγείαν ἐφήλου λίαν καθ-
ορωμένου καὶ μέλανος, ἔμεινεν αὐτοῦ περὶ τὴν κόρην τοῦ
ὀφθαλμοῦ, πομφόλυξ μέγας στερεὸς διάλευκος ἐκκρεμά-
μενος. Ἀλλὰ καὶ οὗτος χάριτι Χριστοῦ διὰ πρεσβειῶν τοῦ
ἁγίου πατρὸς τῷ ἐλαίῳ αὐτοῦ ἐπὶ πλείους ἡμέρας ἀλειφό-
μενος ὑγιώθη.

106 Οὐ μόνον δὲ ἀνθρώπους ὁ πολύσπλαγχνος καὶ
θαυματουργὸς πατὴρ ἡμῶν Πέτρος διὰ τῆς τοῦ ἐλαίου
εὐεργετεῖ ἐπιχρίσεως πᾶσαν νόσον ἀποδιώκων, ἀλλὰ καὶ
κτήνη, ὡς ἔφην, τὰ πρὸς ὑπηρεσίαν ἡμῶν πολλάκις λοι-
μώττοντα καὶ φθειρόμενα, σὺν τῶν δεσποζόντων περιεσώ-
σατο. Ἐν γὰρ τοῖς καταλυδίαν μέρεσιν ἄρχοντός τινος
παντοίων κτηνῶν ἀγέλαι κατεργασθεῖσαι ὑπὸ φθονεροῦ

of his lack of faith and continued to perform his monastic duties enthusiastically with the brothers.

105.1  So our holy father Peter worked many great miracles and other wondrous things for those who were ill, I mean through the application, drinking, or sprinkling of his holy oil. When some children lost their sight due to the blistering of their pupils by some pestilential disease, he granted them the light they had known before with a single application of the oil, wondrously leaving traces of the pustules on their pupils, so that all who saw them were amazed and thanked and praised God, who acted through him.

105.2  Another child from the village of Kakalos, near the monastery, was afflicted with the same disease and the pupil of one of his eyes was already blistered. After he was healed, the rest of his pupil was seen to be black with white specks on it, but a great, solid white bubble remained hanging from his eye around the pupil. But even this was cured by the grace of Christ through the intercession of our holy father, after being anointed with his oil for several days.

106  It is not only people that our most merciful and wonderworking father Peter benefits through the application of his holy oil, by chasing away every illness, but, as I have said, he has also often saved our sick and dying domestic animals, together with their owners. In the region of Lydia herds of all sorts of animals belonging to a lord were dying prematurely after being attacked by an envious

τὲ καὶ γόητος, ἀωρίᾳ ἐθανατοῦντο. Ὡς δὲ ᾔσθετο τὴν ἐπι-
βουλὴν ὁ δεσπότης αὐτῶν τοιαύτην εἶναι, ἀποστείλας
πιστῶς καὶ λαβὼν ἐκ τοῦ θαυματοβρύτου τούτου καὶ ἰα-
ματώδους ἐλαίου, ῥαντίζει αὐτοῦ τὸν οἶκον ἅπαντα καὶ τὰ
ποίμνια, θᾶττον ἐκ παντὸς ἀποσοβήσας τὸν ἐπισκήψαντα
ὄλεθρον ἐξαυτῆς, εἰς πλῆθος πάντων ἐπιδόντων καὶ εὐλογίαν ἀένναον.

107 Γυνὴ δέ τις ἐγκυμονοῦσα τῷ ἕκτῳ μηνὶ αὐτῆς
ἐκτροῦται καὶ ἐνίσταται αὐτῇ τὸ ἔμβρυον τῆς ἑαυτῆς
νηδύος, μὴ ἐκτιτρῶσκον ὅλως ἢ προερχόμενον. Ἀλγυνο-
μένης δὲ αὐτῆς τὰ μάλιστα καὶ ἀπογνωσθείσης παρά τε
ἰατρῶν καὶ ἰδιωτῶν, ἀνδρῶν τε καὶ γυναικῶν, καὶ τῷ παιδὶ
συντεθνήξεσθαι πάντων τὴν μητέρα λογιζομένων, τῇ
ὀγδόῃ ἡμέρᾳ τῶν ὀδυνῶν αὐτῆς τῷ ἁγίῳ ἐλαίῳ ἀλειψα-
μένη, ἐζωώθη ἡ μήτηρ νεκροτοκήσασα καὶ ἐσώθη εὐθὺς ἡ
σωτηρίας ἐξαπορήσασα.

108 Τοῦ οὖν θαυματοποιοῦ πατρὸς τὴν ἐνέργειαν τότε
ἡ σωθεῖσα λογισαμένη καὶ ὅτι μεγίστη ἐστὶν ἡ πρὸς Θεὸν
αὐτοῦ πρεσβεία καὶ εὐαπόδεκτος, τοὺς πίστει αὐτῷ προσιόντας μὴ καταισχύνουσα, τούτοις δὲ ἀεὶ τὰς αἰτήσεις
πρὸς τὸ συμφέρον παρέχουσα, ἔχουσα παρ' ἑαυτῇ παιδί-
σκην ἐκ χρόνων χωλάνασαν, ἐνώπιον τῶν συμπαρόντων
τοῦ ἁγίου ἐλαίου αὐτὴν πιστῶς ἀλειφῆναι προστάττει·
ἧστινος καὶ ἀλειψαμένης, αἱ βάσεις αὐτῆς καὶ τὰ σφυρὰ
ἐξισώθησαν καὶ ἀνωρθώθη αὐθημερόν, τῇ δεσποίνῃ λοχῷ
καὶ τοῖς δι' αὐτὴν παροῦσι φίλοις ἀχωλάντως διακονή-
σασα.

sorcerer. As soon as their owner realized that it was due to this sort of plot, he sent somebody and obtained some of this miraculously flowing, healing oil. He sprinkled his whole house and his flocks with it, and thus immediately drove away the destruction that had fallen on them, and everyone offered up an abundance of endless praise.

107 A woman who was six months pregnant miscarried and the fetus became lodged inside her womb, and did not leave it or come out. She was in excruciating pain and both physicians and laymen, men and women, had lost all hope for her and were all expecting the mother to die with her child. But, on the eighth day of her suffering, she was anointed with the holy oil and was revived, after delivering a stillborn child; and she who had lost hope of salvation was saved.

108 The woman who had been saved thought about the power of our wonder-working father and realized that his intercession before God was both very great and well received, and did not disappoint those who faithfully took refuge in him but always fulfilled their request in a beneficial way. Since she had a servant girl who had been lame for years, she ordered her to be anointed in faith with the holy oil in front of those who were present. After she had been anointed, the girl's feet and ankles were brought to the same level and she stood up the same day, serving her mistress, who was in childbed, and her friends who were there for her, with no lameness.

109 Νικήτας δέ τις δρουγγάριος ἐκ Λυδίας ὑπάρχων ἐκ
παιδὸς γνωστὸς τῷ ἁγίῳ, ὁ καὶ παρόντι αὐτῷ ἐν τῇ παρ-
ούσῃ ζωῇ συναμιλληθεὶς ὡς φιλόθεος, οὗ τῆς οἰκίας πολλοὺς νοσοῦντας αὐτὸν θεραπεῦσαι ἀνεγραψάμεθα καὶ
δεκατέσσαρας τότε δαιμονώσας εἰς ἅπαξ καθαρίσαι θεραπαινίδας καὶ ἐκ πολεμίων ἐχθρῶν καὶ κινδύνων αὐτὸν πολλάκις διαφυλάξαι ἀλώβητον, προσταχθεὶς ἐν μιᾷ παρὰ τοῦ
κατακαιροὺς στρατηγοῦντος διά τινα χρείαν προκαθίσαι
ἐν τῇ κατὰ Μαλάγινα Μεσονήσῳ, τὸν φάρυγγα δεινῶς
ῥευματίζεται καὶ ἀγχόνη ἐκ τούτου παραμικρὸν παραδίδο-
ται. Εἰδὼς δὲ οὗτος ὁ ἔνδοξος ἀνὴρ Νικήτας τὴν τοῦ
ἁγίου πατρὸς εἰς ἐξίασιν ταχυτῆτα, ἀναζεύξας ἐκεῖθεν, μόλις κατέλαβεν τὸ ἅγιον λείψανον συμπνιγόμενος, εὐξάμενος δὲ καὶ ἀλειψάμενος ἐκ τοῦ ἐλαίου τὸν φάρυγγα, τὸ
ἐνοχλοῦν αὐτῷ παραυτὰ καὶ ἄγχον θανατηφόρον πύον
ἐξήμεσεν καὶ ἐξέπτυσεν, ὑγιὴς εὐχαρίστως εἰς τὴν αὐτῷ
τεταγμένην τότε ὑποστρέψας διακονίαν.

110 Πρεσβύτερος δέ τις ἐκ χωρίου Τακώμεως, προσαγορευόμενος Σωφρονᾶς, προσφιλῆν ἔχων σχολάριον ἐκ
Κυταγίου ὁρμώμενον, παρέλαβεν αὐτοῦ τὸν ἵππον, παρα-
καλέσαντος ἕως καιροῦ τοῦ διατρέφειν, τοῦ κυρίου ἑαυτοῦ
πρὸς τὴν βασιλεύουσαν πόλιν εἰς τὴν ἑαυτοῦ στρατείαν
πορευθέντος. Ὁ οὖν πρεσβύτερος, ὡς ἔφην, τοῦ φίλου τὸν
ἵππον παραλαβών, ἡμέρας μὲν αὐτὸν τῇ μονῇ ἐνηφίει,
νυκτὸς δὲ ἔνδον εἰσελαύνων, περιεποιεῖτο τὰ μάλιστα.
Μετὰ δὲ τριακοστὴν ἡμέραν ἀπολυθεὶς ἐπὶ νομὴν ὁ ἵππος
κατὰ συνήθειαν, τῶν γνωρίμων αὐτοῦ ἐξενόμησεν τόπων.
Ὁ οὖν πρεσβύτερος τότε πανταχοῦ τὸν ἵππον ἀναζητήσας

109  A *droungarios* from Lydia called Niketas had known
the saint from childhood, and while the saint was still alive,
he had rivaled him in his love of God. We have already recorded how Peter treated many people from his house who
were sick, cleansed fourteen servant girls at the same time
who were possessed by demons, and often kept Niketas safe
from the attacks of his enemies and dangers in war. On one
occasion this man was ordered by the general of the time to
stand guard in the Mesonesos at Malagina for some reason.
There he suffered from a flux in his throat and was almost
choked to death by it. But this illustrious man, Niketas,
knew how quick the saintly father was in curing illness,
so he withdrew from there and barely reached the saint's
tomb because he was suffocating. After he had prayed and
anointed his throat with the oil, he immediately vomited
and spat out the pus that was troubling and choking him,
and threatening to kill him; well again, he thankfully returned to the job that had been given to him.

110  A priest called Sophronas, from the village of Takomis, had a friend who came from Kytagion who was a *scholarios*. He once took care of his friend's horse since he had
asked him to feed it for a while because his lord was going to
the imperial city for his military service. So, as I have said,
when the priest took his friend's horse, he left it alone
during the day, but brought it inside at night and kept it
very safe. After thirty days, however, when the horse was let
out as usual, it went grazing away from its familiar places.
The priest looked for the horse everywhere but, when he

καὶ μὴ τὸ σύνολον εὑρηκώς, ἀλλ' ἐξαπορήσας, ἀνέρχεται εὐθὺς πρὸς τὸν ἅγιον, τὴν θερμὴν αὐτοῦ ὡς ἐν τούτῳ καὶ ἐν παντὶ ἐπιδεῖξαι αὐτὸν πρεσβείαν ἐξιλεούμενος καὶ τὸ ἀπολωλὸς τάχιστα φανερῶσαι. Πληρώσαντος δὲ αὐτοῦ τὴν πρὸς τὸν ἅγιον ἱκεσίαν καὶ ὑποστρέφοντος, ἀπήντησεν αὐτῷ κατὰ τὴν ὁδὸν ὁ ἵππος, οὐχ ὡς πλανώμενος, ἀλλὰ χάριτι τοῦ ἁγίου πατρὸς ὡς παρά τινος ὑποφορβαίας ἀοράτως περιαγόμενος, ὃν καὶ κρατήσας ὁ πρεσβύτερος τότε, μετὰ μεγίστης χαρᾶς εἰς τὰ ἴδια ἦλθεν, καταπληττόμενος τὸ εὐήκοον τοῦ ἁγίου καὶ ταχινὴν προστασίαν καὶ τοῖς πᾶσι τὸ θαῦμα δημοσιεύων.

III Κωνσταντῖνος σχολάριος +ὁπης+, υἱὸς Βενιαμὶν δομεστίκου τοῦ ἐν τῷ τοῦ πατρὸς *Βίῳ* μνημονευθέντος, ὃς ἐκ χειρὸς Ἰσμαηλιτῶν διὰ πρεσβειῶν αὐτοῦ ἐρρύσθη καὶ διεσώθη, διηγήσατο ἡμῖν ὅτι "κατὰ τῶν Οὔννων ἤγουν Βουλγάρων ἐξερχομένων ἡμῶν ἐν τοῖς μέρεσι τῆς Εὐρώπης καὶ τὸν Εὖρον ποταμὸν περώντων μέγιστον ὄντα, συνέβη κἀμὲ τότε περῶντα τοῦ ἵππου ἀποβληθῆναι καὶ πρὸς αὐτὸ ποῦ τοῦ ποταμοῦ τὸ μεσαίτατον ὥσπερ μόλιβδον ἐν τῷ ὕδατι δῦναι, καὶ μνησθέντος μου ὡς ἐν Ἅιδῃ ὑπάρχοντος τοῦ ἁγίου πατρός, ἐπειπόντος τε 'ἅγιε Πέτρε θαυματουργέ, βοήθει,' θᾶττον ἀβλαβὴς ἀνῆλθον ἐκ μυχοῦ κατωτάτου εἰς τὴν τοῦ ὕδατος πρόσοψιν ὡς ὑπὸ νηὸς ὑπὸ τῆς ὑγρᾶς φύσεως βασταζόμενος ἐπὶ μιᾶς ὥρας διάστημα καὶ μὴ τῷ ῥοίζῳ ἐκείνῳ τῶν ὑδάτων συγκατασυρόμενος ῥεύματι, ἕως ἐλθὸν ἀκάτιον καὶ λαβὸν ἐπὶ τὴν γῆν με διεσώσατο."

couldn't find it at all, he didn't know what to do, so he went straight up to the saint and implored him to make fervent intercession with God, in his case as for all others, and quickly reveal the lost horse. When he was returning after he had finished his prayer to the saint, the horse met him on the road, not as though it was wandering about but as if, by the grace of the saintly father, it was being led by an invisible halter. The priest went home very happily, astounded by the saint's willingness to listen and his swift support; and he told everyone about the miracle.

III A *scholarios,* Constantine, the son of Benjamin the do-*mestikos* who was mentioned in the *Life* of the father and who was rescued and saved from the hands of the Ishmael-ites through the saint's intercession, told us that "when we were on campaign against the Huns, that is, the Bulgarians, in the region of Europe and were crossing the river Euros, which was very wide, it happened that I was thrown from my horse while I was crossing and sank like lead into the water where the river was at its deepest. As I was in hell, I thought of the saintly father and said, 'Saintly wonder-worker Peter, help me!' Immediately I came back to the sur-face of the water from the very bottom of the riverbed and, as though I was in a boat, I was held up by that liquid mate-rial for a whole hour without being submerged by the fast-flowing current of those waters, until a small boat came, picked me up, and brought me safely to land."

112 Βαρσανούφιος δέ τις μοναχὸς καὶ ἡγούμενος τῆς
κατὰ τὴν Φρυγίαν ἤτουν Δαγούτας μονῆς, μιᾶς τῶν ἐν
Ὑπνινῷ, ἐπὶ εἴκοσι καὶ τρία ἔτη βήσσων οὐκ ἀνεκτῶς καὶ
σπαρασσόμενος ἰσχυρῶς, εἰς ἑκτικὸν ἐνέπεσεν πυρετὸν
καὶ θανάσιμον. Πολλοῖς οὖν πολλὰ βουλευσάμενος ἰα-
τροῖς καὶ ἰδιώταις εἰς ἴασιν αὐτοῦ ἐνεργήσασίν τε ἐπὶ δέκα
μῆνας ἐν αὐτῷ ἀνωφελῆ καὶ ἀνήνυτα, ἐκ τῆς ἁπάντων βοηθείας ἀπογνωσθείς, ἦλθεν φερόμενος ὁ εὔελπις πρὸς τὸν
ἅγιον ἢ ζῆσαι ἔτι παρακαλῶν, ἢ εἰ εὐάρεστόν ἐστι τῷ Θεῷ,
δι᾿ εὐχῶν αὐτοῦ τῆς ζωῆς ἀπολυθῆναι. Τοῦτο δὲ γενέσθαι
συμβέβηκεν αὐτῷ πρὸ πεντεκαιδεκάτης ἡμέρας τῆς μνήμης τῆς κοιμήσεως τοῦ ἁγίου. Ὃς καὶ διαρκέσας ὅλην
αὐτὴν τὴν πεντεκαιδεκάτην ἡμέραν καταβεβλημένος
αὐτόθι πολυστένακτος, τῆς ἁγίας ἐνδόξου μνήμης τοῦ
θεοφόρου πατρὸς ἡμῶν Πέτρου καταλαβούσης, πολλοῦ
ἐκεῖσε ὄχλου τότε συρρεύσαντος, ἀναστὰς μεταλαμβάνει
πιστῶς ἐνώπιον πάντων τοῦ ἁγίου ἐλαίου καὶ χρίεται, καὶ
εὐθέως τῶν περιεχόντων αὐτῷ νοσημάτων ἀπολυτροῦται,
ἐρρωμένος πρὸς τὴν μονὴν αὐτοῦ ἀπιών, ὡς τοὺς ὁρῶντας
αὐτὸν θαυμάζειν καὶ λέγειν· "Ἐκ νεκρῶν ἦλθε καὶ παρ᾿
ἐλπίδα ἔζησε ὁ ἡγούμενος διὰ τῆς μεγάλης καὶ ἰσχυρᾶς
τοῦ ἁγίου πατρὸς Πέτρου πρὸς τὸν Θεὸν προσευχῆς καὶ
δεήσεως."

113 Ἕτερος μοναχὸς μονῆς τοῦ Στύλου Νικόλαος ὀνομαζόμενος ἐνεργείᾳ δαιμόνων τὸ φῶς αὐτοῦ τῶν ὀμμάτων
ἐζημιώθη, ὡς τῶν μὲν λοβῶν τῶν ὀφθαλμῶν ὅλως ἀβλα-
βῶν ὁρωμένων, τὴν δὲ τοῦ φωτὸς ἔλλαμψιν οὐκ εἰσδεχο-
μένων. Οὐ μόνον δὲ ἀλλὰ καὶ τὰ ἔγκατα αὐτοῦ πολυαλγῶν

112 Barsanouphios, a monk and abbot of the monastery of Dagouta in Phrygia, one of the ones in Hypninon, had an unbearable cough for twenty-three years and, deeply wracked by it, fell into a lingering and fatal fever. On many occasions, over the course of ten months, he consulted many physicians and laymen in search of a cure, but with no benefit and to no result. When he had despaired of help from anywhere, he was carried to the saint, full of good hopes, asking either to live or to be released from life through his prayers, if that was the will of God. This happened to him fifteen days before the commemoration of the dormition of the saint. When the holy and glorious commemoration of our divinely inspired father Peter arrived and a large crowd had come together there, Barsanouphios, who had spent the whole fifteen days lying there in great distress, stood up, drank with faith from the holy oil in front of everyone, and was anointed. He was relieved immediately of the illnesses which had taken hold of him and left for his monastery in good health, so that those who saw him were amazed and said, "The abbot came back from the dead and is alive beyond hope through the great and powerful prayer and supplication to God of our holy father Peter."

113 Another monk, from the monastery of Stylos, named Nicholas, lost the sight in his eyes through the activity of demons, so that, although his eyeballs appeared undamaged, they were unable to receive the illumination of light. Not only that, but also his intestines were causing him great

ἐδυσχέραινεν. Ἐλθὼν δὲ καὶ παραμείνας ἡμέρας δύο περὶ τὸ λείψανον, μεταλαβών τε τοῦ ἁγίου ἐλαίου καὶ ἀλειψάμενος, ὑγίανεν ὁμοῦ τὰ ἔνδοθεν καὶ ἀνέβλεψεν.

114 Καὶ ἡσυχαστὴς μοναχὸς καλούμενος Θεοφύλακτος, καθ᾽ ἑαυτὸν καθεζόμενος καὶ τὴν ἡσυχίαν πνευματικῶς ἀσπαζόμενος, ἀλγῶν τὸ ἧπαρ καὶ βήσσων ἐπὶ ὅλον ἐνιαυτόν, σπάσας τὰ ἔνδον γέγονεν ἄφνω πολύαλγος καὶ καταβαρής. Ὃς καὶ ὑπὸ τῆς τηλικαύτης βίας τῶν συμπεσόντων αὐτῷ ἀσθενειῶν κατεχόμενος, μετὰ μῆνα τοῦ ἐσχάτου νοσήματος τῆς καταβαρήσεως αὐτοῦ ἐλθὼν πρὸς τὸν θερμὸν καὶ ἀδωροδόκητον ἰατρὸν ὅσιον Πέτρον, ἐκπίνει πιστῶς τῆς ἁγίας αὐτοῦ κανδήλας τὸ ἔλαιον καὶ ἀλείφεται καὶ τῶν συνεχόντων εὐθὺς λυτροῦται παθῶν, ἥπατος, βηχός φημι καὶ τῆς δυσιάτου ἢ καὶ ἀνιάτου καταβαρήσεως.

115 Ἀποτακτικὸς δέ τις ἐκ τῆς μονῆς τοῦ πατρός, ἔτι λαϊκὸς πέλων, καὶ αὐτὸς ὀνομαζόμενος Θεοφύλακτος, ἐπὶ μῆνας ἑπτὰ παραλύσει μελῶν κατεχόμενος, ἁμάξῃ βληθεὶς ἀνέρχεται πρὸς τὸ λείψανον, καὶ τοῦ ἁγίου ἐλαίου ἀλειφθείς, ἐξανέστη καὶ ἥλατο καὶ τοῖς ἐν τῇ μονῇ ἀδελφοῖς διηκόνει διὰ παντὸς προθυμότατα, ὅτι τῷ Θεῷ ἡμῶν δόξα εἰς τοὺς αἰῶνας.

pain. But when he came to the saint's relic and remained there for two days, drank the holy oil, and anointed himself with it, his insides were cured and he could see again.

114 A hesychast monk called Theophylaktos was living alone, spiritually embracing tranquility, but his liver was hurting and he had been coughing for a whole year, when his intestines spasmed and suddenly became very painful and herniated. This man, who was affected so badly by the illnesses which had befallen him, came to holy Peter, the fervent and incorruptible physician, one month after his last illness, the hernia. He drank the oil of his holy lamp with faith, anointed himself, and was immediately relieved from those afflictions that had taken hold of him, I mean his liver, his cough, and his difficult or indeed incurable hernia.

115 A hermit from the father's monastery, when he was still a layman, also called Theophylaktos, suffered from paralysis of his limbs for seven months. After being put on a wagon he came up to the relic and, after he was anointed with the holy oil, he stood up and jumped about, most eagerly serving the brothers in the monastery from then on, because glory unto the ages belongs to our God.

# Abbreviations

*BHG³* = François Halkin, *Bibliotheca hagiographica Graeca,* 3rd ed. (Brussels, 1957). See also François Halkin, *Novum auctarium bibliothecae hagiographicae Graecae* (Brussels, 1984)

*ODB* = Alexander P. Kazhdan et al., eds., *Oxford Dictionary of Byzantium,* 3 vols. (New York, NY, 1991)

PG = Jacques-Paul Migne, *Patrologia cursus completus: Series graeca,* 161 vols. (Paris, 1857–1866)

*PmbZ* = Ralph-Johannes Lilie et al., eds., *Prosopographie der mittelbyzantinischen Zeit. Erste Abteilung (641–867),* 6 vols. (Berlin-New York, 2002)

*TIB* 13 = Klaus Belke, *Bithynien und Hellespont* (*Tabula Imperii Byzantini* Band 13, 1–2) (Wien, 2020)

# Note on the Text

*The Life of Saint Peter of Atroa* survives in two manuscripts:

Glasc. = Glascuensis BE 8.x.5; 10th cent.; folios 46r–48v, 85r–95v, 259r–64v

Marc. = Venetus Marcianus graecus Z 583; 10th cent.; folios 58–95

As has already been made clear in the Introduction, the text of the *Life* was first published by Vitalien Laurent in 1956 as volume 29 of the Subsidia hagiographica series, under the title *La vie merveilleuse de saint Pierre d'Atroa (†837)*. Laurent's original text was based on Marc., but after François Halkin, "Un nouveau ménologe grec de janvier dans un manuscrit de Glasgow," *Analecta Bollandiana* 75 (1957): 66–71, realized that the text was also preserved by Glasc., Laurent published a second volume, *La "Vita retractata" et les miracles posthumes de saint Pierre d'Atroa*, Subsidia hagiographica 31 (Brussels, 1958). This contained an edition of those parts of Glasc. that were missing in Marc., at the same time offering a sort of critical apparatus to all the chapters of his previous edition and enumerating the different readings of Glasc.

Laurent was mistaken in seeing Glasc. as a subsequent it-eration by Sabas of his original text (which is represented for Laurent by Marc.), and it is our belief that Glasc. is in many, but not all, ways the version closer to the original. It is

also clear that the discrepancies between Glasc. and Marc. are so great that any attempt to publish a text combining the evidence of both would be futile. Ideally, we believe, the two versions should be edited separately in their entirety and presented in two parallel columns, offering readers the opportunity to judge for themselves the value and importance of each version; see Athanasios Markopoulos, "Notes et remarques sur la *Vie de saint Pierre d'Atroa*," in *Le saint, le moine et le paysan: Mélanges d'histoire byzantine offerts à M. Kaplan,* ed. O. Delouis, S. Métivier, and P. Pagès, Byzantina Sorbonensia 29 (Paris, 2016), 395–405, especially 401. Unfortunately, such an approach is impossible in the context of the present series. The text we present here, then, is the version of Glasc., printed in its complete form for the first time (since Laurent published only the results of a detailed comparison of the two manuscripts), with the parts missing from this manuscript supplied from the relevant sections of Marc. Points at which the source of the text changes are indicated in the Notes to the Translation; the text of passages where Marc. differs significantly from, or adds to, Glasc. are also provided in those notes.

We have not attempted to carry out any drastic intervention in the text. Certain obvious mistakes in both versions have been corrected. Efforts have also been made to reproduce the Byzantine conventions of spelling and accentuation as far as possible. All changes to Laurent's text are recorded in the Notes to the Text. We have kept all the peculiarities of Byzantine orthography in our edition; thus, for example, forms like ὑπουρίαν (chapter 9.1), ἐπιπολὺ (11.1), προπάντων (11.2), κατασυστήματα (13.1), or ἴδον (19.2) are preserved.

# Notes to the Text

1      ῥυσάμενοι Marc.: ῥυσαμένους Glasc.

2.1     <ὁ> *added by* Marc.

        ἀπαιδίαν Marc.: ἀπαιδείαν Glasc.

2.3     κατείδομεν Polemis-Markopoulos: κατίδωμεν Glasc.

3      ἐγχειρίσαντος Polemis-Markopoulos: ἐγχειρήσαντος Glasc.

        ἐξώσειεν Polemis-Markopoulos: ἐξώσοιεν Glasc.

        ἀμηχανήσαντος: ἀμηχανήσαντα Laurent

6.1     προσαρμόττων Polemis-Markopoulos: προσαρμόττον Glasc.

6.2     ἐγχειρίσαι Polemis-Markopoulos: ἐγχειρῆσαι Glasc.

        <ὡς> *added by* Laurent

        ἀρχιεπίσκοπον Marc.: ἐπίσκοπον Glasc.

6.3     ἐπισκόπων Glasc.: *probably* ἐπισκοπῶν Polemis-Markopoulos

6.9     πρὸς ὃν ἀπεστάλησαν: *possibly* <τὸν> πρὸς ὃν ἀπεστάλησαν

10      τὸν ὑποτακτικὸν Marc.: τῶν ὑποτακτικῶν Glasc.

        κενοδοξοῦντι Polemis-Markopoulos: καινοδοξοῦντι Glasc.

        τοῦ σφάλματος αἴτιος Polemis-Markopoulos: τοῦ σφάλματος
          αἴτιον Glasc.

        πρὸς τὸ μὴ Polemis-Markopoulos: πρὸς τῷ μὴ Glasc.

11.1    ἧς ὧδε Polemis-Markopoulos: εἷς ὧδε Glasc.

        ἔασέ Polemis-Markopoulos: ἔασαί Glasc.

12.2    τὸ <. . .> κατὰ Θεοῦ Polemis-Markopoulos: τὸ κατὰ Θεοῦ Lau-
        rent

        <πρὸς> *added by* Polemis-Markopoulos

12.3    σκιὰ<ν> Polemis-Markopoulos: σκιᾷ Glasc.

        <καὶ> *added by* Marc.

        πεσοῦσα <. . .> Polemis-Markopoulos

13.1    περιδεσμούμενοι Marc.: περιδεσμούμενος Glasc.

16.1    πάλιν <...> Polemis-Markopoulos *with certain doubts*

17    ὥρματο Marc.: ὥρμητο Laurent

18    ἐπιλελησμένους Marc.: ἐπιλελησμένοι Laurent

19.1    ὀξυτόμῳ Polemis-Markopoulos: νυτόμῳ Marc; συντόνῳ Laurent

20.1    τὸν παῖδα Marc.: τῷ παιδὶ Laurent

24.1    προσερρισμένος Polemis-Markopoulos: προσερισμένος Marc.; προσερηρεισμένως Laurent

25    εἰσοικίσθησαν Polemis-Markopoulos: εἰσοικείσθησαν Marc.; εἰσῳκίσθησαν Laurent
       εἰς *deleted by* Polemis-Markopoulos
       ἐκείνῳ Marc. *after correction*: ἐκεῖνο Marc. *before correction*, Laurent
       αὐθίωρον Marc.: αὐθωρὸν Laurent

26.3    εἰδότι Marc.: εἰδότα Laurent

26.4    συνεταῖροι Marc.: συνέταιροι Laurent

29    ἀλλ' ἤν Marc.: *possibly* ἀλλ' ἤ
       αὐτῷ ἔφη Marc.: αὐτὸ ἔφη Laurent

30    Ὅμως Marc.: Ὁμῶς Laurent

32    ἐμεσθεῖσαν Polemis-Markopoulos: αἱμεσθεῖσαν Marc., Laurent

33    καθεζομένῳ Laurent: καθεζομένου Marc.

34    μηκόθεν Marc.: μήκοθεν Laurent

35.2    πνέοντι Marc.: πνέοντα Laurent

36    προσδεόμενος διὰ τὸ Marc.: προσδεομένου δι' αὐτὸν Laurent

37    αὐτῶν μεταλαβεῖν Polemis-Markopoulos: αὐτὸν μεταλαβεῖν Glasc.

38    ὑποπτεύετε Polemis-Markopoulos (*compare* Marc. ἐκπομπεύετε): ὑποπτεύεται Glasc.
       ἀσκητὰς Polemis-Markopoulos: ἀσκηταῖς Glasc.
       κανονικοὶ Glasc., Laurent: *possibly* κοινωνικοὶ Polemis-Markopoulos (*compare* Marc. κοινωνοί)

39.1    κενὴν Polemis-Markopoulos: καινὴν Glasc.

39.2    κατελείφθη Polemis-Markopoulos: κατελήφθη Glasc.

41.1    ἐκτεταμένον Polemis-Markopoulos: ἐκτεταμμένον Glasc.

42     χριστοφρόνως Polemis-Markopoulos (*compare* Marc. χριστο-
φόρως): χρηστοφρόνως Glasc.

43     περιιόντας Polemis-Markopoulos: περιόντας Glasc.

46     ἐπὶ <τὴν ψαλμῳδίαν> χωρεῖν Polemis-Markopoulos: ἐπιχωρεῖν
Glasc.

    εἰς τὸ ἀσβεστοποιῆσαι Polemis-Markopoulos: εἰς τῷ ἀσβεστο-
ποιῆσαι Glasc.

47     διὰ τὸ μὴ παρεῖναι Polemis-Markopoulos: διὰ τῷ μὴ παρεῖναι
Glasc.

    συγχωρήσει σοι Polemis-Markopoulos: συγχωρήσει Glasc.

50.1     πορείαν Polemis-Markopoulos: πορίαν Glasc.

    προσήρεισεν Polemis-Markopoulos: προσείρισεν Glasc.

51     καταλαμβάνει . . . ἐφησυχάζει Marc.: καταλαμβάνειν . . . ἐφησυχάζειν Glasc.; *possibly* Ἐκεῖθεν ὁ ὅσιος {ὡς} ἐβούλετο πρὸς
τὴν ἐν Ὀλύμπῳ καταλαμβάνειν μονὴν αὐτοῦ καὶ ἐν τῷ ἀπὸ
σημείου ἑνὸς σπηλαίῳ καὶ εὐκτηρίῳ ἐφησυχάζειν ὡς εἴθιστο
διαπυρός: διαπύρως?

    εἰκὸς Polemis-Markopoulos: εἰκὼς Glasc.

52     πρὸς τὴν <. . .> Laurent

    δυσωπήσωμεν Marc.: δυσωπήσομεν Laurent

54     ὑγιωθεῖν εἶχον Marc.: ὑγιωθῆναι εἶχον Laurent

58     αὔθωρον Polemis-Markopoulos: αὔθορον Marc.; αὔθωρὸν
Laurent

59     αὐτοῖς Marc.: αὐτοὺς Laurent

63     ἐπειλημμένος <αὐτὸς> Polemis-Markopoulos: ἐπιλιμμένος
Marc.; ἐπειλημμένοι Laurent

    αὐτῶν Marc.: αὐτῆς Laurent

64.2     ἐπιβουλεύοντι Marc.: ἐπιβουλεύοντα Laurent

67     προσαιτὶς Polemis-Markopoulos: προσετὴς Marc.; προσαῖτις
Laurent

68     ἑκάστῳ Marc.: ἕκαστον Laurent

70     ἀπαράκλητον Marc.: ἀπαράκλιτον Laurent

    <οὐ> *added by* Polemis-Markopoulos

    αὔθωρον Polemis-Markopoulos: αὔθορον Marc.; αὔθωρὸν
Laurent

74     <μὴ> *added by* Polemis-Markopoulos

82     Ὅτι δὲ ἐκ πλείστων Marc.: Ὅτε δὲ ἐκ πλείστων Glasc.

83     τελούντων Polemis-Markopoulos: τελοῦντα Glasc.

       ἀπὸ τούτοις Glasc.: *possibly* σὺν τούτοις

       κεκλιμένος Polemis-Markopoulos: κεκλημένος Glasc.

       ἑαυτοῖς Glasc.: ἑαυτοὺς Marc.

       οὕτως Polemis-Markopoulos: οὗτος Glasc.

       Τὸ δὲ τούτοις συνδιαιτᾶσθαι Polemis-Markopoulos: Τῷ δὲ τούτοις συνδιαιτᾶσθαι Glasc.

       τοῦτον Marc.: τοῦτο Glasc.

84.1    ἐγκατέλιπον Marc.: ἐγκατέλειπον Glasc.

       ἐγχείρισον Marc.: ἐγχείρησον Glasc.

       τούτῳ Polemis-Markopoulos: οὕτω Glasc.

84.2    ἐνεχείρισεν Marc.: ἐνεχείρησεν Glasc.

86.1    ἐκθησόμεθα Polemis-Markopoulos: ἐκθησώμεθα Glasc., Marc., Laurent

86.2    ἐκτάσει Polemis-Markopoulos: ἐκστάσει Glasc.

88     ἀλιφεῖσαι Laurent: ἀλειφεῖσαι Glasc.

93     ὑπάρχων: ὑπάρχειν?

94     ὁ καὶ Polemis-Markopoulos: ὃ καὶ Laurent; ᾧ καὶ Glasc.

       <φρόνημα> *added by* Polemis-Markopoulos

95     καταληφθέντας Glasc.: καταλειφθέντας Laurent

96     Βραδύνοντος δὲ: *possibly* Βραδύνοντός τε

       κελλαρί<τ>ου Laurent: κελλαρίου Glasc.

97     κυκλοῦντες αὐτὸ Polemis-Markopoulos: κυκλοῦντες αὐτῷ Glasc.

       ῥυσάμενον . . . ἀπολυτρούμενον Glasc.: ῥυσαμένη . . . ἀπολυτρουμένη Laurent

98     ὅτε: τε Laurent

       ποδοῖν Glasc.: ποδῶν Laurent

       καὶ λαβὼν <. . .> Laurent

99     ἀνενέργητον Glasc.: ἀνενέργητα Laurent

       προσιόντες Laurent: προσιόντω *corrected from* προσιόντων Glasc.

       εἰληφότες διὰ Laurent: εἰληφότος διὰ Glasc.

προσεδρεύσας . . . εὐχαριστήσας Glasc.: προσεδρεύσαντα . . .
εὐχαριστήσαντα Laurent
εἰσελάσαντα Glasc.: εἰσελάσαντι Laurent

100 μονότρητον . . . πολύτρητον . . . πολυτρήτου Laurent: μονότρι-
τον . . . πολύτριτον . . . πολυτρίτου Glasc.

102 σωφρονήσασα Polemis-Markopoulos: σωφρονίσασα Glasc.,
Laurent

104 γηφάγῳ Glasc.: *possibly* ἀδηφάγῳ
ἀλοιφῇ Polemis-Markopoulos: ἀλειφῇ Glasc., Laurent
δὲ αὐτὸν Laurent: δὲ αὐτὸν Glasc.; *possibly* δ᾽ ἑαυτὸν
ἀδελφιδὴν Glasc.: *possibly* ἀδελφιδοῦν

108 λοχῷ Glasc.: λεχῷ Laurent

109 ὁ Polemis-Markopoulos: ὃ Glasc.; ᾧ Laurent
οἰκίας Laurent: οἰκείας Glasc.

110 ἐξενόμησεν Laurent: ἐξενόμισεν Glasc.

111 συγκατασυρόμενος Glasc.: συγκαταβρώμενος Laurent

112 ἤτουν Glasc.: εἴτουν Laurent
αὐτόθι πολυστένακτος: *possibly* αὐτόθι <καὶ> πολυστένακτος

# Notes to the Translation

Pref.   *The hierophants of the mysteries of God*: The same phrase is used in
        Asterius of Amasea, *Oration to Saint Euphemia* 11.2.1, ed. C.
        Datema, *Homilies I–XIV: Text, Introduction and Notes* (Leiden,
        1970), p. 153, lines 22–23.

*in accordance . . . by God*: Compare 1 Peter 4:10.

*about the simplified unity . . . the source of light*: Although similar
phrases are to be encountered in other texts, the author seems
to draw upon pseudo–Dionysius the Areopagite here. Perhaps
closest is *On the Divine Names* 1.3, which refers to "the divine
enlightenments" (θεαρχικὰ φῶτα) and recounts how the mys-
tery of the divinity is, among other things, "a source of deifica-
tion to those who are being deified and of simplicity for those
being made simple and of unity for those who are being unified" (τῶν θεουμένων θεαρχία καὶ τῶν ἁπλουμένων ἁπλότης
καὶ τῶν ἑνιζομένων ἑνότης). Quite similar wording is, however, also found in the prooemium and chapter 3.2 of *On the
Celestial Hierarchy*.

*the unbroken . . . with flesh*: The phrasing closely echoes the doctrinal formulation adopted by the Fourth Ecumenical Council
of Chalcedon in 451; see E. Schwartz, ed., *Acta conciliorum oecu-
menicorum*, vol. 2.1.3 (Berlin, 1935), p. 115, line 34.

*resistance . . . blood*: Compare Hebrews 12:4.

*by the most holy father Jacob . . . a short time afterward*: Marc. reads,
"παρὰ τοῦ μικροῦ καθηγουμένου ταύτης τῆς ποίμνης ὁσιω-
τάτου πατρὸς Ἰακώβου" (by the most holy father Jacob, the
small leader of his flock), which does not seem to make sense.

NOTES TO THE TRANSLATION

On Jacob, who was Peter's nephew and the successor to his uncle, Paul, Peter's brother, as superior of the monastery, see below, chapters 103–4. See further, *PmbZ*, no. 2634, and Vitalien Laurent, *La "Vita retractata" et les miracles posthumes de saint Pierre d'Atroa*, Subsidia hagiographica 31 (Brussels, 1958), 35–36.

*his love of God and his neighbor*: Compare Matthew 22:37–39, Mark 12:30–31, and Luke 10:27.

1.2     *Which are they? . . . other well-respected men*: Marc. reads, "Θεα-σάμενος καὶ παρὰ τῶν εὐεργετηθέντων ἀκηκοώς, εὔδηλα δὲ καὶ σαφέστατα παρὰ τῆς τῶν πανιέρων εὐαποδέκτων ὁσίων ἀνδρῶν ἀψευδοῦς γλώσσης διδαχθεὶς τὰ εὔσημα . . ." (After I saw and heard them from those who received his assistance and after I was taught those notable things in a clear and explicit manner by the trustworthy words of most holy and well-respected holy men . . .).

*to give me speech when I opened my mouth*: See Ephesians 6:19.

*my mind's eye*: See Ephesians 1:18.

*I saw a great church . . . gave me a share of it*: Sabas's vision is somewhat reminiscent of that of Symeon the New Theologian, who saw his elder, Symeon Eulabes, standing at the right hand of Christ. For the original passage, see Richard P. H. Greenfield, trans., *The Life of Saint Symeon the New Theologian,* Dumbarton Oaks Medieval Library 20 (Cambridge, MA, 2013), chapter 5, pp. 12–15. See further, for example, Alexander Golitzin, "Earthly Angels and Heavenly Men: The Old Testament Pseudepigrapha, Niketas Stethatos, and the Tradition of 'Interiorized Apocalyptic' in Eastern Christian Ascetical and Mystical Literature," *Dumbarton Oaks Papers* 55 (2001): 138, where the continuity between Jewish apocalyptic literature, early Christian speculation about the heavenly liturgy, and the problematic of Niketas Stethatos is stressed. The insistence of Sabas on the liturgical dimension of his vision is remarkable. There is also a similar vision in the *Life of Saint Meletios the New* by Nicholas of Methone; see Ioannis Polemis, *Οἱ Βίοι τοῦ ἁγίου Μελετίου τοῦ Νέου* (Athens, 2018), 146–48 (section 33.22–39).

2.1     *of the firstborn . . . into their church*: See Hebrews 12:23.

*Elaia*: Located on the north coast of the gulf of Nikomedeia, around eight miles west of the city. See further, *TIB* 13, p. 546.

*Kosmas and Anna*: See *PmbZ,* nos. 4102 and 446, respectively.

*the prophetess Anna*: The mother of Samuel; see 1 Kings (1 Samuel) 1:1–20.

*although she lived together . . . would be born*: Marc. reads, "Τούτων συνοικουμένων ἕως καιροῦ, ἡ μήτηρ ἄτεκνος διετέλει· λυπου-μένη δὲ τὴν ἀπαιδίαν καὶ τῷ Κυρίῳ ἀνενδότως ἱκετεύουσα προσάξειν ὑπέσχετο τὸ γεννησόμενον ὡς ἄλλη Ἄννα τῷ δω-ρησαμένῳ." (Although his parents had lived together for a long time, his mother remained childless; being distressed by her childlessness and ceaselessly begging the Lord, like another Anna, she promised to offer the child which would be born to the one who would give it to her.)

*hoping to be saved, as the Apostle says*: See 1 Timothy 2:15.

2.2    *a circumcision of the heart*: Romans 2:29. The author refers to the purification rites for the mother, which took place eight days and then forty days after the child's birth. We do not accept Laurent's suggestion that Peter was baptized on the fortieth day after his birth, since the author clearly indicates that his baptism took place afterward (εἶθ' οὕτως).

*regeneration*: Compare Titus 3:5.

*offered . . . Lord*: See 1 Kings (1 Samuel) 1:22–28.

2.3    *the hierarch*: Marc. adds afterward, "θεωρήσας τοῦ παιδὸς τὸ εὔτακτον καὶ περιδέξιον (seeing the child's good behavior and adaptability).

*clipped . . . crown*: This refers to the so-called *oblatus,* a symbolic consecration of young children, widespread in both East and West; see Peter Brown, *The Rise of Western Christendom* (Oxford, 2003), 223.

*increased in wisdom and stature*: Luke 2:52.

*Truly the Spirit of God is in him*: See Genesis 41:38. The phrase, which does not appear in Marc., is also close to one in the apocryphal *Gospel of Thomas* 10, where, after the young Christ cures a child who has cut his hand with an ax, those present exclaim, "Truly the Spirit of God dwells inside this child." It

may not be accidental that Sabas describes a similar miracle
performed by Peter in chapter 45, below.

3    *ceaseless prayer*: Compare 1 Thessalonians 5:17.

*Theotokos*: The Greek term Theotokos (literally, the "God
bearer") is a standard description of Mary in the Orthodox tradition, following its adoption by the Council of Ephesus in 431
CE. The council decreed, in contradiction to Nestorios, the
patriarch of Constantinople, who had claimed that Mary could
be called only Christotokos (Christ bearer), that Mary is the
Theotokos because her Son, Jesus, is both God and man. Sabas
uses the term interchangeably with other phrasing for Mary as
Mother of God.

*Open the gates . . . thanks to the Lord*: Psalms 117(118):19. A similar
miracle is to be found in Sabas, *Life of Ioannikios*, ed., *Acta sanctorum Novembris*, vol. 2, part 1 (Brussels, 1894), 343B.

4.1   *lo and behold a monk . . . passing by*: Marc. reads here, "εὑρήσεις
μοναχὸν ὀνόματι Ἰάκωβον" (and you will find a monk called
Jacob). On this person, see *PmbZ*, no. 2628.

4.2   *Follow me*: Matthew 8:22, 9:9, 19:21, and parallel passages.

*Dagouta*: A mountainous area, probably to be located some ten
to twenty miles south of Mount Olympos (modern Uludağ). It
was thus likely in Bithynia, but perhaps near the border with
Phrygia, which lay to the east. See further, *TIB* 13, pp. 515–16.

*Krypta*: Literally, "Hidden."

*Paul*: See *PmbZ*, no. 5838.

*led him . . . to that great pillar*: The author is alluding to the pillar
of cloud and fire of Exodus 13:21–22.

*Elisha . . . Elijah*: For Elisha as the successor of Elijah, see 3 Kings
(1 Kings) 19:16, 19:19–21; for Elisha's connection to Mount Carmel, see 4 Kings (2 Kings) 2:25 and 4:25.

*Give instruction . . . wiser still*: Proverbs 9:9.

5    *area of Boukellarioi*: The Boukellarion theme (or the theme of
the Boukellarioi) was a large administrative district of Asia Minor, lying to the east and north of the area where Paul was cur-
rently living. See further, *ODB*, vol. 1, pp. 316–17.

*Mantenion*: An area of Paphlagonia, in the province of Honorias;

see Cyril Mango, "St. Anthusa of Mantineon and the Family of Constantine V," *Analecta Bollandiana* 100 (1982): 405.

*hesychasts*: Literally, "seekers of (spiritual) tranquility." At this period and in this context the term is probably being used simply as a synonym for hermits or solitaries. If the more technical meaning is present, it would imply that these men were engaged in the style of monastic prayer and contemplation intended to attain communion with God that later came to be associated with the hesychast movement.

*Eustratios, Theodore, and George*: See *PmbZ*, nos. 1815, 7611, and 2184, respectively.

*it is not enough . . . according to the gospel*: See Matthew 5:15–16 and parallel passages.

*fellow traveler of the Word . . . our Lord*: The same phrase occurs in Gregory of Nazianzus, *Oration* 7.9 and 7.10, ed. Marie-Ange Calvet-Sebasti, *Discours 6–12,* Sources chrétiennes 405 (Paris, 1995), p. 200. Marc. reads, "καὶ συνέμπορος τῶν διὰ τὸ ὄνομα τοῦ Κυρίου ἡμῶν Ἰησοῦ Χριστοῦ καταλειψάντων πάντα καὶ αὐτῷ μόνῳ ἀκολουθησάντων" (and fellow traveler of those who abandoned everything for the name of our Lord Jesus Christ and followed him alone).

6.1    *named him Peter . . . as scripture shows in many places*: See, for example, John 1:42.

*with powerful weapons . . . in obedience to his father*: A slight adaptation of 2 Corinthians 10:4–5.

*as clay to the potter*: See Romans 9:20–21.

6.2    *Byzantion*: The name of the original settlement on the site of Constantinople, which continued to be used by authors, on occasion, throughout its later history. See *ODB*, vol. 1, p. 344.

*and the likeness . . . priestly office*: Marc. reads, "Πρὸς τὴν ἀγγελοειδῆ τῆς θείας ἠθέλησεν αὐτὸν χειροτονίας ἐπιβιβάσαι τάξιν." (He wanted to transfer him to the rank of divine ordination, one which has the appearance of angels.)

*called to mind . . . and act as a priest*: The problem referred to in the text is not addressed by any Church canon directly; however, it was common practice in Byzantion that priests, especially

those who were monks, might not abandon their dioceses in order to exercise their ministry elsewhere.

*Tarasios*: Patriarch of Constantinople (784–806), who was responsible for the restoration of icons under Irene in 787. See further, *ODB*, vol. 3, p. 2011, and *PmbZ*, no. 7235.

*He wrote the following*: Marc. adds, "πρὸς τὸ διὰ τῆς ἑαυτοῦ κελεύσεως ἀποστεῖλαι ἐπίσκοπον τοῦ ποιῆσαι πρεσβύτερον τὸν ὁσιώτατον Πέτρον" (so that, on his orders, he might send a bishop to make the most holy Peter a priest).

6.3    *The letter*: The letters exchanged between Tarasios, Paul, and Basil are not preserved in any other source.

*as a vagrant, in mountains . . . ground*: A slight adaptation of Hebrews 11:38.

*as it seems good to the divine Spirit and your holiness*: See Acts 15:28.

6.4    *Zygos*: It is not clear where exactly this place was located. See *TIB* 13, pp. 1084–85.

*Basil . . . Pezos*: See *PmbZ*, no. 886.

6.6    *the imperial city*: That is, Constantinople. Marc. adds here, "Ὡς οὖν ἔπλεεν" (When he was sailing).

6.7    *that had been sent . . . this is the summary*: The text is abbreviated by Marc. as follows: "καὶ τὴν ἐπικομισθεῖσαν ἐπιστολὴν Ταρασίου τοῦ ἁγιωτάτου πατριάρχου, ἀποστέλλει πρὸς τὸν προμνημονευθέντα ἐπίσκοπον Βασίλειον, γράψας καὶ αὐτὸς τὴν τούτου μαρτυρίαν ἰδιοχείρως καὶ ἐπιδοὺς αὐτοῖς" (along with the letter that he had received from the most holy patriarch Tarasios, and he sent it to the previously mentioned bishop Basil after he had written his testimony to this in his own hand and given it to them).

6.8    *its angel*: Compare, for example, Revelation 2:1.

*being with you . . . in spirit*: See 1 Corinthians 5:3.

6.9    *ordained him . . . At that time a man*: Marc. reads, ". . . καὶ χειροθετεῖ τῆς τριαδικῆς θεότητος ἱερολόγον. Τοῦ δὲ ὁσίου Πέτρου χειροτονουμένου τῇ τοῦ πρεσβυτέρου ἀξίᾳ, ἄνθρωπός . . ." (. . . and ordained him as a speaker of holy things concerning the triadic deity. But when holy Peter was ordained with the dignity of a priest, a man . . .).

NOTES TO THE TRANSLATION

7      *Dagouta*: See above, 4.2.

*Philargyrou*: This is the only reference to this mountain; see Laurent, *La vie*, 84n2.

*since this had fallen asleep*: Marc. presents a different interpretation of how the goat was left behind: "ἀφυπνώσαντος τοῦ ἀλόγου βοσκομένου" (since he had fallen asleep while the animal was grazing).

*told the holy father Paul about it*: Marc. adds here, "Ἔριφος ἐάθη ἐνταῦθα, ἡμῶν μὴ γινωσκόντων." (A kid was left here, without us noticing.)

*She immediately took it*: Marc. phrases this, "Ἡ δὲ παραυτὰ εἰσελθοῦσα, αὐτῇ τῇ ὥρᾳ ἐπιλαβομένη τὸν ἔριφον. . . ." (She immediately came in and took the goat at that very hour. . . .)

*about three miles*: The Greek term used here, *semeion*, is a measure of distance roughly equivalent to a mile.

8      *In the course of . . . reached the river Halys*: The river Halys (modern Kızılırmak) is the longest in Asia Minor. Rising in the southern Pontic Alps, it flows in a vast arc for over eight hundred miles across the eastern and central northern areas before entering the Black Sea near Amisos (Samsun). If Peter and Paul were following the main Byzantine military road, they would have crossed the river at Saniana (Kesikköprü), more than two hundred miles east of Dagouta and around forty miles north of Lake Tatta (Tuz Gölü). See further, Laurent, *La vie*, 86n1.

*the image of God*: Genesis 1:27.

*damaging . . . shoots*: Marc. reads, "κατὰ βοτανῶν καὶ φυτῶν καὶ βλαστημάτων παντοδαπῶν λυμαντικῶς ἐπερχόμενον τὰ πάντα κατήσθιεν" (attacking herbs, plants, and shoots of every kind in a destructive manner, it had eaten everything).

9.1    *church of the prophet Zechariah*: The chapel was located on the plain of Atroa, hence Peter's eponym. On the exact location of Atroa, see Cyril Mango, "The Two Lives of St. Ioannikios and the Bulgarians," in "Okeanos: Essays Presented to Ihor Ševčenko on His Sixtieth Birthday by His Colleagues and Students," ed. Cyril Mango and Omeljan Pritsak, special issue, *Harvard Ukrainian Studies* 8 (1983): 393–404, at 394n7; and *TIB*

13, pp. 434–35. On the monastery of Saint Zechariah, see Laurent, *La vie,* 37–39; M.-F. Auzépy, "Les monastères," in *La Bithynie au Moyen Âge,* ed. B. Geyer and J. Lefort (Paris, 2003), 431–58, at 442–43; and *TIB* 13, pp. 1080–81.

*and to send them . . . heavenly one*: Marc. reads instead, "Ἀπὸ δὲ ταύτης τῆς μάνδρας εἰς τὴν θείαν σκηνὴν καὶ οὐράνιον παραπέμψω, καὶ μετὰ σὲ τὸν σὺν σοὶ Πέτρον καταλιμπάνω διάδοχον." (And I will transfer you from this fold to the divine and heavenly tabernacle, and I will leave behind you your companion Peter as your successor.)

9.2     *In it he gathered . . . secular world*: Marc. reads instead, "ἐχάρη χαρὰν μεγάλην καὶ ἐν ὀλίγῳ καιρῷ συνηθροίσθη θεία συνοδία" (he was very happy and in a short time a divine community was gathered).

*the burdens*: Galatians 6:2.

10     *that true imitator of God*: Marc. reads, "ὁ κατὰ ἀλήθειαν τοῦ θείου μιμητὴς Παύλου" (that true imitator of the divine Paul).

*and who was still lying prostrate . . . physician of our souls*: Marc. reads simply, "Τοῦτο οὖν ποιήσας ὁ ὅσιος Παῦλος καὶ ψυχωφελὴς πατήρ . . ." (After he had done this, the holy and spiritually beneficial Paul . . .).

*Holy Peter . . . mental humility*: Marc. reads, "Ὁ δὲ ὅσιος Πέτρος ἀναστὰς ἀπὸ τῶν ποδῶν τοῦ ὁσίου Παύλου ἐκδυσάμενος τὴν ἱερατικὴν αὐτοῦ στολὴν εἰς τὸ πῦρ ἀπέρριψεν κατὰ τὴν τοῦ μεγάλου πρόσταξιν." (Holy Peter, stood up from the feet of holy Paul, took off his clerical vestment, and threw it into the fire according to the great one's order.)

*accepting the condemnation . . . consigned to the fire*: Marc. reads more simply, "καὶ εἰς νοῦν αὐτοῦ φέρων τὸ παρήκοον" (bringing to mind his disobedience).

*I think . . . dispassionate way*: Marc. reads simply, "ὥστε θαυμάσαι πάντας καὶ δοξάσαι τὸν Θεόν" (so that all were amazed and glorified God).

11.1     *built a little grave-like cell . . . confined himself to it*: The same practice is to be observed in the *Life of Saint Christodoulos of Pat-*

*mos* 72.1–5, by Athanasios, patriarch of Antioch, ed. Ioannis Polemis and Theodora Antonopoulou, *Vitae et miracula sancti Christoduli Patmensis,* Corpus Fontium Historiae Byzantinae, Series Vindobonensis 56 (Vienna, 2021), 236.

*for the word had arrived*: That is, the word of the Lord, telling him his time was up.

*joined with my fathers*: See Acts 13:36.

*being earth, I am returning to the earth*: See Genesis 3:19.

*transfixed with the fear of God*: The Greek carries a sense of "being nailed" or "pierced." The same phrasing is used by Theodore of Stoudios, Μεγάλη κατήχησις 5, ed. A. Papadopoulos-Kerameus, *Theodori Studitae Magna catechesis* (Saint Petersburg, 1904), p. 28, line 12.

*perfect love*: 1 John 4:18.

*your chief shepherd*: That is, the abbot of the monastery. On the office of *hegoumenos* (abbot), see *ODB,* vol. 2, pp. 907–8.

*be subject to him . . . the divine apostle*: See Romans 13:1.

*showing . . . honor*: Compare 1 Peter 3:7.

*Blessed be God*: Ephesians 1:3.

*somebody who is gentle . . . easy yoke of Christ forever*: The passage develops Matthew 11:29–30.

*the rod . . . the staff*: See Psalms 22(23):4.

*openly and proudly declare before Christ*: See Romans 15:17 and Philippians 3:3.

*Behold . . . have given me*: Isaiah 8:18; Hebrews 2:13.

*he surrendered his spirit*: John 19:30.

11.2  *Nikephoros*: Nikephoros I, emperor from 802 until 811. See further, *ODB,* vol. 3, p. 1476.

*Staurakios*: The son and ephemeral successor of Nikephoros I as emperor from July to October 811. Gravely injured in battle against the Bulgarians, he was forced to abdicate a few weeks after the death of his father. See further, *ODB,* vol. 3, pp. 1945–46.

*he did not permit himself*: Marc. reads, "μὴ γευόμενος" (he did not taste).

12.1    *Michael and Theophylaktos*: Michael I Rangabe and his son and
        coemperor Theophylaktos, who reigned between 811 and 813.
        See further *ODB*, vol. 2, p. 1362.

        *that imitator of the devil*: Marc. reads, "πρόδρομος τοῦ Ἀντι-
        χρίστου" (precursor of the Antichrist).

        *a Leo in name and a lion in his headlong assault*: Leo V the Armenian
        (813–820), the emperor who renewed Iconoclasm and exiled
        the iconophile patriarch Nikephoros of Constantinople in 815.
        His name, Leon, means "lion" in Greek. See further on him,
        *ODB*, vol. 2, pp. 1209–10.

        *not resisting the evil one*: See Matthew 5:39.

        *word of Christ*: Marc. adds, "Ἀπὸ τοῦ αἴροντος τὰ σὰ μὴ ἀπαί-
        τει." (Do not ask the one who takes your belongings to give
        them back.)

12.2    *seized the scepter*: Marc. adds, "καὶ κατεπαρθέντος τοῦ Κτίσαν-
        τος" (since he was arrogant toward the Creator).

        *the devil . . . unholy quiver*: An image quite widely used in patristic   ·
        literature for the work of the devil, in particular against Job.

        *the image of God . . . the original*: The idea that honor paid to an
        image is referred to the original is found in a passage of Basil
        the Great (PG 32:149C), which was frequently employed by or-
        thodox writers against the Iconoclasts in this period.

        *the Son who is the exact imprint of God*: The phrasing echoes He-
        brews 1:3.

        *thanks to his compassionate heart*: Luke 1:78.

        *came in his own good time*: See Titus 1:3.

        *the first fruit*: See 1 Corinthians 15:20.

12.3    *deified his image*: See 2 Corinthians 8:9.

        *some of them divided . . . different hypostases*: That is, the followers
        of Nestorios.

        *another proclaimed . . . only one nature*: That is, a Monophysite—
        for example, Eutyches or Severus of Antioch.

        *another foolishly declared . . . from heaven*: For example, Apollina-
        rius of Laodicea. See a relevant passage in George Cedrenus,
        *Historiarum compendium* 291.6–7, ed. L. Tartaglia, *Georgii Ce-*

*dreni Historiarum compendium* (Rome, 2016), vol. 1, p. 464, who attributes this doctrine to Eutyches.

*another dreamed . . . shadow*: For example, Manes. For a catalog of these heretics, see Anastasius of Sinai, *Viae dux* 14, ed. K.-H. Uthemann, *Anastasii Sinaitae Viae dux, Corpus Christianorum Series Graeca* 8 (Turnhout and Leuven, 1981), 259–64. A similar passage, enumerating the various predecessors of the Iconoclasts, is to be found in Sabas, *Life of Ioannikios,* ed. *Acta sanctorum Novembris,* vol. 2, part 1, pp. 334B–35A.

*now he fell . . . beneath the earth*: The devil was identified with death and thus with Hades or hell in Byzantine thought.

*Father . . . name to men*: John 17:6.

*I will send . . . from the Father*: John 14:16.

*the powers of the air*: See Ephesians 2:2.

*which walked on the sea*: See Matthew 14:25, Mark 6:48, and John 6:19.

*who sowed these weeds*: See Matthew 13:25.

12.4    *After Leo had thrown . . . symbol of the cross*: Marc. reads, "Ταῦτα δράσας κατὰ τῆς τοῦ Θεοῦ ἐκκλησίας" (After he had done these things against the church of God).

*together with the symbol of the cross*: This is false, since the sign of the cross was revered by the Iconoclasts.

*against the image*: Marc. reads, "κατὰ τῶν μὴ πειθομένων αὐτοῦ τοῖς δυσσεβέσι προστάγμασι" (against those who would not obey his impious orders).

13.1    *ordered by the holy scripture . . . temptations upon ourselves*: Compare Matthew 26:41, Mark 14:38, and Luke 22:46.

*bonds of love*: Compare Colossians 3:14.

13.2    *the church of John the Theologian in Ephesus*: The famous Basilica of Saint John, rebuilt under Justinian I between 548 and 565 on the site of the purported tomb of John the Evangelist's dormition. See further, *ODB,* vol. 1, p. 706.

*the church of the archangel Michael in Chonai*: Chonai (modern Honaz) was a city in Phrygia near ancient Kolossai. It was the site of a large basilica dedicated to the archangel Michael and

was a center of pilgrimage and trade. See further, *ODB*, vol. 1,
p. 427.

14.1 *Mesolympon*: There is no reference to this place in any other
source, see *TIB* 13, pp. 771–72.

*Moses whose face was glorified*: Compare Exodus 34:30.

*and was seen by those . . . supernaturally in nature*: Marc. reads, "καὶ
ὁρᾷ ἐκεῖσε ὡς ἄλλος Μωϋσῆς τὸ τῆς Χριστοῦ εἰκόνος πρόσω-
πον γαλακτοειδεῖς ἀποστάζον ἱδρῶτας, τῆς ἐν αὐτῷ, ὡς οἶμαι,
τοῦ Παναγίου Πνεύματος χάριτος διαδεικνυούσης αὐτῷ τὰ
μέλλοντα" (and there he saw, like another Moses, the face of
Christ in the icon dripping a milk-like sweat; for I think that
the grace of the Holy Spirit in him was revealing the future to
him).

*like the birds of the gospel*: See Matthew 23:37.

*The shepherd asked . . . monastery, advising, teaching*: Marc. reads,
"μετὰ τὴν ἐκ τῆς μονῆς ἔξοδον ψυχωφελῆ ὀδύνην ἐπυνθάνο-
ντο. Ὁ δὲ ὅσιος ποιμὴν ἐνουθέτει αὐτοὺς διδάσκων. . . ." (they
asked him about the pain that had profited his soul after he left
the monastery. The holy shepherd advised them, teaching. . . .)

*For whoever welcomes . . . barren deeds*: See 2 John 11.

14.2 *one mile*: On the *semeion* as a measure of distance, see the note on
7, above.

15.1 *by the demon*: Marc. adds, "καὶ τῶν ἥμισυ μερῶν τοῦ σώματος
ἀπεστερημένην" (and deprived of half of its body). The Greek
deliberately dehumanizes the possessed boy.

*participant in human nature . . . beastly disability*: As above, in being
deprived of speech, the boy is also depicted as having been
made into an irrational, "dumb" beast by the demonic possession, lacking the power of reason and speech (both comprised
in the same Greek term *logos*), which distinguished a human
being from an animal in Byzantine thought.

*received from God the gift*: For the term τάλαντον ("talent" or
"gift"), see the parable of the talents at Matthew 25:14–30 and
Luke 19:12–28; compare Matthew 18:24–28.

15.2 *wanted all people*: See 1 Timothy 2:4.

*who lived in the world and <. . .>*: From this point until midway through chapter 37 there is a lacuna in Glasc. This is filled by the text of Marc.

16.1  *the mountains of Asia near Hippos*: On this place, see Laurent, *La vie*, 43 and 104–5n1. Although it is impossible to locate exactly, Laurent suggests, from evidence in the text, that it was probably situated to the north of Pergamon (modern Bergama), on the border between Asia and Lydia.

*the previously mentioned deacon John*: See *PmbZ*, no. 3240. Presumably, the "very diligent and virtuous man called John" of 13.2, above.

*the Abba's spring*: The Syriac word *abba*, which means "father," is used quite commonly in Greek hagiography.

17  *the village in which he was born*: That is, Elaia, on which see the note on 2.1, above.

*Follow me*: See Matthew 8:22.

*Paul*: See *PmbZ*, no. 5839.

*not consulting with his flesh and blood*: See Galatians 1:16.

19.1  *he begged the Lord . . . ran like a spring*: A similar miracle is described in Sabas, *Life of Ioannikios*, ed. *Acta sanctorum Novembris*, vol. 2, part 1, p. 380C.

*protection against many ills*: The Greek term *pathos*, here rendered (in the plural) as "ills," brings with it a range of meaning impossible to capture in English. It embraces suffering, illness, disease, and more general misfortune, as well as passion, in the sense of an extreme emotion resulting in behavior or thought that is seen as morally bad.

19.2  *Dagouta*: See above, 4.2.

*half a mile away*: Literally, "two bowshots."

*a few feet away*: Literally, one *orguia*, or fathom, just over six feet.

20.1  *the foot of Olympos near Prousa*: That is, the northern slopes of the mountain. Prousa is the modern city of Bursa.

*Dele*: There is no reference to this location in any other source; see *TIB* 13, p. 532.

*Maurianos, a count*: See *PmbZ*, no. 4892. The title *komes*, or "count,"

at this time indicates a senior official or a subaltern military officer; see *ODB*, vol. 1, pp. 484–85.

20.2    *no power even over pigs*: This claim is based on the gospel story of the Gerasene demoniac, in which the demons enter a herd of pigs at Jesus's command and rush into the lake to be drowned. See Matthew 8:30–32, Mark 5:11–13, and Luke 8:32–33. The same point is made in 79, below.

20.3    *a great pillar and a shepherd . . . has fallen*: See John of Sinai, *Climax,* ed. PG 88:885A–C, where a similar story is recounted. "Rational sheep" is a common Byzantine expression for monks.

22.1    *Apollonia in Maurousias*: On this place, in the upper valley of the river Kaikos (the modern Bakırçay), northwest of Germe (Soma), see Laurent, *La vie,* 116–17nn1–2.

*one of the mountains of the Hellespont . . . the Good Mountain*: On this monastic settlement, mentioned only in the *Life,* see Laurent, *La vie,* 41–43, who follows the logic of the text in placing it in Lydia and argues persuasively that "Hellespont" must thus be a scribal error.

*Nestorians*: Followers of a doctrine developed in the fifth century and condemned at the Council of Ephesus in 431 for placing an overemphasis on the humanity of Christ. It seems possible, but not certain, that Sabas identifies the Nestorians with the Iconoclasts here. See further, Laurent, *La vie,* 117n5.

22.2    *Jesus Christ . . . life and death*: See Acts 3:15.

*Let us go there*: John 14:31.

*was disturbed in his soul*: John 13:21.

*Symeon, stand up*: The original reader would hear in the Greek imperative "ἀνάστηθι" (stand up) an allusion to the resurrection; it might be rendered more archaically as "arise."

23    *shepherd called Athanasios*: See *PmbZ,* no. 677.

*a region of Lydia called Plateia Petra*: Although its exact location is unknown, the place was evidently in the Thrakesion theme; see Laurent, *La vie,* 120n1.

24.1    *The most holy mother of that flock*: That is, the abbess.

26.1    *an exarch called Lamaris*: On this man, see *PmbZ,* no. 4220. As suggested there, the office of exarch in this context may refer

to that of the *strategos,* or military governor, of the Thrakesion theme.

*in the image and likeness of God*: The wording combines two phrases from Genesis 1:26.

*image of God the Father . . . at the predestined time*: See Colossians 1:15 and Titus 1:3. The reference is to Jesus.

*the threefold . . . divinity*: That is, the Holy Trinity.

*not put up any resistance to the evil one*: Matthew 5:39.

26.3 *nothing will separate me*: Compare Romans 8:35.

*will inherit the eternal fire*: See Matthew 25:34–41.

26.4 *arrows of fire*: See Ephesians 6:16.

27 *because they had been deemed . . . sake of the Lord*: A slight adaptation of Acts 5:41.

*silver or gold*: See Acts 3:6, where Peter heals a lame beggar. The same expression is used below, in 67.

28 *Good Mountain*: See note to 22.1, above.

*the monastery of Chareus*: This place is not recorded in any other source; see Laurent, *La vie,* 130n2.

*Patermouthios*: See *PmbZ,* no. 5749.

*the laughingstock of the demons*: The phrase first appears in patristic literature in Chrysostom but was used a number of times by Romanos the Melodist and Theodore of Stoudios.

*what have you to do with us*: Mark 5:7. The phrase reworks that of the Gerasene demoniac to Jesus. It is also used in 36 and 70, below.

*changing your mind concerning the sins of men*: Joel 2:13.

*Take care of yourself*: Exodus 34:12, for example.

29 *Abba Matthias*: See *PmbZ,* no. 4873. On the term "Abba," see above, 16.1.

30 *a monastery called Semnion*: The location is unknown, but see Laurent, *La vie,* 134n1.

31 *some distance away*: The Greek means, literally, about a bowshot away.

33 *Leo the tyrant went to his death*: The emperor Leo V was assassinated on Christmas Day 820, by supporters of Michael II.

*Michael . . . from Amorion*: The emperor Michael II (820–829),

founder of the Amorion dynasty, which is named from his city of origin (now Hisarköy) in Phrygia.

*the tempest*: Numbers 16:48. A similar passage is to be found in Sabas, *Life of Ioannikios,* ed. *Acta sanctorum Novembris,* vol. 2, part 1, p. 355B.

34    *senator . . . consul*: By this period, the term "senator" *(syngkletikos)* designated a rather ephemeral functionary (see *ODB,* vol. 3, pp. 1869–70), and "consul" was an honorific title rather than a functioning office.

35.2   *Stand up*: Mark 5:41–42. The wording parallels that of Jesus's healing of Jairus's daughter.

*terror . . . those present*: Compare Genesis 15:12 and Mark 16:8.

36    *a legion of impure spirits*: Compare Mark 5:9 and Luke 8:30. The description reflects the gospel story of the Gerasene demoniac.

*What have you to do with me*: Mark 5:7. The same phrase is used in 28, above, and 70, below.

*the tyrant Thomas . . . siege of the City*: Thomas the Slav, who rebelled against the emperor (Michael II) in the winter of 820/1 and besieged Constantinople ("the City") from December 821. He was forced to retreat, and was captured and executed in 823. See further *ODB,* vol. 3, p. 2079.

*Christ's holy physicians, the Anargyroi, Kosmas and Damianos*: The principal Byzantine healing saints, who performed their cures without charge and were thus called the *Anargyroi* (without silver). A substantial collection of their miracle stories has survived, recording cures performed at their shrine in the Kosmidion district, which is generally accepted to have lain just outside the northwestern corner of the walls of Constantinople.

*the eastern gate*: Given the location of the shrine of Saints Kosmas and Damianos, the need to exit through this gate seems far from accidental.

*that very hour*: Matthew 9:22, the conclusion of the story of the woman with the issue of blood.

37    *Some of the previously mentioned bishops . . . Peter*: The events of this chapter, as recorded by Sabas, are largely supported by the

account in chapter 33.2 of the *Life of Theodore of Stoudios* by Michael the Monk, ed. and trans. Robert H. Jordan and Rosemary Morris, *The Life and Death of Theodore of Stoudios,* Dumbarton Oaks Medieval Library 70 (Cambridge, MA, 2021), 172–75. Peter, who is there given the epithet Aboukis (probably meaning "without a mouthful"), clearly has an already established reputation for his extreme fasting. As in Sabas's account, he has been accused of sorcery and seeks validation from Theodore (on whom see the note below), who is in exile and staying temporarily at Kreskentios. Theodore is said to have questioned Peter on his lifestyle and then to have "gently urged him to partake occasionally of bread and wine and the other foods eaten in monasteries (because of the tendency of weaker individuals to make accusations), and to wear sandals in wintertime" (p. 173). He is also said to have written to Peter's accusers, rebuking them for their poor judgment and telling them to desist, although the text of the letter is not included there.

*Beelzebul, the leader of the demons*: Matthew 12:24 and Luke 11:15; compare Mark 3:22.

*your holy name should be slandered because of me*: Sabas works together three biblical passages here: Isaiah 52:5, Ezekiel 36:20, and Romans 2:24.

*Let loose*: See Psalms 38:14 (39:13).

*your waves*: See, for example, Psalms 41:8 (42:7). The waves are an image of God's punishment.

*Theodore, the confessor . . . abbot of Stoudios*: Saint Theodore of Stoudios (759–826), a prominent Byzantine cleric who is renowned for his fervent defense of the veneration of images during the second period of Iconoclasm, for his monastic reforms, and for his considerable literary legacy. See further the "Introduction" in Jordan and Morris, *Life and Death,* vii–xvii; *ODB,* vol. 3, pp. 2044–45; and *PmbZ,* no. 7574.

*the area of Kreskentios*: An estate situated on the Gulf of Nikomedeia (İzmit Körfezi); see *TIB* 13, p. 694.

*My brother, I want you to tell me*: At this point the text of Glasc. resumes.

*the forty-day fasts*: That is, the four Lenten fasts of the Byzantine

ecclesiastical calendar: "Great Lent" (preceding Easter) and those before the Nativity, the Dormition of the Virgin, and the feast of Saints Peter and Paul.

*I have only one tunic . . . I have no shoes*: See Matthew 10:10; compare Mark 6:9 and Luke 10:4.

38 *My friends . . . canon of the fathers*: The letter of Theodore of Stoudios to the monks concerning Saint Peter of Atroa was also published by G. Fatouros, *Theodori Studitae Epistulae*, vol. 2, (Berlin, 1992), no. 560, pp. 860–61. There are, however, doubts about its authenticity on linguistic and content grounds, and it is evident that the current version has been at least elaborated by Sabas; see further, Jordan and Morris, *Life and Death*, 357; and Laurent, *La vie*, 148n1.

*not to sharpen your tongue*: Psalms 63:4 (64:3).

*for the one who sanctifies . . . one origin*: Hebrews 2:11.

*who extends . . . mighty works*: Marc. reads, "τὴν θείαν χάριν αὐτοῦ ὡς διὰ τῶν ἀποστόλων ἐν σημείοις καὶ τέρασι καὶ δι' αὐτοῦ νυνὶ ἐκπέμποντος" (who distributes the divine grace through him now as through the apostles with signs and wonders).

*through the apostles . . . mighty works*: See Acts 2:22; see also Acts 14:3.

*He who believes . . . than these*: John 14:12.

*bad opinion*: Compare Hebrews 10:22.

39.1 *a notary called Zechariah*: See *PmbZ*, no. 8631.

*the tyrant Thomas*: Thomas the Slav; see note on 36, above.

*Phygela*: Phygela (modern Kuşadası) was a town near Ephesus that became the main port for the area when the latter's harbor silted up. Since Phygela itself was on the mainland, it seems likely that this narrative refers to the small island (modern Güvercinada) that lies just off the coast and is now connected to the city by a 250-yard man-made causeway, although its striking current fortifications are Ottoman. Compare Laurent, *La vie*, 149–50n3, and *ODB*, vol. 3, p. 1672.

*for the healthy . . . who are ill*: Matthew 9:12.

*an angel . . . opened the doors*: See Acts 12:7–10. Similar miracles are described in Sabas, *Life of Ioannikios*, ed. *Acta sanctorum Novembris*, vol. 2, part 1, pp. 359C and 379B.

*Go home in peace*: See Luke 7:50.

*to the mainland, where the second set of guards*: Marc. reads, "οἱ ἐπὶ τῆς ξηρᾶς διοδεύοντες φύλακες" (the guards who were roaming about on dry land).

39.2     *domestikos*: The term *domestikos* at this time designates a broad range of civilian, military, and ecclesiastical officials; see *ODB*, vol. 1, p. 646.

        *Benjamin*: See *PmbZ*, no. 1009. The same man is mentioned in 111, below.

        *Hagarenes*: A term commonly used by the Byzantines for the Arabs, based on their supposed descent from Abraham's wife Hagar through her son Ishmael. See also the note on 48, below.

39.3     *spatharios*: An honorary title by this time. On this, and the office that it formerly designated, see *ODB*, vol. 3, pp. 1935–36.

        *senator*: See note on 34, above.

41.1     *convent of women . . . father Peter's guidance*: Presumably that mentioned in chapters 23–24 or 31 (or both), above.

        *a group of the enemy*: Probably a reference to a group of partisans of Thomas the Slav.

        *the nuns, seeing this . . . with great faith*: Marc. reads, "καὶ δὴ ἐκεῖναι ταύτην τὴν ἐπιβουλὴν νοήσασαι μετὰ τὸ τέλος τῆς ψαλμῳδίας τῆς ἐκτενῆς ἐναρξάμεναι τῷ παντοδυνάμῳ Θεῷ καθικέτευον καὶ τῷ αὐτοῦ θεράποντι Πέτρῳ ῥυσθῆναι τῆς τοιαύτης ἐπιβουλῆς. Τῶν δὲ παρθένων κραζόντων τό· 'Κύριε ἐλέησον. . . .'" (when they realized this threat, after they had finished singing the Psalms, they began a fervent prayer, and they begged almighty God and his servant Peter to be saved from that plan. When the nuns were crying out "Lord have mercy. . . .")

41.2     *had reduced the plague*: Compare Numbers 17:13, 17:15 (16:48, 16:50).

42       *thought that this was a test of his endurance*: Marc. reads, "ἰδὼν τὸν ἀδελφὸν τῇ ἐπαύριον πάλιν κοπιῶντα" (when he saw the brother was laboring once more the next day).

43       *steward*: The steward (*oikonomos*) of a monastery usually ranked second to the superior in its hierarchy and had responsibility for managing the foundation's properties and estates. See further *ODB*, vol. 3, p. 1517.

44      *One of those children*: Probably Jacob, Peter's nephew, who became abbot of the monastery of Saint Zechariah after the death of Peter's successor, his brother Paul. See chapter 103, below.

*If my Lord God . . . to the world*: Marc. reads, "Ἰάσεταί σε, τέκνον, ὁ Θεός μου καὶ Κύριος, εἰ μὴ πρὸς τὸν κόσμον ἐπαναστρέψῃς πάλιν." (My God and Lord will heal you, child, if you do not go back to the world again.)

*No, my divinely wise father*: Marc. reads, "Μὴ γένοιτό μοι, πάτερ θεόσοφε, ἀλλὰ πρὸς σὲ διαμείνω." (May no such thing happen to me, my divinely wise father, and may I remain with you.)

45      *Theophylaktos from the town of Prevetos*: See *PmbZ*, no. 346. Marc. gives the town's name as Provaton, a place also known by Theophanes the Chronographer; see R. Bondoux, "Les villes," in Geyer and Lefort, *La Bithynie,* 377–409, at 407n428.

*he came to the holy one*: Marc. adds, "παρακαλῶν αὐτὸν τῆς ἰάσεως τυχεῖν· ὁ δὲ μακάριος ποιήσας ἐπὶ τὴν χεῖρα αὐτοῦ εὐχήν" (asking him to receive a cure; and the blessed one, when he had said a prayer over his hand).

46      *Theodoulos*: See *PmbZ*, no. 7986.

*and kept the brother . . . glory to God*: Marc. reads, "ἀβλαβῆ τὸν ἀδελφὸν ἐκ τῆς φάραγγος ἀνήγαγεν" (and pulled the brother out of the ravine unharmed).

*Terror and amazement*: Compare Mark 16:8.

47      *Rhyndakos*: A river in northwest Anatolia (the modern Mustafakemalpaşa, Orhaneli, or Adirnaz River), which flows some thirty to forty miles west of Olympos and feeds Lake Apollonias (Uluabat Gölü) south of the Sea of Marmara. See further, *TIB* 13, pp. 976–77.

*monastery there, named for Saint Porphyrios*: See Laurent, *La vie,* 39–40. As Laurent notes, chapter 76, below, indicates that the monastery must have been situated quite near Lake Apollonias.

*while he himself . . . take care of him*: M has here, "σὺν αὐτοῖς εἰς ἐπίσκεψίν τινων ἀδελφῶν πλησίον αὐτῶν ὄντων ἀπῆρεν· ἐν δὲ τῇ αὐτῇ μονῇ κατέλιπέν τινα ἀδελφὸν Ἀδριανὸν καλούμενον νόσῳ βαρείᾳ συνεχόμενον μετὰ τῶν δύο ὑπηρετῶν αὐτοῦ

Βαρνάβα καὶ Φιλοθέου" (then he left with them and went to visit some brothers who were nearby; but in this monastery, he left a brother called Adrianos, who was seriously ill, with his two servants, Barnabas and Philotheos).

*Adrianos: PmbZ*, no. 100.

*Barnabas and Philotheos:* See *PmbZ*, nos. 808 and 6189, respectively. They are mentioned again in 51 and 94, below.

*I have never thought of looking at:* Marc. adds, "ἢ παρακούειν" (or disobeying).

*our brother Adrianos ... said this to him:* Marc. reads, "Καὶ κελεύσας ὁ ὅσιος ἐξειπεῖν, ὡς βούλεται, τὰ αὑτοῦ ἐλλείμματα, μετὰ τὸ εἰπεῖν ἀπελύθη τοῦ σώματος, τοιαῦτα πρὸς αὐτὸν τοῦ πατρὸς εἰρηκότος. . . ." (The holy father told Adrianos to confess his faults as he wanted to, and, when he had confessed, he departed from his body after the father had said this to him. . . .)

48    *Ishmaelites:* That is, Arabs. The term Ishmaelite is commonly used in Byzantine sources. It derives from Ishmael, the first son of Abraham, who was held to be the ancestor of the Arab people through his second wife, Hagar. Compare the use of "Hagarenes" in 39.2, above.

*to raid the Roman territory:* This most likely refers to raids in the late 820s and 830s by the Arabs who had recently established themselves on Crete. See Laurent, *La vie,* 152n1.

*queen of cities:* That is, Constantinople.

49    *monastery of Baleoi:* The exact name of this monastery is unclear. Although Laurent, *La vie,* 45–46, initially argued that there were two distinct monasteries, Baleioi (named in 50.1 and 80, as well as in 54 with the spelling "Balaioi") and Balea (named here in 49), he subsequently concluded, on the basis of the text of Glasc., that they were probably identical; see Laurent, *La "Vita retractata,"* 44–45. The *TIB* 13, pp. 445–46, agrees on identifying them and places the foundation close to and above the monastery of Saint Zechariah (on which, see above, 9.1).

*who fed five thousand people with five loaves:* Compare the gospel story in Matthew 14:15–21, Mark 6:35–44, Luke 9:12–17, and John 6:5–14.

*And, after everyone ate and was full:* Marc. reads, "Ἀναγα-

γόντων δὲ τὰ βραχύτατα λείψανα τοῦ ἄρτου καὶ τοῦ οἴνου, καὶ ἐν καρδίᾳ αὐτοῦ προσευξάμενος ὁ ὅσιος ηὐλόγησεν αὐτά, καὶ ἐξ ἐκείνου τοῦ ἄρτου ἐμπλησθέντων τῶν πεντεκαίδεκα ἀδελφῶν . . ." (After they had brought the scanty leftovers of the bread and wine, the saint said a prayer in his heart and blessed them, and with that bread the fifteen brothers were full . . . ).

50.1    *modioi*: A variable unit of grain measurement. See further *ODB*, vol. 2, p. 1388.

*but treasure the unperishable . . . endures forever*: John 6:27.

51    *the protonotarios Bardas*: See *PmbZ*, no. 792. His office was probably that of *protonotarios* of a theme, an official responsible for the supply of the army; see *ODB*, vol. 3, p. 1746.

*enter the monastery*: Marc. adds, "διὰ τὸ τῶν ἀδελφῶν σκάνδαλον, ἐμήνυσεν" (so that the brothers might not be caused to stumble, and sent a message).

*Philotheos and Barnabas*: See the note on 47, above.

*a bishop . . . John*: See *PmbZ*, no. 3237.

52    *So he rushed . . . So he quickly sent*: The repetitive and awkward, indeed rather breathless, phrasing here and in the previous sentence reflects that of the Greek.

*my relatives and toward <. . .>*: From this point until midway through chapter 78 there is a lacuna in Glasc. This is filled by the text of Marc.

*one iota*: Luke 16:17; compare Matthew 5:18.

*every illness and disease*: Matthew 4:23, 9:35, and 10:1.

*helping widows*: 1 Timothy 5:16.

*generously distributing*: Romans 12:8.

53    *Receive the Holy Spirit . . . are retained*: John 20:22.

*your sins are forgiven*: Luke 5:23 and 7:48.

54    *Abba*: On this term, see above, the note to 16.1.

55    *in his image and likeness*: Genesis 1:26.

*transformed the water into wine*: See John 2:9.

56    *How can I, a sinner, do that*: See Luke 1:43.

57    *kourator called Eustathios, from the Thrakesion*: See *PmbZ*, no. 1786.

A *kourator* was a manager of imperial estates; see *ODB*, vol. 2,

pp. 1155–56. The Thrakesion was a theme (administrative district) of western Asia Minor. It included the Aegean territories of Ionia and Lydia, along with parts of Phrygia and Caria. Its largest city was Ephesus and its capital probably Chonai. See *ODB,* vol. 3, p. 2080, and J. Haldon, trans., *The "De thematibus (On the Themes)" of Constantine VII Porphyrogenitus* (Liverpool, 2021), 108–13.

*protospatharios called Staurakios*: See *PmbZ,* no. 6891. *Protospatharios* was a senior dignity granted mostly to commanders of themes; see *ODB,* vol. 3, p. 1748.

60 *Kosmas*: See *PmbZ,* no. 4136.

*a dumb and mute spirit*: Mark 9:25.

*into fire and water*: Mark 9:22.

*you do not know what you are asking*: Matthew 20:22.

*his last state will become worse than his first*: 2 Peter 2:20.

61 *Konstantinos*: See *PmbZ,* no. 3946.

*Petzikas . . . Pegadia*: These places, which lie somewhere on the more than fifty-mile route between the monastery of Saint Zechariah, northeast of Olympos, and that of Saint Porphyrios near Lake Apollonias, are not referred to in any other source; see *TIB* 13, pp. 894–95, and 911, respectively.

*twisted the mouths*: The meaning is not entirely clear. It could imply that the demons rendered their victims mute, or perhaps that they made them say inappropriate things.

62 *because of his mercy*: Luke 1:78.

63 *Michael . . . Theophilos*: Michael II died in 829 and was succeeded by his young son, Theophilos (829–842); see *ODB,* vol. 3, p. 2066.

*John, an impious Iconoclast . . . under Leo*: That is, John VII Grammatikos. As his epithet "the Grammarian" suggests, he was a distinguished scholar and rhetorician who later became patriarch of Constantinople (837–843). Although originally an iconodule, he had become an ardent Iconoclast by the time Leo V came to power and was entrusted by him with overseeing the establishment of the doctrinal basis for Iconoclasm and subsequently with the conversion of iconodules. Sabas

here explains the fact that the new emperor Theophilos was a strong supporter of Iconoclasm by citing John's influence over him as his tutor. See *ODB*, vol. 2, p. 1052; *PmbZ*, no. 3199.

*The pseudo-bishop . . . Leo*: See *PmbZ*, no. 4425.

*two or three*: Compare Matthew 18:20.

64.1     *main community*: The Greek term used here, *koinobion,* simply indicates an organized monastic community. In other contexts, however, the term could also take on a polemical tone when the communal pattern of monasticism was being compared with more individualistic interpretations. See further, *ODB*, vol. 2, p. 1136.

*that consul . . . many times before*: See chapters 34–37.

64.3     *Whoever digs a pit for his neighbor will fall into it*: Proverbs 26:27.

65     *Jacob*: See *PmbZ*, no. 2630.

*Anchialos in Macedonia*: Anchialos (modern Pomorie in Bulgaria) was an important Black Sea port; see *ODB,* vol. 2, p. 90. The term "Macedonia" was frequently applied to Thrace in this period.

*Tarasios*: See note on 6.2, above.

66     *Apollonias*: See note on 47, above, on the monastery of Saint Porphyrios, and *TIB* 13, p. 412. The bishop of Apollonias was a suffragan of the metropolitan of Kyzikos at the time; see Laurent, *La vie,* 194n2.

67     *dumbness of my deaf and speechless child*: Use of the pejorative "dumbness" is deliberate here since it catches quite nicely the linkage in Greek between speech and rationality. If the child was speechless, it was also necessarily limited in the rationality or intelligence that made someone human. See also the note to 15.1, above.

*neither gold nor silver*: See Acts 3:6. The same expression is used above, in 27.

*the nearby monastery . . . Saint Kerykos*: See Laurent, *La vie,* 46–47.

68     *a bishop . . . named Paul*: See *PmbZ*, no. 5853. On the theme of the Boukellarioi, see note on 5, above. On Plousias, a suffragan bishopric of Claudiopolis (modern Bolu), see Laurent, *La Vie,* 196n2.

NOTES TO THE TRANSLATION

*Clemens*: See *PmbZ*, no. 3654.

*it is the inferior that is blessed by the superior*: Hebrews 7:7.

*one mile*: Compare above, 14.2 and 42.

70     *the hot springs*: There are many hot springs in the area of Prousa (modern Bursa), for example in the Çekirge district, which lies on the northwestern foothills of Olympos.

       *What have you to do with me*: Mark 5:7. The same phrase is used in 28 and 36, above.

72     *living there in secret*: This seems to imply that Sabas was still living in secret at the monastery when the brothers had scattered to avoid the Iconoclasts.

       *fire prepared*: Matthew 25:41.

73     *Euthymios . . . Smyrna . . . Prinabaris*: On Euthymios, see *PmbZ*, no. 1854. Smyrna is modern Izmir on the west coast of Asia Minor, and Prinabaris is modern Bornova, now a suburb to the northeast of Izmir. See further, Laurent, *La vie*, 202n1.

       *the treasury of his heart*: Luke 6:45.

       *topoteretes*: The Greek term probably indicates at this time a military officer subordinate to the commander of a regiment or theme. See further *ODB*, vol. 3, pp. 2095–96.

75     *seventh year of the reign of Theophilos*: That is, 835 to 836 CE. See Laurent, *La vie*, 206n1.

76     *Ampelis*: See *PmbZ*, no. 219.

       *Sophos*: An unidentified place, but clearly on the shore of Lake Apollonias (Uluabat Gölü); see *TIB* 13, pp. 1011–12.

       *he gave glory . . . who gave such a power*: See Matthew 9:8.

77.1    *notary called Nikostratos*: See *PmbZ*, no. 5631. The term *notarios* (notary) can be applied to a range of lay and ecclesiastical officials who were involved in specialized scribal, secretarial, and legal work. See *ODB*, vol. 3, p. 1495; and in more detail, H. Saradi-Mendelovici, "Byzantine Notaries," *Medieval Prosopography* 9 (1988): 21–49.

77.2    *not repay anyone evil for evil*: Romans 12:17.

78     *Zenobios*: See *PmbZ*, no. 8644.

       *on his arm*: At this point the text of Glasc. resumes.

79     *Menas*: *PmbZ*, no. 4969.

*gradually led him . . . deifying commandments*: Marc. reads, "βουλόμενος ὁμόσκηνον τῆς ποίμνης αὐτοῦ ἀποτελέσαι" (wishing
to make him a member of his flock).

*serpent*: Although the Greek term is *drakon,* literally meaning
"dragon," it was more commonly used for any large snake, including, as here, the devil in his guise as the serpent. The con-
notations of the English "dragon" would thus be misleading
here.

*thinking that . . . efforts at saving himself*: Marc. reads, "διὰ τούτων
οἰόμενος αὐτὸν θροῆσαι" (thinking that through these actions
he might disturb him).

*the serpent with the fishhook of divinity*: Compare Job 40:20.

*no power even over pigs*: See Matthew 8:30–32 and Mark 5:12–13.
The same point is made in 20.2, above.

*cut the hair of his head*: That is, had been tonsured as a monk.

*he was still awake*: Marc. has instead, "οὐ μὴν κοιμωμένου" (while
he had not yet fallen asleep).

80  *Throwing off*: Marc. adds before, "προσευξάμενος πρὸς Κύριον"
(he prayed to the Lord and).

*Ioannikios*: See *PmbZ,* no. 3389.

*will stay in his body . . . wants*: Marc. reads, "ὡς θέλει ἐν σαρκὶ
περιέπεται" (he is treated in his body as he wishes).

81  *delightful mountain . . . the vaults of heaven*: A version of the phrase
"vaults of heaven" is found in Plato, *Phaedrus* 247b, but similar
passages, closer to this one in wording, appear several times in
patristic literature. The same passage is repeated verbatim in
Sabas, *Life of Ioannikios,* ed. *Acta sanctorum Novembris,* vol. 2,
part 1, pp. 370C–71A. On the cosmic mountain, see, for example, R. J. Clifford, *The Cosmic Mountain in Canaan and the Old
Testament* (Cambridge, MA, 1972).

*As the Lord is . . . profit from them*: Marc. reads, "Ταῦτα δέ, ἀδελφοί, ἐγὼ ὁ ἐλάχιστος Σάβας, μαρτυροῦντος τοῦ Κυρίου,
παρὰ τοῦ ἁγίου στόματος τοῦ πατρὸς ἡμῶν Ἰωαννικίου ἀκήκοα περὶ τοῦ μακαρίου καὶ ὁσιωτάτου πατρὸς ἡμῶν Πέτρου
ἐξηγουμένου. Ἀλλ' ἐπὶ τὸ προκείμενον ἐπανέλθωμεν καὶ τὸ
αὐτοῦ μακάριον ἐξαγγείλωμεν τέλος." (These things, brothers, I, the most humble Sabas, heard spoken by the saintly

mouth of our father Ioannikios about our blessed and most
holy father Peter. But let us return to our subject and narrate
his blessed death.)

82 *For, so as to tell . . . doubt this*: Marc. has different phrasing here
and places the chapter break later than Glauc., at the end of
the following: "Κατὰ μίαν γάρ, ὡς ἔφην, ἀδελφοί, τοῦ ἐνιαυτοῦ περίοδον πανεόρτιον καὶ πάνδημον ἦγεν ἡμέραν, τοῖς
ἀδελφοῖς ἄπασι διακονῶν καὶ παριστάμενος ἀκενοδόξως· ἦν
δὲ αὕτη ἡ πρώτη τοῦ ἰαννουαρίου μηνός, ἐν ᾗ ἡ τοῦ Κυρίου
Ἰησοῦ Χριστοῦ καὶ σωτῆρος ἡμῶν ἐπιτελεῖται ἐν σαρκὶ ὀκτα-
ήμερος περιτομὴ καὶ ἡ τοῦ μεγάλου Βασιλείου κοίμησις." (For
on only one day, as I have said, brothers, in the entire year did
he hold a truly great and popular festival, serving and humbly
attending to everyone along with the brothers. That day was
the first of the month of January, on which the eighth-day circumcision in the flesh of our Lord Jesus Christ and Savior is
celebrated, and the dormition of Basil the Great.)

83 *For then indeed . . . sang along with then*: Marc. has, "Ἐν ταύτῃ οὖν
τῇ ἡμέρᾳ τῶν ἀδελφῶν τῆς ἑορτῆς τὸν κανόνα ψαλλόντων
καὶ αὐτὸς ὁ ὅσιος πατὴρ τούτοις ἀνακείμενος ἐν κλίνῃ συν-
έψαλλεν· ἦν γάρ, ὡς προείπομεν, ἀφ' ἡμερῶν νοσήσας." (So
on that day, when the brothers were singing the canon of the
feast, the holy father himself, although lying on a bed, sang
along; for as we said before, he had been ill for some days.)

*singing there*: Marc. adds, "Δεῦτε ἐνθάδε, τέκνα." (Come here,
children!)

*the day of my departure has come already*: 2 Timothy 4:6, a phrase
commonly used in the final addresses of Byzantine saints to
their disciples. See, for example, Athanasios of Antioch, *Life of
Saint Christodoulos of Patmos* 73.5, ed. Polemis and Antonopoulou, *Vitae,* 236. Sabas's account of Peter's death in this and the
following chapter should be compared with that of Paul's in
11.1, above.

*If someone competes . . . the rules*: 2 Timothy 2:5.

*already been said*: Marc. has instead, before the quotation, "λέγει
γὰρ ὁ Ἀπόστολος ὅτι" (for the Apostle says that).

*a temple for the Spirit*: See 1 Corinthians 3:16.

*on the right-hand side*: Matthew 25:34; compare Mark 10:40. The reference in Matthew is to the separation at Judgment Day of the metaphorical sheep from the goats. Those people on the right-hand side of God, the righteous, will pass into the kingdom, but those on the left, the sinners, will depart into the fire.

*Do not say 'welcome'*: 2 John 10–11.

*for anyone who . . . from the king*: Marc. reads, "ὁ γὰρ ἐσθίων μετ’ αὐτῶν μέτοχος αὐτῶν τῆς πίστεώς ἐστιν" (since the one who eats with them is a partner in their faith). The reference in the text of manuscript Glasc. to becoming "a partner in many punishments from the king" seems to be an allusion to the story in 1 Kings (1 Samuel) 20:30–34, where Jonathan, King Saul's son, is accused of being a "partner" (μέτοχος) or "friend" of David, whom Saul wishes to kill, and leaves the table without eating after his father throws a spear at him. On the phrase, "anyone who fraternizes with the king's enemies," also compare John Chrysostom, *Homilies to the Gospel of John*, ed. PG 59:558.2–3.

*by the hope of those good things reserved for you*: Proverbs 24:20.

*Blessed are those . . . kingdom of heaven*: Matthew 5:10.

*the perfect love*: 1 John 4:12–18.

*who is weak . . . indignant*: 2 Corinthians 11:29.

*Christ . . . head of his church*: Ephesians 5:23.

84.1   *shepherd them after him*: Marc. adds, "ἀλλὰ μόνον ἔκλαιον ἀνενδότως ὡς μέλλοντα τὸν πατέρα καταλιμπάνειν αὐτούς" (but they just wept without stopping as their father was going to leave them).

*worthy governor*: Marc. adds, "ἐγὼ γὰρ ἤδη λοιπὸν συντόμως τῶν ἐνθένδε μεθίσταμαι καὶ πρὸς τὸν Κύριόν μου ἀπέρχομαι" (for I am already swiftly departing from this life and going to my Lord).

*being earth . . . to the earth*: Genesis 3:19.

*the one who has gone astray*: Matthew 18:12.

*supporting the one who is feeble*: Ezekiel 34:16.

84.2   *entrust me with the helm in ruling the flock*: The translation preserves the mixed metaphor of the Greek.

*holy things . . . to those who are holy*: A phrase from Saint Basil's liturgy; see PG 31:1649D.

85.1   *who visited us*: See Luke 1:68.

    *one flock*: John 10:16.

    *Protect it from the evil one*: Compare John 17:15.

    *the king of peace*: Hebrews 7:2.

    *the thrice-holy glory*: See Isaiah 6:3.

85.2   *the Lord, to whom I have entrusted you*: Compare Acts 14:23.

    *relinquished his spirit*: John 19:30, describing Jesus on the cross.

    *through grace*: Marc. adds, "Ἐτελειώθη δὲ ὁ ἅγιος καὶ σημειο-
φόρος οὗτος πατὴρ ἡμῶν καὶ ἰσάγγελος Πέτρος μηνὶ ἰαν-
νουαρίῳ πρώτῃ, ἡμέρᾳ δευτέρᾳ, ζήσας ἔτος ἑξηκοστὸν
τρίτον, ἰνδικτιῶνι πεντεκαιδεκάτῃ, ἀπὸ δὲ κτίσεως τῆς τοῦ
κόσμου συστάσεως ͵ϛμε΄, βασιλεύοντος τῆς τῶν Ῥωμαίων
ἀρχῆς Θεοφίλου." (This holy miracle worker, our father Peter,
who was like an angel, died on the first day of January, a Monday, having lived for sixty-three years, in the fifteenth indiction, in the 6345th year from the creation, when Theophilos
was ruling the Roman state.) That is, he died on January 1, 837.

    Marc. then has the following epilogue (chapter 86 in Lau-
rent, *La vie*):

> Ταῦτα, ἀδελφοί, τὰ τῆς ἐνσάρκου ζωῆς τοῦ πατρὸς Πέτρου
> ἀγωνίσματά τε καὶ θαύματα· τὰ δὲ μετὰ τέλους καθ᾽ ἑκάστην
> σημεῖα καὶ τέρατα γενόμενα ἐν τῷ αὐτῷ ἰαματηφόρῳ καὶ
> πανολβίῳ τάφῳ τίς διηγήσασθαι δύναται ἢ ποία γλῶσσα
> ἀπαγγεῖλαι τὰ καθ᾽ ἡμέραν τελούμενα ἀεννάως καὶ ἀφθόνως
> μέχρι τῆς δεῦρο; Τυφλοὶ γὰρ τὸ βλέπειν χάριτι Θεοῦ λαμ-
> βάνουσιν, κωφοὶ τὸ ἀκούειν, λεπροὶ τὴν κάθαρσιν, δαίμονες
> ἀπελαύνονται ἀπὸ τῶν ἀνθρώπων διὰ τῆς ἐπισκιάσεως τοῦ
> ἁγίου, καὶ <οἱ διὰ> πᾶσαν μαλακίαν καὶ νόσον προστρέχον-
> τες πρὸς αὐτὸν ἅπαντες ὥσπερ ἐκ πηγῆς ἀεννάου τὰς αἰτή-
> σεις λαμβάνουσιν. Μεθ᾽ ὧν δοξάσωμεν Κύριον τὸν μόνον
> φιλάνθρωπον, τὸν μόνον εὔσπλαγχνον, τὸν μόνον Σωτῆρα,
> τὸν δοξάσαντα καὶ μεγαλύναντα τοὺς ἁγίους αὐτοῦ ἐν δόξῃ
> καὶ τιμῇ, ἅμα τῷ Πατρὶ καὶ τῷ ἀληθεῖ γεννήτορι σὺν τῷ
> παναγίῳ καὶ ζωοποιῷ Πνεύματι, νῦν καὶ ἀεὶ καὶ εἰς τοὺς
> αἰῶνας τῶν αἰώνων· ἀμήν. Ἐτελειώθη ὁ βίος τοῦ ὁσίου
> πατρὸς ἡμῶν Πέτρου τοῦ θαυματουργοῦ.

(These, my brothers, were the struggles and the miracles of Father Peter's life in the flesh. But who can narrate the signs and wonders which occurred every day after his death at his healing and most blessed grave? Or what tongue can recount those performed ceaselessly and abundantly every day until now? The blind receive the ability to see by the grace of God and deaf men to hear, lepers their cleansing; demons are driven away from men through the overshadowing power of the saint, and all who rush to him because of any disability and disease receive what they ask for, as if from an ever-flowing spring. Together with them, let us glorify our only benevolent Lord, the only merciful one, the only Savior, the one who has glorified and magnified his saints in glory and honor, with his Father, who truly begot him, and with the most Holy and life-giving Spirit, now and always and unto the ages of ages, amen. The life of our holy father Peter the wonderworker is completed.)

86.1   *This is the final point*: Laurent, *La "Vita retractata,"* 134–35, numbers this chapter, which does not appear in Marc., as 86 *bis*.

*which is irrevocable, to put it apostolically*: See Romans 11:29.

86.2   *the extension ... to put it apostolically*: See Acts 4:30.

87   *face-to-face*: 1 Corinthians 13:12.

*fifteenth indiction ... sixty-three years old*: That is, as noted above in the note to 85.2, he died on January 1, 837.

*like deer thirsting*: See Psalms 41:2 (42:1).

*the desert practically resembled a city*: Compare Athanasios of Alexandria, *Life of Saint Antony* 8.8, ed. G. J. M. Bartelink, *Vie d'Antoine*, Sources Chrétiennes 400, rev. ed. (Paris, 2004), 156.

89   *Bartholomaios*: See *PmbZ*, no. 819.

91   *which people like to call the "fly"*: The term *myia* (fly) for a disease of this sort appears to be otherwise unknown; see Laurent, *La "Vita retractata,"* 140n1. It is, however, perhaps worth noting that Aristotle, *Historia animalium* 604.b.19–21, describes the bite of the *mygale* (shrew)—in Greek the two sound rather similar since the gamma is silent—as also producing *phlyktainai* ("pustules" or "boils"), which are dangerous to draft animals.

92  *blind mole rat*: The *asphalax* (blind mole rat) is a subterranean rodent native to eastern Europe and western Asia. The spreading tumor was apparently so named from its resemblance to mole hills.

*who makes dew in fire*: See Daniel 3:50.

94  *Barnabas and Philotheos*: See note on 47, above.

*he lived and moved*: Acts 17:28.

*thought of the flesh*: Romans 8:6.

*freedmen of the Lord*: 1 Corinthians 7:22.

96  *metretai*: A liquid measure equaling one and a half Roman amphorae, or nearly nine gallons.

97  *surrounding it . . . around the throne of God*: See Isaiah 6:1–2.

98  *like another Siloam*: A pool in Jerusalem to which, according to John 9:7, Jesus sent a man who had been born blind to wash, in order to complete his healing.

*and taking <. . .>*: There is a lacuna in the manuscript at this point.

100  *the monastery of Hippos at Dagouta*: On Dagouta see note to 4.2, above. Given that Dagouta was not far from Olympos, the monastery of Hippos mentioned here must thus be distinguished from the area of Hippos referred to in 16.1, above, which was located by Laurent near Pergamon, on the border between Asia and Lydia.

*the same disease on his back*: Presumably a pustule or carbuncle, as in 91, or a tumor, as in 92 and 93.

102  *the holy coffin that destroyed illness*: The Greek term *pathoktonos* might literally be rendered as "passion killing," but it also embraces the full range of *pathos* discussed in the note to "protection against many ills" at 19.1, above.

103  *in a most holy and righteous way*: See Ephesians 4:24.

*Methodios*: Methodios I, who was elected patriarch of Constantinople (843–847) following the death of Theophilos, was a key figure in the restoration of the veneration of icons in 843; see *PmbZ*, no. 4977, and *ODB*, vol. 2, p. 1355.

*the lampstand*: Compare Matthew 5:15, Mark 4:21, and Luke 8:16.

*Ignatios . . . of Nikomedeia*: See *PmbZ*, no. 2669, and Laurent, *La "Vita retractata,"* 152–54n3.

*on the fourth day of the week*: That is, Wednesday. On the issues with this dating, see Laurent, *La "Vita retractata,"* 45. The text then has Paul depart for Nicaea "on the sixth day of the week" (Friday) and arrive "on the seventh day of the week" (Saturday).

*Nicaea*: Nicaea (modern Iznik) was an ancient, storied, and important city situated at the eastern end of Lake Askanios. It was capital of the Opsikion theme and lay on Paul's route to Constantinople via Nikomedeia to the northeast. Paul had only traveled some twenty miles. See further *ODB*, vol. 2, pp. 1463–64.

*Paul departed from his body*: As Laurent, *La "Vita retractata,"* 155n6, indicates, this was August 26, 844.

*Jacob*: On Jacob, see note on the Preface, above.

104     *Andrew*: See *PmbZ*, no. 407.

        *blind mole rat . . . crawls in the earth*: See note on 92, above.

105.2   *Kakalos*: On this village, which evidently lay on the plain to the northeast of Olympos and east of Prousa (Bursa), see Laurent, *La "Vita retractata,"* 159n2, and *TIB* 13, p. 633.

108     *feet and ankles*: Compare the story in Acts 3:7.

109     *droungarios . . . called Niketas*: See *PmbZ*, no. 5480. On this military rank, see *ODB*, vol. 1, p. 663.

        *We have already recorded . . . possessed by demons*: Niketas would appear to be the unnamed "well-off" man who is healed in 24.2, above, and whose fourteen maids are freed from possession by Peter's hair shirt in 25. The wording here makes it seem possible that he is also the unnamed consul whose wife, nephew, and various other household members were cured or helped by Peter in 34–36, above, and who is himself Sabas's source for those stories.

        *in the Mesonesos at Malagina*: Malagina appears to have been situated some fifty miles northeast of Olympos. On the complex identification of this place from these two toponyms, see Laurent, *La "Vita retractata,"* 70–74 and 162nn1–2, and *TIB* 13, pp. 748–51 and 772. On Malagina, see also Bondoux, "Les villes," 394–95.

110     *Sophronas*: See *PmbZ*, no. 6843.

*Takomis*: The location of this place is unknown; see Laurent, *La "Vita retractata,"* 163n4, and *TIB* 13, p. 1024.

*Kytagion*: Kytagion, or Kotyaion (modern Kütahya), lies some sixty miles southwest of Olympos.

*scholarios*: A member of the Byzantine military; originally the term referred to the imperial palace guard, but later took on a broader significance.

*the imperial city*: That is, Constantinople.

111    *Constantine*: See *PmbZ,* no. 4000.

*the son of Benjamin . . . saved from the hands of the Ishmaelites*: For him and this episode, see 39.2, above.

*Huns . . . Bulgarians*: The Bulgarians are frequently called Huns in Byzantine sources. It is unclear which conflict between Byzantion and Bulgaria the author is referring to; Laurent, *La "Vita retractata,"* 165n3, places it around 865 CE.

*Euros*: The river (Evros) in Thrace that marks the modern border between Greece and Turkey.

112    *Barsanouphios, a monk . . . in Hypninon*: See *PmbZ,* no. 818. The location of Hypninon is unknown; see Laurent, *La "Vita retractata,"* 167n3. Given the mention of "the monastery called Hippos at Dagouta" in 100, above, it seems possible, however, that this Hypninon is a corruption of that Hippos, or vice versa.

113    *the monastery of Stylos*: On the potential location of this monastery, see Laurent, *La "Vita retractata,"* 168n1.

*Nicholas*: See *PmbZ,* no. 5592.

114    *Theophylaktos*: See *PmbZ,* no. 8345.

115    *Theophylaktos*: See *PmbZ,* no. 8346.

# Bibliography

### EDITIONS AND TRANSLATIONS

Laurent, Vitalien, ed. and trans. *La vie merveilleuse de saint Pierre d'Atroa.* Brussels, 1956. Edition based on Marc.

———. *La "Vita retractata" et les miracles posthumes de saint Pierre d'Atroa.* Brussels, 1958. Excerpts based on the text in Glasc.

### FURTHER READING

Alexander, Paul J. *The Patriarch Nicephorus of Constantinople.* Oxford, 1958.

Auzépy, Marie-France. *L'histoire des iconoclastes.* Paris, 2007.

Brubaker, Leslie. *Inventing Byzantine Iconoclasm.* London, 2012.

Brubaker, Leslie, and John Haldon. *Byzantium in the Iconoclast Era, c. 680–850: A History.* Cambridge, 2011.

Bryer, Anthony, and Judith Herrin, eds. *Iconoclasm.* Birmingham, 1977.

Chryssostalis, Alexis. *Recherches sur la tradition manuscrite du "Contra Eusebium" de Nicéphore de Constantinople.* Paris, 2012.

Humphreys, Mike, ed. *A Companion to Byzantine Iconoclasm.* Brill, 2021.

Kaplan, Michel. *Les hommes et la terre à Byzance du VIᵉ au XIᵉ siècle.* Paris, 1992.

Parry, Kenneth. *Depicting the Word: Byzantine Iconophile Thought of the Eight and Ninth Centuries.* Leiden, 1996.

Pratsch, Thomas. *Der hagiographische Topos: Griechische Heiligenviten in mittelbyzantinischer Zeit.* Berlin, 2005.

Prieto Domínguez, Óscar. *Literary Circles in Byzantine Iconoclasm: Patrons, Politics and Saints.* Cambridge, 2020.

Talbot, Alice-Mary, ed. *Byzantine Defenders of Images: Eight Saints' Lives in English Translation.* Washington, DC, 1998.

Treadgold, Warren T. *The Byzantine Revival: 780–842.* Stanford, 1988.

# Index